Doria Shafik, Egyptian Feminist

Doria Shafik, Egyptian Feminist
A Woman Apart

CYNTHIA NELSON

The American University in Cairo Press

First published in Egypt in 1996 by
The American University in Cairo Press
113 Sharia Kasr el Aini
Cairo, Egypt

This edition published by arrangement with
University Press of Florida

ISBN 977 424 413 3
Dar el Kutub No. 8271/96

Frontispiece: Doria Shafik, 1952.

Printed in Egypt by International Press

To Aziza and Jehane in memory of their mother

Action de Grâce

Je rends grâce
à Dieu
d'avoir vu le jour
au pays des mystères.
d'avoir grandi
à l'ombre
des palmiers,
d'avoir vécu
dans les bras
du désert
gardien des secrets . . .
d'avoir vu
l'éclat
du disque solaire,
et d'avoir bu
enfant
eaux du Nil
fleuve béni.

Thanksgiving

I render thanks
unto God
to have been born
in the land of mysteries,
to have grown up
in the shadow
of the palms
to have lived
within the arms
of the desert
guardian of secrets . . .
to have seen
the brilliance
of the solar disk
and to have drunk
as a child
from the Nile
sacred river.

—*Doria Shafik, Larmes d'Isis*

To Aziza and Jehane in memory of their mother
Contents

Preface

"The End Is My Beginning"

What we call the beginning is often the end
And to make an end is to make a beginning.
The end is where we start from. And . . .
Every phrase and sentence is an end and a beginning,
Every poem an epitaph. And any action
Is a step to the block, to the fire, down the sea's throat
Or to an illegible stone: and that is where we start.
We die with the dying:
See, they depart, and we go with them.[1]

This is the story of an Egyptian woman who wanted her life "to be a work of art." It is the story of one woman's struggle against those conservative forces within her society—whether cultural, religious, or political—that opposed the full equality of women. It is the story of the encounter between a woman's emergent feminist consciousness, shaped by the values of Islam and humanism, and her society's awakened nationalist identity grounded in the historical realities of the post-World War II era. Doria Shafik was a woman who wanted "to experience it all," to be a public heroine in a society that defined and circumscribed woman primarily in terms of helper, supporter, and moral guide to the family in the domestic sphere. She derived strength, importance, dignity, and self-respect from her own exploits in pursuit of freedom.

There are several reasons, blending the personal and professional, that make the writing of Doria Shafik's life particularly challenging. Paramount is the woman herself. She is complex, contradictory, and controversial. She grew up in a very modest and traditional middle-class Muslim family in the provincial delta towns of Tanta and Mansura during the period when Egypt was passing through the throes of great internal turmoil following World War I, which erupted in the 1919 revolution. During the 1920s and 1930s, educational opportunities for women were slowly beginning to open up, and for some young women like Doria Shafik—endowed with intelligence, ambition, and beauty—education became an outlet from the constraints of tradition, particularly the pressures for an early arranged marriage, and a chance to discover alternative possibilities to a conventional life. Doria exploited that avenue to the fullest and obtained her *Doctorat d'Etat* from the Sorbonne in 1940, achieving the highest accolade, *mention trés honorable*. Although not the first Egyptian woman to receive such a degree, at twenty-nine she was certainly among the youngest. Education may have been an outlet for her craving to achieve, but her ultimate ambition was to enter the public and political arena, and it was within the context of post–World War II Egypt that Doria Shafik catapulted herself into national and international prominence.

During her brief but volcanic eruption onto the public stage of Egypt, she openly challenged every social, cultural, and legal barrier that she viewed as inimical and oppressive to the full equality of the woman in her society, thereby contributing more directly than had the reformers of an earlier generation to the construction of an Egyptian feminist discourse surrounding women's rights and Islam. She presented a radically different model as a leader of the women's movement in Egypt. Her efforts set against the backdrop of postwar social and political upheaval, Doria Shafik attempted to shape a new consciousness for the women of Egypt on several fronts: first, through writing; second, through developing a feminist organization and political party; and finally, through a strategy of direct, militant confrontation.

She expressed her feminist vision through writing and not only founded and edited two prominent women's journals but also authored and coauthored several books in both French and Arabic on the history, development, and renaissance of the social and political rights of the Egyptian woman.[2] She established a feminist organization and a political party through which she challenged the very bastions of male authority under both pre-revolutionary and revolutionary regimes, shaping a feminist consciousness through a strategy of confrontation: storming the Egyptian parliament, attempting to run illegally for parliamentary elections, staging sit-ins to protest the British occupation of Egypt, and finally organizing an eight-day hunger strike for women's rights. She met and spoke openly about "women's rights" not only with the president of her own country, but also with the heads of state of India, Ceylon, Lebanon, Iraq, and Iran; she publicly chastised the president of Pakistan for taking a second wife; she lectured to audiences in Europe, the United States, and the Far and Middle East on the Arab woman's struggle for political equality and human freedom—only to lose her own freedom and civil liberties in 1957 following her dramatic protest against the erosion of democracy in Egypt under the populist regime of Gamal Abdul Nasser.

Although Shafik was silenced and virtually secluded from public life from 1957 until her death in 1975, her image lingers on. Every so often, the contemporary Egyptian press mentions the Bint al-Nil Union or reprints her photograph as a nostalgic reminder of Egypt forty-five years ago. Her name can still evoke strong reactions among certain circles. Following a paper I delivered at an international colloquium in Cairo in 1985, an angry and heated debate among several Egyptian participants erupted over Doria Shafik's role in the history of the women's movement in Egypt. Inji Efflatoun, a well-known painter and leftist critic, publicly declaimed that "Doria Shafik had been a traitor to the Revolution and did not merit having a biography written." What then justifies this biography?

I first became aware of Doria Shafik through a gift of her poetry given me by her daughters, Jehane and Aziza, in June 1983,[3] twenty years after my own arrival in Egypt, twenty-six years after her house arrest and subsequent self-imposed seclusion, and eight years after her death. From reading these poems, I discovered a voice which—despite differences of language, culture, and historical experience—was exploring ontological and existential concerns that seemed so familiar from my reading of the lives of women from other cultures and other times, women who had dared to be different. Although the images and metaphors were taken from her own beloved Egypt, Shafik's themes were those of solitude, alienation, determination, struggle, human freedom, and the search for the Absolute. From the moment I read her poetry and then later her memoirs, I became increasingly conscious of this interplay between solitude, alienation, and creativity which ran through her life and work and which brought her into continual conflict with her family and society. Although her life is an expression of one woman's unique experience in the context of a particular culture and history, her metaphors reach beyond the borders of Egypt to remind us of other women who also challenged the forces that constrained their autonomy and freedom in an unswerving "courage to be." And when thrown back upon herself, Doria listened to and depended upon that inner realm of memory and consciousness, her muse of interior music, her beloved companion through whose consolation she escaped on her flight into the Infinite.

Poetry!
My great comfort
You transform my solitude into Beauty
You extend your hand

When
As a shipwrecked woman on the High Seas
Despairing to find
Even the lightest landmark
To cling to
Overwhelmed by the Tempest
So
I do not know from
Which illumined Heavens
You appeared
Symbol of Love
Symbol of Beauty
I took refuge
In your tenderness
No longer a
Flotsam upon the Sea.[4]

Deeply touched by such poems, I was curious to know more about the woman who wrote them. In 1984, I spent the fall semester teaching at the University of California at Santa Cruz, where I met Akram Khater, a young Lebanese graduate student who was interested in the history of women's movements in the Middle East. We worked together for several months and discovered that scarcely any scholarly attention had been given to the women's movement in Egypt following World War II and no mention at all of Doria Shafik, despite her very active public life during that period. Increasingly I became convinced that a serious biographical study on Doria Shafik was not only relevant to my own intellectual interests but also, given the dearth of scholarly material, long overdue.

Returning to Egypt in the spring of 1985, I broached the idea to her two daughters, spelling out my feelings and intentions in wanting to undertake a biographical study of their mother. Their response was and has continued to be both enthusiastic and encouraging. And it is thanks to their trust that Doria Shafik's personal memoirs and unpublished papers have been generously shared, profound and painful memories have been re-lived, and pathways of understanding have been established.

What draws me to Doria Shafik is not only her meditative and poetic sensibility—from which she drew sustenance and inspiration during moments of personal crisis, especially during those last eighteen years spent in near total seclusion—but also her audacity and courage to fight against the powerful institutions of patriarchy which challenged her own sense of autonomy and freedom. Although her quixotic pursuit to reach for her star beyond society's traditional expectations of what a woman can or cannot do, or be, may have ended in tragedy, her themes reach far beyond the borders of Egypt.

It is this dynamism and tension created between and among the interlocking and sometimes contradictory strands and demands in her life—the cultures of the East and the West, the languages of Arabic and French, the meditative mode of the poet and the activist mode of the feminist; the exigencies of domestic and public responsibility—that contribute to her fascination. But is she more than just a footnote in contemporary Egyptian history?

As C. W. Mills reminds us, "Neither the life of the individual nor the history of a society can be understood without an understanding of both."[5] The writing of Doria Shafik's life is an attempt not only to express something about the shaping of a feminist consciousness but also to reveal something about Egyptian society during a particular moment in its historical unfolding.

As the story of a woman of conscience and a woman of letters, what can her life reveal about the nature and meaning of feminism, feminist consciousness, and feminist movements during Egypt's struggle to liberate itself from the last vestiges of colonial domination after the Second World War? What kind of role model as a "feminist leader" did Doria Shafik offer to her Egyptian, Muslim society, and how was her feminist struggle viewed by that society? What were her views on the relationship between Islam, modernity, and women's rights? How did she express this vision in her feminist discourse? What did it mean to be a product of both French and Arabic cultures in a society experiencing the throes of decolonization and national liberation? What can her life tell us about the conflict of identities in a nationalistic society? What was the nature of her participation in the construction of women's history in this post-World War II, pre-revolutionary, and early revolutionary period in Egypt? In short, how does the life of Doria Shafik intertwine with the life of her society during a particular moment of colonial encounter?

Doria Shafik was a Muslim modernist trying to forge a public, political space for Egyptian women on different grounds than had those women leaders who came before her. She not only challenged dominant Islamic traditions and institutions by demanding full political equality between men and women, a radical position from the point of view of conservative Islamic definitions of women's place; also, by her own example, she tried to redefine women's conceptions of themselves and their place in the wider political system. This is still a burning issue within the Arab and Islamic world, as recent publications will attest.

In Cairo in June 1995, a religious court ruled that a professor of Arabic literature at Cairo University is an apostate on the grounds that his scholarly analyses of the *Quran* are secularist and heretical. Because a Muslim is forbidden to remain married to an apostate, the professor's wife was ordered to divorce her husband, which she patently refused to do. The couple now live in a Scandinavian country to await the ruling on their appeal and to avoid possible assassination by zealous fundamentalists in Egypt.

In Bangladesh a reward of 50,000 rupees was offered in 1993 for the death of Taslima Nasreen, a feminist writer whose novels and poems openly demand human rights for women. A journalist pointed out that "In her latest novel *Lajja* (Shame), Taslima Nasreen challenged her culture not on any political grounds but on the very simple and honest ground that she considers herself not a Muslim but a secular person. This led in September 1993 to an obscure fundamentalist group demanding the arrest and trial of Taslima as an apostate, and a ban on her book."[6]

Egypt of the 1940s and 1950s was in many ways a much more tolerant society than either Egypt or Bangladesh of the 1990s. Despite the resistance to her struggle Shafik could openly engage in a feminist challenge to the religious establishment because she based her critique on the conviction that Islam, when properly understood, offered no barriers to women's rights and freedom. If the religious authorities saw in her feminism the hidden hand of Western colonialism attempting to undermine the Islamic family, they nonetheless did not order her assassination. Nasreen on the other hand publicly renounced her religion, which constitutes as great a threat to the religious authorities today as does her feminist message in her fiction.

As Shafik attempted to unite her aesthetic voice with her activist voice in her struggle for liberation—whether this be on the personal level or in the domain of women's rights or ultimately for human rights—she ignited the imagination of some, incurred the disdain of others, and suffered the wrath and condemnation of many. For over a decade after World War II, she was the focus of public interest on the pages of the national and international press, variously described as the "perfumed leader," a "militant feminist," the "beautiful leader," a "radical," a "danger to the Muslim nation," a "taste of candied chestnut," the woman of the "eighty-eight eyebrows," a "traitor to the revolution," and the "only Man in Egypt." To many of the younger and educated generation after World War II, who were restless to move beyond the confines of family into the public sphere but felt that the women's movement in Egypt had become moribund, Doria Shafik offered a different voice.

*   *   *

Because this biography relies heavily upon Doria Shafik's memoirs—"that highly personal configuration of significance by which a person views his own experience"[7]—the question arises: why not just publish them? The answer is simple. They are unpublishable as they exist: Doria wrote several versions of her memoirs, and thus there is the problem of which version to choose and on what basis. She was more poet than memoirist. Her style is impressionistic, almost pointillistic—in the manner of a sketchbook rather than a photo album. No laborious descriptions, just a brush stroke. And as history, the memoirs can be maddeningly confusing, especially if one is looking for a profound analysis of social and political situations.

Although written at three different moments of her life and not entirely complete (some segments are lost; others are simply unavailable), each version of Shafik's memoirs is like a separate map of the same symbolic landscape, illuminating the central strands of her thought and action within a broader context of history and society. The memoirs allow the biographer to follow the contours of her life, to grasp the myths she generated and the metaphors she chose to construct and interpret that life, to discover what she considered valuable and meaningful in the particular situations of her life and in the individual stages of her past.

She wrote her first version sometime between 1955 and 1956, after her lecture tour of the United States, in response to a specific request from Elizabeth Lawrence, chief editor of what was then called Harper and Brothers. Fascinated by an article she had read about Doria in *Holiday Magazine,* Lawrence wrote asking, "what would you think of writing your personal story that would give you the opportunity to say all the things you believe and are working toward in your public life?"[8]

Attracted by the idea, Doria embarked on a manuscript which she wrote directly in French. The publishers requested an English translation, and by May 1956, Doria had submitted a few chapters of her story. The editor's response was prompt and direct: "The point of view at present seems to me not quite right for American readers to whom your name is an unknown. It is, to be frank, too self-centered. Possibly because you are a woman of ideas and action, it is difficult for you to observe the people and the world around you in a way to make them vivid for foreigners. It would be more interesting to show the conditions in Egypt which prompted you to rebel and work for reform."[9]

When the Suez War erupted on October 29, 1956, all correspondence between Harper and Brothers and Doria Shafik ceased. Although large segments of these early chapters are lost, one can still catch a glimpse of the world which fashioned her and against which she rebelled. More interesting, however, are the metaphors she uses to describe her project of writing her life story:

> In sounding the past, one does not remember according to a pure geometric line because the events get tangled and muddled in the night of time. But at the moment that I least expect it, my memories pour forth

in luminous patches and enlighten me. To write the story of my life is nothing less than to undertake the very conquest of my being. It is not a question of venturing through space toward the conquest of some material spoils. It is something else entirely. Here it is no more a question of length, breadth and depth. Rather one perceives completely new lines in which the angles of flesh and blood intersect within the exciting meandering of the human heart with its loves and hates, hopes and despair. I look back upon my life as a series of incessant combats.

Her second version was begun some time after her house arrest in 1957. Although Doria Shafik never dated her personal documents, it is fairly certain that she completed this version of her memoirs around 1960 because she specifically comments, "for more than three years now, I have been carrying the responsibility for my action to reclaim my freedom and those of my compatriots." This French manuscript consists of nearly 550 typewritten pages and is the most complete of the memoirs. It augments and complements her earlier descriptions of the world in which she grew up, her own parents and family, her years in France during the 1930s, her marriage, and her public life until her political demise in 1957. Throughout it all is the recurrent theme of her passionate struggle to find a meaningful role in a society that would never quite accept her on her own terms. Writing just after her dramatic protest against Gamal Abdul Nasser, under conditions of house arrest and in French—which was her favorite medium of poetic and literary expression—Doria Shafik asserts that "this work, which I have titled *Freedom,* is not a description of events but the expression of the trajectory of a life—a life that is essentially an effort to break the chains that centuries of servitude have imposed on Egypt and the Egyptians. It is an attempt to discover the immediate reasons as well as the most distant origins of the chains of servitude weighing heavily upon me since my early childhood."

The writings of a woman secluded in her apartment, having had her publications destroyed, being forbidden access to publishers, and being banned from travel, one might ask for whom were these memoirs intended? Since French was her medium of expression, only an educated elite within Egypt would have been able to read them. Given the circumstances following her house arrest, there was little chance she would ever get them published in Egypt. Perhaps she wrote them for her daughters and future grandchildren. My own feeling is that she wrote her memoirs as an act of self-preservation from the semi-seclusion and solitude which she endured over nearly eighteen years.

It was during the final stages of this long internal exile that she wrote a third and final version of her life, consisting of nearly 4,200 handwritten pages in English, which she simply titled "Memoirs":

Why am I writing these memoirs? To see clearly into myself. In sounding the past, the present will be brought into focus and then I can look to the future with more clarity. When evoking the future, I don't speak only for myself but also for mankind, never having separated my own destiny from humanity as a whole. In my fight for freedom throughout my life, I have always had the consciousness that my own freedom was inseparable from mankind's freedom. Writing this book will help me to be aware of the essential meaning of the events surrounding me—my own story thus merging with the history of our century. The ultimate hope is to reach the comprehension of man's profound nature through the introspection of my own inner value.

These last memoirs are virtually "stream of consciousness"—incomplete, repetitive, and often difficult to comprehend. Yet they communicate an inner pain and loneliness that is more reflective of an attempt by Shafik to resist her own despair than to "set the record straight" as she had done in her French memoirs of 1960. In essence a rewriting of that French version, they were completed sometime in early 1975, a few months before she took her own life. Writing had always been her weapon against loneliness, but it was a struggle that finally exhausted that very resource.

Unless otherwise annotated, all quotations from Doria Shafik in this volume have been taken from her memoirs, and all translations are my own.

In some measure, Doria Shafik's end was my beginning. Yet for me to have continued upon the journey depended on the assistance of many people along the way. Limitation of space precludes my mentioning them all. However, special recognition and thanks must go to those students, friends, and colleagues who helped in the archival research, the translations, the introductions to key personalities who knew or worked with Doria Shafik, or shared with me their reactions to my work around the seminar tables, lecture halls, and offices. Especially I thank Laila Zaki, Lamia Raie, Reem Saad, Hania Sholkamy, Nevine Ibrahim, and Laurence Moftah for their patient and meticulous help in making sure I understood the nuances of the Arabic and French translations and for guiding me into the history and culture of their own Egyptian society.

My gratitude also goes to Akram Khater, who first stimulated my interest in and helped illuminate my understanding of Arab feminism and nationalism, and to Huda Fahmy, who provided the first public forum for me to share my project with an Egyptian and international audience. I wish to thank my colleagues in the Department of Sociology-Anthropology, especially Mark Kennedy, Nick Hopkins, and Saad Eddin Ibrahim, whose interest and challenging queries always stimulated my thinking. To Tareq and Jacqueline Ismael, Virginia Olesen, Elaine Hagopian, and Suzy Kane, my appreciation for their unwavering moral support during the long and agonizing process of writing.

A sabbatical grant from the American University in Cairo and the Bunting Institute at Radcliffe College were a valuable support in the early stages of the journey.

Most significantly I am indebted to the patience of Raghia Ragheb, Munira Qassem, Ibrahim Abdu, Zaynab Labib, Aida Nasrallah, Mustapha Amin, Inji Efflatoun, Loutfi al-Kholi, and Pierre Seghers, who not only answered my questions but offered insightful comments of their own. For her generosity of spirit, not only for recounting her memories of Doria Shafik to me but also for offering me copies of some of Doria's letters to her grandmother, I acknowledge my particular debt to Sania Sha'rawi Lanfranchi. Special thanks are due to Elizabeth Rodenbeck, whose meticulous and sensitive editing helped put the finishing touches on the manuscript. To El-Said Badawi, my gratitude for his gentle guidance in helping me understand the subtle nuances of the Arabic language. Errors of interpretation are my full responsiblility.

Finally and most profoundly, my blessings to Aida Ibrahim Fahmy, without whose nourishing friendship and unflinching faith in me I could not have sustained the energy and momentum to continue this work, ten years in the making.

CHRONOLOGY

1882   Revolt against foreign dominion led by Colonel Ahmad Pasha Orabi. The Orabi movement is the outcome of the erosion of Khedival power and the imposition of European financial control over the country. It also reflects a weakened Ottoman state and an empire in decline.

1899–1901 Publication of Le Duc d'Harcourt's *L'Egypte et Les Egyptiens* (1893) prompts Qasim Amin to write his two controversial books, *The Emancipation of Women* and *The New Woman*, reflecting the growing internal debate on how to reconcile Islam with modernity.

1908   December 14, Doria is born in Tanta, third child and second daughter of Ahmad Chafik and Ratiba Nassif. Family moves to Mansoura. By this time, three major political groups which are to dominate Egyptian political life until the outbreak of World War I have appeared on the scene. Despite their ideological differences, all three contemplate the establishment of an independent state in Egypt, entertain ideas of social reform, and seek to influence public opinion through the press. The *Hizb al-Watan* (Nationalist Party), led by Mustapha Kamil (1874–1908), advocates through the pages of *al-Liwa* (The standard) the immediate evacuation of all British even if it requires the use of force. The *Hizb al-Umma*, led by Lutfi al-Sayyid (1872–1963), espouses the idea of an Egyptian nation and regards the remolding of laws and institutions in response to the needs of the modern age as the most important task of their time. Al-Sayyid, as editor of *al-Jarida* (The newspaper) contributes to the development of secular liberal ideas at a time when pan-Islamic sentiment still moves the masses. A third political trend known as *as-Salafiya* (an Islamic reform movement), founded by Mohammad Abdu (1849–1905) and catalyzed by Rashid Rida (1865–1935), comes to provide the major opposition to secularism in the early decades of the twentieth century.

1911	Lord Kitchener takes over as high commissioner in Egypt; in 1913, he establishes a legislative assembly.
1914	August 3, outbreak of World War I. Egypt is unilaterally declared a protectorate, an act permanently changing that nation's legal status by detaching it from the Ottoman Sultanate and defining the terms of its future self-government. A new leadership representing the nucleus of a native Egyptian landed and commercial bourgeoisie emerges and demands unconditional national independence. The leader of this new movement is Saad Zaghlul (1857–1927). Son of the mayor of a small village near the provincial capital of Tanta, Zaghlul belongs to an elite group of agriculturalists who are acquiring land and gaining power among the ruins of the domainal system. He frequents the political salon of Princess Nazli and marries the daughter of the prime minister, Safia Mustapha Fahmi Pasha. Although belonging to the old aristocracy, she identifies herself wholly with her husband's nationalist struggle and lives on after his death as the venerated "Mother of the Egyptians."
1915	Doria goes back to Tanta to attend Notre Dame des Apôtres, lives with grandmother Khadiga.
1917	The Russian Revolution.
1918	Armistice declared, the end of World War I. Gamal Abdul Nasser and Anwar Sadat are born.
1919	Fuad marries Nazli Abdul Rahim Sabri (1894–1971), an Egyptian commoner with "foreign" blood. Nazli is the granddaughter of the French Colonel Séve, known as Soliman Pasha al-Fransawi, who was recruited by Muhammad Ali around 1817 to modernize the Egyptian army. She is to bear Fuad one son, Faruq (1920), and four daughters: Fawzia (1921), Faiza (1923), Faika (1926), and Fathia (1930). (Fuad had been previously married to his cousin Princess Chevikar but divorced her in 1898 allegedly because she had not borne him a son.) Zaghlul spearheads the formation of a national delegation (*Wafd al-Misri*) to attend the Paris Peace Conference and put forth the nationalist claim for independence. Zaghloul is not allowed to attend and leads the 1919 national revolution demanding complete independence and the formation of a constitution. Along with Ismail Sidki (1872–1950), he is exiled to Malta.
1920	Doria's mother dies in childbirth, and Doria's forced engagement to nephew of maternal uncle is broken off.

1922   November 28, Britain unilaterally ends protectorate over Egypt and proclaims Sultan Fuad (1868–1936) King Fuad I. The declaration contains provisos, known as the Four Reserved Points, basically assuring continued British control of the Sudan and Egypt's defense, while guaranteeing special protection to the foreign community.

Doria joins her father in Alexandria, enrolls in the mission school of St. Vincent de Paul, and prepares *Brevet Elémentaire*. She changes spelling of her name to Shafik.

1923   Egypt drafts the first Egyptian constitution and holds elections. The constitution establishes a two-chamber parliament: a senate, two-fifths of which are to be appointed by the king, and a chamber of deputies to be elected by universal male suffrage. Huda Sha'rawi returns from the meeting of the International Association of Women in Rome and takes off her veil. Doria enrolls at French Lycée and studies for her baccalaureate.

1924   Egypt's first parliament is elected, along with Prime Minister Zaghlul, who is in the forefront of the attack against the British. Sir Henry Lee Stack, sirdar of the Egyptian army, is assassinated by a group of nationalist extremists ushering in an uninterrupted crisis in domestic politics. Doria passes second part of *bachot* and is awarded silver medal for attaining second highest marks in the country-wide exam.

1925   Sha'rawi founds the Egyptian Feminist Union and establishes its journal, *L'Egyptienne*, with Ceza Nabaraoui as editor-in-chief.

1927   Mustapha al-Nahas (1876–1965) succeeds to the leadership of the Wafd. From this point onward, three groups alternately wield power in Egypt: the palace, the British, and the Wafd, with minority parties manipulating the power struggle between the palace and the Wafd to serve their own interests. Disagreement over the best strategy for dealing with the British erupts within the leadership of the Wafd, leading to the formation of the Liberal Constitutionalist Party by Muhammad Mahmud in 1922 and the People's Party by Ismail Sidki in 1930.

1928   Muslim Brotherhood is founded by Hassan al-Banna. Doria writes to Huda Sha'rawi, meets her in Cairo, and gets scholarship from Ministry of Education. Sha'rawi invites her to speak at Ezbakiya Gardens Theater on May 4, where Doria makes her first public speech for the Egyptian Feminist Union. In August, she sails for France to study at the Sorbonne.

1933   Young Egypt is founded by Ahmed Hussein. Doria obtains *Licence d'Etat* and *Licence Libre*. Returns to Alexandria and stays with her father.

1935   Doria enters Miss Egypt pageant in Alexandria and is runner-up, a fact which attracts huge publicity. Marriage to journalist Ahmad al-Sawi lasts only a few weeks.

1936   Doria divorces al-Sawi and returns to Sorbonne vowing never again to marry. King Fuad dies; Faruq (1920–1965) succeeds to the throne. Anglo-Egyptian Treaty is signed in August. Léon Blum is elected prime minister of France. Fascism on the rise in Europe, Italian troops occupy Addis Ababa. Civil war in Spain.

1936–1939 Palestinian Revolt—5,000 dead. Doria meets Nour al-Din Ragai. They marry in Paris in 1937, honeymoon in England.

1939   Sha'rawi holds first Pan Arab Women's Congress on the Palestine Question. September 1, Germany invades Poland. Outbreak of World War II. Nour finishes his doctorate in law; Doria still needs to defend her two theses. They return to Cairo.

1940   Doria returns to Paris in early spring to defend her theses. Is awarded *Doctorat d'Etat*. Is rebuffed by Egyptian Feminist Union and works as an inspector of French language for the government.

1942   In February, tanks roll up in front of Abdin Palace, and Lampson orders Faruq-appointed pro-British al-Nahas as prime minister. In April, a malaria epidemic breaks out in the southern province of Aswan. November 4, the battle of al-Alamein halts German advance. March 6, Doria gives birth to Aziza.

1944   August 17, Doria gives birth to Jehane. Mme. Marie Reilly becomes children's governess.

1945   Egypt declares war on the Axis, but war ends in May. The United Nations is formed. Prime Minister Ahmad Mahir is assassinated. The Arab League is established. Doria is approached by Princess Chevikar to edit *La Femme Nouvelle*. Doria founds *Bint al-Nil* and publishes first edition in December.

1946   Massive student strikes. Sidki resigns. Doria starts children's magazine, *Katkout*. Meets Pierre Seghers, poet and publisher of resistance literature.

1947   September, cholera epidemic breaks out in the delta province of Sharqiya. November 29, the partition of Palestine. Princess Chevikar dies, and Doria takes over *La Femme Nouvelle*. Huda Sha'rawi dies; Doria is invited to deliver short eulogy.

1948   May 15, Egyptian troops attack Israel unsuccessfully. Palestinians become refugees. Doria founds the Bint al-Nil Union and "goes on the offensive."

1949   Cease-fire, armistice concluded in March. Struggle for national liberation takes various forms. Faruq divorces the popular Queen Farida.

1951   In February, Doria leads a march on parliament, storming the gates demanding rights of suffrage. She is arrested and summoned to appear in court in April, but the case is dismissed sine die. October 8, Wafd unilaterally abrogates Anglo-Egyptian treaty. November through January, violent demonstrations against British occupation. Mossadegh, the first elected prime minister of Iran, visits Cairo.

1952   January 25, British troops kill forty Egyptian police in their quarters in the town of Ismailiya. Doria and Bint al-Nil demonstrate in front of Barclay's Bank. January 26, Egyptian mobs burn foreign clubs and businesses in Cairo (Black Saturday). The king dismisses Nahas, recalls Ali Mahir. In March, Doria registers, illegally, to run for elections. July 23, a military coup. July 26, the king leaves Alexandria. Free Officers annul the 1923 constitution, nationalize the press, abolish political parties, and appoint a fifty-*man* commission to draft a new constitution.

1953   General Naguib is named president. The military Revolutionary Command Council is placed in charge of government.

1954   February 24, Naguib resigns; Nasser takes over as chairman of Revolutionary Command Council. No women on constitutional committee. Martial law reinstated, political parties dissolved, elections postponed. March 12, Doria and eight women from Bint al-Nil stage an eight-day hunger strike at the Press Syndicate to protest omission of women's representation on new constitutional committee. In October, Doria begins round-the-world lecture tour. October 27, attempt on Nasser's life by Muslim Brothers. In November, a new revolutionary tribunal is appointed; Naguib is put under house arrest.

1955   Nasser goes to the Bandung Conference in April and meets Tito, Nehru, and Chou En-lai. Establishment of non-aligned status.

1956   January 16, the new constitution is announced. Women granted the vote, with condition of literacy, but all voluntary and private organizations are suppressed. State co-opts women's voluntary associations and places them under Ministry of Social Affairs. Bint al-Nil, along with all other private associations, collapses. Press turns on Doria and begins a campaign of ridicule. July 26, Nasser announces nationalization of Suez Canal Company. October 29, outbreak of Suez War. Tripartite aggression halted by Eisenhower.

1957   February 6, Doria stages hunger strike at Indian Embassy, demanding the end of dictatorship in Egypt and the withdrawal of Israel from Egyptian soil. She is placed under house arrest. By June, all Doria's magazines cease to exist and her publishing enterprise is closed down. Her name is officially banned from the press. She enters her long period of seclusion in her apartment in Zamalek.

1958   Union with Syria and the formation of the United Arab Republic.

1960   Doria writes a letter to Dag Hammerskjöld protesting impotence of the United Nations to protect "human rights."

1962   Free-enterprise system gives way to a centrally controlled, directed economy. Egyptianization and subsequent nationalization of "enemy property" (largely British, French, and Jewish banks; insurance companies; industrial enterprises; and land holdings).

1965   Mustapha al-Nahas dies; an enormous cortege follows his coffin.

1967   In February, Egypt and Syria sign a mutual-support pact. Israel attacks and annihilates air force during the Six-Day War.

1968   Doria asks for a divorce.

1969   Nasser launches War of Attrition. First grandchild, Nazli, is born to Jehane and Ali.

1970   Black September suppression of Palestinians in Jordan. Nasser mediates. September 28, Nasser dies of a heart attack. Sadat (1918–1981) becomes Egypt's third president.

1971   Sadat successfully survives a major coup against him known as the May 17 Corrective Revolution. Doria visits Aziza in North Carolina and sees her first-born grandson, Sharif.

1973   The October War and negotiations begin with Israel to gain back the Sinai. Sadat initiates his turning to the West and economic liberalization by announcing his "open door" policies. Second granddaughter, Hedayat, is born to Jehane and Ali. Doria beginning to fall into depression; begins writing third version of her memoirs.

1975   September 20, Doria ends her life by throwing herself from her sixth-floor apartment.

The Awakening (1908–1928)

To catch the imponderable thread connecting my very own existence to my own past, as well as to my own country's history and civilization. The Egypt I knew in my early years was an Egypt awakening from a thousand years' sleep, becoming conscious of its long sufferings—that it had rights! And I learned in my early childhood that the Will of woman can supersede the law.

—Shafik, "Memoirs" (1975), 4

1

Between Two Poles (1909–1928)

I find myself again at a huge window, looking out upon the Nile. My governess is holding me and singing a melancholy tune filled with yearning for her native Syria. This view of the river enchants me with its great beauty, overwhelming me with an indescribable feeling of the Infinite—a sort of immanence of the Absolute. I lean out of the window to see where the river ends, but then I feel the painful sensation of restraint as the nimble hands of my governess pull me back to the chair. At the same time I see my mother and grandmother sitting on a large sofa in front of this window, drinking innumerable cups of coffee. Gently and slowly they sip from the small cone-shaped cups as if Time had been stripped of all Motion. If these images return simultaneously, it is for the same reason, for like the Nile, the beauty and the extraordinary presence of my mother dazzled me and conveyed to me my first feeling of the aesthetic. Between these two poles of light my early childhood slips by.

With this nostalgic glance back upon an idyllic scene from her childhood, Doria Shafik opens her memoirs and introduces us not only to the social and historical milieu within which her life unfolded but also to those crucial early experiences which helped shape her into that indefatigable "seeker of the Absolute." It is through her chosen metaphors that we are guided to a deeper understanding of her personality and from which we discover those dominant strands and underlying motifs around which she organized her life.

Born December 14, 1908, in Tanta, the capital of Gharbiya province, in the home of her maternal grandmother, Doria was the third child and second daughter of six children born to Ratiba Nassif "Bey" and Ahmad Chafik "Effendi." Although both parents were natives of Tanta, they belonged to two distinct status groups, a fact revealed by the different titles appearing at the end of their names. Titles were often bestowed on male members of certain powerful families as part of an extensive hierarchical patronage system practiced throughout Egypt when the country was still part of the Turkish Ottoman Sultanate and were coveted marks of status within a society that was rigidly class structured. The most prestigious title, after the elite Royal Family of the Khedive, was that of *Pasha* and was usually reserved for the wealthy and powerful landowners or men in high political positions, whether these were the Turco-Circassian elite or the indigenous Egyptians. *Bey,* a somewhat lesser status, was often granted to men belonging to prominent urban groups, such as lawyers, doctors, and wealthy merchants; or the rural notable families (*al-'ayan*) of the provinces. *Effendi* was usually reserved for the petty civil servants who served in the Khedival government and represented a lower status than *Bey,* but certainly a step higher than the majority of the country's impoverished peasants.

Egypt at the turn of the century was a society in which a multitude of factors combined to create conditions of protracted and intense crisis. The defeat of Ahmad Pasha Orabi in 1882 and the subsequent occupation of Egypt by Great Britain marked the end of one era and the beginning of another in Egyptian modern history. The reform and reconstruction of the Egyptian administration and economy imposed by European financial control over the country not only led to the emergence of near-feudal conditions in which huge social and economic barriers separated social classes; it also meant a further and more rapid fermentation of ideas begun earlier under Muhammad Ali, the founder of the elite Royal Family of Egypt that ended with the abdication of King Faruq in 1952. These conditions of foreign domination provoked profound socioeconomic and political change throughout Egypt during the first quarter of the twentieth century.

Marriages between people from different class backgrounds, while not usual or desired, did occur, particularly when impoverished women of higher status, usually Turco-Circassian, were married off to native Egyptian men of modest means. Due to certain economic and cultural pressure, specifically linked to the family circumstances surrounding Doria's grandmother, Ratiba and Ahmad were forced into such a marriage.

Doria's grandmother, Khadiga, was the granddaughter of one of Tanta's more influential notables, Husayn al-Qasabi, and thus inherited part of the family wealth as well as notable status. When only a child of twelve, Khadiga's family arranged for her marriage to a wealthy man nearly twice her age. By the time she reached her twentieth birthday, she was a widow with three young daughters. As a woman without male heirs, she was prevented by cultural taboos from living on her own, even though the wealth she had inherited from both her husband and her parents would have supported her indepen-

dent existence in great luxury. Women of Khadiga's generation—particularly
those from religiously conservative, Muslim families of the al-'ayan—were
not allowed to live independent lives without endangering their family's reputation in the entire town. Khadiga, therefore, was obliged to live with her elder brother, Abul 'Azz al-Qasabi, known locally as "the pasha" because of his
wealth and very high position in the provincial government. The pasha assumed the guardianship of his sister and her three "orphaned" daughters. Together with his wealthy Turco-Circassian wife, his four daughters, and two
sons, they formed an extended family in his large palace in Tanta. Since there
was never a question of Khadiga's remarrying—"only girls of the street dream
of marrying again after the death of their husbands"—her wealth fell under
the control of her brother. As the absolute master of the family, the pasha
managed her fortune as he liked, without her being able to open her mouth or
demand the least account, "because she was only a woman and meant nothing! She had even to accept her own husband taking a second wife into her
house because she had produced no male heirs."

At the same time, Abul 'Azz's wife believed that it was her prerogative to
arrange the marriages not only of her own daughters but also those of her
husband's sister. For her own daughters, she arranged marriages among those
families who held the same social rank as their father. For the "orphans," she
made other arrangements. Khadiga's eldest daughter, Hafiza, was promised to
an army officer, Ali Chafik, who, although financially comfortable, had neither wealth (that is, land) nor high status. This was considered a shameful
downfall for Khadiga, who upon her own marriage had received several slaves
as a dowry. Because she had no male heirs to protect her own interests or
those of her daughters, Khadiga had to obey her brother (the head of the family) in silence and without protest. As a matter of convenience, the pasha's
wife decided to marry the two sisters at one go. Thus Ratiba, who was barely
fifteen years old, was promised to Ali's younger brother, Ahmad Chafik,
a penniless student at the university finishing his studies in engineering.
To compensate for this financial problem, it was decided that the two young
couples would live together in the household of the elder brother, who would
assume all the financial responsibilities until his younger brother completed
his degree.

A double marriage ceremony, the katb-il-kitab,[1] was arranged immediately.
However, fate intervened, and within a few weeks the army officer was killed
suddenly in an accident, rendering the marriage of Ratiba Nassif to Ahmad
Chafik somewhat meaningless. Even though Ahmad had fallen in love with
his bride upon first seeing her at the contract ceremony, he offered, out of a
fundamental sense of decency and pride, to withdraw from the marriage contract if the pasha demanded it. Neither Khadiga nor her brother would con-

sent to annulling a marriage. That would have meant divorce in front of society and thus would have brought great dishonor to all the family. Khadiga later explained to her granddaughter Doria: "Weighing the two choices, a poor man from a lower class or a family dishonored by divorce, the Pasha decided to accept your father as the lesser of the two evils."

This class difference between her parents was a source of pain to the sensitive child who felt that people around her considered her father not equal to being the husband of a woman as well-born as her mother: "There always seemed to be an unspoken feeling of mortification within Mama, who felt diminished compared to her cousins, the majority of whom had married wealthy landowners. And within Papa, a profound hurt. He loved my mother deeply and had achieved a high level of culture through his own efforts, yet he felt irreconcilably outclassed. A great tragedy existed within my family and they hardly even realized it."

This class difference also heightened Doria's awareness of the particular qualities she admired in each of her parents. From her mother, she developed a love of beauty; from her father, the joy of reading and a deep sense of religious devotion. Although her love for her mother surpassed everything else, Doria was also very fond of her father, whom she describes as "a man of deep intellect and piety with an appearance of timidity and impenetrable reserve who, like myself, adored my mother. I often overheard people say that my mother had fallen on good luck; for however poor the revenues of Papa might have been he was a very kind man and always showed great deference to his wife."

* * *

During the first eighteen years of her life, Doria grew up within three different social and cultural milieus of Egypt, Mansura, Tanta, and Alexandria, each of which would be remembered because of their special significance in her life. For Doria, these towns became identified with three different cultural worlds that evoked contradictory emotional feelings. Mansura always remained the idyllic locale where her mother's loving presence provided Doria with stability and a sense of her own significance. Tanta, on the other hand, represented Khadiga's household, conveying feelings of sadness, separation and estrangement, a sense of chaos and disorder, the oppressive weight of ancient customs and traditions. But Alexandria exposed Doria to the world of ideas, the encounter between East and West. From it she herself would embark for Paris in her ambitious quest for a coveted degree from the Sorbonne.

She spent the first seven or eight years of her childhood in the picturesque town of Mansura, in the province of Daqahliya, where her father had been posted by the government as a civil engineer for the railways. She would later return to Tanta for her schooling. Mansura personified her mother's household, embodying feelings of happiness, love and tenderness, a sense of order and harmony, the Nile's serenity. On its way through Mansura, the Damietta branch of the Nile flowed past her window. Doria's awakening to the pain of separation came about when Ratiba left her husband and children for several months of the year to stay with her mother and unmarried sisters in Tanta: "For half the year my grandmother and her youngest daughter, Hikmat, who at seventeen and unmarried was considered a potential old maid, lived with us in Mansura. The other six months my mother returned to Tanta with grandmother, leaving me and my sisters and brothers under the care of Badia, the Syrian governess, and an array of domestic servants. These frequent separations were exasperating and filled me with a dreadful anxiety. When my mother left, the sun seemed to vanish around me and the days grew long. To forget the pain and to help the time pass I would watch the boats on the Nile glide by my window."

Doria grew up in a basically female-centered household which included her mother, her grandmother, her unmarried Aunt Hikmat, and her orphaned cousin Zohra—whose mother, Hafiza, having lost her husband, Ali, after only a few weeks of marriage, died herself while giving birth. In addition, there was a swarm of servants, among whom was Zaynab, her mother's maid and a key figure in Doria's early life, with whom she felt a very close bond: "I loved Zaynab, she had the gift of the gab and the charm of the story teller and she enraptured us children with her wondrous tales of good and evil spirits." It was Zaynab who told Doria the story of her parents' marriage. It was Zaynab who brought "the sorceress into the house to perform mysterious rituals for Mama and her friends." Ruling over this menagerie of servants and children was Badia, the French-speaking, Syrian nanny. Badia also took care of Doria's older sister Soraya, "who I adored because of her good humor," and her elder brother Gamal, "who had an excessively turbulent and violent temper brought on by a childhood disease which had left him with a very bad limp. His lack of response to affection and his tempestuousness earned him the title 'the lame brat.'" What seems clear in her own mind is that Doria felt she was the favorite child of her mother, while Soraya was the favorite of her grandmother. "My sister called me *La Reine* [the Queen], because of the special attention I received from Mama, who was a sort of Divinity in my eyes, and I was in heaven whenever I could be the center of her attention." Her other siblings, Ali, Muhammad and Layla, were all much younger and, with the exception of Ali, were born after Doria had gone to live in Tanta.

As a child growing up in Mansura on the eve of the First World War, Doria observed that being female involved differential, unequal, and sometimes unjust treatment. Why was she punished when she walked on the side of the

river near the boys' school? Why couldn't she enter the mosque as her brothers did? Why was Zaynab, the maid, beaten and banished to Tanta? Why did
the husband of her mother's friend take a second wife? Why did the sorceress
perform special rituals so that women would have male children? Was there
something bad in being a girl?

Her mother's pregnancy with Ali worried Doria. She had overheard the
servants talking about her mother having a baby, and this awakened her curiosity. She asked Badia, "Why is Mama wearing such large dresses and looking
so heavy and clumsy? How will she have the baby?" Badia told her, "One day
you will find it under the tree, near the window":

> The days passed and the baby didn't appear. I was convinced that as soon
> as the baby appeared, Badia would rush and grab it from the branches
> and carry it immediately to my mother's room. Grandmother arrived
> with her two slaves,[2] Adam, a large black woman who was totally veiled
> and never left the house nor spoke to anyone, and Lala Fayruz, a wom-
> anish looking eunuch with large tinted lips, a red fez and the voice of a
> child. Why does a woman have the name of a man? Why does a man
> have a voice like a child? Badia said I asked too many questions! A few
> days later grandmother and the "wise woman" are in my mother's room
> and I hear her cries. Soon I hear Zaynab shouting: "It's a boy!" I ran to
> the window but I understood nothing as the most absolute calm reigned
> at the tree. A few weeks later mother came out of her room and I saw
> that she had regained her svelte figure and I wondered if there wasn't
> some connection between her thinness and the arrival of the baby and
> posed the question to Badia who slapped me across the face forbidding
> me to ask the same question again. What had I done to deserve such a
> reprimand?

This response to her innocent question so upset her that it inhibited her from
approaching her father "with the heap of questions that worried me. I wanted
to ask him what God looked like? Was he like the round, white rock near the
bridge or like the trees by the window? Afraid of exposing myself to other
smacks I decided not to ask any more questions"—not even when she participated in the naming ceremony of her new-born brother a few days later.

Throughout Egypt, especially among traditional families in the rural areas,
during a special ceremony called the *siboua* (literally meaning "the seventh
day after birth") children, males usually, are the center of a joyous celebration
and given their names. Ali was named after his uncle, the army officer who
had died tragically, shortly after marrying Ratiba's sister. The ritual, which
involves a great deal of cultural symbolism, accentuates the social value of
males. "In an elaborate procession Ali was taken from Mama's room and car-

ried by Lala Fayruz through two rows of lighted candles held by the children (males on one side females on the other) to the Rabbi who was waiting to carry out the circumcision. The servants trilled their ululation; incense hung heavily in the air and songs were sung—all in celebration of the birth of a boy." She wondered about the day of her own birth—"a day no doubt filled with great gloom. Are boys truly better than girls? This question would torment me for a long time. But the sting of the slap guarded my tongue."

In addition to observing traditional rituals within her immediate family, Doria also listened to stories of women's lives told by her mother's friends, the wives of the town notables who "flocked to our house attracted to mother who was like the radiant sun of the universe. Every Monday afternoon when the ladies of Mansura visited, the entire household bustled with movement as everything was turned upside down and father was banished to his library." During these gatherings, Doria listened to the women tell their life stories and was astonished at how powerfully the institutions of polygamy and divorce and the values of shame and honor were embedded in the fabric of society and how heavily they weighed on the lives of these women:

An oppressive and agitated atmosphere reigned that Monday in the sitting room of our house in Mansura. It was as if a beloved friend had died. They were all there: Mama, Grandmother, my unmarried Aunt Hikmat, the ladies of Mansura, Zaynab and the itinerant peddler looking shamefaced as if she had committed a great crime! The cause of this gloom was the news that the wife of the town prosecutor, Mama's friend, had just learned that her husband had taken a second wife, because she had failed to produce a male heir. The peddler had been given a large sum of money to procure the services of a local sorceress who had promised to use her special powers to bring a son from this pregnancy. But instead of the desired male, the woman gave birth to twin daughters, augmenting to nine the number of her female children. Now faced with a second wife in her household she shouted. "I want a divorce!" With that shout an icy silence fell over the room. I remained transfixed with astonishment, not only at the violent reaction of this woman who up until now was considered a sort of simpleton incapable of taking any serious action, but also at the energetic opposition to her announced decision by the women around her. Grandmother whose attachment to the past could not be severed so easily led the campaign. "I don't understand you women of today insisting on exclusiveness. You are making a mountain out of a molehill. By taking a second wife the husband reduces the burden on the woman. I remember when my husband took another wife, I was pleased to have a friend in my rival. For I was sick to death of the company of slaves, eunuchs and servants. I had someone to talk to. And even when he took a third wife we all banded together against him, the common enemy. Never pronounce the word divorce! It signifies dishonor for you and your daughters who will never see the shadow of a suitor if you act in this way." My grandmother's words seemed to act as a whip over the other women as the thought of their daughters being old maids sank in and they all rallied round her. "Forget this idea," my mother counseled, "You must fight to regain your husband's love." "To fail once or even many times does not mean you will always fail," concluded grandmother. So they decided to ask the peddler woman to find her sorceress again.

Doria grew up not only listening to these women's unhappy tales of domestic life but also sensing her mother's inferiority complex in front of certain relatives within their extended family structure. Whenever her Aunt Aziza, Ratiba's best friend and wealthy cousin from Cairo would visit them in Mansura, bringing news of the latest fashions and political events from the capital, "the whole household was turned inside out in preparation. It was necessary that Tante Zaza, who was married to a rich lawyer from Cairo, see that our lifestyle was that of a rich family. Always this same complex with my mother."

Although Doria was aware that women were being treated unfairly, she also realized that in the bosom of her own family, her mother totally dominated her father and even herself. Her mother and grandmother could get all they wanted by manipulating her father into feeling that everything had been his idea in the first place. His complete and utterly selfless devotion to his wife was the envy of many of the women in Mansura:

> Better a kind husband than a rich and tyrannical one. Mama could never get used to the idea that she was married to a simple functionary who had no other revenue than his salary. Her lavish attempts to maintain appearances in front of her rich cousins led to a continual exhaustion of the financial resources of the household—until the point of bankruptcy. There were never sufficient funds from my father's modest salary to maintain the lavish style in which my mother entertained. This became the chief source of friction between my parents as well as creating within me a great feeling of insecurity. I felt somewhat deceived that Mama attached more importance to her innumerable friends, to the Monday receptions, to the visits of Grandmother, to the cousins from Cairo who came with their children, than she did to our comfort or that of Papa.

Not only was Doria an unhappy witness to the social inequality "reigning within the bosom of my own family"; she also felt the sting of humiliation in being relegated to a class category inferior to her own self image: "I always had the tendency to place things and people into categories and classes. And as

I nearly always figured out that I was not on the class level that I imagined, I suffered terribly."

She noticed that "our home like the homes of all the other less wealthy people in Mansura, was situated on the banks of the diversionary canal, called the little river, while those of the great landowners were all along the banks of the great river." She was made to feel that the nationality of one's governess could also be the basis for lowered social status. The most wealthy families could afford to hire an English governess, which was the case with her Aunt Aziza. She felt demeaned "when one day my cousin threw me a haughty look, scorning Badia, who was but a simple Syrian. I was mortified not only because I loved Badia but because this governess hierarchy relegated me to the less wealthy or rather the more poor. My cousin could attend the prestigious French Lycée in Cairo while I had to enroll in the miserable Italian nuns' school in Mansura."

These early childhood encounters with the yoke of social and gender inequality must have provoked within Doria some very deep, personal feelings of outrage and indignation and probably did more than anything else to aggravate her impulsive temperament to revolt. While questioning (within herself, to be sure) the reasons behind these social inequities, she seemed equally preoccupied with trying to understand the meaning of God. There were so many diverse interpretations of the divinity expressed by those around her. There was the God of Zaynab, who "always blended His name along with the pantheon of underworld spirits and jinns to assure her protection from the evil eye or the veracity of her words." There was the God of her Christian governess and the nun's church that "thanks to the stained-glass windows allowed me to imagine God in a human form." There was the God of her grandmother, "who prayed five times a day to some invisible person demanding regularly, at the end of each prayer, the protection of her two remaining daughters." Her mother hardly mentioned God at all, but Doria believed that "my mother's beauty was testimony enough to His existence." Finally there was the God of her pious father, "the most formidable of all, the God who did not pardon":

> The interpretation that my father gave to us of the divinity was so abstract that I could not understand a thing. It was absolutely forbidden for us to represent God under any material form whatsoever. I would break my head trying to represent a line so very fine that it would escape matter. But always I would stumble on a material object. I was very often disturbed thinking about this during the night. Then one day while watching the river moving toward the invisible, beyond the distant shore, I had the intuition that God must be there. Often when I awoke at dawn to the chant of the muezzin,[3] I was filled with this profound emotion, a

harmony blending with a sense of quietude. I forgot every oppression. Not understanding what had passed through me I remained overwhelmed by nothing less than an indescribable symphony. Everything, like the minaret, which I could see from my window on the opposite side of the little river, seemed to soar up in the direction of heaven, in prayer. The breaking forth of this religious sentiment filled me with a sense of the beautiful.

During her early childhood, Doria never felt the same sense of harmony with other people that she experienced in the presence of her mother and the river. Even when she was playing "rough games" with the other children, games she wanted to join, "I always had this unbearable sensation of feeling like a stranger. I experienced a great trauma in discovering myself *un être à part*— not like everybody else. It tortured me to find that I was too thoughtful for my age. Being too young, I did not understand the irreconcilable opposition in me between dreams and action. An antagonism that took me a very long time and many battles to resolve. Whereas the others played simply, my reflections preoccupied me to the point of paralysis, depriving me of that ease which I instinctively tried to grasp. I was unhappy."

This sense of estrangement was accentuated by her mother's frequent and long absences. Doria was left under the care of Badia and the domestic servants and, in her solitude, would often slip into a mood of withdrawal, "listening to songs of the boatmen on the Nile which enchanted me and helped dissipate my misery. They were like a lament and blended perfectly with the chants of the muezzin."

*   *   *

A most painful moment of separation occurred when Doria was around six or seven years old. Her parents decided to send her to Tanta to live with her grandmother so that she could attend the highly respected French Mission School, Notre Dame des Apôtres. Foreign schools, particularly French mission schools, played a prominent role in the education of a certain class of Egyptian women during the latter part of the nineteenth and the early part of the twentieth centuries. When Doria entered primary school, more than half of all young women registered in schools throughout the country were in foreign sectarian schools—most of them Coptic, Greek, or Jewish—to which very few Muslim families sent their girls. The number of French mission schools was nearly triple that of the British, even though the country was a British protectorate. It was only in 1873 that the first Muslim girls' school (al-Saniya) was founded under the patronage of Haunt, Ismail Pasha's third wife. Few upper-class families appear to have taken advantage of this school because at the beginning, "girls were recruited from among the white slaves belonging to the different families related to the ruler and from the families of the palace officials. The foreign aristocratic families employed European teachers privately, a practice not widely adopted by the Egyptian people."[4] By the end of World War I, it was becoming increasingly more prestigious and culturally acceptable for middle-class Muslim families to educate their daughters in foreign schools. However, the objective was not to prepare such a young woman for an independent life. It was to equip her with those proper and desirable assets that would make her a "Lady of the Salon" and thus an attractive prospect for a good arranged marriage.

The decision to send Doria to Notre Dame des Apôtres had as much to do with her mother's social-class aspirations for her daughter (after all, she herself had attended this school) as it did with the actual lack of governmental schools for women in the provinces as this time. There is no question that this decision would influence the future course of Doria's life. On one level, this early educational experience contributed to her bias toward French language and culture, alienating her from the more dominant Arabic cultural and linguistic roots of Egyptian society. On another level, it intensified her sense of abandonment by her mother.

When she learned that she would have to leave Mansura, she was filled with misgivings: "I could not imagine how it would be possible to leave Mama, my ultimate source of joy, my source of light without whom everything in me and around me became dark." But her mother persuaded her that it would be in her best interest to go to this school, which was far superior to the one in Mansura. In fact Doria felt stifled by the Italian nuns' school, "where nothing had ever attracted me except the immense garden where we played all too briefly and the grand piano in the parlor on which despite the lessons, I never could quite create the right sounds. I paid more attention to the music from the chapel than my lessons and received innumerable raps on the knuckles." Doria attempted to compensate for her unhappiness at the thought of being separated from her mother by telling herself that she would at least be reunited with her sister, Soraya, who had been sent to Tanta two years earlier. Despite their sibling jealousies over parental attentions, Doria missed her sister's vivacity and was looking forward to being "happily established in Grandmother's house and perhaps in Grandmother's heart as well."

Accompanied by her mother and Badia, Doria traveled the thirty-five miles from Mansura to Tanta by train. When she arrived at this melting pot of the Delta—the heroic capital of Gharbiya province and the third largest industrial and commercial city in Egypt[5]—her dream that "Tanta might be even more beautiful than Mansura" was shattered by a first impression that seemed to augur the bleak life that lay ahead of her: "The streets seemed dirty and the people had ghost-like faces. Tanta was a town without color, without light and above all without the Nile. Nothing but a miserably shallow and muddy canal. Was it chiefly the absence of Mama and the Nile? Or was it perhaps an intuition of the unhappiness that was awaiting me?"

Her grandmother was now living in her own house. Since her daughters Ratiba and Hikmat were now married and her older daughter as well as older brother had died, Khadiga al-Qasabi was no longer forcibly obliged to live under male tutelage. Although she could have benefited more in a material sense by living within the household of her wealthy and forceful uncle, al-Sa'id al-Qasabi (1860–1927), son of the powerful Husayn al-Qasabi, she was allowed to live independently in her own house on part of the family estate she inherited after her brother's death. In Doria's eyes, this decision reflected a "contempt for material values," an attitude that Doria always admired in her maternal grandmother. The fact that Khadiga was allowed to do this suggests a certain relaxation on the seclusion of widows. A more fundamental reason for her decision is probably linked to the status difference that existed between Khadiga and her uncle. Although he had political power ("On February 23, 1924, al-Sa'id al-Qasabi was elected senator from Tanta"), he lacked social status ("He was black and wore a gallabiya").[6] In Egyptian parlance, to "wear a gallabiya" (a loose-fitting robe, the traditional dress of peasant males) usually meant that one was of the underprivileged class and also illiterate. To hint at his skin color was to suggest his black "slave" origins.

Although uncle and niece were linked agnatically through Husayn al-Qasabi, they did not share the same mother. Among certain wealthy, rural notable families of Husayn's generation, it was not unusual for a man to have several wives as well as concubines. In fact, it was common family knowledge that al-Sa'id was the offspring of the union between his father and a black concubine slave, which automatically made him Khadiga's social inferior. Despite this "status inferiority" and the fact that he was also illiterate, al-Sa'id al-Qasabi was still able to amass a large fortune through the cultivation and sale of cotton during the war years. He was able to "buy" his way into a dominant social position through the avenue of politics. During the stormy years following World War I that were characterized by national uprisings and the rise to power of Saad Zaghlul and the Wafd, al-Sa'id rapidly became a very prominent personality in Tanta: "People were whispering that al-Sa'id had filled his pockets with Grandmother's fortune and in its turn the Wafd party had fed its treasury with al-Sa'id's money. And rumors affirmed that al-Sa'id's millions were the only reason that he had been chosen by the Wafd party as a parliamentary candidate of Gharbiya governorate. When I compare this powerful, though illiterate, man to my brilliant father, whose name never appeared in the papers, I was nauseated at the unjust power of money."

If Tanta could evoke her mood of revulsion as personified in someone like al-Sa'id al-Qasabi, it could equally spark her feelings of religious sensibility as embodied in the figure of the thirteenth-century Shaykh al-Sayed Ahmad al-Badawi, one of Egypt's most holy and venerated Sufi shaykhs. Although born in Fez, Morocco (A.H. 596, Islamic calendar), al-Badawi's ancestral lineage goes back to a religious family in Mecca. He received intensive religious training as a youth and later turned to mysticism. After making the pilgrimage to Mecca, he traveled to Iraq to meet Sufi leaders there and eventually settled down in Tanta. It is believed that he possessed miraculous powers of healing, and still today, tens of thousands of people pour into Tanta in late October for the celebration of his annual *Moulid,* or festival, marking his birth. A mosque named after him and constructed over his tomb attracts many pilgrims throughout the year and accentuates the sacred origins of the town itself. Three weeks prior to al-Badawi's birthday in October, thousands of people from all parts of Egypt and even from countries as far away as Pakistan and India flock to Tanta, set up their tent-like pavilions around the city, and engage in religious rituals, including recitations from the Quran, the slaughter of calves whose meat is distributed to the poor, and the telling of mystical, religious stories, accompanied by the playing of tambourines. Sufi religious leaders sway rhythmically while chanting Quranic verses and odes to the Prophet Muhammad.

Zaynab, her mother's servant, once took Doria to Shaykh al-Badawi's *Moulid.* She describes in her memoirs her feelings upon visiting his tomb:

All along the streets on the sidewalks are immense heaps of *hommos* [chickpeas] gathered into pyramids illuminating the town like so many lamps of shining yellow. Sidewalks are crowded with vendors selling al-Badawi's *halawa semsimeya* [candy made of sesame and roasted chickpeas]. Groups of young men dressed in *gallabiyas* chanting verses from the Quran circulate around the tomb carrying on their shoulders large green drapes covered with religious inscriptions. In the interior of the mosque there is a large silver grille encircling the tomb of the Shaykh. The sick crowded around to touch his tomb in the hopes of being healed. Zaynab points out to me the special place in the corner of the mosque that is reserved for Grandmother and her uncle. Because of their lineage connections to al-Badawi (and thus to the Prophet himself) they have the honor of being buried there. While listening to the religious songs I felt transported beyond the crowds. These songs that I was hearing for the first time were not unknown to me. They seemed to arise from my own depths. Then I remembered the church of Mansura where my governess used to take me every Sunday until my father discovered and forbade it. The songs of the church blended intimately with the songs of the Quran evoking the feeling of God's infinite mercy. The faith of these pilgrims evoked the profound beliefs of my father. I was deeply moved.

Except for these brief moments of inner harmony evoked by religion and her mother's visits, Doria always felt ill at ease in her grandmother's house, where "I lived as a stranger." There seemed to be "a tribal atmosphere where the interests of the community dominated those of the individual." She felt helpless. Even the house was constructed as a labyrinth so that "in order to go from the kitchen to the dining room you had to go through the bedrooms and in order to go from the bedrooms to the bathroom you had to go through the dining room. An uninterrupted stream of busy people scurried up and down the numerous hidden staircases so that you couldn't climb two steps without bumping into a servant or a door. I felt like a boat going adrift. An unvoiced revolt against the negation of my self started to rise within me! My torments began."

Another source of confusion arising from her early childhood experiences centered around the meaning of love and how severely a woman could be punished for admitting to "being in love." One year during *Sham al-Nessim* —a holiday associated with the planting season, its name literally meaning "the breathing of spring"[7]—when Doria returned with her grandmother to Mansura to enjoy a long school vacation with her family, she was witness to the disaster that befalls a woman who publicly reveals her love. Badia, the governess, was allegedly jealous of Zaynab's vitality and charm and, therefore, reported to her mistress that Zaynab had sent a note wrapped around a gift of chocolate to the neighbor's cook:

My mother's first reaction was to dismiss the affair with a smile but Grandmother was scandalized and our household erupted into a tempest. Zaynab shut herself in the bathroom beating her cheeks and pulling her hair and crying: "If only the 'master' (meaning my father) doesn't find out." One knew the intransigence of Papa on the question of honor. It was the duty of the man to safeguard the honor of the family. Zaynab's own brothers swore to kill her. When father returned from work and found out what had happened he beat Zaynab without pity. It was the first time I had ever seen my father, usually so timid and sweet, actually strike someone. I was very upset. Is it a sin to love? How could I explain the very great love that Papa has for Mama. Why is this love permitted and not that of Zaynab for the cook, which seemed equally touched by the Absolute? This problem tormented me: Why is something so beautiful as love prohibited? What would I be without Mama's love? My questions remained unanswered but I took my precautions: Never speak from the balcony to the neighbor's son.

More disturbing to Doria was to witness the fate that awaited Zaynab following her fall from grace. Ratiba and her mother arranged to marry her off, not to the cook but to an old, one-eyed former servant of Khadiga's who owned a small carpentry shop in Tanta and was not himself married. The plan was to offer him thirty pounds of Zaynab's own savings on the condition that he marry a "dishonored" girl:

Zaynab, who was so much the source of gaiety and life within the household that she was always in demand by the ladies and children to tell stories and enact veritable pieces of theater, became very sad. All her dreams of beauty and of love vanished. She was now destined to pass the rest of her life with a husband three times her age, who mistreated her at every turn. I often overheard Zaynab complain to her mother who repeated the same refrain again and again: The only things that the woman can resort to are patience and resignation! After a short time I don't remember seeing Zaynab again, she had been delivered over to her unhappiness—her destiny—to use the language consonant with the atmosphere of fatalism in which I grew up.

Although her own father was kind and gentle toward his wife, Doria grew up in an atmosphere where women, rich or poor, suffered in their marriages and lived at the mercy of man and the "whims of his tyranny, a tyranny that had become second nature." Al-Sa'id al-Qasabi seemed a living proof:

His first wife was a black ex-slave whom he regularly forced to abort through harsh beatings. Because he himself was the black son of a black concubine and had suffered great humiliation during his childhood, he did not want a black son. "My sons will be white," he had declared. Whereupon the wife prayed to God that he would never have a child. And God executed that prayer. For in taking three consecutive wives he did not produce an heir. The fourth, a Lebanese, had been chosen because her sisters had each given their husband seven sons. However despite recourse to sorceresses and midwives no heirs appeared. Her life was spent in the monotony of the greatest luxury, totally lacking in any spiritual nourishment. In time this luxury became as intolerable as the greatest misery. I wondered who suffered the most of these two women: The wealthy Lebanese or the poor Zaynab? It was not easy to answer.

Doria's observations of oppression and injustice were not limited to the institution of marriage. Notre Dame des Apôtres disappointed her with its harsh discipline, "generally found in religious institutions." She recalls being slapped by one of the sisters for reading a book that was "not for my age" and being wrongly accused of taking someone else's pen and being embarrassed by her rich cousins attending the same school for not being a "daughter of landowners." She seems to have compensated for these cheerless experiences by identifying with the "songs coming from the chapel," which, although different, reminded her of the call to prayer from the minaret:

> The call to prayer from the minaret awakened a memory of a past glory. The song from the chapel invaded me with the splendor of the unknown. Behind those stained-glass windows of a million colors (I see them still) was the world of dreams. Flights toward the immeasurable, the Absolute. As Muslim students we were not allowed access into the chapel,[8] hence I never saw the interior, which concealed the immensity of my dreams. I remember the indescribable effect of the shimmering lights of the stained glass windows that served as an intermediary between my flashing imagination and that which I supposed to be there, beyond the real. All the beauty of the dream. The music from the chapel transmitted a new vision, a new language.

Her aesthetic sensitivities were profoundly shaped by these two great religious traditions which permeated her early childhood.

However, it was *Ramadan*—the holy month of fasting for all Muslims whose observance constitutes one of the five pillars of Islam—that most symbolized her identification as Muslim: "It was that moment of the year during which the spirit of religion permeated every object and every word, to the degree that the poetry of the Quran itself raised human existence to the level of the Absolute." For Doria the exalted moments of *Ramadan* were always associated with the blind Quran singer who used to pass the entire month at her grandmother's:

> To hear her sing was to savor the life of the beyond. I often sat near her on the couch (out of respect for the Quran she did not sit on the floor like the other servants). As soon as the divine words rang out, silence was imposed and it was never broken until the singer gave the signal. I used to ask her to sing the verse about Miriam (Mary, the mother of Jesus). I listened to her with profound emotion, delighted that silence substituted for the great disorder that habitually reigned in Grandmother's house. I felt transported onto another plane where there was nothing except order, harmony, love and peace of the soul. At the moment when the anguish of the Virgin was sung, I nearly stopped breathing. Her sufferings were carried with such grace that I loved suffering![9]

A presentiment of my childhood was that through suffering and love one arrives at the Sublime.

The feast days following *Ramadan* were usually periods of great joy for Doria because her parents always came to join the family celebration at her grandmother's farm outside Tanta. It was during one of the feasts of *Grand Bairam*[10] that Doria became aware of her mother's very serious heart condition, deepening her foreboding of disaster.

Her mother, who was in her early thirties, was expecting her seventh child, even though she suffered from frequent cardiac crises and had been repeatedly warned by doctors that having more children would most certainly result in her death:

> The feast began badly for me. At dawn all the children had been assembled on the terrace to assist in the sacrifice of the sheep.[11] We arrived at the moment the throat was slit and I fainted. Too sensitive. Words resounded in my ears as if someone had said I was incurably ill. But as long as Mama was there my pains did not last long. Her presence, even the fact of her existence (although far from me) was a balm. When the shock of the morning began to wear off toward the end of the day, there came another event that was much worse. The doctor was summoned in great haste. My father had a very worried look on his face. But the fact that Mama was always radiant and never stayed in her bed reassured me. A momentary illness, I convinced myself, but an indescribable anxiety invaded me. Is it possible that Mama could die? No! God would not allow it! And above all Grandmother prayed five times a day. I decided that I would also pray. This was one of the blackest nights of my life. I overheard Mama talking to Papa: "Before I die I would like to assure the future of Doria, as I have done for Soraya." (My elder sister had been engaged earlier to one of father's nephews who was studying medicine in Cairo). "With my two eldest married off, each in her turn could look after Layla." Mama's words cut through me like a knife. Papa reprimanded her tenderly assuring her that she was in good health. The tears in her voice revealed the horrible truth.

Within a few days, an engagement was arranged between Doria and a nephew of al-Sa'id al-Qasabi, "a man I had seen once and only from a distance during the marriage of Aunt Hikmat. He was rich, and for my mother that was sufficient guarantee for my future security." The marriage would be consummated only after the nephew's return from Germany where he was completing his medical studies and when Doria would have reached her sixteenth birthday. How did she feel? "A ring was put on my finger and with it was the collapse of all my dreams of a free future! A door had been slammed on the unknown and its unsuspected riches. Distressed, I felt marriage was nothing but a mere expedient undertaken in dreadful circumstances."

Doria, who had not yet passed her thirteenth birthday, could not displease her mother, whose very existence seemed tenuous. She thus "made no protest against that which had been decided for my future" and endured her fate with painful resignation. She returned to school and anxiously awaited the summer holidays when the family would again be reunited on the farm and Doria would have the chance to be near her beloved mother. But what appeared to be the start of a happy family reunion would end in a cruel nightmare:

> I was so happy! I simply couldn't believe that I would be with my mother for two whole months. I remained close to her side so as not to lose one moment of our time together. All the family surrounded us. The brightness of her beauty and incomparable high spirits drove away any dark thoughts about my future. She was captivating. At thirty-four she was in the prime of her beauty. One morning toward dawn the morbid sounds of women shrieking awakened me and I ran towards Grandmother's room. A servant stopped me and announced: "Your mother is dead!" The abyss opened under my feet. Vainly I searched for tears. Stupefied, I was suspended in the void!

This loss of her mother was the single most excruciating experience of Doria's childhood. Recalling that moment in her memoirs nearly thirty-five years later, she wrote, "Such a day remains in my memory as a profound and incurable trauma, a wound so huge that it marked, with its desolation, the whole of my life. I feel I am returning to an immense emptiness of sadness. My pen slides away from my fingers as if loath to continue. Terrified. To return to this Time, so decisive in my young existence, is painful." And in the midst of these sentences, she penned in French this short verse: "Tous ces murs si hauts si sombres qui s'écroulent sur moi!" [All these walls so high, so gloomy, are crumbling in upon me!].

*   *   *

Doria, along with the other children and the cook, was immediately sent back to Tanta, where her mother would be buried in the family tomb. In the frenzy that ensued, the cook mistakenly bought third-class tickets, creating a situation which further added to Doria's gloom and her creeping realization that now she was "an orphan." As she entered her grandmother's house, she was overpowered by the cries, tears, and laments of the women friends and relatives who had come from near and far to offer their condolences. She observed the dignified silence of the men gathered in the large tent set up outside the house—men who "retained a sort of stoicism in face of death"—in contrast to the frenzied shrieking of the women within the house, who "gave the impression of having caught fire." And throughout these painful moments, not one person took her into their arms to comfort or console her. No one seemed to notice the lost and lonely child forgotten amid the tumult:

> All these women, including the servants, were beating their faces in the traditional gesture of sadness, and wearing black. Where did all these women come from—so numerous, in the rooms, on the staircase, everywhere that it became impossible to circulate? The house became an immense black blot, as did my heart! Grandmother in the midst of this madness was the living image of desolation. Resigned to the will of God! I tried to reach her but I was prevented. I had the sensation of being shipwrecked in the midst of a sea of black veils. Suddenly the howling of the women increased as the coffin departed, accompanied only by the men. I tried to get to a window to see Mama one last time. But how to get through this mad crowd? I was pushed back. I thought of the terrace, I stumbled on the staircase. A waif.

Following his wife's death, Ahmad Chafik was transferred to Cairo. He left his three sons and youngest daughter, Layla, in the care of Badia in Mansura, while Doria and her elder sister Soraya remained with their grandmother in Tanta. The next two years were very miserable for Doria, who felt not only the loss of her mother but also the complete dislocation of her family. She cannot remember the family "ever being all together again" except for very short periods of time, and for the rest of her life, she never went back to Mansura: "Nothing in the world would make me set foot in this town where a thousand details would evoke the past without end." From that moment, her father "closed in upon himself and his sadness, honoring to the end of his days his absolute love of my mother." But according to Doria, "This somber solitude that my father had consciously chosen was not completely negative or empty of content. After my mother's death, pledging himself entirely to the education of his children, he did his utmost for each of them. Imposing on himself total abnegation he channeled toward his children his infinite love for my mother. It was only later, reading the work of Balzac, that I saw in my father that grand figure Père Goriot."

With this further separation from her family, Doria felt even more lonely and lost. This town that she had never liked from the very beginning became even more intolerable after her mother's death. Her grandmother became the epitome of human sadness at its most tragic—seeking solace in religion, praying the customary five times a day and passing every Friday at her daughter's tomb, taking Doria with her. But Doria cried so much that she stopped accompanying her grandmother. According to her younger sister, Layla, "Doria was so totally broken-hearted that she cried continually and shut herself into her room for days on end, not talking to anyone."[12] In her own memoirs Doria describes herself as "Being lost in the desert, without a guide. I felt I was becoming this great sick being. A being on the margin of her surroundings, who ceased being interested in that which preoccupied others . . . and who little by little saw others losing interest in her. Discovering myself at the edge of the abyss . . . by instinct I reacted. To be able to turn my back on my grief. . . I don't say forget. I needed to act. I threw myself completely into the preparation of my exams."

School became an outlet for her despair, and she excelled to such an extent that at the end of the term she skipped a class, finishing her certificate of studies within the same year as her sister. This pleased her father, who "visited me often in Tanta smiling at my scholarly success." Then Soraya's fiancé, having completed his studies in England, returned. At age sixteen her sister, who had little interest in further studies, married and moved to Alexandria, where her father had also been transferred. Her sister's marriage made Doria conscious of the eventual return from Germany of her own betrothed, and the idea of an arranged marriage haunted her and created an "intolerable oppression as each day passed by. But how to get out of it?"

Doria thought of leaving Tanta to go and live with her father in Alexandria but did not want to hurt her grandmother, "who found in me the image of her daughter." Doria never doubted, however, that the "moment would come when this obsession with leaving would carry me away." Biding her time until the proper moment, Doria wrote to her father asking him to take her with him to Cairo to pass the *Bairam* holidays. Her father happily agreed and took the opportunity to show her the ancient monuments that were the "marvel of our capital": "I rediscovered the Nile, my great friend, almost not daring to look at it in such a strong light. The Pyramids welcomed me from the distant land of my ancestors! At the foot of the Sphinx my heart beat as I, drowned in his look, heard his words: 'Doria don't ever despair.'"

Whether her father sensed her unhappiness or Doria asked him directly is not clear. But shortly after her visit, her father told Khadiga that he wanted to take Doria back to Alexandria to live with him. The grandmother objected, however, saying that to have Doria was to have a small part of her daughter. Doria finally summoned all her courage and, with a feeling of liberation, told her grandmother that "I want to live with Papa and I ask you to announce to al-Sa'id al-Qasabi that I renounce this marriage to his nephew." Doria exerted her will. The engagement was broken off, and she went to Alexandria with her father.

* * *

Alexandria opened a new chapter in Doria's life. Everything about the city contrasted sharply with Tanta. By the time of her arrival in 1924, little survived of the ancient Greek city which was now known by the Arabic name *Iskandariyah*.[13] Alexandria offered Doria a place of emotional refuge and renewal for which, after the turmoil of Tanta, her own sensitive and poetic soul hungered. Where Tanta was dark and closed in upon its traditions, Alexandria was light and open to new ideas. Where Tanta was encircled by land, Alexandria was almost surrounded by water—on the north by the Mediterranean, on the south by Lake Mereotis. When Doria glimpsed the sea for the first time, it brought back fond memories of the Nile and Mansura, and she spent hours watching it: "Its immensity bestowed upon me a sort of messenger from the Absolute. I discovered nature in its profound beauty, whispering to my heart, creating marvelous dreams of crossing to the other side."

Doria was enrolled in the French mission school of St. Vincent de Paul, where she prepared for the elementary certificate known as the Brevet *élémentaire*.[14] While studying at this school, Doria met a young Greek girl whom she immediately nicknamed "Pugnose," who became Doria's first and only childhood friend. What drew them together was their shared ambition to excel in their studies. Doria was able to skip one year and sit for her exam at the same time as her friend. When they went to Cairo for the public exam, Pugnose was terrified. To give comfort to her young friend, Doria filled out the forms and changed the spelling of her last name from Chafik to Shafik, so that she could sit near her friend. This spelling remained with her for the rest of her life. They both passed with first-class distinction, but Doria still did not feel satisfied. A "great void still persisted within me that nothing seemed able to fill since Mama's death."

She thought about becoming a secretary and explored the possibilities of studying shorthand and typing at one of the foreign institutes in Alexandria, but her father and Soraya reacted negatively: "No man of good family would marry you. People will look down upon you." But she wanted to do something with her life. She wanted to have a career: "And if I were to have a career I decided it would have to be a brilliant career." As a way of preparing herself for this "unknown career," she decided to register for the French baccalaureate, or *bachot*. The only route to this diploma was to enroll in the boys' French lycée of Alexandria for a two- or three-year course of study. But for Doria, who was "in a great hurry to connect to a future that I always believed to be fleeing in front of me," that was too long a time to wait. Also the prospect of facing several long summer months with nothing to do prompted her to prepare immediately for her exams, hoping to pass in a few months what others took over a year to accomplish. She convinced Pugnose to join her in this "true adventure with all the risks, the emotions and the inexorable discipline of work that was imposed upon us." After four months of intense study, they succeeded passing the first part of their exams, with Doria coming out among the top three in the country. Doria recounts that when one of the outside examiners who had come to hear the oral examination heard her answering a question, he asked what school had prepared her. One of the priests answered, "the French mission school." The professor expressed surprise, since he knew that the school had no curriculum available for girls. "We shall from now on," the priest answered.

Again, Doria's success was not enough to assuage her nagging sense of emptiness. She and Pugnose decided to sit for the second part of their *bachot*, which demanded another year of intensive study. They selected philosophy, a subject that would require the services of a special tutor. Realizing the best professor was at the Lycée, Doria wrote a letter imploring him to tutor them at home. He obligingly accepted, and her father agreed to pay his nominal fee on behalf of both girls. Doria developed a schoolgirl crush on the handsome Belgian professor and for the first time in her young life experienced the sensation of falling in love: "From the very first lesson I do not know what confused feelings invaded my heart. A sort of very sweet music blended with disquiet, I would say even anguish, plagued me. I felt somewhat like a shipwrecked soul finding land! However, I saw the danger of this voyage that would lead nowhere. My professor was three times my age, of a different religion, a different culture and worse, married! I resolved, as they say in Arabic, to put a stone on my heart and conquer my feelings."

Doria passed brilliantly, placing second in the country. But she never saw her professor again. She was awarded a silver medal of commendation. At sixteen, she also was the youngest in the country to obtain the *bachot*.[15] Yet her success did not seem to dispel the nagging sense of void, idleness, and depression which continued to haunt her. Even among her extended family, she believed herself to be an outsider: "One evening after dinner at Tante Aziza's, I inadvertently overheard a conversation between my aunt and one of her friends who alluded to me as an orphan, telling my aunt that it was absolutely necessary to find me a husband. The effect on me was disastrous. Again I felt this terrible impression of being a waif, like the day when my mother died. My grief returned."

About this time, two of her brothers were sent to Europe to pursue their studies in engineering—Gamal to Berlin and Ali to England. The governess had married and left the family, and it was automatically assumed that Doria would take care of her father and youngest brother, Muhammad, and manage the household. She did so, but continually felt that there had to be something more to life. She wanted to pursue her own dream of going abroad to continue her studies as much as to get away from the daily reminders of her inferior social status vis-à-vis her rich cousins: "I often asked myself why my sisters, who belonged to the same family as I, never felt this terrible sensation of being estranged from my cousins."

* * *

By 1928, the idea of leaving for Paris and the Sorbonne had become an obsession for Doria, and she was more than ever resolved "to get away from the memories and the pain of estrangement; to tear myself away from all these nightmares." But there seemed to be too many obstacles to overcome: "How could I abandon my father and younger brother? How could I convince a family as conservative as mine, especially Grandmother, to accept a plan that would seem nothing less than my downfall?" The overwhelming barrier was financial, as her father had already committed whatever resources he had to sending his two sons to Europe. This essentially meant that Doria would have to wait years until their return before she could have her chance unless she could obtain a scholarship. She believed that "in Egypt one could obtain nothing without being backed or helped out by someone who had connections." She had to find her own contacts "because I could not count on the husbands of my aunts. For a long time I had ceased to be understood by these people."

Without mentioning her plans to anyone, she once again took matters into her own hands and wrote a letter to the esteemed Huda Hanum Sha'rawi (1879–1947), a woman who was seriously trying to bring an end to veiling and seclusion and open the doors of higher education and professional work to women of all classes. As the daughter of Sultan Pasha, one of the richest landowners in Egypt, and the wife of Ali Sha'rawi, a leading member of the newly formed Wafd party, she was endowed with all the potential that social status, wealth, and power can confer—assets that she did not hesitate to use in her own struggle to improve the status of women. With the assistance of Ceza Nabaraoui (1888–1984), her *fille spirituelle*, Sha'rawi organized and founded the first feminist organization in the Arab world, through which she spearheaded a drive to push for social reforms such as equal rights in education, the abolition of prostitution, the abolition of the veil, and the raising of the age of marriage to sixteen for women and eighteen for men. She submitted petitions to parliament advocating reform in the Islamic Personal Status Law, specifically demanding the abolition of polygamy; respect for a woman's rights to divorce under conditions specified in the Sharia; and an increase in the age of children remaining in the mother's custody after a divorce. These reform measures lay dormant in parliament until Doria Shafik resuscitated the struggle for equal rights a quarter of a century later.[16]

Shortly before Doria moved to Alexandria, Sha'rawi gained national recognition in 1923, following her public and dramatic act of removing her veil as she disembarked from the boat returning from Italy, where she had led the first Egyptian delegation to the International Alliance of Women. She thus signaled to Egyptians that a new era for women was beginning. During the late 1920s her efforts on behalf of women's rights were gaining national attention not only among the educated elite in Cairo but in the provinces as well. Doria recalls a family incident that first brought the name of Huda Sha'rawi to her attention and made her aware that alternative possibilities were opening up for Egyptian women: "Behind the shutters, Grandmother awaited the arrival of my aunt, saying, 'I see the governess but where is Zaza?' Because she was unveiled Tante Aziza was mistaken for the governess. When Grandmother recognized her unveiled niece, she was shocked! When the initial emotions died down, I realized that Tante Aziza's gesture was not an isolated event. The winds of change were erupting in Cairo. A signal for women had been initiated by a certain Huda Sha'rawi and I felt joy that a woman had at last opened a way along the route. From afar and without my knowing it, Huda Sha'rawi entered my life!"

Evidently touched by Doria's letter, Sha'rawi immediately cabled the ardent young woman, inviting her to come to her palace in Cairo within the week. Ahmad Chafik, resigned to his daughter's habit of deciding things on her own, gave his consent for her to travel alone to meet the celebrated Egyptian feminist:

She welcomed me with such charm and simplicity that she immediately won my heart. I found in her a warmth that resembled that of a mother, who would take my hand and guide me towards my future. She saw how moved I was and did everything to make me feel at ease. "I am happy to see you are so clever and I am pleased that a girl of your standard will represent Egypt abroad," she said. "Then you think I can go?" "Why not? Tomorrow someone will speak about you at the Ministry of Education." She saw so much emotion and gratitude on my face that she asked me: "Why this ardent desire to study abroad?" I was near to tears. She noticed it and, without waiting for the answer, quickly changed the subject. She spoke to me about the causes which led her towards the path of feminism. She told me about the unhappiness she had experienced within the harem when a newly-married thirteen-year-old girl and almost a prisoner in her own home. For the first time I realized that this lady, although rich, beautiful, having everything, had suffered. I also realized that there had to be other values beyond the material ones. Liberty was the profound goal of her "feminism." I left her palace with an exalted sense of calm, convinced that nothing really worthwhile can be accomplished without suffering. She was an example of how the will of a woman can overcome the law. An example which would forever remain in my memory and my heart.

Doria Shafik's first encounter with Huda Sha'rawi marked the beginning of an inspiring yet controversial relationship that would unfold over the next twenty years, not only linking her life to the women's movement in Egypt but also helping to shape her own feminist consciousness.

The year of their first meeting, 1928, also marked the twentieth anniversary of the death of Qasim Amin (1863–1908). Qasim Amin, the son of an aristocratic Turkish father and respectable middle-class Egyptian mother, was sent to France on a scholarship in 1882 to study law. It was during his years in France that he met and worked with the exiled Egyptian Shaykh Muhammad Abdu and the popular Islamic reformer and political agitator Jamal al-Din al-Afghani—both of whom had a profound impact on Amin's own ideas about the necessity for reform in Islam. Amin argued that society could raise the status of women primarily through encouraging their education, a reformist idea earlier put forth by Muhammad Abdu. The whole question of changing the personal status law or encouraging women to participate in the political life of the country was not touched upon. At the turn of the century, Qasim Amin forced an agonizing reappraisal of Islam around the "woman question." In response to a particularly harsh attack on the morality of the Egyptians contained in Le Duc d'Harcourt's L'Egypte et les Egyptiens (1893), Amin wrote an apologist rebuttal defending Islamic customs—a defense that brought the whole question of the "emancipation of women" into sharp and immediate focus and provoked a polemical debate that would dominate public discourse in Egyptian society for the next several decades. He became a dominant figure in this struggle and—on the basis of his two controversial books, The Emancipation of Women (1899) and The New Woman (1901)—is described by some as Egypt's "first feminist."

Some contemporary feminist scholars, arguing that Amin's role is exaggerated, point out that during the final decades of the nineteenth century, there existed a considerable repertoire of Egyptian women's writings articulating an awakened feminist consciousness.[17] Nevertheless, in 1928 he was still perceived as a staunch supporter of women's emancipation and, as part of the celebration to commemorate his contributions to that end, a national contest was held to select the best essay written by a young Egyptian woman honoring his memory. Doria won the contest and was invited by Huda Sha'rawi to speak at the theater of Ezbakiya Gardens on May 4. Sha'rawi opened the celebration with a eulogy to Qasim Amin expressing what she felt he represented to Egypt and to Egyptian women. Sitting on the stage next to the founder and president of Egypt's first Feminist Union, Doria listened in rapt attention to this remarkable woman who had now become her benefactress. Sha'rawi's words only added fuel to Doria's burning ambition to escape those painful childhood years of estrangement: "Gentlemen, if we honor today the remarkable gifts of Qasim Amin and particularly his fight for the emancipation of the Egyptian woman, it is because we are firmly convinced that his sentiments in this regard, his battles in the defense of women and his pleas for the necessity to educate them were inspired uniquely by his respect for justice and his love for equality, as well as his country and by the noble desire to raise the prestige of Egypt among all nations. It is this same goal that Egyptian women have assigned to their feminist movement."[18]

As if echoing her heroine's voice Doria stood before her audience and for the first time publicly proclaimed her feminist vision. It was an extraordinary speech for a girl of nineteen, showing Doria's amazing grace and courage:

Madam Huda Sha'rawi: One of your protégées has come from far to participate at this anniversary as much celebrated as painful. Qasim Amin Bey is a name which has been engraved in our hearts with gratitude eternally. Has he not been our guide in the darkness? I will try to be one of his disciples whose example will teach women to fend for themselves in spite of the necessities of material life. What miseries the depths of the harems have concealed for so long! What experience can one acquire if one has simply made a trip from one part of the house to the other? And in her torpor, the woman was not aware of her own captivity; having always led the same life, she did not think she could liberate herself. I ask myself why certain men persist in isolating women? Do they believe that age-old traditions can be adapted to the current of modern life? Or is it that they do not understand the absolute value of liberty? Perhaps we should lock them up for one or two years for them to get the idea of what they impose on women. . . . Perhaps our distant ancestors, who burned their daughters alive, were a little more humane because when they took away liberty they took away life. You men, when you decide to let women out, you cover their faces with lugubrious black veils so that they can't see the world except through a cloud. And when you tire of the first wife, you believe you were wrong in your choice, so you take a second, and a third. It is useless to continue your search. They will always have the same nature—devious and ignorant.

Let man ask himself just once: What is a woman? She is a reasonable human being just like himself. Some men, anticipating the battle that would erupt if women were placed on a par with men, have argued against the instruction of young girls. They argue that within a few years we would have to deal with pedants who, with their science would come to dispute our position with us. You are mistaken gentlemen. You would deal with enlightened wives who with true affection would serve your home from the heart. Would you content yourselves with a heart without any knowledge of life? Do you believe that a woman could truly love you if she did not understand you? And for her to understand you, mustn't she be educated? Young girls of today, are they not the mothers of the future? Does an ignorant mother know how to give her child a clear idea about infinity, duty, justice? Would she know how to explain the course of the planets, if she herself takes them for brilliant pearls, scattered on a black ceiling? One young woman assured me the other day that a moon exists for each particular town. In this case, if men have the fancy to create a new town, God will have to create a new moon. That is where the deductions of ignorant women lead us. It's in the unselfish love of the mother, in this true love of the husband, that one sees the reflection of divine religion. You men construct walls around your daughters, you multiply the number of gates and guards, but you forget that walls are never high enough for feminine ruse. To enable them to communicate with the outside world, your daughters have an old woman or a domestic servant. You show them the world through the windows of their imagination so they see only illusions. And at the first opportunity they fall into the abyss. Why don't you use religion as your support? Give your daughters a good conscience and let them out into the world![19]

The day after her performance at Ezbakiya Gardens, Doria received word that her scholarship from the Ministry of Education was arranged. Her financial problems were solved. But how to settle the family dilemmas? How could she leave Egypt with no one to care for her father? As luck would have it, her sister's husband was going to be transferred to a hospital in Alexandria within the year, and Doria, who was staying with her sister during her visit to Cairo, convinced Soraya to move with her husband and infant into her father's house, a plan that suited everybody.

All that remained to be done was to convince her grandmother, who was more of a stumbling block than her father. The news of Doria's plans to leave for France startled her: "'Madness! The departure of this young girl to go and live in exile among the Druze!'[20] For my grandmother all non-Muslims were Druze! 'And where is the man who would want her when she returns?'" This last innuendo that she would remain an old maid began to haunt her: "Perhaps Grandmother was right. I also saw the possibility of finding myself alone until the end of my days without a man to help me. *Tant pis!* I would go no matter what the price! But I had to get her blessing. I couldn't leave without it. Finally she relented after all my entreaties and kisses on her cheeks and hands."

By August, Doria was on a ship headed for France, leaving her family and country to venture forth into the unknown. Ahmad Chafik was pleased and proud. And before she embarked, father and daughter went to Tanta to visit Ratiba's tomb: "For the first time I did not cry. I felt the strange sensation of being the continuation of my mother's life. She was not dead, but living forever within me. This strange sensation of being on the threshold of realizing a great dream, unacknowledged but vaguely felt by generations of oppressed women, a secret buried deep within their hearts, which little by little, as within my own, would become the day of liberation."

The Turning Point (1928–1944)

We are witnessing the great turning point that constitutes the crisis traversed by the woman of today: a passage from one moment to another moment of her history, a substitution of a new reality for another reality.

—*Shafik, "Memoirs" (1930), 20*

2

To Want and to Dare (1928–1932)

Oh, mysterious Sphinx, what do you want of me? You dominate all and your strong shoulders represent all the glory of ancient grandeur. Before you I feel myself so small in spite of all there is to be proud of. Many times I have gazed into the mirror of my consciousness and heard your voice: "Only you Know, only you Can, only you Want and only you Dare." Four words which contain all perfection. Could I guess the eternal enigma that you have posed to humanity?[1]

Doria was only nineteen years old when, along with eleven other young Egyptian women and a British chaperone, she boarded the ship in Alexandria and sailed for Europe. Although not the first group of Egyptian women to have been sent to Europe for higher education, they did constitute an impressive array of talent and ambition, as their subsequent contributions to Egyptian society testify.[2] They all were in their the early twenties, most were graduates from al-Saniya (the first government school for women established by the wife of Khedive Ismail in 1873), and like Doria, they were operating under the auspices of the Ministry of Education's Cultural and Educational Mission Abroad program. But instead of heading for England "to study fields such as geography, home economics, medicine and business, subjects deemed practical for women's education," Doria was to avow, "I was on my way to Paris to study philosophy." She described her traveling companions as having "clever eyes and high spirits," and she seemed to like them. She enjoyed the experience, feeling that "the spring of life was smiling upon me." Daring to break tradition, "I escaped from the sleeping British chaperone with one of my newfound companions to attend a dancing party on the deck."

Doria harbored no self-doubts or second thoughts about leaving Egypt for France, and one can imagine her at the ship's railing looking forward toward Marseilles rather than backward toward Alexandria with a sense of determination, inspired not only by the thought of Qasim Amin but also by the knowledge that the mantle of approval had been bestowed upon her by Huda Sha'rawi herself. In a touching letter written to her benefactress on August 17, 1928, we catch a glimpse of Doria's inner mood and frame of mind.

Very Dear Madam:

I truly regret not having been able to write you before my departure because I did not know the name of the ship until I saw it: then it was too late. I am very happy with my journey and the sea has been very calm; perhaps it has understood that this is my first voyage and did not want to cause me any trouble. My affection toward Egypt has doubled since my departure; perhaps I have always loved my country as much, but I was unaware of all that love until I left it. The homeland is more than a mother: it nurtures us even when we are ungrateful. It is for that reason I have not only wanted to serve my country to the best of my ability, but also to enhance my power to prove to her all the love that wells up within me. God has helped me in my ambition; He has chosen you to replace the one that is no more and I am sincerely grateful to you for all that you have done for me. I have learned something further: before serving one's country, it is useful to leave it, in order to become aware of all the devotion that one carries in oneself for the motherland. I have chattered too much and your time is precious. But I need to be able to converse with you at length. I would chat more but I am waiting to get to Paris. I kiss your hands with all the tenderness and gratitude that I feel toward you.[3]

As an echo to Doria's letter and a signal to the Egyptian public that a new generation of young women, with Doria Shafik as one of its leaders, was fulfilling the dream of Qasim Amin, *L'Egyptienne* published Doria's photograph in the frontispiece of their September 1928 issue. There could not be a clearer public affirmation of Doria's expected future role in the vanguard of the Egyptian women's movement than this statement in the very pages of the journal representing that movement:

We are happy to announce to our readers that among the students sent on mission last month by the Egyptian government in order to specialize in the different branches of feminine education one finds the name of our young friend: Mlle. Doria Ahmad Shafik. Our readers will undoubtedly remember the success of this congenial young speaker at the evening commemorating Qasim Amin Bey. On the occasion of her departure we have the pleasure of publishing the photo of this valiant feminist who so ardently desires the emancipation of women and who, in order to attain it, has dedicated herself to the education of Egyptian youth. In wishing her all the success that she deserves, we hope to see her one day in the ranks of the militants who will achieve the final victory of their noble cause.

Doria's romantic notions about France were tarnished somewhat while docking in Marseilles, "this radical city where the commune was proclaimed." She discovered "that with a few cigarettes my companions could avoid the customs. Marseilles' radicalism did not seem so radical after all!" She was enthralled by the French countryside: "For the first time I saw mountains and marveled at their picturesque green and magnificent heights, conveying a sense of the infinite. I felt again that intense "aesthetic emotion" that had filled me when I first saw the sea. So anxious was I to arrive in the City of Light that the Paris-Marseilles train seemed to crawl." But again she was somewhat disappointed by that first encounter: "How let down I was by the gloomy obscurity of the Gare de Lyon. In my quest to greet this free life (forgetting that our chains pursue us) I only wanted to see Light." The secretary of the Egyptian office in charge of the students in Paris had come to meet her: "Already a jailer! I felt an intense desire to break completely with the past. But impossible and I knew it!"

Doria bade farewell to her traveling companions as the chaperone turned her over to the care of the secretary, whom Doria found "kind and well mannered." The director of the Paris office of the Egyptian educational mission had decided that it would be best for Doria to live with a family in a French boarding house, a *pension de famille*, until the other Egyptian mission students returned from their summer holidays in October, at which time she would join her compatriots. The secretary took Doria by taxi to a *pension de famille* located in the Auteuil district: "While we went along the secretary told me stories to put me at ease. From time to time when he laughed to himself I laughed too, so as not to disappoint him; but I wanted so much to be alone, to savor this important moment in my life—my first contact with Paris at dawn. The streets were silent and a light rain was falling like a hundred soft kisses upon my cheek."

The taxi stopped in front of a large building in the elegant Auteuil district where Doria was introduced to a middle-aged widow who had established the pension in order to take care of her two sons and two unmarried daughters. This was Doria's new "family," with whom she would live for the next two months. They were joined each evening for dinner by other family friends, including a young French poet studying at the Sorbonne. An immediate attraction developed between them: "In his poetic attitude toward life I felt an echo of my own dreams. A ray of hope was kindled in my heart, hinting that there might be a possible reconciliation between me and life. It was obvious that the poet took an interest in me which made me happy, but my joy was tempered by the dreadful fear that the news might reach the director. But what connection could there be between the pension and the director? I tried to rid myself of this anxiety."

During her first weeks, Doria was drawn more and more into the Parisian atmosphere surrounding her, despite her homesickness: "The active and noisy household didn't make me feel uncomfortable. It was a different type of turbulence from that of Grandmother's house. It somehow seemed more civilized. At least at table they didn't all try to speak at once. The atmosphere was more poetic and the friendly table conversation with the boarders helped me get to know the people of Paris."

At her first meeting with the director of the Egyptian education office, Doria faced a situation in which she challenged his authority. One of the stipulated conditions of her scholarship from the Ministry of Education was that she study one of the "branches of feminine education." She was assigned history and geography, subjects which the ministry felt were "more suitable for women who would become future teachers" but which Doria detested. When she confided her "horror of geography" to the director, he responded, "And of what do you not have 'horror'?" "Philosophy!" came her defiant answer. "It is not what you like or dislike," returned the administrator; "It is the government's decision. One cannot change the order of the minister!" "I could tell from his smile and mercurial manner," Doria was later to write, "that this man would not put himself out to help me." Before she left his office that day, the director gave Doria some worldly advice: "I must warn you. Avoid speaking to young men! Pay attention to your reputation! Behave yourself, or else you will be sent back to Egypt!" "Anyway I will study philosophy!" she silently whispered to herself as she leapt down the stairs four at a time; "I didn't come this far to give up! I shall study what I want to and nothing else!"

Believing that it might be in bad taste to request another favor from Huda Sha'rawi so soon, Doria turned to Dr. Taha Husayn (1889–1965), the famous blind Egyptian nationalist and liberal reformer of the twenties and thirties who had studied at the Sorbonne and then served as dean of the faculty of arts at the National University in Cairo.[4] It was he who was responsible for admitting the first women students to the university in 1928, and his French-born wife was a member of Huda Sha'rawi's Egyptian Feminist Union. She decided to cable him for help. Within days, the director received a telegram from the Ministry of Education in Cairo advising him to change Doria's program at her pleasure: "This was my victory. But I paid for it dearly. The director became my enemy!"

She had succeeded in realizing one of her cherished dreams, registering for the course in philosophy a week later:

> I was so excited as I mounted the large stairway, passing under the clock tower of the Sorbonne into the immense hall surrounded by amphitheaters. The mystery of the medieval cathedrals came to mind and I thought of the Sorbonne's intellect blended with the religious splendors of the past. I entered the Sorbonne as if entering a sanctuary. I reached the secretariat and was asked to pay only 80 francs. I am not costing my government very much, I thought! I left the university radiant. I am at the Sorbonne and I am in the philosophy section!"

As bold and self-confident as Doria was in challenging barriers to her intellectual ambitions, in matters of the heart she seemed more constrained and less willing to disregard the Muslim, middle-class values that constituted her sense of "moral propriety"—a fact exemplified by her friendship with the young French student whom she had met at the pension. As a way of amusing herself, or "lightening her heart," as she described it, Doria would often stroll through the streets of the Latin Quarter, enthralled by her discovery of "her new homeland with its books, mountains of books!" Balzac, Baudelaire, Rousseau, Hegel, Marx, and Poe were some of her favorite purchases.

She loved music as well. Having studied the piano as a child, she attempted to learn the violoncello while in Paris, "but my fingers could never make those notes achieve that sublime sound." She often bought gramophone records and wiled away the hours in the pension listening to her favorite composer, Robert Schumann. Returning home one afternoon "with my recent purchase of Schumann's *Rêveries*,"[5] she encountered the French poet in the drawing room. He expressed interest in her choice of music and asked if he might listen with her:

> In silence we listened to the pathos of the music. "Do you know," he said, "you evoke a certain Poetry around you! You are as mysterious as the Sphinx." The next day I received this poem:

Reine	Queen
des Temps Anciens	of Ancient Times
revenue	returned
parmi nous	among us
vous incarnez	you incarnate
l'Egypte	Egypt
le Nil	the Nile
l'ineffable	the ineffable

grandeur	grandeur
de siècles	of centuries
révolus.	past.

Her encounter with this young poet and the discovery that they both shared a love of the aesthetic inspired Doria to write her own poetry: "Feeling this intense urge to write, we exchanged poems and I was happy to discover that I, too, was a poet."

It was through poetry that a tender friendship developed between them, and it was through this friendship that Doria was introduced to the Parisian world of art. But at the same time, she did not feel entirely free in her relationship with the young Frenchman:

> In that brief moment of hesitation I experienced when the poet first invited me to accompany him to the opening of an art exhibition, I remembered the words of the director. Reputation! Be wise! They reverberated in my head like a hammer. What is reputation? What is it to be wise? If I followed the advice of the director it would mean nothing other than losing that for which my being longed. To be in contact with the most fundamental of human values—Art and Love. My desire to attend the exhibit with the poet was so strong. I wanted to learn how to look at a painting! To touch in some way that world of dreams to which the painting would transport me. I did not hesitate for long.

It was while looking at some paintings by George Rouault that she was reminded of "that melancholy train ride to Tanta" following the death of her mother. But being with the poet made her "hope that the wounds of my childhood would begin to heal." That is all we learn about Doria's relationship with the French poet—whose name we never learn—while she was living in the pension.

In October, when students were returning from summer holidays, the director of the Egyptian mission summoned Doria to his office to introduce her to three Egyptian girls (two sisters and their friend) with whom she was now obliged to live in an apartment especially rented by the Egyptian government for its female students. Doria was not happy with this ultimatum: "Why the devil must I live in the Bois de Boulogne so far from the Sorbonne instead of in the Latin Quarter where I had always dreamed of being?" But she prudently decided not to argue the point, having so recently challenged the director about her program of study, rationalizing that "necessity has its laws."

Her sadness at leaving the pension and the daily contact with her poet was heightened by the realization that she had so little in common with her Egyptian compatriots. But the poet told her that if she would agree, they could continue to exchange poetry and attend exhibits from time to time: "I accepted with every intention of going along with it." She felt ill at ease in her new surroundings. Without a room of her own in which to study, or soul mates with whom she could discuss art and poetry, she became increasingly unhappy and withdrawn: "I found the uproar of Grandmother's house including Tanta's tribal life transplanted into the heart of Paris! I felt I had returned to the old chains. I was in a prison without bars. Feeling on the verge of a depression I threw myself into my studies."

Her course of study at this time included philosophy, sociology, and mental illness. But she became "so upset at seeing the plight of the inmates at St. Anne's Hospital, sometimes imagining their symptoms within myself that I switched to aesthetics." She had made some friends among her colleagues in philosophy, and through them, she was introduced to some white Russian refugees, mostly Georgians, with whom she felt a shared cultural understanding. Still, the atmosphere in her apartment was frustrating to her: "I did my best to avoid friction but the jealousies intensified particularly when my brother, Gamal, came to visit me and I was oblivious to the evident romantic interest in him by one of the sisters. After a while I lived in a sort of isolation, with tension building up to bursting point among my house mates."

Often during these moments of estrangement and unhappiness, Doria would escape to the inner world of the imagination and express her despair and loneliness through the metaphors of her poems and essays. Although not her best writings, these early pieces are important for what they reveal about her self-image and inner feelings. Through them, we catch a glimpse of her nostalgia for the Nile: "Alone next to the waves that pass, no sound reaches you except the heavy roaring of the always majestic Nile, the echo of Infinity from the desert, that mysterious silence where the human soul finds a point of contact with Eternity; a sublime and mournful kiss between perfection and the still imperfect human being; between man and Divinity, a kiss that leaves an indelible mark within the silence of the desert." And we witness her attempt to build and nourish a sense of self confidence: "Do not despair you are still young and the truly strong souls are the ones forged by suffering. Above your despair place hope beyond all reach."

In an essay Doria wrote during her first year in Paris, we catch a glimpse of a nascent self-consciousness as she constructs a dialogue between the mighty Sphinx and the child of the Nile:

Shake off your slumber, child. Why do you still sleep? From where are you coming and what do you dream as you gaze upon these waves passing by?

Sphinx, I would like to be like thee, regarding the universe from on high and seeing nothing except infinity that circles everywhere under the multiple forms of mere mortals. The Nile gave birth to me and Madam Sha'rawi Pasha became my protectress. The Nile, overflowing with life, sparkling between the banks that nature has traced, has thrown up a human wreck upon its shores, a wreck waiting for a hand to lift it up and imbue it with a consciousness of life that lies dormant within. Oh Nile, sire of my ancestors, thy spirit courses within my veins. I would like to propel myself over thy waters where thou wouldst carry me, gently floating, following thy course to the sea where I would merge with infinity. But instead thou hast thrown me upon the shores indicating another path for me. It is very painful, the obstacles are numerous and the blows are often grievous.

Paltry being, who traverses the desert, you do not know your way because you do not know yourself. You bleed, human being, and your wound is all the more painful because you do not know where it is. It is throughout your being and you will always bleed until you know yourself.

Sphinx, only thou knowest. Tell me the secret of human nature. Thou wilt spare me a very painful way!

Poor human being, who are you in comparison to the Past?

I dare answer: "I am the being that wants to touch true knowledge with her own hand."

In the midst of the somber night, which began its doleful wailing, the child of the Nile heard a voice which echoed from the desert: "Child, raise yourself and move forward and you will understand. It is not in the age of roses that the Sphinx will answer you. You are indeed far away, but if you despair, you will die!"

The child of the Nile arose and slowly moved forward keeping the head of the mysterious Sphinx in view. A voice in the distance called out: "Courage, Child, and I shall answer you."[6]

The contrapuntal themes of Doria's world seem etched into the metaphors of this essay. The mystical bond between herself and the Nile, the mournful kiss between perfection and the imperfect human being, the reconciliation of dreams merging with infinity, the trauma of being thrown into the world with its painful obstacles and grievous blows but then the forging of strong souls by suffering, the despair countered by this being who wants to touch true knowledge with her own hand, to Hope! Know! Will! Dare! These four words poetically woven within her essay presage an attitude toward life that illuminated her path later on.

In another essay, she muses on the question "Does a woman have a right to philosophize?" In attempting to answer her own query, she articulates what she believed "is the great drama bursting forth to which the modern era may bear witness: the sensitivity of the woman; the intellect of the man—two contradictory aspects within a single being." Through her defense of woman's right to philosophize, Doria is not merely arguing for the right to study one subject as opposed to another; she is offering us her ideas on the crisis challenging the woman of the modern era: "If it is true that every reality is the truth of the moment, then we are witnessing the great turning point that constitutes the crisis traversed by the woman of today: a passage from one moment to another moment of her history, a substitution of a new reality for another reality."[7]

What is this new reality that the woman must substitute for the other reality? What is the nature of this passage? What was Doria's image of the "new woman"? How did she connect this to woman's right to philosophize? Exploring passages from her essays, we discover the profound influence of the ideas of Jean-Jacques Rousseau (1712–1778) on Doria's thinking as she explored the philosophical underpinnings of her own evolving feminist consciousness. His dictum that man is by nature virtuous, free, and happy, and has been corrupted by society; his emphasis on moral purity and sexual chastity; and his belief in importance of maintaining one's principles—all struck a responsive chord within her own value system. So absorbed by Rousseau was she that she focused her first degree at the Sorbonne on his life and works. Her essay "Une Femme a-t-elle le Droit de Philosopher?" opens by addressing male readers in particular:

Be reassured, gentlemen, to philosophize is something other than sterile meditation. The modern epoch requires a philosophy more real than pure rationalism. Rousseau has revealed to us the true values of Nature by which Man could live in face of the paradoxes that are by necessity inherent in this world, a world where man, toy of his own passions, allows Chance to have right over his Will, where the human being becomes the irony of the universe and awaits the inevitability of his Fate.

How can we move from a romantic conception of things to a new realism? The triumph of this struggle against passion, is it so simple? How is the repression of the great Romantic wave possible? Woman has confined herself to this world of "Feeling" of Rousseau to the exclusion of clear knowledge. Being a toy of her own passion she has become the toy of those who want to live love. For a long time woman has adopted this sentimental attitude, which undoubtedly had its charm with you, gentlemen.

Now one must consider a new woman very different from the old. It is time that a new realism wipe away these tears, from now on useless and even paradoxical.

Realism as I understand it consists of getting rid, as much as possible, of illusions of the imagination and as a condition of this effort to conserve the desire of Being, this cry of the Self. It is from this Self that I set out and ridding it of all hallucination, I introduce it into the world of pure knowledge. I ask for a return from this sentient wandering. I ask for a passage from the complaints of Rousseau to a social adaptation that prepares the return to realism.

Doria seems to mean by the phrase "a return from this sentient wandering" a passage from a first stage, where woman abounds in sensitivity, to a second stage, where woman explains the universe for herself:

There are moments of respite in human life where, by reflection upon the self, it is possible to observe oneself objectively. This self that is passionate can, by looking back upon itself, study objectively the passionate Being that it was. This Being with a Janus face is simultaneously both an "I" and a "me." It is this being, in all its (indefinable) complexity, which must constitute the proper object of philosophy. Woman must, insomuch as she is intuitive, be able by looking back upon her past, to regard this intuition objectively. This calm of reason is indispensable to the present feminine epoch.

Doria reveals a certain "modernist" outlook in her attempt to grapple with one of the fundamental issues in philosophy: the relationship between intuition (immediate, spontaneous, subjective knowledge) and reason (distanced, systematic, objectified knowledge).

She explores this question within the context of the situation facing women who, like herself, are caught between two philosophical moments:

The opposition of the woman of yesterday to the woman of today reflects the great opposition of an intuitive philosophy to a more systematic philosophy. I mean a philosophy of presentiment where mystery reigns, but one in which the harmonious base is glimpsed by the human heart. Perhaps it is there wherein lies great philosophy? Anyway there is another philosophy that is venerated much less than this latter one but has the advantage of being incontestably realistic. It is a philosophy concerned with the multiple problems posed at every moment to the individual to which the only solution is Action. To philosophize one must first live; but only living would be insufficient. It is indispensable to turn inward and consider the living being that one is.

For Doria, the feminist problematic involves the possibility of uniting apparently contradictory modes of knowing, which leads her to consider the relationship between art and positivism, a very contemporary issue: "Art and Positive philosophy? Is such a unity even possible? The essence of art rests above all in the spontaneity of the work itself; the artist cannot predict the goal except very vaguely and the goal can only be seen once the work is completed. Positive philosophy on the other hand is contrary to Art. It demands above all a work of discrimination and analysis, aiming at a principle of clarity, eliminating everything that is confused. It seeks systematization. How to unite these two domains?"

With that question it becomes clear that Doria does not intend to leave the argument as a mere opposition between women of two different eras or between two different philosophical positions. She wants nothing less than to find a true synthesis:

How could I explain to myself the synthesis of an intuitive and systematic conception of the universe? A concrete response is suggested to me by the woman of the present era. She has come through a great crisis of growth, a crisis characteristic of a passage from one stage to another. There always remains a spark in the ashes from what has been burned. Likewise woman who systematizes will save from the intuitive being that she was, the embers of the center of her passions in order to reconstitute a new passion: that of Knowing! As magic has given birth to science (the analogy permits me to say) so the woman of today, daughter of the woman of yesterday, preserves within her that which she was, but she lives with a new life. How can woman, in being artist, pretend to pure knowledge? She is herself a work of art! In this work she is no longer placed as an object of contemplation. Her goal is knowledge. She wants to conceive clearly that which she has produced spontaneously. She wants to introduce the spirit of system into that which by its essence, defies analysis. She sees the possibility of blending Intuition and Concept. And in this, one cannot refuse her the Right to Philosophize!

There is a definite "modernity" in the manner in which Doria has structured the crisis posed in the successive moments of feminine history when a new adaptation is substituted for the old. Although in this essay she is not analyzing any particular historical reality where this transition is taking place, she nonetheless reveals a certain insight into the problem she is confronting as a woman intellectual who desires the right to be recognized in this world "where so many authorities (daughters of centuries past) would like to ridicule her."

She believed in her right to choose, at the same time conscious of the struggle involved:

> Objections will be made that it is a pity that woman loses that which characterizes her as woman, in throwing herself in the path of man! That it is against the possibility of all future life that the woman wishes above everything to be equal to man! Why do you, gentlemen, infer that the future will be what the past and the present have suggested to you? Perhaps you miss the gentle companion of former days and, projecting her image into the future, you would want it reborn? The character of the living is not to lament something that is inevitably dead but to deduce a future which must be new and completely alive.

Woman as a work of art! That phrase was not just a casual metaphor. Doria believed this with her entire being, and in one sense, it reflected her own self-image as the new woman of the post–World War I era.

Paris in 1930 was the fashion capital of the Western world, and Doria obviously enjoyed clothes. Possessed of an astute sense of fashion, she knew how to make the most of her striking appearance. Therefore she did not consider it a contradiction to be writing essays on philosophy at the same time as she was modeling dresses for one of her Egyptian colleagues studying haute couture at the Ecole Normale.

In a letter written to Ceza Nabaraoui in May 1930, Doria reveals what she might have meant by the New Woman as "two aspects in one Being":

Dear Mlle. Nabaraoui:

> We have dispatched to you, along with this letter, two photographs and the "philosophical" article from one of us. In the two photographs Alia Kamal and Doria Shafik are modeling dresses created by Alia Kamal. The shawl that the latter is holding in her hand is entirely sketched and made by her; her dress is rose tulle (the model is one of her creations). Next time she will send you one of her portraits in the lounging pajamas of which she has created the genre. Presently she is preparing for her second diploma in cutting and sewing at the Institute of Paris.
>
> We also draw your attention to the fact that Doria Shafik has received the grade "with mention" in her exams in: (1) Psychology; (2) Ethics and Sociology; and (3) General Philosophy and Logic. Presently she is preparing for the fourth certificate that ends with the *licence d'enseignement* and hopes that the French government (with the approval of the Egyptian government) will accept the admission of an Egyptian woman among the candidates for the Agrégation de Philosophie, given the fact that up until now the Agrégation is reserved only for the French.[8]

For Doria to have aspired to enter the state competitive examination for recruitment of secondary-school teachers in France is indicative of her ambitions. Whether she actually received the permission to enter this examination and, if so, whether she succeeded in obtaining the *Aggrégation* is not known. Clearly coming through this letter, however, is Doria's desire to overcome yet another barrier preventing her from being allowed to pursue her goal. Only this time by using the pages of the reputable *L'Egyptienne,* and with the tacit support of its editorial board, she tried to influence the French government!

Her essays provided one outlet for her deepening sense of loneliness. Another was the anticipated visits of Huda Sha'rawi, who would always contact her when passing through Paris. Once, Doria was in Switzerland conducting research on Rousseau. Her sadness at having missed her benefactress is revealed in the following letter: "Dear Excellence: Upon my return from Switzerland I found the card that your Excellence left for me. I was so happy to have received a small word from you and regret not having been able to see you before you left Paris. The Egyptian woman could not be more worthily represented than by your maternal hands. With my best wishes for good health and my inexpressible gratitude. Doria Shafik."[9]

Meanwhile life in the apartment near the Bois de Boulogne was becoming intolerable for Doria. The incident that unleashed the storm between her and her housemates was Doria's discovery of the disappearance of her French friend's poems. When she confronted her companions, they did not deny that they had taken them but seemed to relish telling her that they had sent them to the director of the Egyptian mission! Doria was visibly shaken by this event which "disgusted and disheartened me. Decidedly the human being is not as good as I had wanted to believe. Did they really believe they were doing the right thing? I kept asking myself: What harm is there in writing and receiving poems?"

She was summoned immediately to the director's office. "I suppose you know what we have to talk about?" he asked her. She answered that she did not. "The director looked askance at me, saying: 'Anyway, I think you will have to get ready to go back to Egypt! You know perfectly well you cannot continue to have your scholarship!'" Doria was outraged, but she didn't waste any time feeling sorry for herself. She took immediate action: "In a flash my decision was taken: to the devil with the lot of them—compatriots, director, scholarship, the government! I would work just like my poor companions at the Sorbonne, and then I would do with my life exactly as I pleased! Without a reproach, without a word of good-bye, I packed my things and left. I was liberated."

Perhaps the romantically inclined would have preferred a scenario in which Doria returns to the pension and finds her French poet, and together they struggle through life at the Sorbonne in blissful poverty writing love poems to each other. However, this was not Doria's way of liberation when she felt the weight of preconceived ideas constraining her. "The prejudices! All the past with its centuries of customs and beliefs, which one could not destroy with a single gesture. The centuries were still there in the depths of my being!"

So instead of returning to the pension in Auteuil, Doria took a taxi and headed directly for the International House on 93 Boulevard St. Michel. She knew about the International House as it bordered the Rue des Ecoles where she used to take the Metro back to her apartment in the Bois de Boulogne, "an address I uttered randomly without even knowing if they had a free room." Counting her money, she realized she could live for a month—"on one meal a day if I asked to pay the rent of the room at the end of the month. By then I would find work."

Her material circumstances did not worry her because she felt liberated from an oppressive atmosphere: "Through the window of the taxi taking me to the Latin Quarter and the International House, I saw Paris as if for the first time. A sensation of freedom, of quietude, however relative. My Egyptian milieu, with its machinations and jealousies, had succeeded in making me associate the word Love with Terror. I wrote the poet not to send me any more poems, not to contact me and urged him to forget the whole affair. I had to."

She was starting a new page in her life, one that would bring her into contact with women from all over the world—women who, like herself, were breaking out of traditional societies and seeking training and knowledge in fields that were hitherto closed to them, women who wanted to be free to follow their own destinies and for one reason or another were drawn to Paris. Her entry into the International House was a mark of her bravado, because she was not sure of retaining her scholarship and thus would have no immediate means of support. Upon arriving at the reception desk, she asked to meet the director, and within a few minutes she was in the presence of both the French and the American directors: "They looked me over sympathetically when I told them my nationality, the nature of my studies and that I wanted a room. They asked if I was on a scholarship and since I had received no official statement to the contrary I said 'Yes.' That was met with nodding approval but when they said I would have to wait a year, I couldn't control my disappointment. Sensing my predicament they agreed to make immediate arrangements. I had won the first round!"

Before being shown to her room, Doria was asked to fill out a questionnaire about her background, interests, and area of study, and she was shown the rules of the house. When she read that "Girls returning to the house after midnight will find the doors locked," she mused: "No mention of punishment.

Girls had only to come late if they wanted to stay out all night! What liberalism!!"

Her room, with its rustic furniture and simple decor, attracted her immediately, and she pulled her books out of her suitcase and placed them in the bookcase:

> For the first time I saw all my philosophy books shelved together. In spite of my worries I felt an inner calm. The order and elegance of the room conveyed tranquillity. The murmuring of the traffic and the lights dancing below the window on Boulevard St. Michel seemed to be welcoming me. The tears in my eyes were not of despair, but rather from a sense of hope. I would postpone any worries about my future until I knew the decision of the Egyptian Ministry of Education. I wrote a letter to my father giving him my new address without mentioning any of the recent events. And with a quiet soul I went to sleep.

Doria felt in her element at the International House, "surrounded by young women from the four corners of the earth, each one with her own customs, her own problems and despite our differences there was a synthesis, a basic tolerance."

Her closest companions were three women from each continent of the world: "a Martiniquian, a Moroccan and an Iranian," whom she met by chance during her first meal in the International House:

> By a sort of elective affinity I sat at a table where three came respectively from Africa, Asia and Central America. Later they became my best friends. Like me each of my companions had their problems—more or less complicated. In this ensemble the life of the Americans seemed to glide along an easy path. I did not envy them. Struggle had always seemed a necessity for a person to approach her fullness of being. The Orientals were always more tormented. The Iranian, my best friend, resourceful and brilliant, did not know what she wanted. She was somehow lost between the East where she was born and the West where she was raised; between the distant past from where she came and a present offering itself to her in all its freshness but with which she could not come to grips (oppressed by I do not know what invisible hand). The Martiniquian (mulatto and beautiful) had only one dream, a veritable obsession: to marry a "white"! The Moroccan was a woman with great energy and adapted to everything but always with a look of anxiety in her eyes. There were the others: the Georgian whose family had fled the Russian revolution and who led her life "as the wind blows." She had too much ability to adapt and she always kept life on the surface. The Romanian

who was simply wicked and the Greek who was born under a tragic star—three times engaged and three times jilted. I realized that my country was not the only place where women suffered.

What attracted Doria to these women was her awareness that they all shared certain things in common:

> we each had the experience of being misunderstood in our own countries, being intellectually more ambitious than our countrymen; we each had our oriental nature emphasizing a poetic attitude toward life in this very Americanized atmosphere of the International House; and we were all very superstitious. I read Hafez[10] to know my fortune. We were seekers of the Unknown. Apparently we had come in quest of diplomas but in reality we had come in quest of the Absolute. Like me these girls had left their homes, their country, their family, seeking to pass beyond family and the fatherland!

Within a week of her flight from the Bois de Boulogne, Doria received news that instead of her abrupt recall to Egypt, the director actually congratulated her for "being in such good hands" and informed her that the authorities had allowed her to retain her scholarship. She also received a letter from her father "containing some reproaches but filled with great tenderness." Echoes of her essay reverberated in Doria's mind: "To Want and To Dare! Never hesitate to act when the feeling of injustice revolts us. To give one's measure with all good faith, the rest will follow as a logical consequence."

Elated at her news, Doria reflected on her sensation of emancipation. She was filled with confidence; she had tested her will and succeeded in imposing it on the director of the office in Paris as well as on those from whom he received his orders: "All this coming to me from an act of the faith I carried within me through the centuries from the Levant. I was aware in my heart of a new synthesis between the east and the west, between the past and the future. A feeling, in which I could have no doubt, invaded me like a light. In this atmosphere of confidence I set to work."

She realized, however, that victory had its price. She had to renounce her poet:

> Yes. I had won my fight, through my own will. But what had been the price of such a victory? The price had been too high. My victory left me hurt. As I had lost my mother's infinite love, I had lost again the genuine love promised by the springtime of my existence. I had a growing awareness of my desolation. I was feeling so terribly alone, drowned beneath the indifference of Paris. Again I found an outlet to my distress in my studies. I had two years ahead of me and I decided to make them ones of

hard work and to forget my suffering. I had to forget love, tenderness. Sometimes when feeling this void in my life, I rewrote some of the poems I had written and memorized before they were stolen.

Paroles d'une Poupée de Sucre	Words of a Sugar Doll
C'est la fête	It is the feast
du Prophète	of the Prophet
Moulid al-Nabi[11]	Moulid al-Nabi
des milliers de poupées	thousands of
de sucre	sugar dolls
comme moi	like me
étalées	displayed
le long des rues	along the streets
couleur de vie . . .	all colors of life . . .
Un enfant me regarde	A child looks at me
ses copains	his pals
mangent	eating
les yeux, la bouche, le coeur	the eyes, the mouth, the heart
de leurs	of their
poupées	dolls
Mais lui	But he
est pauvre	is too poor
il ne peut payer . . .	he cannot pay . . .
D'ailleurs	Besides
il ne veut point manger	He'd rather not eat
Il me regarde	But look at me instead
Sans me flatter	Without flattering myself
je le crois	I believe he's
amoureux . . .	in Love . . .
Même s'il pouvait payer	Even if he could pay
l'accès	enough for
aux poupées	the dolls
Je suis sûre	I am sure
qu'il préférerait	he'd prefer
mon regard langoureux	my languorous look
à tous les mets	to all the food
Se gardant bien	Guarding so well
ma bouche	my mouth
de la croquer	to munch it
Sauvant ainsi les mots trés doux	Thus preserving the very tender words
que je dirai . . .	I would speak . . .

Quant à ma taille trés fine	As for my waist so slender
pas question	no question
de l'enlacer	of clasping it
entre ses doigts	between his fingers
je craquerais.	I would crack to the touch.
En cela	In this
voyez-vous	don't you see
je ressemble	I resemble
au bonheur des humains	the happiness of humanity
Il s'évanouit	As soon as
aussitôt	one grasps it
qu'on le tient.	it ceases to be.

During these two years at the International House, Doria led a rather solitary existence: "At university I kept so much to myself that I earned the nickname of Sphinx. This feeling of being a stranger to life, not allowed to have happiness like others remained with me. I had to construct my own path, so as not to be drowned beneath the sense of fatality that had haunted me since childhood. To construct this path, I needed a zone of solitude for thinking, for preparing for my future, toward what I was not sure, only that I had a mission. So in spite of the friendships I formed during this time, I remained at a distance from my surroundings, isolating my heart."

However, there were excursions planned by the International House. To encourage the girls to work hard, the management arranged a month-long stay in a rest house called Le Moulin, in the little village of Peyriou in the southeastern region of Savoy near Aix les Bains. Doria's group—the Moroccan, Iranian, and Martiniquian—were among those chosen during her first year there. Also with the group was a Greek girl who, according to Doria,

obviously disliked me. We were continually in each other's company. Quite often I found myself near the Greek at table and noticed in her black eyes a certain unhappiness. I learned from my friends that the Greek had come from a very poor family, lost two sisters from tuberculosis and had been twice engaged only to have been jilted. I sensed her inner sadness and began to sympathize with her. She turned to me and said: "But you don't look as if you've suffered." I answered: "That is because I never despair. But I do know what unhappiness is." I told her about my mother's death when I was still a child, and suddenly there was a bond between us. I noticed that she admired the yellow suit I was wearing and without humiliating her I suggested that with her blonde hair, the suit would look so much better on her. "Do you really think so?" And I realized with pleasure that she had not been insulted and was taking my hesitant offer as the sincere gift of a new friend. She became firmly established in our group. I was happy. A year later she was engaged and jilted anew. Only this time she was pregnant. One evening she came to my room showing me a letter from her fiancé who had left France. "What can I do?" she repeated. "I can't even have an abortion. It is too late." "Don't cry," I said. "You will have your baby and you will never be alone!"

Doria convinced the directors of the International House to pay for the Greek girl's stay in a maternity home until the birth of the baby. A few months later, she obtained her diploma in medicine and in front of society described herself as a divorced woman with a young child. Doria was elated to have helped her solve her problem. Despite her sense of estrangement and isolation, Doria was not without compassion or sensitivity to those around her, and she responded particularly to the challenge of winning over those from whom she felt a certain hostility.

At the Sorbonne, Doria worked hard. She had chosen a difficult program and had decided to sit the exams for two degrees, the Licence libre and the Licence d'état. For the Licence d'état she needed to pass a Latin language examination, a well-nigh impossible task as she was almost totally ignorant of this language. Her strategy for passing this exam displays a certain clever dissimulation:

I knew that even if I studied Latin seriously and took extra lessons, I ran the great risk of failing the exam. I knew what a tragedy it would be if I failed. I would risk being sent back to Egypt without finishing my studies. So I compromised! I decided to take both the examinations for the Licence d'état and the Licence libre to make sure that I obtained at least one degree. So I started studying Latin, but it was like moving mountains. "You can't drink a language like a spoonful of soup," said my Iranian friend. It was a challenge and made me more and more determined to make the grade. I studied certain passages which had been given at similar examinations in previous years. As luck would have it a passage I had prepared was on the exam but to my dismay it contained an additional five lines that I had not prepared. These five lines would betray me! I knew that if I tried to complete the passage, it would be obvious to the examiner that something was wrong. So I decided to leave them out altogether. It was the only way. The examiner, finding all but five lines, very accurately translated, would no doubt think that I hadn't had time to finish! The result came—I had passed with full credit!

Doria's gambit prevailed. She passed her exams with distinction and obtained her Licence d'état. This single-minded capacity to commit herself totally to achieving her goals would prove to be both her great strength and her Achilles heel. In her pursuit of knowledge, such determination and discipline were an enormous asset. Within the domain of her public and political life, such burning ambition could generate quite different consequences. But this was just the beginning of her quest:

> A dream began to take shape which would allow me to teach at the Sorbonne itself. I would one day become a professor at the National University of France. But I would have to renew my scholarship first and that required that I return to Egypt. I was somewhat apprehensive about this new contact with my country. Many events had created a huge abyss between Egypt and me. The painful events which had darkened my childhood had been exacerbated by the attitude toward me of my three compatriots in Paris. But when I saw my name in print describing the "great scholarly success of an Egyptian girl in Paris," I felt triumphant. I made plans to return to Egypt, believing that the nightmare would be over."

Before leaving France, in July 1932, however, she wrote a letter to her heroine and protectress, Huda Sha'rawi: "Excellence: I am incapable of showing you my thankfulness for all your kindness on my behalf. I waited impatiently for the moment of seeing you this year in Europe to convey to you, orally, my profound gratitude. I hope to be able to do this soon in Cairo, because I have made my request by cable this morning to the Ministry, to have the authorization to pass my vacation in Egypt. Awaiting this happy moment, I kiss your hands. Respectfully, Your devoted, D. Shafik."[12]

Despite her unqualified success and joyful anticipation of returning to her family, Doria was very worried about what might be waiting for her:

> I had the feeling that what I was leaving behind me, the International House, the Latin Quarter, the Sorbonne, was much closer to me than what I was going to find at home. Although I wanted to return to Egypt to see my family, whom I missed very much, it was nevertheless in Paris that, for the first time, I had won out over the hostile world around me. In spite of the isolation, the huge loveless emptiness and my feelings of loneliness; in spite of the desolation, I felt a tremendous moral compensation I had imposed my will and fulfilled my own dream: I had studied philosophy and I had obtained my Licence d'état at the Sorbonne."

3

In Search of Love (1932–1936)

O, my homeland
Here I have returned
Will you welcome me
This time
with
A little more love?

A soul in agony because it thirsts for the Infinite. The Immensity. How
to grasp it? Forgetting time and everything that the measure beats, the
young woman wants to live in wholeness: a sympathy between herself
and the universe; a genuine dream that seeks harmony between the storm
that overturns the self, and this other storm which never ceases to give
existence to the universe: a fight and always a fight. Between lived reality and being: Love! A word that will never die away except with the
human being! But today love of whom and love of what?[1]

This passage—from the essay "Rêverie d'une femme d'aujourd'hui," which
Doria wrote in 1932 on board ship while returning to Alexandria—seems almost clairvoyant in its anticipation of what she would experience on a personal level once back in her homeland. On the political level, however, she was
completely unaware of the growing forces that had begun to transform Egypt
into a different society than the one she had left four years ago. The worst
economic depression of modern times and its repercussions were being felt
throughout Egypt as the gulf between the palace and the politicians widened,
forcing the dispossessed to seek political power outside the normal channels.
The continuing challenge of Westernization to traditional Islamic values deep-
ened the crisis among Egyptian intellectuals. Religious reform had come to a
dead end as a rising nationalism coupled with a new radical conservatism began to take hold of society.

During the early thirties, new social groups, crystallizing around these different political moods, launched campaigns for the purification of Egyptian social and political life from European culture and values. On the one hand was the Muslim Brotherhood, founded in 1928 by Hasan al-Banna, an elementary school teacher from Isma'iliyah. The Brotherhood began as a modest lay Muslim moral and religious association, but as it became a powerful movement to counter the spread of secularism and what was perceived as moral and religious laxity resulting from the processes of modernization and the imitation of foreign life-styles, it attracted hundreds of thousands of adherents from both the dispossessed urban masses and the permanently poverty-stricken rural population. Al-Banna and the Brotherhood had an unswerving faith that Islam was perfect and provided all the answers to the problems of mankind and a deep conviction that Islam was in mortal danger from the hostile machinations of the British occupiers and the blind puppets, the Wafdist government. In the words of al-Banna:

> My Brothers: You are not a benevolent society, nor a political party, nor a local organization having limited purposes. Rather, you are a new soul in the heart of this nation to give it life by means of the Quran; you are a new light which shines to destroy the darkness of materialism through knowing God; and you are the strong voice which rises to recall the message of the Prophet. . . . You should feel ourselves the bearers of the burden which all others have refused. When asked what it is for which you call, reply that it is Islam, the message of Muhammad, the religion that contains within it government, and has as one of its obligations freedom. If you are told you are political, answer that Islam admits no such distinction. If you are accused of being revolutionaries, say "We are voices for right and for peace which we dearly believe and of which we are proud. If you rise against us or stand in the path of our message, then we are permitted to defend ourselves against your injustice." If they insist on pursuing their oppression, say to them, "Peace be upon you, we will ignore the ignorant."[2]

On the other hand was the appearance of a new extremist nationalist association, Misr al-Fatah (Young Egypt), launched by Ahmad Husayn, a lawyer, in 1933. Inspired by the discipline and self-esteem demonstrated by the fascist states in Europe, this group attracted young students of secondary schools in Cairo, Alexandria, and other major towns. These were organized into a paramilitary youth movement, the Green Shirts, to demonstrate against the manifestations of adopted European civilization. Young Egypt emphasized the importance of religious belief and its derivative, morality, and argued that women should receive more education since they produce the future greatness of Egypt and its heroes. They proclaimed that they were to be the new generation of Egypt and demanded that they be given rein to eliminate foreign privileges in the country and to nationalize foreign companies.

Both the Muslim Brotherhood and Young Egypt shared an opposition to the manifestations in Egypt of adopted European civilization. Both agitated against foreign schools and the activities of Christian missions, and both attacked the work of European orientalists.[3] It was also during this period that the illegal Communist Party, outlawed as a political organization since its appearance in the 1920s, experienced a revival and a number of other minority parties split off from the Wafd. All these groups, despite their ideological differences, were united in their rejection of Wafdist style of "liberalism," which was perceived as a form of appeasement to the British.

Doria returned to Egypt at a crucial period in the country's political evolution, when hope for the development in parliamentary government was permanently damaged. More important, this period laid the foundations for a more violent political climate in Egypt as leaders became alienated from the monarchy and the public alienated from all normal, orderly government. Ismail Sidki (1875–1950) emerged as the "strong man" of Egyptian politics as he headed the government from 1930 to 1933. Faced with managing the affairs of the country at a time of worsening economic crisis, he dissolved parliament, abolished the Constitution of 1923, and promulgated a new constitution with stronger executive powers, through which he ruled Egypt with an iron fist in what some have described as one of the harshest periods in Egypt's modern political history. During this period of heightened nationalist fervor, any suggestion of accommodation to European ways, let alone to British rule, was tantamount to treason. Part of Sidki's unpopularity can also be attributed to his firm conviction that Egypt should remain part of the Western world. He was an evolutionist and a moderate who believed in hard negotiations, not physical violence, as a mode of dealing with one's adversary. And he had the reputation among the British of being a very tough negotiator. However, during this period, elections were often accompanied by violence and bloodshed as opposition to the government erupted across the country. This spate of demonstrations drew a sharp British warning to both the government and the Wafd about security conditions in the country, especially as their deterioration affected the lives and property of foreign residents. In 1933, Sidki was ultimately dismissed by the king, and Ali Mahir, as the king's man, was appointed prime minister in his stead.

As Doria searched the quay for her waiting family, she saw her father "with tears in his eyes, visibly and profoundly moved to see me again after so many years, and my sisters were thrilled with my Parisian elegance." Doria moved back into her father's home—which housed not only Soraya, her husband and young son, but also Layla and her two brothers. Since her father traveled frequently, working on engineering jobs that took him away from Alexandria for long periods, Doria was more in the company of her brothers and sisters, who naturally assumed she had come home to stay. She deferred any discussion about her future ambition to return to the Sorbonne, "as I didn't want to rush things." Much to her astonishment, she found that a prospective husband had been picked out for her and was awaiting her return from Paris: "But where has he seen me?" she asked her father. "He's seen your picture in the newspapers. He's quite rich, from a good family and well educated," he answered. "What more could a girl ask for?" commented Soraya.

Doria was in a quandary. Although this process of marriage brokerage did not at all correspond to her own ideas about personal freedom to choose a husband, "which I thought should be based on genuine love," she was not altogether prepared to dismiss the idea outright. Given the society's tremendous emphasis on arranged marriages, the family pressure and cultural expectation of filial obedience to male authority, Doria rationalized that "perhaps accepting my family's choice would be one way of breaking down the wall that I had built around myself to avoid being hurt again. And even if I wasn't expecting true happiness anymore following the events surrounding the French poet, this proposal opened up a possible reconciliation between me and the life around me."

A meeting was arranged between Doria and the young man, an engineer and an acquaintance of her brother's, who also seemed to get along very well with her father. One senses that Doria was torn between her sense of loyalty to her father and the desire to please him, and her own inner feeling that something was amiss about the whole process: "It was like being in the *suq* [market], bargaining around the very essence of my life." Also she did not find her suitor particularly attractive. "But with your vivid imagination you can imagine him handsome," comforted her brother, Gamal. "Marriage is a matter of habit," proclaimed Ali. "After two or three months it would be the same, handsome or not handsome." "Better an ugly face than a slim pocketbook," added Soraya.

Doria struggled to reach some emotional détente in her life: "I wanted to relax the too rigid directives on my life, to set my heart free from the isolation that I felt." So she thought seriously about the situation. "I couldn't dismiss the young man immediately as he did have some fine qualities." But what did she really want from marriage?

Happiness? I had renounced that since my disillusionment in Paris. Perhaps I was expecting only a reconciliation with life, a reconciliation allowing me to free my own heart from solitude. And if that was the only thing I was expecting from marriage, there was no reason in the world to refuse this man. Perhaps it would be an opportunity to adapt myself to my country and to live the normal life of other girls of my age. This would be a way of entering the conventional life of Egypt and cease being considered as someone out of the ordinary. I had suffered a great deal from being looked upon as different from others. I wanted to put an end to the many questions and discussions by people around me as to why I should study? Why should I want a job? Why didn't I want to stay at home and get married!? Only girls from very poor families ever had to work; and girls of a higher class who studied at university were those who were too ugly to find a husband! I was an enigma to my surroundings. Nobody was able to pigeonhole me into a specific category. One way to solve this problem was to get married and thus enter into the definite category, "married woman." It would be the common denominator between me and my fellow countrywomen.

Passively, and contrary to her very nature, Doria acquiesced and accepted the proposal of marriage, but with great ambivalence: "I thought of accepting the idea of just being engaged, but to delay the actual marriage until my return at the end of my studies." She let the young engineer know, through her brother, that she had agreed to the marriage, and he immediately began showering her with an enormous diamond ring and other jewels "in order to seal my word." When she saw these gifts, she had the unpleasant impression that "I had, in effect, sold myself by agreeing to marry without love," and she began to feel some remorse for having given a promise to the young man, particularly since he seemed to be "much more enamored as the weeks went by. I tried to fall in love with him but I couldn't."

Doria felt more and more that she had entered into a relationship that would only lead to disaster if she did not act swiftly and decisively to put an end to the whole charade: "The suffering that my fiancé would endure would be less than a marriage without love on my part." Her father was extremely disappointed when she told him she wanted to return the jewels and put an end to the engagement: "But he didn't try to dissuade me. He knew that when I came to a decision it was after serious thought and that I never changed my mind afterwards. On the other hand he had great respect for other people's freedom, never interfering in their own wishes or decisions." Finally it was her brother-in-law who took charge of the affair and officially broke off the engagement, leaving Doria with "a feeling of liberation." Once again, when a choice had to be made between her sense of freedom and conforming to expectation, Doria chose her independence, refusing to be defined and manipulated by the expectations of the cultural traditions dictating what a woman should or should not be and do.

It was during this time that she met Ceza Nabaraoui, who had arranged an interview for an article for *L'Egyptienne*. In a letter from Ceza to Huda Sha'rawi, we learn how very much Doria was still the focus of their interest: "Doria Shafik is at this moment in Egypt. I had an appointment with her the other day at the seaside. She is always the same: simple and charming. She asked me if you had received her telegram of thanks. Not knowing what to report to you, she is going to send me an article that she wrote for *L'Egyptienne* during the crossing. I am going to see her again and do an interview. She has obtained the authorization from the ministry to return to France to prepare her doctorate, but her family are trying to dissuade her from leaving."[4]

It is in this context that Doria's "Rêverie d'une femme d'aujourd'hui" can best be understood. Writing the essay during a period of emotional ambivalence, Doria describes the quandary of the modern woman, and it is no accident that her title is reminiscent of "my master, Rousseau," to whom she pays homage.[5] In a vein similar to her earlier essay in which she conversed with the Sphinx, Doria repeats her question "Qui es tu?" As she formulates an answer, she describes the young woman's inner struggle to maintain a sense of autonomy. Through her metaphors, we grasp something of the "true meaning of my own life":

> A young heart thinking only of the true, the tragic, the sublime. Youthful and old at the same time, a human being who questions "who are you"? To myself I am an unknown: the one who would know herself would no longer be a human! What can I grasp of myself outside this material and social crust? If one could transpose the formula of Descartes into the order of life and say: "I Fight Therefore I Am," then every act would perhaps have a meaning. In this fight, our dreamer is engaged: reverie, yes, but a living reverie, because the ideas that manipulate her are experienced ideas! It is always the same problem, a solution forcibly suspended, a relentless fight that dies and is reborn: There lies humanity. There is the woman of today.[6]

To the more conservative forces within her society, such philosophical musings were often perceived as egocentric, and later, during her confrontations with the voices of reaction, Doria Shafik would be criticized for her Western, self-centered exhibitionism. Such reactionary voices, coming not only from the Muslim Brothers but also from the conservative Islamic clergy and the government, were condemning the appearance of young Egyptian women on the beaches of Alexandria. In response to these criticisms, Ceza Nabaraoui wrote: "Great changes have taken place within Egyptian customs and mores during the space of these past ten years. And simultaneously a great press campaign has been mounted by certain elements in society to represent our beaches as places of perdition from which our young women must be turned away. What a chasm for those who have known women of another time jealously hidden in the shadow of the harems, to see the young women of today playing in the full light of the benefits of the fresh air of liberty."[7]

Arguing that the gambling casinos and houses of prostitution patronized by young men from high society, which neither the government nor the clergy attempted to close down, were a greater threat to public morality than the young women enjoying the healthy sun and sea of the beaches of Alexandria, Nabaraoui maintained:

> Aided by this spirit of regression which has reigned in official circles for some time now, we read in the press the most absurd articles on the utility of the veil, the dangers of higher education for women and the mixing of the sexes which are leading women to licentiousness and in turning them away from their mission. One could say that the authors of these writings knowingly want to ignore the irresistible power of modern ideas particularly that of the emancipation of women. But what serious arguments can they oppose to this movement when, in their academic achievements, these young women have distinguished themselves by their brilliant talents, their application and their model conduct?

And who did Nabaraoui select as a symbol to counteract reactionary sentiments and provide evidence that the young women students sent on mission to Europe "represent our highest hopes for the future of Egypt?" He continued:

> I found among them on the beach of Stanley Bay, Mlle. Doria Shafik who so brilliantly gained her license to teach at the Sorbonne, and Karima al-Said who obtained a diploma of honor in history from Westfield College. While chatting with Mlle. Doria Shafik, she explained to me her reasons for preferring philosophy to any other field of study. "It is because," she told me, "this study opens our intellectual horizons to more extensive views. It also forms our character and enriches us through accurate knowledge." According to Doria "the higher instruction of young girls would permit the education of a new generation of women, more conscious of their responsibility and the duties that proceed from it." The moral crisis that the young woman is passing through today as a result of these modernistic currents does not seem to frighten her too much. She sincerely believes that "the woman, solidly instructed, could master these modern currents by fighting the materialistic tendencies of our day with her idealistic faith."[8]

By mid-October, 1932, Doria had returned to Paris to resume her studies. In a letter to Huda Sha'rawi written from the International House, she expressed her delight at having been able to see her before leaving Egypt. She went on: "I resume my studies more seriously then ever, taking as guide the example of courage that you never cease to give us in order to raise up the Egyptian woman. I have read with a very great joy the articles concerning the 'Last Harems,' because through them I became aware of all that you have been able to do for the woman of our epoch. I end in kissing your hands respectfully and sending you from here my grateful souvenir. Your devoted, D. Shafik."[9] In another letter written two years later, we learn that Huda Sha'rawi had visited Doria in Paris: "Excellence, Thank you again for the very agreeable evening yesterday. I was happy to have seen you and to see Egypt represented in your person. I would dearly love to see you again before your departure but knowing that your spare time is limited, I do not dare to bother you. Allow, Excellence, that I respectfully kiss your hands. Your devoted, D. Shafik."[10]

*   *   *

Doria's summer holidays were usually spent in Alexandria, which by the mid-thirties had become the playground not only for affluent Cairene families escaping the summer heat, but also for the wealthy European tourists who were pouring into Egypt. In the summer of 1935, a beauty pageant to select the young woman who would represent Egypt in the international competition for Miss Universe was held in Alexandria. Never before had an Egyptian Muslim woman entered this contest, and Doria decided to compete without informing or requesting the consent of her father. For Doria, this decision was consistent with the image of the New Woman she had developed in her essay "Does a Woman Have the Right to Philosophize?" The New Woman represented the unity of beauty (the feminine) and intellect (the masculine) within one single being. And life itself was to be a work of art: "In Paris I had asserted myself in the intellectual sphere. Now I wanted to assert myself in the feminine sphere. It was as if nature, in a sort of immanent justice, having deprived me of the power of class, status and wealth had compensated me with these qualities."

The Miss Egypt beauty pageant was a golden opportunity for Doria to put her ideas to the test. But to enter such a contest was not an easy decision for her. She realized that as a Muslim woman from a provincial and conservative background, she "was risking my reputation" by doing so. And she realized that the whole adventure might seem frivolous from an outsider's point of view. But when she set the matter within the context of her own arguments, she saw that there was nothing flighty in it, and she decided to enter the competition: "I knew that my father would be against my entering such an exhibition and that it might hurt him to know of my action. I resolved not to tell him and since he was out of town at the time it wasn't necessary. If I won he would be proud and if I failed he would never know anything about it."

According to an article published at the time, "there were fifty contestants on that Saturday evening, August 15, 1935, who filed in front of the jury for ten to twelve hours, and the refrain was always the same: walk slowly; pass again; show your legs; next! It is 1:00 a.m. in the morning. It is very warm and we are all perspiring. The jury retires to make its choice. Miss Egypt and her three Maids of Honor are elected."[11] Doria as the first Maid of Honor placed second to the winner, Charlotte Wassef, who subsequently went on to Paris to win the Miss Universe Pageant of 1935. However, it was as much for her beauty as the fact that Doria was the first and only young Muslim woman ever to participate that created a stir among the journalists.

The French magazine *La Réforme Illustrée* published an interview that gives us a glance not only at Doria Shafik's public image but at her self-image as well:

A dark-complexioned young woman of tall and slender stature, who gives one the impression of a calm, reflective person with a resolute will, spiced by a touch of audacity, Mademoiselle Doria as a Muslim has great merit to have entered in a beauty contest. She confided to me that she entered without the knowledge of her family. "What motivated you to take part in this pageant?" Mlle. Shafik answered me betraying by her voice and gesture that she had known how it would all turn out. "I wanted to amuse myself a little, to see the people, to feel the commotion around me, to deviate from the commonplace for an evening. Moreover the contest was serious. When my family learned that I had not been elected Miss Egypt they congratulated me, realizing that my father would never have let me go to Europe to participate in the world contest. I am also happy not to have to regret a beautiful voyage!" Mlle. Shafik leaves one with the strong, clear impression of a very cultivated young woman. Conversation with her easily takes a philosophic turn. When I asked her to define for me her ideal, her ambition, she answered me with this sibylline phrase: "It is for those things that I do not have and I desire; if I had them, I would consider that my ideal had been attained!" And with a touch of irony, she adds, "*Glissez mortels.*"[12]

The Egyptian Arabic press was much more critical of Doria's participation in this pageant, and her name "was splashed all over the newspapers." As a result, she received letters from her previous teachers from the Mission schools in Tanta and Alexandria, "criticizing me for acting in a way not proper to my upbringing." There was a virulent campaign against her; the strongest criticism was that "I was a Muslim girl who had acted against Islam!" This particular accusation upset her for the pain she felt it would cause her father: "But I discovered his great moral integrity and noble spirit when he came to my defense, assuring me that the slanderous campaign had nothing to do with Islam. He explained that the true spirit of Islam was liberal and tolerant; that Islam was not against beauty adding, with a quote from the Quran, that the Prophet himself was described as the most beautiful of God's creatures."

But out of this uproar and notoriety, Doria found herself enmeshed in yet another proposal of marriage, which in her memoirs she describes as a version of Sartre's *La Nausée*! It appears that Doria perhaps fell victim to her own idealism. The young man who appeared on the scene and offered himself as Doria's ardent suitor was none other than the popular Ahmad al-Sawi Muhammad, founder and owner of one of Egypt's favorite social magazines of the period, *Magalati* (My review). Al-Sawi was also a gifted journalist known for his enlightened and progressive articles in defense of the cause of women. He had studied journalism in Paris before entering the Sorbonne, where he received a diploma in social studies in 1927. He was also among that group of young intellectuals (those who had traveled to France for higher studies) who formed a coterie around Huda Sha'rawi. Doria met al-Sawi in the context of the Miss Universe pageant, and shortly thereafter, their engagement was announced. She bitterly recalls this experience:

> In the uproar of the polemic around me an Egyptian journalist who was then owner of a successful magazine came to worm his way into my life. Though ugly as sin, he was most charming and I shut my eyes to his ugliness imagining him under the mask of a Cyrano de Bergerac. Our house was literally invaded with red flowers. He spoke to me of Paris and I thought I found in him the soul of a poet. I was taken up in a sort of whirlwind. Everything happened so quickly. There was no question of my reflecting before entering into this new adventure. With dizzying speed we had signed the marriage contract.

So sensational was this engagement that for the first time in Egypt, the photograph of a bride and groom appeared on the front pages of the Egyptian press. As Mustapha Amin recounts:[13]

> One morning *al-Ahram* newspaper came out with two large pictures in four columns on the front page with the caption "A Happy Union." The readers were quite surprised for this was the first time that *al-Ahram* had published a picture of a bride and groom on the first page. Even the news of the marriage of King Fuad to Queen Nazli, when Fuad was the ruler, was published by the dignified *al-Ahram* newspaper on the page

of local news on the inside, not on the front page. The readers were even more surprised when they read that the groom was the beloved young writer, Ahmad al-Sawi Muhammad, who wrote the column, "Brief and To the Point" on the front page of *al-Ahram*. Al-Sawi was not handsome but his writing about love and passion and beauty made his image in the minds of the young female readers appear as their dream or Romeo or Valentino, or Clark Gable, or Robert Taylor. The bride on the other hand was Miss Doria Shafik who had a degree in literature and who had got a diploma at the Sorbonne in Paris and about whose beauty and brilliance all society was talking. The readers were even more astonished when they read that the wedding party had taken place at the Alexandria summer mansion of Mme. Huda Sha'rawi, the leader of the women's movement in Egypt, and the value of the *mahr* had been twenty-five piasters only.[14] This was the marriage of the season especially since the two protagonists were supporters of the demand for the rights of women. Signing the contract took place in complete secrecy and no word leaked out, no rumors to any newspaper or magazine and *al-Ahram* got the exclusive story.[15]

Photographs of Doria and Ahmad appear next to those of Huda Sha'rawi's young cousin, Hurria Idris, and her groom in the September issue of *L'Egyptienne*, under the caption "a modern couple." What is of particular interest in this account is the emphasis on the attitude of the modern couple as a new example of the equal status of man and woman. Instead of the hundreds or thousands of pounds that would have been expected from a man marrying the cousin of Huda Sha'rawi, the bride agreed to accept, as a point of honor, only twenty-five piasters as dowry (*mahr*) (worth about fifty cents at that time), which is the minimum required by law in a contract of marriage. In order that this concession not be considered an easy way of dissolving the marriage, the remainder of the dowry payable to the wife in case of divorce (*muta'akhkhir*) had been fixed, by the groom himself, at 300 Egyptian pounds. The following principle is established in this contractual arrangment: the bride, by accepting a small amount of money as *mahr*, facilitates the marriage; the groom, by contracting to pay a substantial *muta'akhkhir*, imposes a certain barrier to seeking an easy divorce. Occurring in a highly publicized marriage blessed by Huda Sha'rawi, this example of a more egalitarian marriage contract sent out a clear message to Egyptian society.

However, something went wrong between Doria and Ahmad almost immediately. As Amin related:

But the marriage which produced such a great storm didn't last. In fact the divorce happened before the wedding procession. Ahmad al-Sawi was a European on the outside and a *sa'idi*[16] on the inside. He was born in Aswan and educated in Paris. He was liberated in what he wrote and conservative in his house. Doria Shafik was influenced by her studies at the Sorbonne and demanded for the Egyptian woman all the rights of the French woman. She wanted her to be someone who voted and could act as a representative and a minister. Al-Sawi had no objections to any woman in Egypt being a minister or an ambassador except his own wife. Her place was in the house so the divorce was inevitable. Doria Shafik took the shock of the divorce with remarkable courage and she said to me at the time that "this is the smallest sacrifice that I make to enable me to keep to my principles."[17]

Doria's reconstruction of those events as written in her memoirs conveys a feeling of her having been profoundly deceived:

We had a huge engagement party and I was so happy to see Mme. Huda Sha'rawi again. Everyone thought it was a successful union: a true merger of modern minds. I had a strange presentiment of something wrong in the whole affair but tried to convince myself that I was mistaken. Since my fiancé had failed to offer me an engagement ring, which was customary between couples at that time, my father gave me the money to purchase one, something my fiancé was aware of. One day he came to visit me with a small packet in his hand. Thinking it was a gift, I was astonished when I opened it to find a photograph of myself taken during the pageant when I was wearing a strapless evening dress. The way the photo had been faked it looked as if I were not wearing a dress at all! I could not understand the meaning of this. He turned to me and said: "If I do not receive the money" (alluding to what my father had given me) "then this photo will be published in all the newspapers and you will not be able to show your face or walk in the street. Your reputation will be lost for good!" Then he waited for an answer. It was as if someone had plunged a knife into my heart. My mind played for time and I told him I would have to go to the bank. "Then I shall return tomorrow." He picked up the photograph and left.

It is difficult to understand why al-Sawi wanted to blackmail Doria in this way, and her memoirs do not give us much of a clue. Mustapha Amin observed that al-Sawi was "French on the outside but a *sa'idi* in his heart." When it came to his own wife, all al-Sawi's liberal beliefs about the freedom of women went out the window. Realizing that Doria had a mind of her own and was not about to shut herself up in his upper Egyptian household, he perhaps thought he could threaten her into submission. Shocked by "a terrible sense of oppression—again at the edge of the abyss," Doria despaired: "how shall I escape from this nightmare?"

Although the *katb-il-kitab* had taken place, the marriage had not been consummated. Doria was nevertheless considered "married" in front of society. But unlike her mother a generation before, who acceded to the pressures of society's view about divorce, Doria set about to see if she could get this marriage annulled. The word "divorce" troubled her father deeply, for he believed her reputation would be greatly affected, and he advised his daughter "to handle the situation amiably. Two engagements and two ruptures (one in a divorce) in less than two months would be shattering!" But Doria was "terrified by the horror of what had happened and wanted a divorce at any price." The situation was complicated, since according to Islamic law, there can be no divorce if the husband refuses—unless the woman, during the signature of the marriage contract, has stipulated that she has the right to divorce:

> I went to Tante Aziza, whose husband was a very well known and powerful lawyer who assured me not to worry. And indeed within twenty-four hours, the "blackmailing fiancé" evidently was afraid and accepted the divorce. This liberation *in extremis* left me with a bitter taste, a sort of nausea. I had the sensation that something was wrong in my country in which the bondage which women suffered was only one manifestation. I didn't try to analyze this sensation as I was concentrating all my efforts on bearing up under the weight of this latest wound, without bending.

As Doria was recovering from her personal catastrophe in 1936, the sixteen-year-old Faruq succeeded to the throne of Egypt, following the death of his father, King Fuad I. Ali Mahir, strong man of Egyptian politics and close to the palace, returned from England with Faruq, who had been sent by his father to Sandhurst for study. Faruq, young and inexperienced, was surrounded by many who sought to maneuver themselves into advantageous positions within palace politics. Because of his close palace connections, Ali Mahir was appointed prime minister. According to Doria, "Nazli, the Queen Mother, feeling the sense of liberation from a tyrannical and oppressive husband, decided to take her revenge on life." By this, Doria meant that Nazli began to assert her newfound power as mother to Faruq and surrounded herself with persons she felt would support her goals. Specifically she empowered the young Ahmad Hassanayn, who, as the favorite former tutor to the young king, was believed to have a strong influence over his pupil. Others around the king took umbrage at Hassanayn's advantage, and the intrigues within the palace flourished.

It was during this period that Doria, without then being aware or conscious of what exactly was going on, first became entangled with the palace and its machinations:

It had been decided that the queen-mother should henceforth have a social activity and it was therefore necessary for her to have an educated person work closely with her. The choice fell upon me. My nomination to the post was nearly official when, suddenly, the whole affair fell through. How had it begun and how had it ended? My name had been suggested by Murad Muhsin, chief of the royal treasury, who had great influence at the palace. His wife had known my mother (and admired her) and had seen me as an infant in Mansura. Within the palace I was therefore completely identified as being on the side of Murad Muhsin since I had obtained this post through his mediation. My appointment would aid him a great deal (seeing the influence I would have with the queen-mother) in his fight against Ahmad Hassanayn whose increasing power was disturbing him. But the latter had foreseen this maneuver and had thwarted it. I had no idea about all this when an appointment was made for me to meet the queen-mother. From the first moment that I entered the salon of the palace where I waited for her majesty to enter, I had the impression of suffocation. There was an oppressive atmosphere and I had the crazy desire to slam the doors and leave. Patience! Finally a lady in waiting arrived and in confused and confusing language interviewed me for an hour. Immediately I sensed an intrigue. But what? Finally after allusions and innuendoes she hinted I was too young! I started to leave and she did not restrain me.

It seemed that everywhere Doria turned or every time she tried to become reconciled with her surroundings, her effort ended in her being hurt or wounded by some scheme that she perceived as not of her own making: "What had happened to me with al-Sawi could not be the result of pure chance or an inability to adapt on my part. A profound sickness was eating away at my country, advancing at a steady pace even within the depths of our social structure. I could not know its nature but I felt it; I could foretell it. I had to leave."

So once again Doria decided to return to that haven where she had always found sustenance and strength to face the hurt and wounds of her social existence—back to the world of the intellect, the world of the Sorbonne and the pursuit of philosophy. But this time, "my departure is not a running away or an escape but a quest—a conquest, an acquisition of knowledge! I would leave again for Paris! I would have the highest degree in the world. I would arm myself to the teeth, with all the powerful weapons of knowledge! Then and only then would I be able to find the way to freedom."

She had no difficulty obtaining a new scholarship to prepare for the Doctorat d'état in philosophy at the Sorbonne. She felt optimistic that she was on her way toward the fulfillment of an ardent dream. But at the same time, she realized there was "a gigantic abyss separating me from my country. I had done my best to reconcile myself to Egypt and I had failed. I thought that the reason for this had been, perhaps, the great distance between my idealistic illusions on the one hand and Egypt's effective reality on the other. And I asked myself: How can I draw my country nearer to me?" Doria asked herself the question in stilted English, and later in her memoirs she provided an answer: "If I had failed to adapt my own "dimensions" to those of my country, wouldn't it be possible to do the opposite—to adapt my country's 'dimensions' to my own?" Were Doria's words arrogant, or did they reveal a prescient conviction that she was destined to carry out some "mission" in the life of her country? "I had the persistent presentiment," Doria says, "that some day—later—I would achieve some great deed for my country. But at the same time I was conscious of immense difficulties hindering the adaptation of those high principles to life's realities."

The dominant theme coming across the pages of Doria's memoirs as she recalled these moments is her realization that life, although endowing her with great possibilities, was also going to exact a great price. As if to draw a parallel between herself and the poet's suffering in the midst of his earthbound life, she quotes Baudelaire's poem "The Albatross":

Le Poète est semblable au prince des nuées
Qui hante la tempête et se rit de l'archer;
Exilé sur le sol au milieu des huées
Ses ailes de géant l'empêchent de marcher.

The Poet is like the Prince of the clouds;
Who haunts the storm and laughs at the archer;
Exiled on earth amidst the hoots of the crowd
His giant's wings prevent him from walking.

To be endowed with great potential meant at the same time to be exposed to great suffering: "For the rule of Great Nature makes us understand," Doria concluded, "that we can have nothing without paying the price, and that the higher the goal, the higher must be its price."

Like the albatross, Doria was on a quest, the exact nature of which was still unclear to her, "except that it was a human mission, in the profound sense of that term, meaning the very essence of man. I had to begin my preparation for it at once. I knew I must devote myself to attaining the highest knowledge;

but at the same time subject myself to the strongest discipline." Doria was thinking more of her future than her past: "I hadn't time to lick my wounds. My heart was obsessed with the idea of returning to Paris, the Sorbonne and becoming one of the most educated woman in the world—only then would I be liberated from the past and myself." And in August of 1936, at the age of twenty-seven, Doria once more set sail for France, feeling "there is a sort of immanent justice, facilitating certain things in compensation for others."

*   *   *

As Doria was leaving in quest of her own liberation from her oppressive past, a naive and inexperienced sixteen-year-old boy had just ascended the throne of Egypt, opening the way for the never-ending machinations and struggles for power among himself, the British, and the Wafd.[18] The mounting Axis threat in Europe, underscored by Italy's invasion and subsequent annexation of Ethiopia and the intensification of fascist propaganda in Egypt, motivated the British to respond more flexibly to Egyptian efforts to eradicate the vestiges of colonial occupation. Combined with the fact that Mustapha al-Nahas—who had succeeded to the leadership of the Wafd party following Zaghlul's death in 1927—had been constitutionally elected back into power, the appropriate circumstances were created to bring about the signing of the Anglo-Egyptian treaty in August 1936. The specific conditions of this treaty included: that Great Britain would recognize Egypt's complete sovereignty (except for a clause allowing Britain to maintain a military presence on the Suez Canal for twenty years); that the Sudan would continue to be administered by both Egypt and Great Britain; and that foreigners and minorities would henceforth be the responsibility of the Egyptian government.

The outbreak of the Palestinian Revolt (1936–1939) brought the Palestinian Question into prominence and gave added impetus to the conservative religious reaction against Europe. During this period in Palestine, there were 400,000 Jews—out of a total population of approximately 1,400,000. Over the course of the Arab revolt, 5,000 Arabs and Jews died, and over 15,000 were wounded. The British put down the revolt, exiled its leadership, disarmed the Palestinians, and armed the Jews. A torrent of immigrants flooded into Palestine from Europe. By 1939, the battle cry "Go to Palestine!" had raised the number of Jews coming into Palestine to nearly 15,000 a year.[19] Both the Muslim Brothers and Young Egypt called for closer cooperation with the Arabs struggling against Zionism in Palestine. Huda Sha'rawi, who was to devote the rest of her life to the Palestinian cause, held the first Pan Arab Women's Congress on the Palestine Question in 1939.

While the British were negotiating with the Zionists to make Palestine a "national home" for the Jews of the world, they were successfully concluding the Anglo-Egyptian Treaty, which allowed the English to station troops on the Suez Canal. Although the treaty was accepted by a wide range of the public, there was intense opposition to it among the groups outside the political mainstream (that is, the Communists on the left and the Fascists on the right). Over time, the treaty became the symbol for popular resistance to the hated British occupation as nationalist feelings for independence erupted throughout Egypt over the next two decades. Ahmad Husayn modeled his Young Egypt organization after the fascist structures in Europe and attracted many young Egyptians. Communist groups had begun to organize clandestinely, while Hasan al-Banna's Muslim Brothers became stronger and more militant.

Because she was abroad during most of these years, Doria did not understand "the full meaning of these disorders around me in this prewar period, except for the feeling of impending chaos."

4

Return to the City of Light (1936–1939)

J'ai souvent eu faim	I have often been hungry
dans la ville de Paris.	in the city of Paris.
J'y cherchais	There I searched for
l'instruction	knowledge and
J'y apprenais	learned
la philosophie.	Philosophy.
J'aspirais à la vie	I longed for a life
dans le sens absolu,	in the absolute sense,
dégagée, purifiée	released, purified
de ce qui l'avilit.	from that which debased it.
J'ai longtemps quété	For a long time I have
l'Infini.	searched for Infinity.
Et je demeure	And still I remain
"Chercheuse d'Absolu"	"Seeker of the Absolute"
Comme autrefois	as in the past
dans la ville	in the city
de Paris.	of Paris.[1]

Genuinely relieved and happy to be back in the city where she felt "all the hidden forces gathering in my heart, calling me irresistibly toward a new awareness and outlook on life," Doria looked upon Paris as if she were "awakening from the nightmare of the previous events." Believing that marriage was synonymous with pain and deception, she pledged herself to celibacy and vowed to dedicate herself completely to "the pursuit of the intellect wherein I could please myself." The quest for the Absolute became her dominant obsession as she sought to rediscover and seize the quintessence of her City of Light. For the next three years, she would savor the Parisian milieu—think, speak, and write in the French language, study the heritage of western European philosophy and civilization, meet men and women from different parts of the world and slowly become aware of the political upheavals in Europe occurring in the face of the successful aggression of fascism. These years in Paris critically shaped and gave content to Doria's emerging feminist consciousness and aesthetic attitude.

The Paris of the thirties, by anybody's standard, was a colorful place with new ideas and ideologies springing up, most notably those filtering in from America and Russia. From the West came the "American way of life," typified not only in the material power of Henry Ford but equally in the new music of jazz personified in the figure of Josephine Baker, who had taken Paris and France by storm throughout the twenties and thirties.[2] Ideas about the alleged freedom and equality between the sexes were challenging the French Catholic tradition. Anais Nin was writing her diaries,[3] and Henry Miller, Ernest Hemingway, and Scott Fitzgerald were attacking philistine sexual attitudes and creating a new genre of literary expression. American expatriates poured into Paris to attend the salon of Miss Gertrude Stein and live cheaply and freely on the Left Bank.

From the east came the Soviet "experiment" with its rejection of bourgeois values, remaking society and carrying on the program of the revolution. Marxism emerged as a serious intellectual force in the wake of the Great Depression. The "red decade," or at least the "pink" one, had begun. It was also during the thirties that many French writers became interested in Communism. They had grown weary of the despair and skepticism of the esthetes of the earlier generation and wrote them off as irresponsible. Conversion from gloom and alienation to hope and social purpose seemed a miracle at the time.

During the thirties, it was taken for granted that art has a social content and that artists ought to work for social change. Dadaism—symbolizing outrage against bourgeois sentiments, morals, and patriotism—was giving way to surrealism, a social and artistic movement which debated the proper role of the intellectual in a changing society.[4] Prominent leaders of the surrealist movement were the poets André Breton, Louis Aragon, Paul Eluard, and Pierre Reverdy. Drawn more to the themes of human freedom than to left wing ideological partisanship, these writers nevertheless became Doria's favorite reading.

The Left was in the ascendant, and radicals, socialists, and Communists were united in the defense of the Third Republic against the Fascist leagues, Hitler, and the interests of the "two hundred families that ruled France." Léon Blum— the elegant lawyer, drama critic, and debater—became the new prime minister of the Popular Front in 1936. It was he who appointed the first woman, Mme. Brunschvicg, wife of Doria's philosophy teacher at the Sorbonne, to a ministerial post. And at that historical moment, she was more celebrated than her husband. Civil war broke out in Spain in 1936 and became a symbol of the unending and hitherto successful aggression of fascism. Reaction against fascism and nazism not only provided a rallying point for the shattered morale of European intellectuals but also made it clear to Doria that people were being oppressed and losing their freedom—a cause dear to her heart that was to appear again and again in the different contexts of her later struggle.

*   *   *

Upon her arrival in Paris, she took up residence once again at the International House. All of her former colleagues had left, and she was not very interested in cultivating new friends—"none of them seemed as interesting as my old companions." There were many more "effete Americans pursuing general surveys of western civilization," which Doria felt was not serious study. She wondered "why the Sorbonne gave academic diplomas for secondary school subjects!" However, she discovered that her Georgian friend, Elsa, was still living with her family in Paris and taking courses at the Sorbonne. She used to come to the International House from time to time to take her meals with Doria: "I had always been fond of Elsa, who was very oriental and, like the Egyptians, had a marvelous zest for life." Their friendship developed and brought Doria in touch with Elsa's entourage, an "exotic group of political refugees from Stalinist Russia and Eastern Europe for the most part" and a Parisian life-style completely different from that which she had encountered at the *Pension de Famille,* the apartment in the Bois de Boulogne or the International House: "The fiery spirit of my Georgian companion, her excessive love of life, brought me into contact with reality. I often took my lunch with her family and the exiles. It was a veritable magic tour."

The exiles, as she called them, were mostly from the Russian elite, including officers of the tsarist army who had fled to Paris after the 1917 revolution. Lunchtimes were spent arguing about the various social and political forces spreading throughout Europe. Doria observed a "general feeling of indifference, political skepticism and negativism in the discourse of international politics" among her Georgian friend's entourage: "I felt a certain malaise yet events themselves created a sense of tension, dread, violence, chauvinism and the continual infraction of international law." She further recalled:

These discussions sometimes became very embittered among the young Georgians but I was intrigued. Some would argue against Communism (which seemed natural to me as they had been forced to leave their country); but others argued for it, although they had also fled. I did not understand these latter ones. Or rather I refused to go too deeply into certain subjects, which I intuitively felt would have deceived or disappointed me. My commitment to the Absolute very often turned me away from facing the raw coarseness of reality. A sort of reserve, (aesthetic I would say), keeping me at the edges of truth each time the latter, blending with the exigencies of life, risked, if I probed too closely, colliding with my taste for the Infinite. An attitude that would remain with me as a rule of life, for a long time. It was this that would contribute to delaying my contribution to the political life of my country. Politics do not often allow such grand loftiness as the Absolute imposes!

The realm of politics and the concept of the Absolute, two poles around which Doria Shafik created and expressed herself throughout her life, had taken root during those early childhood years in Mansura and Tanta. Both were strengthened and given direction during her years at the Sorbonne: "All my life I can recall looking at people and the world around me from this aesthetic angle. During my earlier years at the Sorbonne I had been drawn to the philosophy of Rousseau like a moth toward the flame. I felt his idea of pantheism, the universal harmony between nature and man, was but another name for what I call the aesthetic feeling. Of what does it consist? What is the profound nature of this sublime emotion which seizes us in front of beauty and to what end can this sentiment lead us?"

With only a month to choose how these questions might find concrete expression in her doctoral work, she set out to formulate the specific topics by making an appointment with her major professor of aesthetics, Victor Basch, a political activist as well as an academician: "Making up part of a group of French aestheticians that included Lalo, Souriau and Fouillon, Basch (a grand arrogant figure, difficult with students) had a very interesting political past. At the time of the Dreyfus Affair, between 1897–1906, he was a friend of Jaures, that is a militant in the Party of the Dreyfuists."[5] Doria recalled her discussion with him on the aesthetic sentiment in Kant's philosophy for her final oral examination for her Licence d'état three years earlier but was apprehensive that he would not remember her. When she met him in his study,

He was just the same, with his large black bow in place of a tie and his hair, as always, a little longer than normal. I was struck by his face that seemed more tormented than ever (possibly a presentiment of what was going to happen to the Jews of France after the invasion of the Germans). "You have changed, Sphinx," he said. "A mature young woman now." I was happy that he had remembered me. I explained to him my interest in the aesthetic sentiment and asked his advice. "Why don't you try to do something on the philosophy of the art of your own country? You have at your disposal a very rich art with an unmatched history. Being an Egyptian you must feel about it more profoundly than any other subject." It was like a revelation to me and I wondered why I had not thought about it myself. Then suddenly the idea came to me for my second topic. Why shouldn't I write about the women of my country as well. I would study the conditions of the "Liberation" of the Egyptian woman in particular and Muslim women in general. "Very good idea," he said. "Now you must refine your ideas, determine the respective titles of your theses and choose the professors with whom you will work." I left him feeling that I had found my way.

Doria plunged immediately and feverishly into her work because she realized that the terms set by the Egyptian Ministry of Education for her scholarship, allowed her only three years to complete her doctorate. Characteristically she was in a hurry because she had to finish her two theses in half the time it takes most other students. Her choice of research topics reflected her own existential situation of living in the very different cultural and intellectual worlds of France and Egypt. Through her two theses she attempted to bridge these distinct traditions. On the one hand, she blended European aesthetic philosophy with a study of ancient Egyptian art, and on the other, she reconciled the question of women's rights with Islamic religion. In so doing she was also giving shape to her own modes of being-in-the-world—the poetic and the political.

Her first thesis challenged the prevailing scholarship about ancient Egyptian art, which argued that the ancient Egyptians aimed solely toward a utilitarian end, the conquest of eternity, and that their art, in serving a religious purpose, did not constitute art for its own sake:

> Most of the critics of ancient Egyptian art were concerned with its utilitarianism, i.e. that art was aimed at an end which was not itself, that is, not disinterested. Art's finality is its spontaneity, its creativity. I was wondering if all art was really utilitarian. Whether artistic production could become, for the artist, a pure aesthetic pleasure having nothing to do with function. What about music, poetry, objects belonging to everyday temporal existence? Couldn't ancient Egyptian art have begun as utilitarian and then surpassed itself in order to become disinterested?

It was in answer to that question that Doria wrote *L'Art pour l'art dans l'Egypte antique*. The research she undertook "influenced not only my own spiritual formation but also played an important role in the construction of my own life's directives"—particularly on what she would call her "aesthetic attitude toward life based fundamentally on the primacy of sentiment" for which she credits Rousseau, who "had a great influence on me through the supremacy he accorded to the 'heart.' The primacy of feeling and harmony I see as basic universals. My aesthetic feeling is based on the three conditions: inner harmony, disinterestedness and universality." To the major Western philosophies of art and aesthetics she fused the ancient Egyptian poetics such as the legend of Isis and Osiris, symbols that pervade a good deal of her poetry.

For her second thesis, "I decided to concentrate on a topic that was close to my heart, that had obsessed me for a long time and on which the selection was almost imposed as if by necessity—the conditions under which Muslim women lived in my country and their sufferings, to which I had been witness as a child growing up. I would write on the woman and religious rights in contemporary Egypt."

She wrote to her father asking him to send her relevant Arabic books but she had to improve her classical Arabic in order to read the materials sent to her. Her literary Arabic was weak because, like many women of her background and generation, she had a French education and French was considered the language of social status and culture. She found an Egyptian professor from al-Azhar University who was studying in Paris, and he agreed to give her some lessons. With her subjects chosen, she set about learning not only Arabic but also German, English, and Greek in order to read the necessary texts on the philosophy of aesthetics, history of art, Egyptology, and sociology. This was no mean task, given the fact that she had limited time. Even she wondered how she was going to accomplish all this in three years!

Doria's professors were internationally recognized scholars, several belonging to the Académie Française. Emile Brehier, Doria's philosophy professor and chairman of her thesis-defense committee, was regarded as France's leading scholar on Descartes. He had also taught one year (1925) at the Egyptian National University. Maurice Halbwachs, the noted social psychologist and disciple of Durkheim, was the major advisor on her second thesis. (He died in a German concentration camp in the early forties.) Charles Lalo, co-advisor on her first thesis, and Victor Basch were her professors of aesthetics. Lalo was a disciple of Basch, and both were members of a group of French aestheticians who founded the French Committee for the League of the Rights of Man in the 1930s and were deeply involved in opposing the Fascists. Raymond Weill, her major advisor, with whom she experienced the most difficulty, was a well-known archaeologist, highly respected for his excavations and historical studies on ancient Egypt. He was the president of the French Society of Egyptology. Doria also studied philosophy under Léon Brunschvicg, the great authority on Pascal who was regarded by his peers as the "philosopher of the spirit" and a personal friend of Henri Bergson.

Doria credited these professors—several of whom were involved in international political struggles going on in France during the 1930s—with having

been "the most important intellectual and spiritual influences of my Paris studies." Through Brunschvicg Doria read Schopenhauer, Nietzsche, and Hegel,
and was exposed to Henri Bergson, whose doctrines were still dazzling the
audiences at his public lectures of the Collège de France.[6] They steeped Doria
in the Western philosophies of humanism, liberalism, intuitionism, and ratio-
nal idealism—ideological values that, given her own quest for the Absolute,
must have seemed very attractive as she was working out her own philosophical stance. To her, Western philosophy expressed "the increasing liberation of
thought from material matter which began with the signing of the Magna
Carta[7] when the religious values of the medieval period gave way to the political values through the concept of Liberty the Supremacy of Law and the
Rights of Man, culminating with the aesthetic values of the Renaissance. Eventually these values become linked. The essential aesthetic value attributed to
Liberty in western philosophy has exercised a great influence on my own political formation and became the fundamental principle of my political attitude."

*   *   *

As respite from her long hours of study, Doria would lunch with her Georgian
friend, Elsa. One afternoon while they were lunching at a restaurant on Place
St. Michel, "where they served magnificent oysters," she encountered the
young French poet from whom she thought she had detached herself:

I had broken all ties and emotional feelings. Upon seeing him enter, I felt
my blood turn cold. He hesitated a moment and Elsa, sensing my perplexity, asked what was wrong. Her gaiety encouraged the poet, who
came to sit with us. He was surprised that I had returned to Paris and
asked how I was getting along. The three of us chatted together before
he left. A few days later I received this poem:

Il y avait au-dessus de Paris	There were so many stars
tant d'étoiles!!	over Paris
Tant de voix	As well as a voice
se mêlaient dans	that mingled
le silence du souvenir	with the silence of memory
De la Place Saint-Michel	The colors of
les couleurs	Place St. Michel
s'écaillant en larmes	are flaked into tears
Tout était si loin et si près	Everything so far, so near.
A jamais si présent	Never so present
Que le temps de la vie se voyait	As the time of life
pris au piège	seen

Et qu'une voix	caught in the trap
toujours fidèle	And a voice
se souvenait.	always faithful
	is remembered.

Doria read and reread these verses, which seemed to her "to come from heaven, from a distant region with the aura of the Absolute, where alone one can have access to the heart of man. I also rediscovered my past, only without the wounds and hurts. I perceived the sun was rising again for the first time since Mama's death."

But she hesitated in answering, and another letter arrived several days later—this time it was not a poem but a proposal of marriage:

I was perplexed. What should I do? How to sacrifice a true happiness offered at the moment I least expected? How to abandon it at the risk of never finding it again? And if I came to renounce it how would I live in obscurity after so much Light? Upon reflection I uncovered one by one the reasons for my hesitation. First of all, the pain it would cause my father. I didn't have the right after so much self-denial on his part to cause him the least sadness. Then there was the difference in religion and upbringing that could one day shackle a sentiment so near to the Absolute and which I wanted to protect in all its clarity and beauty. On the other hand how could I evade my obligation to my country that, although it had made me suffer—or perhaps because it had made me suffer—required that I return to try to remedy the deep roots of the social apathy that was the cause of these sufferings? Finally I felt my profound wound would never close if I did not return to the very scene of the abyss in order to heal it. Taking my courage in both hands I wrote a letter in which I crossed off my happiness. After I had sent the letter my confusion was so great that for the first time I wanted to die. I even thought about committing suicide, but thinking of my father I renounced it.

The last we hear about her French poet is a later and slightly different version of the circumstances surrounding his proposal of marriage. It took place during what must have been her last rendezvous with the poet at the exhibition of "Masters of Independent Art," held at the Petit Palais art museum in 1937. Doria describes the experience through her reactions to the paintings of the artists on exhibit:

Picasso! Braque! The atmosphere of a dream. Not retaining anything but the essence! Not seeing anything but the Invisible, the Unknown. That which communicates to the very soul of things. Georges Rouault!

Bringing me back to my childhood! From the black contours transmitting lights that speak to me. Around me the paintings are dancing. And a barely audible voice whispers in my ear: "Why don't we get married?!" Happiness came running toward me, her hands full of rubies and emeralds. However, I did not respond. I thought about my mission (what mission I couldn't say) but it was there in my heart. Everywhere. So hard to please! Not tolerating happiness. The silence was prolonged. The paintings became tortured. The strings of a violin shatter sending me the last song as he murmured, "Forget what I was just saying!"

That is all she ever wrote about the poet—except a few lines that appear several years later in a volume of her collected poetry and reverberate like a distant echo:

L'Amour perdu	Love Lost
Au loin	Far away
à l'horizon	on the horizon
une ombre s'évanouit	a shadow vanished
et disparait	and disappeared
sans bruit	without a sound

Doria decided to leave the International House, hoping that the change in atmosphere would help her weather this crisis. She moved into a small pension on Rue Richelet Drouot in order to be nearer to the Bibliothèque Nationale, where she threw herself into working on her two theses to forget her emotional pain. Elsa came often, and "her gay spirit prevented me from thinking too much about recent events." Over the next several months, Doria divided her time between the Bibliothèque Nationale, the Louvre, and Elsa's home. But her life was lonely. She tried to concentrate on intellectual pursuits, but they did not completely satisfy her, and she yearned for some equation in her life that would "bridge the gap between pure intellect and pure emotion. I avoided thinking about love and marriage as I associated these words only with pain and had therefore focused all my attention on the doctorate. I was severe on myself, imposing a complete isolation around my heart, removing myself from any possibility of another relationship. From such a harsh discipline I felt a profound loneliness. Despite my hard work I was unable to fill the vacuum in my heart."

It was during this moment of deep loneliness that Doria learned from Egyptian friends of Elsa that the son of Tante Aziza, Nour al-Din Ragai, had arrived from Cairo. He had passed his exams so brilliantly that Cairo University had granted him a scholarship to pursue his doctorate in commercial law at the University of Paris. His arrival could not have been more fortuitous for

Doria, who by now had convinced herself that loneliness was to be her lot in life. As one of the children that frequently accompanied Tante Aziza during her visits to Mansura, Nour had known Doria since childhood. She remembered the time when "Nour as a young lad sold his jacket and fez to the man at the kiosk in order to buy candy when he didn't have the money." Nour's father was the eminent lawyer who had helped Doria during the al-Sawi affair, and she recalled with gratitude the "great kindness and sympathy that my cousin had shown me during this tragic situation." However it wasn't until several weeks after his arrival that Doria and Nour met quite by accident when she and Elsa had gone to the branch office of the Egyptian Bank of Paris: "He welcomed us enthusiastically and I introduced him to my friend, who whispered to me: 'I'm absolutely mad about him!' It was true, he was extremely good looking and full of charm and had tremendous success with women both in Cairo and now in Paris. Apparently for the first several months he was in Paris he was having such a good time that he neglected to inform the director of his arrival or register at the university."

The arrival of her cousin was like a breath of fresh air for Doria. As soon as they met, he invited the two young women to a café in the Latin Quarter. Noticing that Doria ordered black coffee rather than alcohol, he followed suit. Doria was impressed by his wish to keep her company and commented that she was so afraid of potential rumors and social pressures coming from the Egyptian community in Paris that "I remained scrupulously correct from a Muslim point of view." How revealing of her suspicions toward her countrymen, whose penchant for gossip about a woman's reputation had the power to control her own behavior: "I felt oppressed by these attitudes." The presence of her cousin in Paris was a source of great emotional comfort to her, and she "had a feeling of quietude being with him. I trusted him. It was comforting to have someone fend for me. I had the feeling of not being alone anymore."

But the idea of marriage was far from her thoughts until one day they bumped into the director of Egyptian students, who invited them to his office for a cup of coffee. At one moment, when Nour was out of the room, the director turned to Doria and asked, "Is he only your cousin or your future husband?" "The question surprised me," Doria was later to write, "but then the director was always asking insensitive questions and I recalled my resolution not to get married before finishing my doctorate. In any case I would never marry a Don Juan, and a born gambler. There would be too many problems. And anyway he is not a man with domestic ideas and that settled the question for me for the time being."

Nour made Doria come out of her self-imposed seclusion as he introduced her to a life-style that contrasted sharply with the cloistered life of the graduate research student at the Sorbonne. He was definitely a bon vivant who enjoyed the good life. He once invited Doria to his favorite Parisian nightclub, Le Grand Feu, which according to her was "like entering another world":

Beautiful women, elegantly dressed and covered with jewels. The people were truly enjoying themselves. Bursts of laughter, soft music, indirect lighting—the whole place was plunged into a languid atmosphere. Nour was absolutely at ease and obviously well known among the patrons. We danced and upon returning to our table we found a very pretty French woman whom Nour asked to join us. When I was introduced as Nour's cousin, she stared at me in disbelief. At first I thought she was a fellow law student. I was impressed by her audacity in moving back and forth among the tables chatting easily to everyone and I thought: I could never do that! Her presence electrified the atmosphere. When the lights dimmed, a spotlight focused on the stage and there was Nour's friend, a well known singer as it turned out. As she sang "Take Me in Your Arms," she threw challenging glances at Nour. I felt that if we didn't leave before the end of the song, it would be the end between us. I suggested that we leave and Nour immediately called for the bill and we left. As we reached my pension, he asked, "Shall we meet tomorrow?" "If you like!"

The following morning Doria received a threatening phone call from the singer asking her to leave Nour alone. This audacity and jealousy amazed Doria, who, defiantly accepting the challenge, realized yet again that "whenever something good comes into my life it is always accompanied by struggle."

Nour and Doria became constant companions, and she found herself more and more surrounded by his Egyptian friends, with whom she did not feel completely at ease. Recalling those painful experiences with her compatriots both in Egypt and the Bois de Boulogne, Doria feared rumors. But through her relationship with Nour, she began to realize "the possibility of a new reconciliation between Egypt and myself. Nour was taking me out of my pure intellectuality. His great dynamism was helping me to integrate intellect with feeling, with life. I was feeling a new wholeness, a synthesis. I wasn't alone anymore." Nour represented for Doria something that her French poet could never offer, the possibility of harmonizing the intellectual and emotional sides to her character. Nour was a bridge between herself and Egypt.

One senses a certain vulnerability and insecurity within Doria, who was not a person who could easily reveal her deeper emotional feelings. Her constant association of marriage with reconciliation to Egypt also suggests that she had not completely turned her back on her own cultural heritage with its traditional expectations. However, her feelings for Nour went deeper than a mere "accommodation" to Egypt, for she was clearly aware of her ever increasing attachment to him. One day, taking Doria quite by surprise, Nour asked her to marry him. "Marriage is a serious step, one must give it serious thought," said Doria a little primly. "I have thought about it," Nour replied. "I have to sort things out," she demurred.

Doria's ambivalent feelings toward marriage created a dilemma for her. Although she felt a deep attraction to her cousin, she was acutely aware of their very different personalities and life-styles. His happy-go-lucky outlook contrasted sharply with her sense of life as a continual struggle: "But I discovered that we had one point in common that drew us together: our crazy love for Freedom, although our interpretation of that concept differed greatly. For me Freedom always meant a severe discipline to prepare myself for the ultimate goal of being set free. For Nour it meant essentially to experience life to its fullest."

In her memoirs, she penned these paradoxical feelings:

I always had the greatest sympathy for my cousin but events were rushing at me with such speed that I felt the sensation of advancing without rest into a perpetual storm. My perplexity was at its peak. Why hesitate over agreeing to marry this young man after whom all the beautiful girls were running, who not only was handsome but possessed such a brightness of mind that he was always first in his class at the university without ever taking the trouble to study? But on the other hand how to accept without hesitation, when one sees in advance the worries that a marriage with a Don Juan could engender? Was I going to rush into this grand adventure when I still had not fully recovered from recent events? From another angle, how would it be possible to synchronize our two lives, when I was in full conflict with my destiny while he had not yet had his first combat (because, until then, chance had provided him with everything he wanted)? Then I remembered the little boy in Mansura who, forbidden to buy candy, sold his coat and fez to get the money, not so much for the candy but because it had been forbidden to him. And I asked myself what he would do with me one day when I would no longer be a thing forbidden to him. To accept such a marriage would be to accept to have to conquer my husband every day, it would be to act in such a way that he would have to conquer me every day also. It would be to venture into a war without end and with an uncertain result.

Or perhaps it was the only possible solution for me, to take my destiny in my hands by marrying not only an Egyptian of this power and of this caliber, but also an Egyptian from my own family where all the memories were there pestering me. I myself would go to meet them and finally fight it out. It was this battle, and this battle alone, that would make it possible for me to conquer the past. As soon as I realized this, my hesitations disappeared instantly. This marriage appeared to me as a liberation!

A marriage with Nour represented both a confrontation with and a liberation from all those oppressions of her past that tormented her. She believed marriage was possible because "Nour provided me with that emotional security for which I searched and hoped so ardently. I was now profoundly convinced that I was right in accepting Nour's proposal. Knowing that in Egypt and only in Egypt would my future be played out, such a marriage would help me adapt to the conditions of my country. It was my best chance of reconciliation with Egypt and without dwelling further on the difficulties that our marriage would inevitably involve, I accepted this new adventure."

If this marriage held out the prospect of reconciliation, it also meant the continuation of "those profound directives of my life woven on a thread of struggle." Doria and Nour's first challenge was "to break the habitual constraints under which Egyptian women 'suffered' marriage. To marry outside all social pressure and power of tradition was to build our life together with our own hands. And it was to place me on the margin of all those customs that for so long were such a burden for me." The second challenge was whether to inform their relations before the marriage. To be married in France rather than Egypt was already a most unorthodox step, but to do so without informing their parents was an audacious break with Muslim Egyptian tradition. They decided not to tell them until after the ceremony had been completed. According to Doria, Tante Aziza "was extremely possessive of her son. She had already selected a young, wealthy and beautiful Egyptian girl for Nour to marry. If she hears I'm marrying her son she'll do everything to prevent it. Everything rested in his hands. The girl was his for the asking."

Being seven years older than Nour (she was twenty-nine and he twenty-two in 1937) and from a less wealthy family, Doria felt a certain sense of vulnerability and insecurity, although she was considered by many as a great beauty in her own right. The fact that Nour "chose me above everyone gave me confidence in myself!" But in a very fundamental sense, Doria had also chosen Nour. This was no arranged marriage despite the fact that they were cousins and traditionally could have been expected to marry each other. Doria felt she was breaking tradition by offering an example to others of "how an Egyptian woman can assume responsibility in choosing her own husband and thus seek freedom! To be married in Paris, without one's family, alone, without dowry or jewels or material assets (which is the first condition of marriage in Egypt), was for me the ultimate symbol. It was freedom in my own eyes, freedom from all the outworn social conventions which had so enslaved Egyptian women. But I was also aware that to marry under such conditions would create a scandal in Egypt."

There was the question of Doria's scholarship and the continuation of her studies after her marriage. Being a man, Nour would have no difficulty in retaining his scholarship and, as a married man, would even qualify for additional living expenses. However, Doria's situation was different. There had never been a married Egyptian woman on scholarship before. In fact, there were not even regulations to offer guidance in the face of such contingencies. Nour felt that Doria did not need to keep her scholarship as he had sufficient resources to support them both. But Doria didn't see the problem in the same light:

> I understood that Nour, like all Egyptian men, intended to be "master" in his own home. I had my own ideas about independence and I never liked to depend on anyone, even the one I had chosen to be my life partner. There is this need for absolute freedom which has been the strongest root of my being. We argued for hours and finally agreed upon a daring but possible plan of action: (1) Nour would cable the rector of Cairo University to obtain consent for the marriage mentioning my name so that they would know that he was not marrying a foreigner; (2) I would cable the Ministry of Education simply to ask permission to marry and not mention anything about the scholarship.

When they received joint copies of the telegrams from the rector and the minister approving their plan to marry as well as allowing them both to retain their scholarships, Doria was overjoyed: "I truly believed in miracles!" The final hurdle to be overcome was convincing the Egyptian ambassador that they were serious in their plan to marry. Three separate dates were agreed upon, only to be passed over, forgotten, or broken before the ambassador organized the proper arrangements for the *katb il-kitab* through the Egyptian consulate in October 1937.

In reading Doria's memoirs recounting this important moment in her life, one is struck by the profound difference between her own marriage and that of her mother as she tries to synthesize both her Eastern and her Western values:

> At the moment before placing my signature on the marriage contract a reflex on my part proved that I was not yet as liberated from my superstitions as I had thought. When the consul asked me if I wanted to have the right of divorce stipulated in the contract,[8] I quickly responded No! I feared that any such expression of reservation about our marriage on my part would only carry ill luck. I remained the superstitious Oriental believing in the power of the word. But while I signed the contract without dowry (except for the symbolic twenty-five piasters),[9] without diamonds, without trousseau, I felt I was engaging in an act of faith! a faith

in a future of the liberation of the Egyptian woman from these outmoded customs. And I experienced a magnificent feeling of EQUALITY
with my husband!

Doria's sense of freedom and equality experienced during the signing of
the contract was carried over into her marriage with Nour. Yet from the outset
of their conjugal life together, she realized that

despite my husband's great charm he would not be easy to live with.
From the very first week our domestic life had the flavor of controversy,
which, in some absurd way, created a certain solidarity to our marriage,
keeping it vital and intact. It was certainly not monotonous. This was
partly due to the argumentative temperament of my husband. If I would
say black, he would say white. I resolved the dilemma by saying white
when I wanted black until he caught on and I would revert back to saying what I really wanted. Our daily life became a game. The two of us
interested each other!

The decision for a winter honeymoon in London was also reached through
playing this game. Wanting to go to London, Doria said to Nour: "We could
go to Switzerland or anywhere but London. So he chose London!" Arriving
too early in the morning to be allowed into their pension, they were told by
the porter to come back in two hours. Since everything else in the district was
closed, Nour started to complain bitterly:

"These British are too stiff and inflexible. They adore rules! Imagine
that there are no coffee houses open! It is too cold to walk around and
what are we going to do until the pension opens?" Annoyed at his grum-
bling and contradictory attitude I realized that it would get me nowhere
to be always sweet with him. I remembered an old uncle of mine giving
advice to a bridegroom saying: "If you don't assert your authority during the first day of your marriage, you never will." If that is how an
Egyptian male thinks you should treat a woman, then I decided to adopt
it with my man. When he complained again about walking in the cold I
answered: "Keep quiet! And if you are not happy then go to the devil!"
    He looked at me half surprised, half amused: "I didn't know I had
married a madwoman!" He began to laugh, saying sweetly: "We mustn't
argue, Doria."
    I had won! And I had also set the tone of my behavior towards him—
neither too sweet nor too abrupt.

At the same time that Doria commented on "setting the tone," she was also
wondering "how would I hold our marriage together successfully? I knew that
my husband often lost the sense of the value of things he possessed. And I

realized that in order to keep his interest in me alive, I would have to give him the feeling that he was winning me every day!"

A few days after the honeymooners arrived in London, they were surrounded by the Egyptian colony and, given Nour's gregariousness and charm, inundated with an avalanche of invitations from many of their relatives and friends studying there. For the first time, Doria seemed happy to be amid these gatherings: "I felt a sense of having returned to the very heart of Egypt and I particularly missed the Nile as if it were a living person."

While in London, Doria continued her research by studying documents on ancient Egyptian art at the British Museum, touring the exhibits of art and archaeology in the galleries, and visiting the various monuments throughout the city. She also met several English people and listened to their political talk about the approaching cataclysm that was engulfing Europe. She sensed a political and moral anxiety permeating the country "which left a gap in the ancient and strong traditions of Great Britain. As in Paris, London conveyed the feeling of a city on the brink of a catastrophe with this one difference: In Paris the response to the 'brink' was to *act at politics* through an effervescent dialogue. Whereas in London *political action* seem to proceed with methodical momentum. The British kept cool in serious circumstances to gain time when necessary. But both capitals seemed to be trying to convince themselves that peace was possible."

After a fortnight, Nour and Doria returned to Paris and settled down to the disciplined work necessary for them both to complete their doctorates before the impending storm of war overtook them. On November 20, 1937, Doria wrote to Huda Sha'rawi requesting her assistance in providing material for her thesis on women and religious rights in Islam. The stationery carried their address as 39 Rue Pascal, Paris XII:

Excellence,

Excuse me for abusing the precious time of Your Excellence and keeping your attention for some minutes to read my letter, but I am sure that you will welcome it with your usual kindness which has left an unforgettable memory engraved in my heart.

I am taking the liberty of asking Your Excellence a question concerning my *doctorat-ès-lettres* which I have the intention of presenting to the Sorbonne within several months. One of my two theses treats of: "The evolution of the Egyptian woman in the twentieth century." Given that the focus of my research will be the feminist movement in Egypt, its foundation, its development and the very important events that it set in motion. Your Excellence would be the most important person to inform me on this subject, seeing that this movement finds in you its most noble founder.

I would therefore greatly appreciate it, if it is not too much to ask of Your Excellency, if you could send me some documents concerning the principal stages of the feminist movement in Egypt, also the principal social reforms of which it has been the direct cause.

Shortly thereafter, Nour and Doria moved into a boarding house belonging to a former baroness from Egypt in the elegant Auteuil section of the Bois de Boulogne, where "we were the only commoners in the place." Having learned that Tante Aziza was furious over the marriage of her son, Doria became doubly anxious that Nour pass his exams "as I didn't want a rain of accusations to fall upon my head." For weeks "we locked ourselves up in our rooms taking our meals alone. Nour studied seriously and even let his beard grow so as not to be tempted to go out with his Egyptian friends." After three weeks, Nour sat for his exams and passed brilliantly. But Doria—while very happy that Nour had succeeded—realized that "this boarding house had become far too worldly for serious study" and longed to return to the Latin Quarter. Nour agreed, and they moved again to the Madison Hotel opposite the Church of St. Germain des Près: "I loved the place. There was a feeling in the air of the echoes of things brought back from a vanished time. The presence of students was rejuvenating. We would take our coffee every day at the Café des Deux Magots and I was curious about the many 'failed geniuses' that frequented this café. They were brilliant but seemed to have accomplished nothing in their lives and I wondered why? Perhaps they lacked the will. Brains without will power can't accomplish a thing."

The Egyptian colony filled Nour's everyday life, but to Doria, the constant stream of friends coming and going hindered her work. She still did not feel at ease among them: "There was a certain distance between me and my own people. Was it that I was subconsciously associating them with my own unhappy memories and experiences? It wouldn't do any good to analyze my feelings too deeply. So I tried to dismiss the thought and made an effort to suit my personality to my husband's friends. It was necessary to preserve our ménage." Their lives continued in this way for several months, but life in the hotel was becoming too active for Doria, who felt "that time was flying and we had so little in which to finish our doctorates."

They decided to move once again, but this time to a quieter locale, and found their own private apartment closer to the Sorbonne, near the Rue St. Jacques. They hired a French cook-housekeeper to handle domestic affairs while Doria concentrated on finishing her two theses. However, the visits of Nour's Egyptian friends continued to increase, and Doria finally resigned herself to the fact that "My husband was happy with his friends around him. I understood that I would just have to get used to it and do my studies in spite of the activity around me." From the autumn of 1937 until the spring of 1939, international conditions were deteriorating, and the threat of war was ever more imminent. Nour was finishing up his thesis on commercial law while Doria was still struggling with her two.

She encountered some difficulty with her Egyptology professor, who, when reviewing a preliminary draft of her manuscript, commented: "Nonsense! I don't understand all this talk about stones." She began to explain that it was a philosophic interpretation of the art. "Interrupting me he said: 'What's all this trash about its philosophic value? There is nothing in a stone but a stone with a date and a place—that is all. This is not interesting.' And he threw the manuscript back at me." Doria felt that his reaction was less associated with her particular views and more with the fact that she had stopped attending his classes: "as nothing new was coming out of his course I found that I was no longer benefiting and because I did not have time to lose I simply dropped the course."

In a quandary, she called her ex-professor of philosophy, Emile Brehier, who agreed to meet her at once: "Welcoming me in a warm and fatherly way, 'The Sphinx looks unhappy today,' he said as he saw tears streaming down my cheeks. I told him the story and he informed me that it was strictly against university policy to change professors. He offered a solution: 'Since your thesis overlaps the domains of both archaeology and aesthetics you are entitled to have two professors on your committee.' He suggested my ex-professor of aesthetics, Charles Lalo, and wrote a special letter to the dean of the faculty, thus offering a solution to my problem."

In the spring of 1939, Nour finished and successfully defended his thesis.[10] He returned to Egypt immediately, not only because a teaching post was waiting for him at the Fuad I University in Cairo but also because he wanted to break the ice with his mother and pave the way for Doria's later return: "It was our first separation and we were both very upset. But we knew it was only for a short while." Doria remained with Elsa, her Georgian friend, "as there was absolutely no question of my living alone in our flat while Nour was not in Paris!"

For Doria, the political atmosphere reigning in Paris created the impression that "chaos, malaise and disintegration seemed to dominate the political scene finding an echo of universal negativism in artistic circles." This contradiction between her own arguments in support of "art for art's sake" in the midst of the political and artistic turmoil going on in France at the time was particularly poignant: "There was no synthesis, no transmission of profound moral values inspired by aesthetic feeling." The surrealist movement, with its philosophy of negation of existing notions and standards of what constituted artistic value, was at its zenith. Many of these ideas must have contrasted sharply with Doria's own notions of the aesthetic which she was developing in her thesis. It was during this period of political and artistic convulsion that Doria completed the final drafts of her work and submitted them to her professors, whose evaluations provided her not only with an insight into the nature of the critical spirit within the Sorbonne but also with an independent judgment on the quality and value of her work.

Commenting on her principal thesis, Raymond Weill criticized her lack of specialization in Egyptology but noticed her strengths as well:

> The work is good on the whole, particularly on the level of philosophy. Some further scholarly documentation in archaeology could enhance her philosophical argument. The citations are awkward and references to Egyptian texts insufficient. On the order of history the general lines are correct and in accord with the facts and the mechanism of evolution. One appreciates the abundance of illustrated documents borrowed from collections of recent and incomplete monuments. In total, the thesis could be accepted following the additions, corrections and retouches that we have noted. The endorsement for printing could be given to this work under the condition that these revisions are executed and controlled by the examiners prior to printing.[11]

Her published thesis was later reviewed by the eminent Jean Capart, who criticized her references and her insufficient archaeological background: "I do not wish to be too severe since it is a matter of the work of a beginner who was wrong to attack a problem for which she was not sufficiently prepared."[12] But how like Doria to take on the challenge of a task for which she may not have been "sufficiently prepared"!

Regarding her complementary thesis on the woman and religious rights, Maurice Halbwachs wrote:

> This study is seriously conducted from beginning to end and rests on an analysis of a quantity of very representative texts well chosen and ingeniously related. The principal interest appears to us to be in making us completely aware of a debate at once theological and moral, which is developed in the religious framework following the rules of an accomplished traditional dialectic adapted to the conditions of modern life. Mme. Ragai is a Muslim very respectful of orthodoxy and the Quran, who is still in contact with professors of al-Azhar University; but at the same time she has been closely tied to the women's emancipation movement: from there emerges an engaging contrast between a formalism (a little disconcerting for the western mind) and a very lively feeling of contemporary moral and social aspirations. One will regret without doubt that

this work rests on a somewhat narrow sociological and historical base, being at times too bookish, that it lacks concrete notation and description—those that have been extracted are only from contemporary Egyptian, primarily literary, works. At least there was an attempt, particularly in the last annex, to pull out some results from the rare available statistics. There is an effort to defend an original thesis on the relation between religion and social conditions in today's Egypt. By its contents and its composition it is a very appreciable work and I propose to accord to Mme. Ragai the authorization to print it.[13]

There can be no doubt that the years spent in France during the late thirties were crucial in shaping Doria's aesthetic-philosophical as well as her feminist-political outlook. Her two theses express this fact very clearly. The first argues for the existence of the aesthetic attitude underlying the everyday world of the ancient Egyptians, reinforcing her own value commitment to the principle of synergy between art and life. Her second thesis, described by one of her readers "as one of the most forceful arguments for women's rights I have ever heard," became the blueprint for her feminist struggle in the years ahead as she tried to create a bridge between humanism and Islam in her demand for equal rights.

Her Sorbonne education did much to enhance her own quest for philosophical freedom which was grounded in the ideas of Islamic reformers like Muhammad Abdu, Qasim Amin, and the Egyptian secularists. The emphasis on the individual over the collective and the primacy of the will of the individual in human action by the French liberal humanist tradition seemed consistent with her own moral value system. However, in another very real sense, these years at the Sorbonne led to Doria's cultural and political estrangement from events unfolding in her own country during the thirties.

The Mustapha al-Nahas government had fallen through the manipulation of Ali Mahir, who replaced Ismail Sidki as the "strong man" of Egyptian politics during these critical prewar years. As prime minister, Ali Mahir formed a nationalist, anti-British government, and his openly fascist sympathies created several crises in relation to Britain, who soon took a firmer hand. The country was placed under martial law, censorship instituted, and diplomatic relations with Germany and Italy broken, although many Egyptians supported the Axis powers simply because they were in conflict with England.

As Doria was becoming more deeply immersed in the study of French culture, history, and politics, the oppressed and disenchanted forces in Egypt were reacting negatively to the "failed liberal experiment," and the Egyptian masses were becoming more and more disaffected with the inability of the Wafd, the palace, and the minority parties to address the basic issues: national liberation, social and economic reform, and wider political representation. Even the leadership of the Egyptian Feminist Union was shifting its focus away from an exclusive concern with women's rights to the broader question of independence and the establishment of a real democratic regime.

In July 1939, while Doria was finalizing her theses for publication and preparing to leave Paris, Ceza Nabaraoui, seated next to a delegate from the Society of Jewish Women of Palestine, was delivering a speech in Copenhagen to the delegates of the Twelfth Congress of the International Alliance of Women on the important role of youth in Egyptian society: "In a country like ours where the number of illiterates is still very large, youth represents an intellectual elite whose enlightened opinion is respected by the masses, giving expression to their unknown hopes. Conscious of the immense hopes placed in them, our youth are trained from now on to the noble mission which has fallen to them by their capacities and their learning, to free their country from all foreign tutelage, economic as well as political."[14]

In August 1939, on the eve of Doria's return to Egypt, the non-aggression pact between Germany and Russia was signed, preparing the way for their invasion of Poland in September. Britain finally and formally declared war on September 9, and World War II erupted, while *la drôle de guerre* unfolded in France: "When I left Paris I was very anxious, not knowing if I would ever be able to return. If war should break out I would have to wait years for my oral defense for the Doctorat d'état and my dreams would be shattered."

A Stranger in Her Own Land (1939–1942)

Women from all walks of life found in me something to reproach. Society women reproached me because of my advanced education. They accused me of being a snob. When I got my doctorate they never forgave me. They found fault with my clothes whose simplicity contrasted to their more ornate styles. The intellectuals reproached me for spending money on clothes and attending receptions, which they felt was not dignified for my advanced education; the middle-class reproached me for associating with the aristocracy; the upper bourgeoisie reproached me for defying their class and wanting to have a career and work for a salary; the religious fanatics reproached me for breaking old harem traditions. "She sets a bad example for our girls. She will demolish our homes. Why does she want to work anyway since she has a husband to house and keep her?"

As the SS *Esperia* eased into the harbor on that sultry August afternoon in 1939, Doria Shafik was not the least preoccupied with the profound political changes that were taking place in Egypt and the consequences these would have for her own life. Any anxiety about the impending war in Europe was overshadowed by her happiness at seeing the beauty of the Alexandrian skyline swathed in a harmony of pastels created by the last rays of the setting sun, at hearing the melodious voices of the traders hawking their wares on the docks and smelling the delicate odors of the spice markets permeating the air. She was returning home feeling a certain sense of satisfaction at having managed to resolve the apparently irreconcilable contradiction between her personal quest, "in search of the Absolute," and family pressures to conform to the traditional cultural expectations of her society. Not only had she attained the highest academic degree at one of the most prestigious universities in the Western world, but she had also chosen her own husband, a man who loved her and wanted her for herself. That she had married an Egyptian, a Muslim, and her cousin—rather than a Frenchman, a Christian, and a stranger—suggests that despite her many years in France, she had not completely broken with her society's cultural values and traditions. On the contrary, marrying a man with Nour's obvious charm and irrepressible sociability had enabled her to narrow the gap she felt existed between herself and her society. She may have bent the rules by not seeking parental approval, refusing the *mahr*, and marrying in a foreign country; but her choice of life partner was culturally consistent with Egyptian middle-class values. Overjoyed to be reunited with her husband and family, Doria allowed herself to believe that "for the first time in my life happiness is a lasting possibility."

Each of her brothers and sisters was either married or engaged and settled in his or her own home. Gamal had married Zohra, the cousin who was orphaned at birth, and was living in Mahalla with their new baby. Her younger sister Layla was engaged, and Ahmad Chafik—resigned to a quiet and retired life after his wife's death, "never dreaming of changing"—continued to live with Soraya, his eldest daughter, her husband, and their small son in Alexandria. Her youngest brother, Muhammad, had finished his studies in Germany and obtained a post as a police officer. Ali, her middle brother, had just returned from England with his engineering diploma and a young English bride: "No one found fault with his having taken a foreign wife; after all he was a man, not a woman, and could do as he pleased!"

Following a few weeks' visit in Alexandria with her family, Nour and Doria came to Cairo, where his family gave them a large traditional Egyptian wedding. They spent their first month living with Nour's mother and father. Although Nour had rented an unfurnished apartment on the Corniche overlooking Doria's beloved Nile, they were unable to move in immediately because it was being redecorated. Nour found it quite natural to accept his mother's invitation to live with her until the flat was completed. This situation was not exactly appealing to Doria but to insist on living on their own in a hotel would have been considered culturally shameful and personally insensitive: "My father, having provided for my trousseau and knowing that the welcome of my in-laws would not be very favorable, cautioned me with his characteristic gentleness, not to be too long in establishing my own home." Sensing how very happy Nour was to have her back, "as a profound friendship characterized our relationship since the very beginning of our marriage," she wanted to avoid starting off life in Egypt by a misunderstanding with her husband and agreed: "For my part I was apprehensive about living under the same roof with my mother-in-law, even though she was my mother's cousin and best friend, and had grown up in the same household in Tanta. She received me rather coolly, since she had never forgiven me for having married her son without her consent or permission, outside all our customs!"

Doria felt a "certàin discomfort that stifled" her and wondered whether there wasn't some other reason than having married Nour without her permission that created Tante Aziza's grim mood:

> I knew that, in spite of the grand luxury in which she lived with her husband, she was never truly *en rapport* with him. But she could not face the idea of a separation. Women of her generation still clung to the tradition of accepting their destiny without believing in the possibility of changing it. But she drew great satisfaction in consecrating herself totally to raising her six children and placed all her hopes in them. As Nour was her favorite and the first son to marry, it was automatic that the one who took him away from her would be the object of her dislike. Added to this was the fact that her only daughter had been so unhappy with the husband chosen for her that her father felt it better she divorce and return to her paternal home than suffer such unhappiness. Thus Tante Aziza comparing the poor luck of her daughter with my good fortune was doubly annoyed.

Doria wanted to leave her in-laws as soon as possible because she was sensitive to this "atmosphere of intrigue and machination reminiscent of those old harems of Egypt, and it evoked painful memories of the past." She recalled one incident concerning a bottle of French perfume that she had given to her mother-in-law when she first arrived. Several weeks later, the bottle was returned to her by a servant, who told Doria that her mistress didn't wish to keep it. Doria noticed that its contents had obviously been doctored: "My sister warned me that this was surely an act of sorcery presumably to make my husband come to hate me."

Finally their flat was ready, and the couple cheerfully moved into their first real home together, a magnificent apartment with a large terrace overlooking Doria's beloved Nile: "Although it wasn't the main branch of the river, it was still my marvelous Nile. I felt the river's presence as one feels the true presence of a living person. Looking out on the Nile from my terrace I felt a strange quietude. I was discovering again, through the Nile's flowing currents, my mother's smile, her irreplaceable presence. I felt at home again as in Mansura."

In the months that followed, Nour was busily and happily involved with his teaching at the faculty of law at King Fuad I University. Over the years, he earned himself the reputation of a brilliant professor of commercial law. However, as a well-known sympathizer of the Wafd party, Nour was perceived by some of the more radical university students of that period as "somewhat reactionary."[1] Meanwhile Doria, waiting for news from Paris about the date of her formal dissertation defense, bided her time in a pattern of life that filled her with a sense of aimlessness: "My life was nothing but a routine of getting up, eating, going and coming as I liked. The rhythm of my week was punctuated by the large Friday lunches with the in-laws, a family tradition to which I submitted out of necessity. In a word, I was without any real social activity which would allow me to take a position in the midst of the development and future of my country, a future with which I felt irrevocably connected. Without work in which I could find refuge, I felt lost."

Not a person to be satisfied with sitting idly at home, Doria became increasingly anxious to participate in the public sphere. Hence when the Ministry of Education contacted her and offered her a position as inspector of French language for all the secondary schools in Egypt, Doria willingly accepted. The Egyptian government expected the students they had supported to work for them after completing their studies. To be an inspector of French language required that Doria travel periodically throughout the country to visit those secondary schools where French was taught and assess whether the quality of language comprehension and expression were meeting the standards of the French educational system. It was an occupation that further strengthened the public perception that Shafik was more French than Egyptian.

Doria harbored secret ambitions to teach philosophy at the national university, but since she had not yet officially received her degree, she felt she could not present herself. The offer from the ministry was an interim solution: "I thought I had nothing to lose in accepting. Not to mention the financial independence it would give me. I had run up debts through a taste for beautiful things, a trait I inherited from my mother. I furnished our apartment on the Nile, and outfitted myself in *le dernier cri* from Paris. Needless to say these extravagances placed a great strain on Nour's pocketbook. So I accepted. It was something to occupy me until I had my doctorate in hand and could teach at the university."

Although she had been away from Egypt during most of the 1930s, she was aware of what was happening within the country and what the consequences would be if war were to break out between Germany and the Allies in Europe. She had hardly begun to work when the news broke of Germany's invasion of Poland, signaling the outbreak of World War II. "I was thunderstruck: first by the violence that was spreading throughout the world and especially in Egypt; second at the realization that politicians were nothing more than liars creating the disintegration of human values; and thirdly, by the fact that France in a state of war would mean the postponement *sine die* of my thesis defense. My dreams were vanishing."

For the next several months, Doria continued to work for the ministry until she received a letter from the Sorbonne advising her that the date for the defense of her theses had been set for March 9, 1940:

> I decided to leave at once! I went to the under-secretary at the Ministry of Education to request a leave to go to Paris. He said: "Return to your work and when a decision is reached we will inform you." I told him I didn't have a minute to lose. He insisted that I go back to work, warning: "If in 24 hours you are not back at work you will be dismissed!" "You can consider me dismissed as of now for I will not return to work!" I left slamming the door. Before returning home I went to the travel agent and booked my passage to Paris! Later that day the under-secretary met Nour and asked him: "Could you tell me how you manage Doria?" Nour laughed and responded: "And who told you that I dominate Doria?"

Doria was back in Paris at the end of February 1940, during a period when the internal political situation in both Egypt and France was passing through what she described as the "decomposition of moral values." Doria stayed with Elsa, whose house was now flooded by refugees, mostly Georgians fleeing the Stalinist regime of the Soviet Union, and European Jews fleeing the fascist regime of Germany. She remarked how many of Elsa's Georgian friends had married "rich American women"—a fact which seemed to symbolize for Doria the depths of the psychological emptiness that was tormenting Paris during this phony war which was adding its tumult to the disorder already reigning: "The Paris I saw in the spring of 1940, was a Paris on its way to losing its soul! There were continuous blackouts although there were never any attacks. But this vacuum of a war's living reality was worse than an assault. A psychological emptiness—new habits, lavish spending on extravagances. A tormented Paris."

The magic day, toward which Doria had directed all her efforts over these past several years, had finally arrived. On a Saturday afternoon at three o'clock, she entered the grand hall of the Sorbonne to defend her theses for the Doctorat d'état in philosophy. What was she feeling, and what did this moment mean to her?

> I was terribly anxious. I didn't sleep well the night before, worrying that Professor Weill would take his revenge. I decided to read some surahs from the Quran. I selected Surah Yassin because as a child I had learned that if one read this surah forty times one would achieve that which one most wanted. After reading it through several times I felt comforted and took a sleeping draught and slept until morning. I invited Elsa to have

lunch with me at the Dupont Latin, knowing that her gay spirits would put me in a good mood. She suggested that I have a glass of wine, "It will help you marshal your arguments." I said it might have the reverse effect. "Ridiculous!" and she ordered champagne. As I was sipping a glass, who did I notice not far from our table but Professor Lalo dressed in his frock-coat adorned with the Legion of Honor. He cast an anxious glance in the direction of the bottle and sent me a note admonishing, "Don't forget you have your defense in one hour!" The amphitheater of the Sorbonne was crowded with my many friends; the Georgian colony, some Egyptians, including the director of the Egyptian mission; several French acquaintances including the publisher of my theses and that special public who regularly attend every defense at the Sorbonne. I was alone on the chair with the audience behind me and the five man jury on a huge platform in front of me. I felt as though I was the accused in a court of law and I alone had to defend myself. There was Emile Brehier, France's greatest authority on the history of philosophy, as the president of the Jury, flanked by Charles Lalo with Raymond Weill on his right and Maurice Halbwachs and Emile Bayet on his left. My eyes met those of Weill for a moment and I felt uneasy sensing his forthcoming attack. Promptly at three o'clock Brehier opened the defense with words of encouragement. Lalo began with questions that I could answer promptly and explicitly so much so that my Georgian friend decided to prescribe champagne before every defense! Then came the turn of the Egyptologist. My heart was pounding and he began "Madame I want to tell you that your book is very interesting. . . . My only reproach is that you did not discuss with me everything before writing it." I was astonished. It was like a miracle. Things were going in my favor. There was a fifteen-minute break between the two theses and following my defense of women and religious rights, Bayet commented, "Madame, your thesis is the best defense of women's rights existing or ever likely to exist. You have proved things about Islam about which there can be no doubt. You have succeeded in correcting our erroneous ideas about Islam. You can consider yourself as the lawyer of Muslim women in general and the Egyptian woman in particular." This phrase impressed me deeply. After several hours, the jury finally adjourned to discuss the results. I was tired but I felt calm. The jury returned and the president announced: "Madame Doria Shafik has been graduated Doctorat ès-Lettres in Philosophy from the Sorbonne with *Mention Trés Honorable*."

At the Sorbonne during this time, "A thesis of state within the Parisian intellectual milieu is always a small event; but a thesis of state undertaken by a woman is a rare enough event that it produces a certain sensation. If the woman is a foreigner and young it creates a sentiment of curiosity: one wants to see how she will pull herself out of it. Because one knows that the test will be difficult and one has even seen men lose bearing and courage."[2]

An Egyptian friend of Nour's who was in the audience during Doria's defense recalls

a very beautiful girl, very sure of herself, who defended her theses very well. It was extraordinary. She made a big impression on the public and on myself as well. Her French was excellent and she was very distinguished. I also remember how ceremonial the occasion was, very different from those of us getting our doctorates from the faculty of law where one just sat alone with one's professor and talked about one's thesis and that was it. At the Sorbonne there was this big amphitheater with five professors asking questions. It was extraordinary to listen to this girl defending herself.[3]

The chairman of the jury, evaluating Doria's defense, commented on "how much the jury appreciated the ease of her explanatory statements, the intelligence and correctness of her responses in the argumentation."[4] Back in Egypt, *L'Egyptienne* published Doria's picture, acknowledging her Doctorat ès-lettres *avec mention trés honorable*: "Our most cordial congratulations to the young doctor of letters, hope of the Egyptian university and the Egyptian feminist movement."[5]

Doria considered her successful defense and the final securing of this coveted degree to be one of her most important conquests. Some of her critics, however, disdainfully rejected the notion that Doria Shafik had ever obtained her doctorate. "And even if she had," one argued, "the award was due more to her feminine charm than to any scholarly merit."[6] Despite the public affirmation in *L'Egyptienne*, her critics tended to see her beauty as denoting an intellectual superficiality, an image against which she continually had to struggle. This contradiction between what Doria believed herself to be and her public image contributed to an increasing sense of estrangement from her own society.

Expecting to be met with cheers and accolades as she stepped off the boat in Alexandria, Doria instead encountered a complete lack of interest among her family, "except my father who was deeply touched that I had dedicated my primary thesis to him and to the memory of my mother. I saw the sad look in his eyes reflecting his isolation now that all his children had grown up and left." Deciding that the solution to his melancholy would be to take another wife, Doria set about finding him a bride, which she did. Also realizing that her younger sister, Layla, "was in need of a groom, having suffered two broken engagements," Doria managed to find a suitable husband for her. Despite this rather assertive and forceful manner in "taking charge" of her father's and sister's lives, Doria demonstrated her commitment to the social value of marriage. Remembering her own marriage during this early period, Doria described her "deepening love for Nour, whose tenderness and kindness has been a great help in narrowing the chasm between me and Egypt." This chasm or abyss, which she frequently refers to when writing about her relationship to Egyptian society, was also connected to the social and political disorder developing in Egypt following her return in the spring of 1940. She believed, somewhat naively perhaps, that the doctorate she had set out to attain some twelve years earlier would overcome this dilemma. But to the contrary, "My diplomas, which I carried triumphantly believing them a magic key opening all doors, proved themselves to be a great handicap in the end, because of the jealousies that soon appeared. Instead of seeing the streets strewn with flowers and hearing the expected applause, I felt icy hostility and indeed hate, unleashed against me."

Doria's mood was echoed in the growing malaise she felt Egypt was passing through as the country drifted toward war: "We were caving in under this gigantic tide that was invading my country, producing the greatest confusion between certain intrusive ideas and the most profound Egyptian values on every level—national, social, religious, moral. From then on confusion increased progressively until in the end it dominated the great majority of minds and hearts."

The war years in Egypt stimulated a *prise de conscience* not only among the growing masses of Egyptian people who were becoming more organized and demanding of their rights to national independence and social justice, but also within Doria, who sought desperately to find a meaningful place within her country's destiny and thus to narrow the gap between herself and her society: "I encountered an atmosphere of insecurity that did not result in the immediate realization of my dreams. My eagerness to fulfill my destiny in the blink of an eye (a personal flaw I found hard to shed) collided with a hostile milieu and added to an already critical period. These two confusions in my heart became one; an instinctive integration that always made my pulse throb in sympathy with my country."

When Doria returned to Egypt, she automatically assumed that she would fulfill her long-held ambition and secure a position on the faculty of literature at the national university: "If the doctorate in philosophy that I had obtained from the Sorbonne was the required diploma for those destined to teach this subject at the University of Paris, all the more reason for me to be professor of philosophy at the national university. It was logical." But Dr. Ahmad Amin

(1886–1954),[7] then dean of the Faculty of Letters, refused to give her a post, allegedly because he would not take responsibility for appointing a beautiful female teacher to the faculty. According to Doria:

> I still had all my illusions believing that it was sufficient to speak logi-cally in order to be understood. I made an appointment with the dean of the faculty of letters, a graduate of al-Azhar University, conservative by principle, anti-feminist by temperament—the woman's place was by the hearth and no other. I was simply but elegantly dressed in the latest Paris fashion. Just before entering his office I wanted to put on a bit more perfume, when the whole bottle spilled over my dress, creating a dizzying aura to my arrival. I approached, unconscious of the tempest that my meeting would unleash. Our eyes met like the clash of two armies. His reaction to me was one of astonishment, defiance, contempt, even hatred. Why for goodness sake? To begin with, no gesture on his part to invite me to sit down. I waited standing, already ill at ease. I opened the conversation but could not sustain it very long. Without his having to say a word I grasped his categorical refusal and left with a heavy heart.

It was not that Doria Shafik was a woman that prompted Amin to refuse her application. He was convinced that someone with her temperament, her au-dacity, her French modernity would place the image of the newly founded Egyptian university at risk. For the same reason he summarily dismissed the fantastic and erudite Dr. Zaki Mahmud Mubarak. Known as *al-dakatira* (the doctors) in the plural because he had acquired so many degrees, Zaki Mubarak had studied at the Sorbonne. He was something of a Bohemian, but sincere and talented, and according to Jacques Berque, "one of the most genuine intel-lectuals of his country and age.[8] Conservative in his habits, the retiring and deeply sensitive Ahmad Amin spent the greater part of his life clad in the traditional *amma* (turban) and caftan worn by Azharite shaykhs. Yet his pro-lific intellectual writings centered in the social and cultural implications of modernization. Although Amin was an advocate of social and literary reform, his traditional background was such that to have hired Doria would have been anathema to his beliefs concerning the spiritual and cultural values of the East. For him, Doria was "too modern," and the drama of her entrance into his office convinced him that she embodied those Western traits that were most inimical to the East. It is no wonder that there was absolutely no basis of com-munication between them. Each represented an entirely different outlook on the world.

Several decades later in a volume dedicated to outstanding Egyptian women, Abd al-Halim commented:

> It is strange that Dr. Ahmad Amin who was one of the first to write about the mission of Islam in his famous series of books, *The Dawn of Islam, The Morning of Islam* and *The Afternoon of Islam* refused a post to Dr. Doria Shafik, who obtained the doctorate for a dissertation whose subject was *Women in Islam*. But the man knew that Doria Shafik, precisely she, had been preceded by a reputation in the field of defending the rights of women and he was afraid that her presence at the university would stir up a violent storm which would be hard to quell, especially since Doria Shafik was indeed strikingly beautiful and distinguished by her youthful vigor. Therefore he closed this door to her, a door through which many beautiful women and many very active women and even very revolutionary women and very notorious or famous women would later pass.[9]

Doria tried one more time to realize her ambition and, knowing that the university was under the aegis of the Ministry of Education, she thought the minister himself might be persuaded to intervene with the dean and plead her case. However, when she broached the subject with him, he smiled and explained that the dean had called him shortly after his meeting with her and categorically threatened "that the day Doria Shafik puts her foot into this university is the day that I put my feet out!"[10]

Soon after this incident she tried to join the Egyptian Feminist Union, believing that by getting involved in their activities she would find an outlet for her own malaise: "I returned to Egypt with a weapon in my hand not only to defend myself and my own rights, but also to defend the rights of the women in my country. Is it not in liberating women that I can liberate myself?"

Given Doria's profound respect and gratitude for the woman who had been so kind to her and helped her attain the dream of her life, it was only natural that she should think of joining Huda Sha'rawi's organization. She made an appointment to visit her benefactress wishing also to present her with a copy of *La Femme et Le Droit Religieux de L'Egypte Contemporaine*, which Doria had dedicated "To Her Excellency, Madame Sha'rawi Pasha, President of the Feminist Movement in Egypt." Believing that contact had not been broken despite the years in Paris, "I felt the time had come to be a member, that a collaboration between us seemed in the nature of things since we shared the same ideas, the same flame." However, her zeal in meeting Huda Sha'rawi once again soon turned to disappointment:

She seemed genuinely pleased to meet me. I found her still radiant. I was moved to find myself again in her salon. It reminded me of my first encounter with her and she welcomed me with open arms. I attended a few meetings but those around her created a barrier until finally there was no contact whatsoever between me and this woman whom I so admired. I soon felt the intrigues (so current as a mode of action in the orient, particularly within the feminine milieu) around Huda Sha'rawi's entourage, that were aimed at distancing me from her. Now that I look back at things from the vantage of hindsight I realized that it was Mme. Sha'rawi's secretary who was at the center of these intrigues. For it was she who, when I later established my own feminist union after Huda Sha'rawi died, initiated premeditated attacks against me. I never became a member of Huda Sha'rawi's Feminist Union.

This negative response to her quest to find a public role for herself only added to Doria's increasing sense of alienation. Her hopes were thwarted by the very same person who, only a few months earlier, had described her in the pages of *L'Egyptienne* as the "hope of the Egyptian university and the Egyptian feminist movement" but who now seemed to harbor a deep-seated hostility. The secretary in question was Ceza Nabaraoui, the *fille spirituelle* and close confidant of Huda Sha'rawi, who would later become one of Doria's sharpest public critics. When one considers how ardently Doria had been praised and encouraged by Huda Sha'rawi and the Egyptian Feminist Union—especially Ceza, who had lionized her during the thirties by publishing her essays, photographs and academic achievements in issues of *L'Egyptienne*—one is puzzled by this estrangement.

Undoubtedly Ahmad al-Sawi played an important role in turning Huda Sha'rawi against Doria. Following the failure of their very public marriage, he needed to "save face" by portraying Doria in a less-than-favorable light. Being a central figure among the entourage that surrounded Huda Sha'rawi, al-Sawi had every opportunity to construct his own stories. Why Huda Sha'rawi would listen to only one side of the affair is an interesting question. "One frailty of Huda Hanum," commented her daughter-in-law, "was listening to those who were close to her ear and once she had formed an unfavorable judgment about someone, it was not easy for her to change her mind. I used to ask her, 'Why don't you see Doria and hear her side of the story?' But she could be very stubborn."[11] The popular Egyptian journalist Mustapha Amin also remarked that when he asked Doria why she didn't respond to the critical articles that al-Sawi was publishing in his daily *Magalati*, she shrewdly answered, "If I respond it will appear but once, but he can publish his articles every day of the month. It is better not to comment."[12]

Whatever might have been al-Sawi's particular version of the circumstances surrounding the divorce, it was more than likely that Doria's provincial middle-class background—coupled with her advanced university degrees and her own proud, assertive, and audacious personality—had made her unwelcome in the eyes of some of the more conservative women of this class conscious Turco-Circassian society to whom status, wealth, and power were so important. For Doria, it must have been quite painful to be rebuffed by the very woman who had been her benefactress and lifelong heroine. Yet Doria's memoirs neither dwell on this disappointment nor analyze in any great depth what she felt might have been the circumstances behind this hostile and negative attitude, except to allude to the "ruse of the weak and the jealousies among the entourage of Huda Sha'rawi. I only knew that it was impossible for me to become a member of the Egyptian Feminist Union. Thanks to the clever maneuvers of her entourage, I was positively estranged from Huda Sha'rawi."

Her failure to obtain the coveted teaching position at the university, followed by the disappointment at not being accepted into Huda Sha'rawi's Egyptian Feminist Union, increased Doria's sense of rejection. Had it not been for Nour's vivid presence in her life at this time, one wonders whether Doria would have persisted in her quest: "My husband had a sense of humor, happily! And he was broadminded. He was my support. I needed one in this immense solitude where, without giving the appearance of doing so, I lived in my own country. I advanced as if on quicksand, lost and distracted. I did not feel at all at home. Even the very essence of my French culture and education seemed to fall into disuse. What could be the cause of this discord between me and the milieu in which I was destined to live?" This question haunted her throughout her life and she continually pondered over it.

It was not in Doria's character to sit around licking her wounds nor to engage in public recriminations against those who rejected her or became her most severe public critics. Rather she reacted to these setbacks by seeking other avenues by which to achieve her ambition. She returned to her work with the Ministry of Education, aware that in the eyes of many she would be viewed as having fallen from grace: a woman from a more or less affluent milieu exposed herself to a great deal of criticism and even contempt if she worked. Within some classes in Egyptian society, if a woman worked for a salary, it signified that her husband was not financially capable of providing for his wife's material support. Women from the elite classes may have worked for social service or benevolent organizations, but that was perceived as voluntary noblesse oblige. Only women from the middle or lower classes would work for a salary, and for a woman from an upper bourgeois family to do so was to descend from the status of society lady to that of a woman who needed to work. Doria, who was simultaneously both a society lady and a working woman, challenged the taken-for-granted notions of her milieu. She felt that any woman who wanted to work in whatever field should be encouraged to do so and dismissed society's criticism as "the remnant of a cultural attitude that was pure silliness."

Throughout the early years of the war, Doria continued to travel up and down the country, from Alexandria to Aswan, coming in contact with a younger generation of middle-class Egyptian women who were entering schools in ever-increasing numbers. Wherever she went, she created interest and excitement. Layla Takla, now one of Egypt's most prominent parliamentarians, recalls Doria Shafik visiting her school: "I was sixteen and to me she was stunningly beautiful. She wore a fashionable red suit and we all crowded around her. As she talked with us, she would briefly turn her head to the photographer and then return her attention to us. I thought at the time that here was a woman who was intelligent, feminine, and a public figure at the same time. She was someone we admired."[13] These young women made her more aware of the political conditions and ideological currents permeating the country during these critical years. However, her work as an inspector became monotonous—"same landscape, same curriculum, same teachers. The repetitiveness was boring me to death. And I who dreamed of becoming a heroine one day!" Although she stayed on with the ministry throughout the war years, believing it was "my responsibility to share the load in my country's evolution," Doria became increasingly more impatient with the routine of the work: "I felt I was working at something below my level of education and I was depressed at the injustice. I felt the abyss between my work and my Self. I didn't see any way out." To relieve her boredom, she began to write short essays and articles for some of the locally published French newspapers, such as *La Bourse Egyptienne*, but only with the permission of the minister of education, who cautioned her "not to write anything political."

News from Tanta in the early days of January 1942 announcing her grandmother Khadiga's death accentuated Doria's personal sense of ennui, plunging her into a despondent mood:

It was like an eclipse of the sun, reviving the feelings of loss and despair after the tragedy of my mother's death. Although never truly happy in Tanta, I always considered Grandmother a noble figure, endowed with high moral and social qualities not to mention her sense of humor and indescribable charm and goodness. She was the embodiment of legend-

ary Arab generosity, remaining until the end of her life the great benefactress, even when nearly all her wealth had been exhausted. For me,
Grandmother's death marked the end of an era when moral values still
held meaning for Egyptians.

Several years later, Doria wrote an essay comparing the women of her generation with those of her grandmother's and queried: "Have we gained or have
we lost in disavowing our customs and traditions? Between our grandmothers
and ourselves, in which direction is the scale of happiness turning?"[14] Her
grandmother's death symbolized the end of the *belle époque,* but it came at a
moment in Doria's personal life when things began to take a turn for the better.

6

The Turning Point (1942–1944)

I had to wait until circumstances were right for action. I was aware that
I had no position permitting me to play a significant social, political or
moral role in my society. I was not rich like Huda Sha'rawi, which might
have allowed me to impose myself. But I had faith!

As the Axis air raids on Egypt intensified and Rommel's Afrika Corps advanced menacingly toward Alexandria, pressure on Egyptian political leaders
increased, and the anxious British involved themselves more and more in the
domestic affairs of the country. On the pretext of hunting out Axis agents and
guarding the physical and moral safety of their army, the British sharply increased military security, deepening the crisis in Anglo-Egyptian relations and
intensifying the deep hostility toward them already pervasive among the Egyptian people. As General Muhammad Naguib (1908–1984), Egypt's first president following the 1952 military takeover, observed: "Their troops marched
through the streets of Cairo singing obscene songs about our King, a man
whom few of us admired, but who nevertheless, was as much a national symbol as our flag. Faruq was never so popular as when he was being insulted in
public by British troops, for we knew, as they knew, that by insulting our
unfortunate King they were insulting the Egyptian people as a whole. They
molested our women, assaulted our men, and committed acts of vandalism in
public places."[1]

At the same time, the volatile populace, suffering from food shortages and
high prices, were growing increasingly disillusioned with their own government, their profligate king, the power-hungry palace entourage, and the once-
powerful Wafd, now perceived to be in sympathy with the hated British. Egypt
was caught between the supporters of the allies on the one hand and those
who placed their hopes in the axis powers, thinking they would rid the country of the despised British occupation, on the other. Several Egyptian political

groups made clandestine contacts with Rommel, promising to foment internal revolt and facilitate his eventual victory. Most significant among these
groups was an underground movement known as "The Free Officers," which
included Gamal Abdul Nasser and Anwar Sadat, the masterminds of the 1952
coup d'état, which eventually overthrew the monarchy.

The British, wishing to protect their vital interests, imposed and deposed
governments under threat of tanks and bayonets, humiliating the king and
the Wafd alike. The most flagrant display of disregard for legitimate nationalist feelings and intrusion into Egyptian domestic affairs was the famous ultimatum of February 4, 1942, delivered by the British ambassador, Sir Miles
Lampson, to King Faruq demanding the replacement of the pro-axis prime
minister, Ali Mahir, with the pro-British Nahas Pasha of the Wafd. The king
and Lampson negotiated for two days, Faruq lobbying for a coalition under
Nahas rather than an exclusively Wafdist government. The allies were becoming increasingly alarmed by the critical situation in the western desert.
This prompted Lampson to act: "Unless I hear by five o'clock this afternoon
that Nahas has been asked to form a new government, His Majesty Faruq
must accept the consequences."[2] By nine in the evening, there had been no
response. On Lampson's orders, a column of tanks and several hundred mo-
torized troops surrounded Abdin Palace. Faruq was offered abdication papers
or the chance to approve the appointment of Nahas. For Egyptians, this was an
abrogation of the 1936 Treaty. For the British, it was a necessity of war. Ali
Mahir was exiled internally and Anwar Sadat and Aziz al-Masri were later
arrested and jailed for being German agents.

* * *

If these war years were marked by political crises and growing social unrest,
for Doria they were years in which she experienced the joy of personal happiness and the promise of fulfillment. On March 6, one month after the British
delivered their infamous ultimatum to the king, Doria gave birth to her first
child, Aziza, an event that offered her "a sense of reconciliation with life"
despite the disappointment among her husband's family that she had not produced a son: "When I assured my mother-in-law that I was extremely delighted to have a girl she looked at me with an air of disbelief. As if to say:
Hypocrite!"

The arrival of Aziza was a turning point in Doria's sense of fulfillment:
"With Aziza's birth, I found again the brightness of the sun and that absolute
love which had disappeared with my mother's death. What did it matter if I
was conveying such boundless love—and not receiving it as in my early childhood? Wasn't it always the same absolute feeling in its sublime and crystal-
line purity? I was happy! My daughter's birth sweetened my life."

Soon after the birth of his daughter, Nour decided to go into private law practice, motivated partly by the necessity to augment the family income but also to support his expensive taste for gambling and Doria's love of beautiful things. But perhaps the major reason that drew him into private practice was his own talent and zest for his profession. Doria claimed some credit in prompting Nour's decision: "A conflict over the rent arose between a tenant and the Jewish family who owned our building. Being friends with both I suggested they discuss the issue with Nour. He brilliantly reconciled the adversaries and they were so pleased with him that they brought him other clients. As he succeeded so well Nour decided to devote himself more completely to being a lawyer rather than just teaching about law. And our financial difficulties came to an end!"

During the crucial summer of 1942, as Rommel's army slowly advanced toward Alexandria, domestic political disorders intensified, and propaganda reports predicting the imminent entrance of German troops into Cairo were rampant. Virulent anti-British feelings led many Egyptians to welcome the prospect of an eventual occupation by the Germans. But Doria "could not understand how the Egyptian people could be happy at the prospect of a German occupation. German propaganda led Egyptians to believe that Rommel's victory would give Egypt her ideal of freedom. I felt terribly lonely in my presentiment of danger."

As news spread that Rommel had penetrated the Allied defenses and was about to enter the city, Doria became alarmed. But amid the general panic, she firmly held her ground: "That July day when Rommel began a new attack against the British in Alam Halfa, I was sitting on my terrace with my baby daughter Aziza, who was nearly four months old. She was smiling up at me. Her smile always made me forget all my anxieties. But that day, I couldn't help feeling something terribly oppressive in the air. . . . It was as if birds of prey were filling Egypt's sky. On the terrace opposite mine, I noticed my neighbors two little boys. . . ." The boys' mother, who was no particular friend of Doria's, rushed out to gather them up and shouted:

"Leave Cairo at once. In a few hours all the bridges will be blown up and you'll never be able to find milk for your daughter."

"What happened?"

"Rommel will be in Alexandria in a few hours. The British army can't stop him. The Royal Air Force could have held him up but my husband says that even they are too weak to be effective."

"What are you planning to do?"

"I'll leave Cairo at once and take the children to India."

She went inside, pulling her children with her. I kept my daughter close to my heart as if fearing a separation. What could I do? I didn't like the idea of running away. It would be cowardly. I tried to ring up my husband, but couldn't find him. I took some milk cans and rushed down to the flat of an elderly lady. I found her surrounded by some palace ladies and her friend, the wife of a former prime minister. They were ready to leave.

"You must go to your husband's family farm, Doria."

I left without deciding what to do. On the staircase I had the idea of going to the flat of Chalim, the Jewish owner of the building. I wondered if he was leaving too. I found him in the hall surrounded by his wife and children. They were calm.

"Are you leaving?" I asked one of the daughters.

"No," she said.

I thought that if the Jews weren't leaving Cairo, in spite of the probable persecution in store for them, I didn't see why I should. I went back up to my terrace and waited there with my daughter in my arms. When Nour arrived, suggesting that we leave Cairo immediately for the farm in Beni Suef, I persuaded him that it would be better for us to stay.

On November 4, 1942, the fate Egypt as well as of the world was decided during the strategic battle of al-Alamein. For the world, it meant a decisive shift in the trajectory of the war in favor of the Allied forces. For Egypt, it practically sealed the fate of the Wafd party and "the liberal experiment." When the threat of Rommel had evaporated and the tide of war turned in favor of the Allies, Nahas was dismissed and the Wafd would never again emerge as a dominant force in the political life of Egypt. Nahas fell from grace in October 1944, partly due to the publication of Makram Ebeid's famous *Black Book*, which implicated Nahas's wife, Zaynab al-Wakil, in corruption. With the dismissal of the Wafd, the Sa'dists came to power, with Ahmad Mahir as prime minister. Throughout the remainder of the war, Egypt made an important contribution to the allied effort, but the country remained neutral until February 26, 1945, when Egypt finally declared war on the Axis powers.

The party's popularity plummeted, and the country never forgave Nahas for the national humiliation to which he had acquiesced. The British lost whatever good will they had enjoyed, because their coercive action had confirmed that Egypt's independence was a sham. From this point on, the question of national independence became the major issue over which there would be fierce struggle in Egyptian political life.

*   *   *

As the year drew to a close, Doria resumed her work as inspector of French for the Ministry of Education. Entrusting the care of her infant daughter to a young Greek nursemaid, she began traveling around Egypt again. During one of her tours, she passed through Tanta, where another personal catastrophe befell her. As she was waiting for the train,

> I met my father by chance at the railway station. He had come to Tanta to visit his sister who had some personal problems. My train to Cairo had not yet arrived so we decided to have some coffee together at the station buffet. I was so happy to see my father, whom I greatly admired for his morality and absolutely genuine nature. I ordered coffee as he went to wash his hands. When he came back to the table I noticed a sort of tremulousness in his expression and movements. In a few seconds his face turned ashen, vanishing under his skin, suddenly aged. Then, in the throes of terrible pain, he fell to the floor, his face regaining his usual serenity. I thought he had fainted. Everything happened in less than a minute. I was terrified. I shouted for help and was immediately surrounded by the crowds. I was fighting my way out to find a doctor when my sister Soraya's husband appeared on the scene. As a doctor for the Egyptian railways, at that moment he was on a tour of medical inspection of Tanta's station. He heard the commotion and hurried over, but had no idea his uncle was involved. As I cradled my father's head in my arms he injected something into his arm and listened for a pulse. "Nothing!" he said, turning towards me.

For Doria the loss of both her grandmother and father within the same year seemed to reflect the increasing disorder and deteriorating conditions engulfing the country, and the king in particular: "Their deaths symbolized the disappearance of a time when moral principles, based on real concern, guided men's action." Nour's tenderness and affection after her father's death, however, "was like a balm upon my childhood wounds. He was doing his best to make me forget the past. Such circumstances consolidated our reciprocal and profound esteem and the great affection that we felt for each other."

Within two years, Jehane was born, and her arrival again filled Doria "with an indescribable feeling of immeasurable love, intensifying the meaning of my own life." Once more, Doria associates in her writing the feeling of the mother-daughter bond with that of absolute love:

> Whether one gives or one receives, it is this act of the total gift of self that makes life worth living. My daughters' very existence was a marvelous echo to my own feelings and aspirations. I was so happy to have girls. They were so near to my heart. In the infinity of my love for them I rediscovered the indescribable tenderness, lost seemingly beyond recall after the death of my mother. Their presence was a sort of blessing.

The daughters of Doria Shafik—Aziza, age 12 (left), and Jehane, age 10.

When they smiled at me the whole universe was within my arms welcoming me, consoling me and conveying an inner quietude to my tormented soul.

Following Jehane's birth, Doria needed to find someone to whom she could entrust the care of both her daughters, now that she had her work as well as a very active social life with Nour. The Greek nursemaid was unable to cope with the demands of Doria's powerful personality and the two young infants. It was then that Mme. Marie Reilly, an Irish spinster in her late fifties who spoke very little Arabic but excellent French, joined the Ragai household and became the children's beloved governess for the next twelve years.

Mme. Marie, along with her older sister and many other unmarried European women after the First World War, came to Cairo to work in upper-middle-class Egyptian homes. She had never stayed long in any one household. But when she first saw Jehane, who smiled and spontaneously opened her arms to the reserved, middle-aged stranger, she was enchanted, and a deep bond of love and affection developed between them which was to last until Mme. Marie's death in 1975. Doria also developed a profound respect and fondness for Mme. Marie, and thanks to her loving and affectionate care of Aziza and Jehane, Doria was released from major household responsibilities to pursue "an historic role I sensed waiting for me in public life."

*   *   *

But the time was not yet ripe. The Second World War was drawing to a close, and Doria had not found an outlet that would engage her mind, her ambition, and her will. She became restless with what she felt was an aimless and empty life: "I could not complain about the social and economic standard of my life but it was devoid of political content." Despite the outward appearances of a happy marriage and a busy social life, Doria became obsessed by this "desire to fulfill a mission," which was accentuated by a deepening sense of alien-ation. Outsiders might have concluded, as many did, that her life was a tre-mendous success. She lived in a lovely apartment overlooking the Nile, she was often described as one of the most elegantly dressed women in Cairo, she was happily married and had two healthy and beautiful daughters who were the sunshine of her life:

> My life with my husband was happy! He was very kind to me. His high spirits added to his drive and created an agreeable atmosphere in our household. He was helping me to be patient. Yet in my heart, in spite of all the factors helping to make my life a happy one, I still felt a dreadful emptiness. There was a sort of nothingness underlying the briskness of my whole existence. I had the feeling something was missing. I tried to understand the reason for this feeling of uprootedness—"deracination"— of being in surroundings which logically should have made me utterly happy. Yet this sense of emptiness, what could be the cause? The early death of my mother? An unhappy childhood which passed without ten-derness as a day without sun? The wretched days in Paris with the girls at the Bois de Boulogne? The frustrated desire to play a role in Egypt's political life? I always felt that, outside politics, my existence could not have substantial value.

Doria and Nour decided to join the Automobile Club, which was perhaps the most prestigious social club of Cairene "high society" during the war, pri-marily because it was the favorite gambling milieu for young King Faruq and his palace entourage. An ardent card player and gambler himself, Nour was often invited to play at the king's table, a privilege which usually resulted in heavy financial loss for the young lawyer. Doria found herself thrown in with a group of women she did not like, nor did she feel particularly welcome among them. At the beginning, she had joined this milieu primarily to accompany her husband, who enjoyed the socializing and card playing. But as time passed, she had become disenchanted and bored:

> There, surrounded by his partisans, King Faruq, in whose company Queen Farida had not been seen for some time, passed most of his evenings. I

was received with coldness by the ladies of the club, disdained as a sort of intruder, because I was not as rich as they were. In diplomas I surpassed them which annoyed them, though in elegance we were equal. They all hated each other, but in me, for the first time, they found a common target allowing them to team up against me in a sort of tacit accord. . . . However I stood firm. I remained! Moreover I found a kind of shelter from their hostility in the enthusiastic welcome of the male members of the club. I created my own ambiance in this society which hated me and which I, in turn, despised. Each evening was a battle terminating in victory or defeat. What did it matter? The essential point was to be engaged in the combat—conducted as it was in a frigid calm.

The more she felt alienated from the women, the more Doria moved toward the male members of the club, many of whom held positions of power and with whom she entered into political discussions. They opened her eyes to what she called "the politics of the period": "In the very depths of my heart there was always this profound wish to work for my country's future. To play such a role I had to become aware of everything happening in Egypt. I felt that Cairo's Automobile Club was the best place to learn what was going on."

What was smoldering within society since the days of Zaghlul, and was ready to erupt anew as soon as the war ended, was the struggle against British imperialism. According to Naguib, "As always there was the British threat, which increased in proportion as the strategic importance of Egypt increased in the defense of the British Empire. During the war we suffered countless humiliations at the hands of the British, who failed, and still fail, to understand that our national interests are not, and can never be, the same as theirs. Of no country did the British demand more than they did of Egypt and of no country were they less considerate. They expected Egyptians to behave as loyal allies while being treated as conquered subjects."[3]

While Doria was discussing Egypt's economic and political conditions with the male elite at the Automobile Club, the Egyptian masses, who had suffered under the adverse economic conditions of wartime, were listening to a different set of voices fomenting new social and political movements. Their cumulative disenchantment soon found expression in a series of student demonstrations and workers' strikes. The yearning for independence was the great common denominator uniting these different forces.

These events did not go unnoticed by Doria, who was more than aware of the oppressive and unjust conditions in the country—conditions which she believed were spawned as much by an outdated social system as by the tyranny of a colonial regime. Attracted by neither the extreme right nor the radical left, she was more the reformer than the revolutionary. Nevertheless, she felt that there was a role for women to play in this broader national struggle, and she set down her feminist philosophy and vision in a short treatise, *La Femme Nouvelle en Egypte* (1944)—her first conscious attempt since her thesis to articulate the social situation of the Egyptian woman.

By writing in French, she was directing her message to the educated Egyptian elite, the class she wanted to catalyze and lead as the vanguard of social change for the poorer majority of the Egyptian masses. She began by challenging Westerners' orientalist view of Egyptian women:

> The social situation of the Egyptian woman is in a general way very little understood in the world. Westerners are still impressed by the writings of those early travelers, who first probed the East. These very unscientific writings might, through a great stretch of the imagination, provide a portrait of the Egyptian woman of an earlier time. But they certainly distort the idea of the Egyptian woman on which the West bases its views today. She has evolved so fast that one can hardly recognize her. Compared with her sister of the beginning of the twentieth century the Egyptian woman of today is a totally different woman with new ideas, different habits and unlimited ambition. It is with the particular goal of clarifying this issue that I have written this book. I focus on the social situation of the Egyptian woman as it was not so long ago, as it is in our day, and as she hopes it will be in the future.[4]

Through her portrayal of the new woman in Egypt, we catch a glimpse of her own self-image and feminist consciousness at a moment when Egyptian society was struggling toward its own national independence:

> As every oriental woman who respects herself knows, the new woman does not like to be measured. "Everything or nothing," is her motto. With one immense stride she passes from the most complete ignorance to the most striking scholarly success; from the most hermetically sealed cloisters to the most brilliant social life. She advances, always advances . . . perhaps one day she will succeed in putting her two feet into parliament! Perhaps she will obtain a ministerial portfolio [Such as Mme. Brunschvicg under Blum!] Perhaps she will become a world celebrity! It might be healthy for her to forget for a moment the panoply of her own brilliance and to open her heart and ask impartially: What have I done and what am I going to become? What is my true role? Have I failed in my vocation? Have I trampled the duties that nature set out for me? Have I imposed a task too heavy for my fragile shoulders or too different from my true destiny? One of the first questions posed for the [educated] women is the safeguarding of her femininity; another is the role of woman in public life, and a third is the role of woman in society. Feminism in the true sense of the word is the total comprehension between

man and woman, not a perpetual fight between the two sexes. As for the statement that "women normally constituted and not too ugly are not made to be politicians, diplomats, generals or drum majors" I am revolted! You forget Cleopatra, the most beautiful diplomat and politician, and Joan of Arc the charming warrior. The feminine genius is not necessarily accompanied by ugliness. One finds equally that nearly all exceptional women whose names have come down in history, have been unhappy. That is their affair. One must believe that they preferred an unhappy and meaningful life to a complacent but stupid one. "Nothing renders us so great as great suffering," as the poet says.[5]

Doria called on the elite women of the palace and the upper classes to mobilize their considerable moral and material resources to bring about change and transformation in the appalling conditions of the masses. For Doria, the educated elite woman had a special mission, to bridge the immense gap between the women of the upper classes and those of the poor. She argued that it is the particular responsibility and obligation of the feminine elite to change and transform those traditional socio-cultural and legal barriers inimical to woman's free and full participation in the life of the country. That she could engage in public criticism of customs oppressive to women in her society was due to her conviction—the argument she had made in her doctoral thesis—that Islam, if properly understood, offered no barrier to women's freedom: "We are like a huge machine whose cogs fail to mesh. There has been too much progress at the top of society and none at all at the bottom. Yet it is on this basis that the solid foundations of any society, and particularly of female society, are laid, and it is from this layer of society that the majority of mothers come. Here is an issue to which we should devote the greatest attention."[6]

Exemplifying the kind of action elite women could take to narrow the gap between the classes were the "good works" of Princess Chevikar, the first wife of the late King Fuad I,[7] to whom Doria dedicated her book in commendation for "the example she has set, when malaria raged in upper Egypt and introduced the severest misery there, Her Highness Princess Chevikar was one of the first to address herself to the terrible affliction. Her 'beau geste' is all the more meaningful as our present day Egypt is in great need of help. Her Highness Princess Chevikar calls out to the rich and all those who can serve to help the others, those upon whom fortune has not smiled."[8]

This personal homage toward a personality whose reputation in Egyptian society was shrouded in palace scandal and intrigue, particularly around the figure of the young King Faruq, was viewed among the growing social forces in opposition to the palace as a public act inimical to the national struggle. In addition, Doria's unequivocal call for a strategy of social reform through "noblesse oblige" stigmatized her as an "aristocrat," an epithet she would find difficult to shed in the ensuing years.

Doria's plea in the mid-1940s "for the elite women to band together to fight the three scourges of ignorance, disease and poverty" was based on her recognition and admiration of the positive efforts of the social reformers of an earlier generation. Beginning in the late nineteenth century and continuing throughout the war years, social welfare services were provided in Egypt through the private initiative and the family wealth of committed and energetic women from both the palace and Egypt's upper classes. It was through the generosity of Princess Ayn al-Hayat that the major philanthropic organizations of Egypt known as Mabarra Muhammad Ali al-Kabir and La Femme Nouvelle were founded in 1910 and 1919, respectively.[9]

Several women of Egypt's wealthiest elite generously endowed private organizations or supported those already in place. Luminaries such as Mme. Hidayat Afifi Barakat (daughter of the palace chamberlain), Fatma Sirry (sister of a prime minister), and Amina Sidki (daughter of Ismail Sidki) were the driving force behind two of the most active organizations, Mabarra Muhammad Ali and La Femme Nouvelle. Mme. Nahid Sirry, great aunt to Queen Farida and wife of the prime minister, Husayn Sirry, presided over the Red Crescent Society throughout the war years until 1952. Huda Sha'rawi herself had been a member of the La Femme Nouvelle Association until 1923 when, in opposition to Chevikar, she left to found her own Egyptian Feminist Union. To Doria, these philanthropic organizations "mark a decisive stage in the social history of modern Egypt. Not only do they render great service but also prepare the way for those who want to serve their country."[10]

The 1940s was a period when governments, along with their different prime ministers, were appointed and dissolved with such frequency that no basic state-supported institutional structure of social welfare was ever developed to aid the poor and destitute. It was basically these privately endowed philanthropic organizations, grounded in an ideology of noblesse oblige, that provided major social and health services that the government was either unable or unwilling to perform. The Mabarra Muhammad Ali al-Kabir alone was responsible for the establishment of several dozen hospitals, small dispensaries, and clinics that offered health services to the needy throughout the poorest districts of Cairo and the rural provinces. La Femme Nouvelle Association concentrated its efforts on the establishment of training centers for illiterate women of all ages not only to teach reading and writing but also to develop income-generating skills such as dressmaking and carpet-weaving that would allow women to earn their own independent income.

Both in ideology and membership, these benevolent societies projected a completely different feminist goal in Egypt than either the Egyptian Feminist

Union or the more clandestine, political associations that were beginning to attract a number of sons and daughters from both the Egyptian masses and the elite families. Progressive voices argued that liberal capitalism could never banish the three scourges of Egypt because it was founded on injustice and exploitation and thus incapable of liberating the productive forces necessary for their destruction. Drawn to the Soviet Union as their model and Karl Marx as their guide, many young students, including the daughters of the wealthy upper bourgeoisie studying at the French Lycée, like Inji Efflatoun, or the working class studying at the national university, like Latifa Zayyat,[11] were attracted into the various left-wing communist organizations that emerged in Egypt during the closing months of the war. The lives of Doria Shafik and Inji Efflatoun would intertwine, briefly yet dramatically, during this period of struggle for liberation. They held diametrically opposed ideological solutions to the challenges facing Egypt, and each represented very different metaphors surrounding the nationalist-feminist struggle that was about to erupt. As the war ended, Egypt entered a protracted period of social and political upheaval that would alter the consciousness of an entire generation.

The Egyptian women's movement during this early post-war period was ripe for the emergence of a different and more radical feminist voice that would attempt to link the women's struggle to other political and social concerns, such as the nationalist movement and the class struggle. Doria comments in her memoirs: "Egypt was not free. The British still controlled the political strings. The palace had imposed a virtual dictatorship upon Egypt. Political parties were following demagogic methods. The Muslim Brothers were using religious feelings to reach sinister political aims of complete domination of the country, and women had no political rights whatsoever." Although Doria had argued for the mobilization of the upper classes through philanthropic organizations to combat disease, poverty, and illiteracy, she was not unaware that more politically oriented organizations on both the left and the right were attracting a growing number of younger, educated middle-class women and men into their ranks to fight for national liberation. Doria also wanted to be connected to the evolving political events, but neither the Egyptian Feminist Union nor the extremist political groups appealed to her growing sense of mission. As the war was drawing to a close, she was looking for a way to forge a public role for herself.

The Struggle (1945–1954)

My country was in such a state of convulsion that one could not forecast all the accumulated storms. I felt compelled to enter into the fray. It was not a question of simple curiosity but one of profound desire, blended with anguish, to touch with my own hands this great evil from which my country suffered and whose cause I could not yet grasp.

—Shafik, "Memoirs" (1960), 164

7

Into the Limelight (1945–1947)

I needed more experience of real life from which my long studies and
my tendency to meditation (even to dreaming) had isolated me. What I
needed finally was a certain vantage point, a sort of foothold from which
it would be possible for me to take up a position, before venturing on
this mission which the future was soon to reveal to me.

The year 1945 began on a note of violence when, moments after announcing that Egypt had declared war on the Axis powers, Prime Minister Ahmad
Mahir was assassinated in parliament by a young lawyer, Mahmud al-'Isawi,
a member of the National Party. Egypt was then in a paradoxical situation.
Although the country had made an important contribution to the Allied effort, it had remained neutral until February 26, 1945. The decision to declare
war was made primarily because Egypt wanted to plead its case for independence in front of the newly created United Nations, scheduled to meet in San
Francisco in April of that year. This event heralded a turning point in the
country's history. For the majority of the Egyptian people, who were looking
forward to building their country, the aftermath of the Second World War
meant staggering inflation, acute shortages, and increasing joblessness—problems which intensified their polarization: "Social injustices, the most flagrant
of which was the abyss between the diverse social classes widened from day to
day and the growing insolence of wealth accentuated more and more the humiliation of the poor."

Despite the formal termination of the Second World War, the Cold War,
which divided the world and shaped Egypt's role in regional and international
politics for the next five decades, began to unfold.[1] The British maintained
their dominance throughout the Nile Valley, despite their rhetoric about political independence for Egypt after the war, thus fueling the nationalist struggle

among young Egyptians who were becoming more radicalized as well as more organized in their demands for national independence and social justice.

Nationalist feelings were running high as the clamor for liberation from colonial occupation and domination swept through Egypt. It was a time when a whole generation—a disillusioned generation—was awakened to political awareness. It was a time when people felt that the destiny of Egypt could be decided at any moment. It was a time of political chaos when the forces that led to the 1952 military coup were taking shape. The "liberal experiment" was being besieged, and Egyptians were swelling the ranks of fascist, communist, nationalist, and religious fundamentalist parties and groups. British troops were routing out suspected terrorist leaders: "From the national point of view one can say that from May 1945 to July 1952 Egypt lived in terror, with the severest restrictions on the freedom of assembly, speech and the press. Egypt was in a pre-revolutionary mood. It was one of the saddest periods in her history . . . desolated by a terrible cholera epidemic, international isolation and unpopularity abroad, defeat and anarchy at home."[2]

It was precisely during those early months of 1945 that Doria Shafik took advantage of a "certain situation" which would enable her to construct a new career for herself, eventually leading her into a course of events that even she could not have anticipated. Quite unexpectedly one afternoon, a friend of Nour's, whose wife was a lady-in-waiting to Princess Chevikar, approached Doria with a message saying the princess wanted her to serve as editor-in-chief of a new cultural and literary magazine that the princess wanted to publish. Doria was somewhat baffled as to why she was being invited to assume this formidable responsibility since she had no formal experience in either journalism or publishing. Was this Chevikar's appreciation for Doria's dedication in her recently published book? Was it, at last, some public recognition of her degree from the Sorbonne? Was it connected to her husband's presence at the Automobile Club, where he played cards at Faruq's table?

As Doria later learned, it was actually linked to intrigues between two palace cliques surrounding Chevikar:

> One belonging to a group of sycophants of Chevikar's seventh husband some thirty years her junior, who wanted to grab the limelight from the princess. And an opposing group, headed by Chevikar's personal secretary, who suggested that a new magazine be founded that would increase the publicity around the princess and the work of her well-known philanthropic association, La Femme Nouvelle. Because some of my own articles were being published in the Egyptian French press at that time, my name was recommended for the position of editor-in-chief of the new magazine, to be called after her famous benevolent society.

Why would Doria accept full responsibility for establishing and editing a cultural and literary magazine when she had absolutely no experience in journalism or publishing? She simply relished the challenge. This was not the first time (nor would it be the last) that she would venture forth in unknown waters, full of bravado and confidence. By accepting Chevikar's offer at a time when most Egyptians were disenchanted with the monarchy, Doria identified herself with the person considered most directly responsible for initiating the young Faruq into a life of debauchery and corruption. It was a step which also distanced her further from mainstream public opinion, especially among the women of the Egyptian Feminist Union, who believed that the notorious Chevikar was attempting to compete with their beloved heroine.

By the end of the war, the conflict between these two powerful women, Princess Chevikar and Huda Sha'rawi, epitomized the growing rift emerging among the elite. On the one hand was the Turkish princess, a woman brought up in imperial palaces whose hatred and rancor towards the Egyptian royal family after her divorce from the late King Fuad centered in the queen. Chevikar considered Nazli a usurper to her rightful place as queen of Egypt and sought her revenge through Nazli's son, Faruq. Queen Nazli, who had been kept in almost total seclusion by Fuad until his death in 1936, is said to have broken all rules of royal decorum trying to compensate for her years of palace imprisonment. Some have argued that it was as much his mother's flagrant life-style, causing Faruq great personal pain and embarrassment, as it was Chevikar's desire for revenge that contributed to his own undisciplined conduct. Chevikar's name and palace were synonymous with the center of aristocratic life in Cairo, and through her many sumptuous receptions and parties, the princess seemed to be asserting that hers was the true royal house of Egypt.

On the other hand was the Egyptian Huda Hanum Sha'rawi, a nationalist heroine whose name appeared alongside those of leaders of women's movement in America, France, England, and Italy. Political leaders of different ideologies in the Arab world honored her. To devoted followers of Huda Sha'rawi like Amina al-Sa'id, "all this incited the jealousy of the Turkish Chevikar, who desired to become the equal of Huda Sha'rawi. And the only way to do this was to garner King Faruq's trust and friendship. By keeping him a puppet on a string she gathered rich and ambitious people around her like flies around the rivers of money and power."[3]

Although aware that joining Chevikar would probably alienate her from Huda Sha'rawi's group as well as from those middle-class women she most wanted to attract, Doria was convinced this offer from the wealthy and powerful princess presented an opportunity she could not easily pass up: "To refuse, wasn't it to expose oneself to remaining in the shade? One doesn't get an offer like this every day. Now it was necessary, at any price, to acquire a certain notoriety that would give me sufficient authority to allow me, later on, to establish myself! A way leading me to a possible resolution of this irresistible urge." If Doria harbored any doubts about accepting the offer to be editor-in-chief of *La Femme Nouvelle,* it was more directly linked to her feelings of rejection by Huda Sha'rawi: "I would have preferred to work with Huda Sha'rawi for whom I had the greatest esteem not to mention profound gratitude for her help at the beginning of my career. But there was this inevitable rupture and I felt it useless to refuse the chance I was being offered to form a new career, one that would be more in accord with my temperament and disposition. So I accepted the Princess' offer."

Having made up her mind, she launched herself into this new challenge with great gusto, despite her lack of experience: "I knew nothing about journalism and yet overnight I became editor-in-chief of a yet-to-be published magazine. I was completely ignorant as to the process of production. I did not know what was meant by *cliché,* or what a printing press looked like, not to mention a *mise en page* or advertising." But lack of experience never inhibited Doria. She was putting into practice her own motto written over fifteen years earlier: "to know, to be able, to want and to dare." This spontaneity, bravado, and profound belief in her own capacity to succeed were all she needed. She would learn as she went along.

However, the palace surroundings and the situation she had got herself into both attracted and repelled her: "The first person I met in the palace of Her Highness was the husband who made me think of a gigolo, many years younger than his wife. Then I met the princess, looking terribly thin but with laughing eyes, the last vestiges of a vanished beauty. She emerged from the salon, where the opulent ladies of the committee of La Femme Nouvelle Association lolled around on sofas filling them by the cubic meter."

Chevikar's dining room served as her office, and the dining-room table was her desk. The atmosphere was chaotic. Chevikar's husband, the ladies-in-waiting, as well as the women of the committee, were all interfering and giving her advice: "As a training in patience I couldn't have fallen on a better test. I spent more time moving the operation in and out of the palace dining room than I did in the production of the magazine. The staff were the many friends of Chevikar: foreigners, Egyptians, men and women of all nationalities, each wanting to interfere, each wanting a favor. It was a hullabaloo. The atmosphere duplicated that surrounding King Faruq at the Automobile Club, intrigues and machinations in the midst of alarming political disorder."

Her most difficult problem was not so much having to learn a new profession as it was working in an environment that clashed with her own temperament. To work in this palace milieu meant that Doria had "to bow before Her Highness and live in an atmosphere of intrigue mirroring the decadence of society at large." Although she would have preferred a salary, "Chevikar assumed that anyone's time and effort devoted to the projects of her benevolent association were purely voluntary." Doria was made an honorary member of the administrative council of La Femme Nouvelle Association, a gesture which did not endear her to the other ladies. While the magazine was separate from the activities of the welfare association, the older women were not very sympathetic toward this daring and highly educated younger middle-class woman.

Membership on the administrative council of La Femme Nouvelle Association read like a veritable "Who's Who" of Egyptian high society, all wives or daughters of prominent political families who seemed openly hostile to Doria's presence: "The Princess welcomed me warmly but the narrow-minded ladies of the committee, like those of the Automobile Club, looked at me sideways. I had the sensation of being an intruder. I entered with my diplomas, as uncomfortable as an ugly duckling." She struggled to assert herself among those very women whom she had described in her book as "the vanguard closing the gap between the classes."

To work in this milieu also meant that Doria witnessed the daily contradictions between wealth and poverty, separated only by the palace gates:

> I was invited to stay on for lunch and, as we ate off gold plates surrounded by luxury, I thought of the beggars right outside the palace doors and remembered the image of the "silent ones" that my grandmother used to feed. How great is the abyss separating the classes in Egypt! I felt something had to be done to save the majority of Egyptians from their wretchedness. But how? Where to begin? I realized the enormous difficulties in the path of any reform. I had to wait. I needed time to prepare the groundwork for my own plan which was still not even clear in my head.

Despite these difficulties, Doria decided not to quit, believing "that if I were to be able to help my country, I needed an important position and La Femme Nouvelle magazine was the only road open to me leading in that direction. I had found a situation from which I could launch my own mission later on." However, this expediency would extract its price. Many Egyptians criticized Doria for her close association with a class that was becoming increasingly callous and insensitive to the sufferings of the poor majority. Her continued association with the notorious princess and her entourage, her editorship of a French magazine, as well as her friendship with Princess Faiza, sister of King Faruq, led many Egyptians to view Doria as just another of those "ladies of the salon de thé." To Huda Sha'rawi, anyone having to do with Chevikar or her projects was immediately labeled as the enemy, a stance justifying the Egyptian Feminist Union's continued disapproval and public criticism of Doria during the postwar years. Among the women of the more progressive left, like Inji Efflatoun, Doria's association with the palace branded her as just "too bourgeois to be taken seriously."[4]

Nour continued to be a great source of comfort and reassurance. Their relationship during this period seemed to be based on a strong bond of love and friendship through which each offered the other companionship, support, and respect. Doria accompanied Nour to his gambling parties at the Automobile Club, and he in turn accompanied Doria to her receptions at Chevikar's palace: "It was comforting because, as always, everyone liked him. We made a group of friends there, but Chevikar's palace became more than a center of social activity, it took on a political role linked to deceptions and debauchery. And I found myself in the midst of intrigues regarding *La Femme Nouvelle* magazine. And it was within this atmosphere that I had to face my first real challenge in Egypt."

Given the heightened feelings of nationalism during this politically sensitive moment in Egypt, Doria had to confront the rising criticism that she was not truly Egyptian. Her association with Chevikar, her ties to a French publication, and her fashionable French wardrobe did nothing to assuage this negative public image. Rumors that she had anti-nationalist tendencies circulated around her. Her frequent appearances at the Automobile Club, her contact with foreigners, her facility and predilection for the French language led to the accusation that she must be collaborating with the colonialists: "'Wasn't she writing in French? Wasn't she editing a French magazine? Didn't she receive her education in France?' I was deeply affected by these rumors—I felt a terrible abyss was opening up between me and my country—perhaps deeper than before. I decided not to answer my enemies' attacks. But the rumors kept spreading—endangering my career. I was accused of being French!"

Again she considered quitting her job at the magazine because of the milieu in Chevikar's palace, "where I felt increasingly ill at ease, but I knew that I was not welcome within the Egyptian Feminist Union where the atmosphere had been poisoned against me. The women around Huda Sha'rawi had taken every opportunity to point out my ingratitude: 'Look at this Doria Shafik, in whom you had so much faith, working with your enemies!' I had no other alternative but to remain with and have the support of Princess Chevikar."

However, all these public criticisms against Doria's national identity deeply affected her personal pride, and she decided "to do something about it before my critics gained the upper hand." Her adversaries unknowingly provoked her to take a course of action that would move her yet another step closer to finding that mission she always felt was waiting for her: "The irrefutable response to this mounting public attack against me was obvious. Before succumbing to the deluge I would turn their arguments against me to my own advantage. I would found a journal in the Arabic language!" But how would she do this and what did she want this journal to accomplish?

*   *   *

The birth of *Bint al-Nil* marked Doria's formal entrance onto the stage of professional journalism. Assuredly she was not the first to establish an Arabic women's magazine in the region, as the tradition dates back to the nineteenth century. Indeed the publication was heir to a half-century-old tradition of women's journals in Egypt that originated with *al-Fatah*, founded in 1892 by Hind Nawfal.[5] But during those turbulent postwar years, *Bint al-Nil* was the first women's journal in Arabic self-consciously oriented toward and devoted to the goal of "being a vehicle for educating Egyptian and Arab women in the profound sense of that term—awakening their consciousness." The story surrounding Doria's becoming the owner, publisher, and editor of the first postwar Arabic women's magazine illustrates how a particular feminist consciousness was shaped by that very fact; the magazine itself introduced a different feminine discourse into Egyptian journalism.

Bint al-Nil—printed on fine-quality glossy paper—included articles on women's issues, suggestions on nutrition, and advice on how to raise young children, in addition to colored photographs of the latest fashions in Paris. The new publication was the brainchild of three people: Doria, Nour, and Dr. Ibrahim Abdu, the doyen of Egyptian journalism who would coauthor with Doria two books on the women's movement in Egypt.[6] As an old friend of Nour's, dating back to their student days at King Fuad I University, Abdu first met Doria in 1939 when he went to Paris to conduct research on the history of journalism in Egypt from the Napoleonic period. Nour introduced him to his new bride, and from then on, the three were very close friends. In a personal interview a year before his death, Abdu related:

> The idea of *Bint al-Nil* first took root just after the war, when Doria discussed with Nour and me her plans to create a first class journal for women in Arabic. Huda Sha'rawi's journal, *L'Egyptienne*, was no longer being published and another, *Fatat al-Sharq*, was not considered very serious. I remember that evening, as we sat on the balcony of their Corniche apartment overlooking the Nile, when Doria, watching her beloved river flow by, suddenly turned to us and proclaimed excitedly: "I shall name our magazine *Bint al-Nil*!" Nour not only put up some money but also arranged for the purchase of the paper upon which the journal was printed. The main problem confronting the production of

the magazine during this early postwar period was finding the paper, not readily available on the market, and what was available was expensive (forty Egyptian pounds the ream). As the English were still running things in the country, it was necessary to purchase through them. Nour had a British friend who expedited procuring the paper at only five Egyptian pounds the ream. The first issue, selling at five piasters, appeared on the stands on November 1, 1945. Within the first two hours all 5,000 copies were sold out. By 1952 the circulation had doubled but so had its price.[7]

From December 1945 until 1949, the price remained at five piasters, the same price as L'Egyptienne. Then it rose to ten piasters and remained at that price until the government forced its closure in 1957. Considering that the daily al-Ahram newspaper was selling nearly 110,000 copies a day for only five millemes (that is, one-half a piaster), it is more than likely that the readers of Bint al-Nil were of the more affluent, educated, small middle class rather than of the majority, the urban masses or the peasantry, where the poverty level was high and the literacy rate very low, especially among women. The Turco-Circassian elite did not read Arabic.

Doria's story of the founding of Bint al-Nil emphasizes more her goals and objectives in wanting to establish such a magazine and underplays the significant role played by her husband and Abdu:

I wanted a magazine exclusively for women, especially Egyptian and Arab women. One that would concentrate on their problems since so many erroneous interpretations of the Quran were causing great injustices towards Arab women. A women's magazine could be of great help to the progress of my country as well as of all Muslim countries through reaching women among the broader Arabic-reading public with Bint al-Nil's message. Such a magazine could play a positive role in the evolution of my country. But where was the money to come from? There was no question of asking my husband to finance my magazine although our income had actually increased considerably since he set up a law office in addition to his post as professor of law at Cairo University. But our standard of living had also risen—not to mention the expense of bringing up our two daughters. Nour also liked to gamble, so we never managed to save anything. The new magazine had to be an integral part of my life! As to the name, Bint al-Nil, it was not an artificial invention, but a true reality. It sprang throbbing from the song of the boatmen of al-Bahr al-Seghir in Mansura, a song that more than once was my childhood companion and which now rose by itself to the surface of my thoughts as an act of faith. In fact I had the profound feeling that I was the Daughter of the Nile!

Doria was not averse to using the connections she had cultivated through her association with *La Femme Nouvelle* to persuade the largest publicity firm in Cairo (Société Orientale de Publicité) to put itself at her disposal: "They thought they could get nearer to the princess through me." She even tried to engage the same publisher as *La Femme Nouvelle*, "but he was a businessman first and foremost while I wanted to produce a work of art. We couldn't agree on anything. So I decided to do it alone. I needed a license, an apartment with furnishings for an office with two rooms and money for paper, printing and publicity. I had to begin with a pair of empty pockets."

This last statement appears somewhat ingenuous, since we know she had Nour's continued financial support. It was also rumored that Princess Chevikar had donated a large sum of money to Doria to found *Bint al-Nil*. Amina al-Sa'id, a somewhat younger contemporary of Doria's, claimed that Chevikar had first asked her to found the magazine:

> I had been invited to a reception at Chevikar's palace to honor those working in the social services. She pinned the tag of membership to the Mabarra Muhammad Ali Organization on me, and announced that she was giving me the sum of 15,000 Egyptian pounds, to found the *Bint al-Nil* magazine, promising to give me whatever the magazine would need in terms of elegant advertisements and guaranteeing enormous profits. [This is a grossly exaggerated sum that would be the equivalent of nearly 3,000,000 Egyptian pounds today.] I confess that when I heard those words I felt that the world was turning around under my feet. I was terribly frightened that Huda Sha'rawi would think I had cheated her by becoming a member of an organization presided over by her arch enemy "because of the material gain." My suffering was compounded when the newspapers reported on their front pages that I had joined the Mabarra Muhammad Ali Society and was going to found a feminist magazine called *Bint al-Nil*. Once she read the news in *al-Ahram*, Mme. Sha'rawi returned to Cairo from upper Egypt. When she arrived she telephoned me and angrily asked me to meet her immediately. After she heard my story she gave me a paper and pen and told me to write to Chevikar and refuse to accept membership in her society as well as any role in the founding of a magazine which intended to challenge *L'Egyptienne.* I wrote my refusal and sent it instantly to Princess Chevikar. A storm of anger broke out among Chevikar's entourage but the princess was not desperate and began to search for someone else and in the end she finally chose Dr. Doria Shafik.[8]

Al-Sa'id's interpretation is somewhat misleading for several reasons. First Sha'rawi's *L'Egyptienne* had ceased publication by 1940; hence *Bint al-Nil* could not very well have been in direct competition. Second, *Bint al-Nil* never was published under the patronage of Chevikar, unlike *La Femme Nouvelle,* a fact which suggests that al-Sa'id may have confused the two journals. Third, if any such offer was ever extended (according to Sabat, "Doria received a donation of two thousand pounds from Chevikar to found *Bint al-Nil"*), her ardent desire to assert her Egyptian identity would have categorically disallowed having her magazine under the aegis of the Turkish, French-speaking Chevikar. And finally, Shafik herself makes abundantly clear that the point of founding *Bint al-Nil* was to dissociate herself from Chevikar's influence: "The new magazine would be published in my own name and under my full responsibility. It would have a definite plan and market value. I wanted no repetition of *La Femme Nouvelle* with everybody's fingers in the pie. To be successful, a magazine in Arabic could not logically be edited under the same conditions as *La Femme Nouvelle.* I needed a freer atmosphere where it would be possible to give my full measure."

Doria did not need to go very far to find the necessary capital. She obtained a banker's guarantee, presumably with Nour's backing—convinced that she would be able to repay it from the revenue of the sale of the new magazine. And indeed the income from the first issue allowed her to pay off her initial debts, to move the magazine from a small apartment on Ibn Tha'lab Street to a larger suite in the center of town at 48 Kasr al-Nil Street, and to hire additional staff. When she launched *Bint al-Nil,* she resigned her post as a French language inspector "because the demands of this new profession that deals with the multitude of human beings, gave me no time to continue working for the Ministry of Education. I was very satisfied with my new career. It brought a balance to my sufferings in other fields. In journalism I found the dynamism which the monotony of Egyptian social life couldn't bring me. It was lively. Every day a new day, a new fight toward the understanding of events and their meaning."

It is clear that Nour was very instrumental in helping her get started. Not only did she freely discuss her ideas and plans with her husband, but she also depended on his financial support and moral encouragement to help her sustain this journal as well as other projects she would promote over the next twelve years. And Abdu's expertise as general supervisor of the magazine from 1945–1952 helped assure the survival of *Bint al-Nil* in the early years of its existence. He also assisted Doria in coordinating and helping her write her editorials related to women's rights issues. In fact, Doria was dependent on others to translate her writing from French into Arabic. Through his connections at the national university, Abdu hired Khalil Sabat, one of his students who had an excellent command of both French and Arabic, to assist on the magazine: "I was Doria's editorial secretary and wrote and translated materials for *Bint al-Nil* as well as a children's magazine *al-Katkout* (Little Chick) she also published. Doria could read Arabic and speak the colloquial dialect fluently but she was unable to express her ideas directly into literary Arabic. I translated Doria's notes and ideas into Arabic for Abdu to put in final editorial form."[9]

Abdu's assistance had a direct influence on the nature of the editorial messages appearing under Doria Shafik's signature during the first two years of *Bint al-Nil*'s publication. In fact, the ideology expressed in those early editorials is in obvious contradiction to that of later years. Abdu admitted, "Those first editorials of 1946 do not truly reflect the sentiments and words of Doria Shafik. They are mine! I wrote down those ideas, not Doria!" When pressed to explain the circumstances which necessitated this more cautious approach, he responded: "I had a difficult time toning down Doria's confrontational approach. During this period the shaykhs of al-Azhar were strongly and publicly against women going to university with men and entering those professions that were exclusively man's work, such as medicine, law, engineering and science. So as not to incite the al-Azharites' immediate wrath and violent opposition to *Bint al-Nil*, I thought a better strategy was to go step-by-step at a more moderate pace. Also as a university professor at that time, I was more in touch with the explosive political situation than Doria."[10]

The first issue of *Bint al-Nil* appeared during a period when Egyptian society was experiencing dramatic acts of violence, including assassinations and widespread student and worker demonstrations. The national question fanned discontent already festering as a result of the painfully slow movement of social reform—discontent which only two months later erupted with the massive student strike of February 1946. Thousands of students assembled at Cairo University and marched toward Abdin Palace, shouting "No negotiation before evacuation." This culminated in a bloody confrontation with police resulting in the deaths of dozens of students and the wounding of several hundred others. The clash set off a general workers' strike throughout the country, provoking the British (in armored cars) to open fire on the crowds. In retaliation, foreign shops and clubs were attacked and destroyed. Many more died, and hundreds were wounded. March 4, 1946, was designated a day of mourning. The prime minister was forced to resign, and Ismail Sidki, "the strong man of Egyptian politics," was brought back.

The next months witnessed the arrest of hundreds of journalists, intellectuals, political and labor leaders, students, and professionals on charges of communist activity. According to Jean and Simone Lacouture, analysts of the period, "Ismail Sidki applied the term 'communist' to anyone he felt was too liberal or radical or who criticized the status quo and wanted to change. The Sidki-Bevin treaty that he negotiated with the British was strongly criticized by many Egyptians, because it did not achieve what all were hoping for—full independence—and by the end of 1946 Sidki was ultimately forced to resign."[11]

While these events fanned social unrest, the more conservative voice of Abdu filters through the editorials of *Bint al-Nil*:

> I don't, however, think that our active women should be asking for equality because this will not serve the purpose of our movement. Equality will not help the Egyptian woman. What we should be pursuing are our rights. Equality will only deprive us of many privileges we presently enjoy as well as burden us, as women, especially when we take our sensitive and flexible nature into consideration. To me equality will only mean that women lose much of the exceptional treatment they enjoy under the present circumstances. Nature has created a distinction between men and women which is difficult to negate. Women were created most importantly of all to bear children. If we equate her with men we would be liberating her from her natural responsibilities. This role that nature has cast women in makes equality between men and women not feasible. The religious laws [Shari'a] were imposed on men for the sake of women. They were created to guard women and their rights before and after divorce; so how can we ask for equality when all religions have differentiated between the sexes. Socially and biologically she needs special treatment. Instead of asking for equality, we should be asking for a change in the legislation that has been unfair to women.[12]

> Our nation is an orphan; one that does not know where to turn. The political parties of this nation are constantly at odds. It is not the objective of this journal in any way to take part in these discussions: we only ask to know the reasons behind such controversy. We are not a politically oriented group but we do have husbands and children in this nation and therefore seek to understand it better. Our leaders draw their support, prestige and power from the people and so they owe them an explanation of what is happening and must also give them reassurance and security. We as mothers and wives must perform our duties before we can ask for our rights. Some of us can offer our leaders advice and assistance to help them solve the problems which have been partly complicated because men alone were left to solve them. A measure of self-denial and dedication is needed. It is the duty of every mother, wife and daughter to call for better understanding and a spirit of love to prevail between our leaders. The mission of women in general is to sow a spirit of love and understanding as well as a proclamation of noble emotions among both young and old alike.

> If our leaders do not pay any attention to us then this means that

they are abusing us and therefore they do not deserve to represent us. Who knows, perhaps prosperity will come at the hands of those who wear bracelets.[13]

In April 1946, Doria accepted an invitation from Luly Abu al-Huda—daughter of the former prime minister of Jordan, graduate of Oxford, and currently the president of the Society for Women's Solidarity in Palestine—to come to Jerusalem for a three-day visit to deliver a series of lectures on the Egyptian woman. Doria had met this young woman at Oxford in 1939, while Doria was completing her research at the Bodleian Library for her thesis. Luly had not married and had been working in Jerusalem with Hind al-Hussayni, the daughter of Amin al-Hussayni, the mufti of Palestine. "I liked the cities of Jerusalem (and Bethlehem)," Doria was to record in her memoirs, "although the large scale Jewish infiltration had already devastated much of Palestine." For the first time in her life, Doria was asked to deliver her public lectures in Arabic, and she was very apprehensive: "I had never before lectured in the Arabic language. All my education had been in French! To my great surprise I got along very well and was not too handicapped by the language. This event encouraged me!"

She was also very impressed by what she experienced in Palestine and, upon her return to Cairo, wrote an editorial for *Bint al-Nil*, in which she lauded the role that Luly Abu al-Huda and other educated women were playing in the social and political affairs of their country:

They are always right beside the men of Palestine during troubled times. This is a true reflection of the strength of the women's movement in Palestine. These are women who helped and supported not just Arab women from Palestine, but Arab women everywhere. They are a powerful force in Palestine and an emblem for true nationalism for all women. In every town and village there is a leader to be found heading the women's movement. She is usually helped by the local school teachers and headmistresses who are all affiliated with the Society for Women's Solidarity. It is not a contrived movement since women there read as much as men do. Knowledge to them is something sacred. No wonder this land is the cradle of science and the origin of the spiritual ideas that drive the world today. I was surprised that the majority of those attending my lecture were veiled women. I was impressed by the Palestinians' pride. I didn't see a single beggar on the village street and I was impressed by the cleanliness and orderliness of the streets and houses. It touched me that the housewives paid such attention to their homes in Palestine. I really like Palestine and as time goes by, my feelings become stronger because these people have given the world a good image of the Arabs! I am sure that no westerner or invader can belittle the efforts of these people.[14]

As we read this editorial today, after years of devastating wars in that country, we cannot but be saddened by the irony. Doria was a witness to a proud and dignified people only eighteen months before the United Nations partitioned their land and the Israeli militia inflicted upon them a humiliating defeat.

So impressed was she by her experience that after her return from Palestine her editorials focused more on the broader political upheavals such as the Egyptian demand for the evacuation of foreign troops. In July 1946 *Bint al-Nil* writes:

It is the wish of every citizen these days to see the evacuation of enemy forces from our land. It will require sacrifice no matter what the cost. The women of Egypt share equally with men in knowing the rights of their country. The other evacuation I am calling for is a necessary companion to political independence. I am calling for the evacuation of poverty, sickness and ignorance. We women are in a position to contribute to the creation of a modern Egypt; to the remedy of Egypt's three problems by making the poor productive, the sick well and the ignorant aware. You, my lady, in your household, in your neighborhood, in your village, are able to participate in building a new generation. You have a responsibility which is greater than that of the government. One should not deal with poverty out of charity. In giving we should not encourage laziness but offer work opportunities. I am calling upon all female citizens to reflect upon the matter with me. Here in *Bint al-Nil* I am willing to publish the opinions and suggestions that any reader wishes to send. I am directing this invitation to all those who wish to see our nation independent from these problems.[15]

As *Bint al-Nil* became more successful, the Zaidan brothers of Dar al-Hilal,[16] the oldest and most powerful publishing house in Egypt, approached Doria with a proposal to buy her out. They offered her a share in the income as well as the position of editor-in-chief: "But I refused. It was not the money for its own sake, but what that money could do. All my life I have never had the slightest interest in money but the large income enabled me to cope with the material difficulties. With the income and control of *Bint al-Nil* I could continue my fight. I wanted to put my own ideas into the magazine according to my own ideals and not what I would be ordered to put in it if I had sold it." The publishing firm persisted, "threatening me with the challenge that if I continued to refuse, they'd fight me in the market, hinting that I would never be able to compete with them." Doria's success in launching her own feminist magazine also helped her gain editorial autonomy of *La Femme Nouvelle*. With these two magazines under her control, she would be able to communicate her own ideological message to her readers.

* * *

Princess Chevikar's death in early February 1947 placed the future of *La Femme Nouvelle* in question. The internal struggle that ensued precipitated Doria into action, enabling her to manipulate the scene to her advantage and gain ultimate control. Princess Faiza, Faruq's sister, replaced Chevikar as the president of La Femme Nouvelle Association. Doria records:

> The ladies of the committee felt this would be my downfall. They tried to abolish the magazine. I was very upset because the magazine was like my own child. But I was not in a position to do anything! Faiza was young, alert and had a strong personality. The ladies rushed to her side and I remained in the corner, silent. I always felt uncomfortable in the presence of so many ladies all talking at once. Faiza was also feeling overpowered but as she was surrounded we could not exchange sympathetic glances. Princess Aisha, Faiza's cousin and a great friend of mine, came in and stood near me. I told her that the ladies wanted to abolish the magazine and this had to be brought to Faiza's attention now or never. Aisha spoke up, "I hear, your Highness, that the magazine is being stopped!" Faiza responded: "What a pity! It is such a beautiful magazine and so essential for the publicity of our Association. We must do something about it!" Hidayat Barakat, one of the ladies of the committee and general secretary of the association retorted: "We can't continue because the costs are so enormous." As I was not in charge of the accounts nor informed about expenses I was amazed, because I knew that Chevikar's husband and his entourage had made a profit from it. If the ladies did not interfere with its production, the magazine would pay for itself. I turned to Aisha and said: "If I have complete responsibility it will cost the association nothing!" Aisha asked if I were ready to assume the costs of the license and everything else? "Yes!" Aisha presented the idea to Faiza who turned to me and asked if I were ready to do this. "Yes!" They had been hoist by their own petard. Their machinations had been turned into a triumph for me. After the meeting one of the ladies asked me for a ride home and while we were driving she turned to me and said: "Doria, you are crazy to accept such a responsibility." "Whenever I do something interesting people say that I am crazy!" The ladies immediately started their intrigues and I learned that Faruq had ordered the magazine to be continued under the aegis of La Femme Nouvelle Association. But it was too late! The license had been delivered to me!

La Femme Nouvelle was officially transferred to the *Bint al-Nil* office, and over the ensuing years under the guidance of "professional journalists rather than amateurs," it earned a national and international reputation as a cultural and literary magazine of high quality. The price of *La Femme Nouvelle* was initially twenty-five piasters. Beginning with the enlarged and more luxurious production of the Arabesque edition of 1949, the price doubled to fifty piasters, restricting readership to the more affluent French speaking elite of Egypt and the Middle East. All income after expenses went to the support of the activities of La Femme Nouvelle Association: "I wanted to give *La Femme Nouvelle* a special character, an artistic focus. Each edition would concentrate on some aspect of Egyptian heritage—an expression of Egypt's artistic creativity!"

The first issue published under Doria's license and Princess Faiza's patronage appeared in December 1947. The foreword—appearing under the signature of Her Royal Highness Princess Faiza, patroness of *La Femme Nouvelle*, but most probably written by Doria—signaled a new departure: "At such an interesting period as our own in which the most diverse spirits tend to come together and establish understanding, I wanted a review capable of reflecting our state of mind, and of putting us in touch with the rest of the world. A review which would be the mirror of our present progress, and the echo of a very old civilization which is being reborn and which will never die."[17]

This analogy between the rebirth of a civilization and the emergence of *La Femme Nouvelle* resonates throughout Doria's editorials and in many ways reflects her own self-image:

For us who have struggled to create and to safeguard *La Femme Nouvelle* this is a moving day, the day on which she is born again, beautiful, pure, confident. She returns from far away but she goes forward surely, rich in the beauty of her past!! The repository of so many deeds and so much glory, in the very heart of space and time she has her place. Charged with a mission, it is important to us that she reflect a true image of Egypt, of the whole Orient. Charged with a message, it is important that she convey our love of humanity. *La Femme Nouvelle* reappears today, as if resurrected, with a great role to play—that of reflecting our present renaissance, of putting us in touch with other countries, and thus serving as a bond between ourselves and the rest of the world. In this way the West will know Egypt in her reality, with her varied aspects, her mysteries, her traditions, her manners and customs. Up till now, almost all the works produced on Egypt are in foreign languages, and written by foreigners, either passing through or living in Egypt. This was Egypt seen from the "outside," as one might say. But with *La Femme Nouvelle* we offer a description of our Egypt from what may be called the "inside." We tell you about her as we would tell you about our mother whose arms have cradled us. *La Femme Nouvelle* will reveal to us what remains of our past riches. I do not refer only to antiquities and material riches, but to those manifold immaterial treasures, to the many moral values, which are passed on in the hearts of successive generations. *La Femme Nouvelle* will unearth and study and reveal these innumerable legacies of the past. And all this, fused with the contributions of other nations, will produce the most original effects, with the subtle gradations of the diverse hues of its local color.[18]

Bint al-Nil and *La Femme Nouvelle* not only epitomize Doria's attempt to fashion a new image of and for the Egyptian and Arab woman during the critical postwar period; they also reveal how the aesthetic and the activist, those dual and competing strands to her life, are woven more intimately and profoundly into her experience as she seeks to discover her destiny. If *La Femme Nouvelle* was Doria's aesthetic/cultural voice turned outward to the Occident with the goal "of conveying the true image of Egyptian greatness," then *Bint al-Nil* was Doria's activist/feminist voice turned inward to the Egyptian and Arab women of the nascent middle-class with the aim of "awakening woman's consciousness to her basic rights and responsibilities." Both magazines centered around the construction of identity, whether cultural or sexual, evincing not only Doria's personal struggles but also her disquiet over the general debate in society at large between pan-Islamists and Egyptianists as to the more appropriate ideology for the political future of Egypt.

Through the pages of *La Femme Nouvelle* Doria addressed the West, but also the foreign, French-speaking, native elite, whose negative and stereotyped image of Egypt and Egyptian women she wanted to change. The metaphors she used to describe the New Woman is that of message and messenger, bond and bridge: "Our readers will be, so to speak, members of a grand family, that of the New Woman, the one who works without respite. The one who has no other goal but the continued progress of the oriental woman. She will be this messenger directing herself toward the West and will make it hear her voice. In one immense stride, she will throw a magnificent bridge between the East and the West":[19]

The New Woman is a message, an unusual message arising from the distant mists of history and advancing into the future; a message that reveals hidden treasures and relieves Egypt from the burden of so many secrets that she alone has borne for six thousand years! a message that probes freely into the depths of time; a message of those endless and innumerable unknown riches, of hidden treasures. The New Woman is a message of an art that gives life to stone and instills life into the inert. But she is also a messenger that reveals the changing aspect of Egypt and its renaissance.[20]

Doria argued that East and West are not hermetically sealed entities but, on the contrary, act to complete one another, and the new woman enriches herself not only with her own past but with her manifold relations with other civilizations, especially French civilization: "There was a time when East and West were two inscrutable worlds, two irreconcilable monads evolving along two parallel roads and never meeting. Through space and time, various civilizations shake hands, understand one another, unite and complete one another. This edition essentially bears witness to this reconciliation, to this rapprochement, often unexpected, and yet so harmonious. *La Femme Nouvelle* will serve as a bond between the intellectual and artistic life of Egypt and the west."[21]

By focusing on Egyptian culture, Doria was also depicting the renaissance of Egypt. Through its aesthetic heritage, its poetry, painting, theater, and music, Doria was also trying to reveal Egypt from the inside, with all its hidden traditions, manners, and customs. *La Femme Nouvelle* reveals the East as it is with its incomparable past. Through her editorials, one feels she is expressing something about her own self-image:

Like Spring, the new woman is a beginning. Her structure is undetermined, undefined; however she is rich with this indeterminateness, this indefiniteness. She is still in the pure form which is continually searching for her substance before reaching any stability or firmness. Like spring she is enthusiastic. Always ready to start forward afresh. She knows that she can overcome any difficulty. You must only have the will and be determined on something. Kant was right when he said that the power of the will is the essence of the human being. *La Femme Nouvelle* rejects the word impossible. It is essential that this impetus or dash remains. It is essential that *La Femme Nouvelle* always be a beginning, always advancing and improving. It is essential that every issue be a new discovery, each step a step forward. Avoid old mistakes and past errors.[22]

In contrast to *La Femme Nouvelle*, *Bint al-Nil* had another focus and objective. Doria wanted to wake up educated men and women to their duty and responsibilities in solving the nation's problems: "I was dealing with problems very close to the Egyptian woman's essential existence." The letters of her readers started to "flow toward me by the hundreds, as if by the effect of immanent justice, reassuring me. Indissoluble links already united us. These women writing to me about the problems that tormented them, opened up their hearts and as I read their letters I was filled with the most profound emotion." She used one letter as a basis for an editorial that comments on how outmoded methods of bringing up children create certain complexes:

> One of our Palestinian readers, not yet twenty years old and from a privileged family, who experiences no financial problems, wrote that she suffered from deep depression and other emotional problems. I think this letter is representative of the great number of very sad letters that I receive in *Bint al-Nil* and is a reflection of the situation today of many young women in our households in Egypt and in the Arab East. The psychological problems that are the topic of this article have their origins in the way we bring up our children, making our children fear us by shouting and beating them. This only serves to instill complexes that increase as they grow older. Quarreling parents and family breakdowns also cause psychological problems. These psychological problems may be sexual in origin and may only require advice whether medical or otherwise. They may be rooted in the milieu in which the young girl finds herself. Some of the richest and grandest houses are really graves for souls that do not know how to remedy their problems. There are probably other sources for these problems but in the case of our young reader, I think that her country's political situation contributes to her problems. She and her peers are facing a situation of continuous strife that stand between them and their well-being.[23]

In response to these problems "facing our youth which can be averted if we rear our children in a way which is different to that in which we were raised," Doria founded a magazine which she named *al-Katkout*, "whose aim was to educate while being amusing. It would be especially helpful for mothers with small children. We should not force a sad heritage on posterity."

Doria practiced her own advice and, despite a very busy professional life, made it a point to lunch at home every day with her husband and children. For the daughters, this time when their mother came home was one of their fondest memories of early childhood. As Jehane recalls:

> We didn't see her all that much in those early years. The happiest moment of the day was when she came home in the mid afternoon. I would look forward every day to three or three thirty and we would rush to see her. It was a very special time. Regularly, every day! I remember once at school (I always used to be first or second in class), and I was fifth. I was in tears when I came home with my report card and told Mummy that I was fifth. She took me in her arms and hugged me and said: "It doesn't matter at all. You do your best and these things still happen." She was always very, very affectionate with us. When Aziza was growing up, she

would go to Mummy's bed in the morning and put her head in her lap and Mummy would stroke Aziza's hair. I would follow and both of us would sit near her on her bed and she would talk to us. All through our growing up she was always very tender with us.[24]

Doria's older daughter, Aziza, describes the bond she knew with her mother:

She wasn't what you would describe as a typical mother, in the Western sense, who would sit down and help with the homework or play games with us. I don't remember her ever playing games. However I remember more vividly her sitting down and talking things over with me. Once we had someone working for us whom I didn't like. She was not our governess but someone who took care of us and I was afraid of this person. My mother would sit down with me and we'd discuss why I was worried or why I was afraid and she would alleviate my anxiety. I felt her absence most markedly during the summer holidays when we were sent off to Alexandria to one of my aunts where we would spend two or three months. It was wonderful whenever my parents came up for a weekend or spent one or two days with us. It was the highlight of the summer. I missed her presence. This was also true for my father. They were both away a lot as we were growing up.

As Doria became more involved with her publications and Nour with his law practice, there was always an array of guests for lunch or dinner. Aziza comments: "My mother and father knew a lot of people, journalists, publishers, lawyers, you know, people who were active in the politics of the country at the time. Many of them came home for lunch. So it was a very stimulating setting for us and, after all, it was their life."[25]

Her continued close association with Princess Faiza ("with whom I shared a common enemy, the King!") also increased public criticism among Egyptian journalists. The princess and her Turkish husband, Bulent Muhammad Ali Raouf, were frequent dinner guests at the Ragai home, where the daughters recall "being annoyed at having our noses pinched every time Faiza came to visit, although she thought it was great fun." This palace connection gave Doria "all the news before the other journalists, which made them jealous. So a general newspaper attack was launched against me. She is a snob! She is too sophisticated! She looks more like a mannequin than she does a businesswoman! Rumors were also spreading to harm my private life. What could I do? Nothing! Wait! I decided not to answer any attack, written or otherwise!"

Doria now divided her time and energies between her new career and the joys of motherhood: "My daughter, Aziza, was going to kindergarten. Jehane was just beginning to walk. I was happy! I was reliving my own childhood."

However, as she began to devote more and more of her time to the publication and promotion of her two magazines, she spent less and less time at home, relying on Mme. Marie to care for the children and a domestic servant and cook to run the household. Her mornings were filled with editorial meetings and planning her publications, while Nour was busy with his law practice and teaching. Their evenings would be spent at the Automobile Club until, finding the atmosphere there increasingly distasteful, Doria gradually stopped going: "Intrigues were instigated by my enemies concerning my husband's involvement with other women. It was haunting me, obsessing my heart, creating an uneasiness and anxiety. The beginnings of an estrangement."

*　*　*

By the end of 1947, two devastating national disasters had occurred that had profound repercussions on Egyptian political life and helped push Doria closer to defining her future mission. In September, a cholera epidemic broke out in Sharqiya province in lower Egypt, taking the lives of tens of thousands of Egyptians over the next several months. As during the malaria epidemic of 1944, when the country had faced another major crisis, the elite women responded to their country's call when the Ministry of Health asked the women of the Mabarra Muhammad Ali and Red Crescent societies to mobilize their resources and establish vaccine centers throughout lower and upper Egypt. Their efforts contributed in no small way to helping to bring cholera under control within the next few months. In response to this epidemic and the increased demands for more health and social services for the impoverished masses, political leaders were forced to place public health reform on the top of their national agenda.[26]

On November 29, 1947, when cholera was still threatening to run out of control, a second and more politically dangerous crisis arose. The United Nations passed a resolution prescribing the partition of Palestine into a Jewish and an Arab state. With Egypt as a founding member of the Arab League, the Egyptian delegation voted against the UN resolution, and thus the Egyptian government became committed to participate in any collective Arab action against implementation of the resolution in Palestine. The British, who had been governing Palestine under a League of Nations mandate since 1923, refused to supervise its implementation, stating that their troops (the only forces capable of maintaining peace) would evacuate the country on May 15, 1948. In fact, the repercussions of the *nakba* (catastrophe), as most Arabs have defined this event, are still reverberating throughout the Middle East, nearly fifty years later, in the tragedy of the Gulf War, the opening of an Arab-Israeli Peace Conference, and the signing of a PLO-Israeli accord bear witness.

The day after the United Nations resolution was announced, the Arabs launched a guerrilla war, inaugurating a period of political unrest and violence that has endured throughout Palestine and the region for nearly five decades. Repudiating the international resolution, the Arabs rejected what they regarded as an amputation of their territory and a confirmation that they were being sacrificed to a project of colonization. From their point of view, a foreign colony had succeeded in seizing part of their territory and driving out its native Arab inhabitants—and this with the support of the entire Western world led by the United States and the Soviet Union.

It was during this volatile historical moment that a chance encounter with Huda Sha'rawi finally pointed the way for Doria. Although effectively distanced from her benefactress since her return from the Sorbonne, Doria nevertheless respected and admired Huda Hanum Sha'rawi as the symbol par excellence of the protective mother and inspiring leader: "We met quite accidentally at Groppi's.[27] I spontaneously ran up to greet her. She was accompanied by her *fille spirituelle,* who was not at all pleased by the warm welcome I received and turned her back on me. But Huda Hanum greeted me with a big smile and asked how I was keeping. 'Why haven't you been to see me, Doria?' 'I didn't want to disturb you.' 'You know that you are always welcome. I receive guests every Tuesday. Please come and see me.'"

Doria was elated to feel on good terms once again with "this great lady" and promised to visit her the following week. However, she never did, because Huda Sha'rawi died a few days later from heart failure. According to her granddaughter, "The major catalyst to my grandmother's death was her shock and disillusion over the United Nations resolution to partition Palestine. She had devoted the last decade of her life struggling for the Palestinian cause and this resolution broke her heart."[28]

Two very remarkable women—each of whom had played a crucial, although very different, role in shaping Doria's ardent desire to find a niche for herself in the public domain—had now passed away. Chevikar's death in early February at the age of seventy-one had catapulted Doria into taking over the publication of *La Femme Nouvelle.* Huda Sha'rawi's sudden heart failure at the age of sixty-eight on the eve of Doria's birthday was coincidence enough to convince Doria that destiny had finally charted the direction of her mission. With the death of Huda Sha'rawi, one chapter in the history of the women's movement in Egypt came to a close. Another was about to begin. Alive, Huda Sha'rawi had enabled Doria to fulfill her burning ambition to study at the Sorbonne. Her death spurred Doria on to assume the mantle of leadership in the Egyptian woman's struggle to obtain full political rights.

It is customary in Egypt to extend condolences to the relatives and friends of the deceased on the fortieth day after the death. Given her fame, Huda Sha'rawi was publicly honored at a ceremony held at the meeting hall of the

Egyptian Feminist Union in January 1948. Along with a number of other tes-
timonials by prominent Egyptian men and women, Doria delivered a personal
and touching eulogy to Huda Sha'rawi, which not only paid homage to the
leader of the generation who, twenty years earlier, had listened to her ardent
dreams and responded, but also left the audience with little doubt about her
own future intentions: "All of us are a part of her. Our struggle would have
faded away and its effect would have been lost if it hadn't been for her inspiration, her light. We were in the harem until our leader took us out of its darkness! And here we are, pioneers, surrendering to God's will, counting her glorious actions and following her footsteps."[29]

That Doria was invited to speak at this august occasion and that she was
introduced by the honorific title *Hanum*—a Turkish word used to express po-
liteness and deference to a lady of society and to acknowledge her membership among the elite in society—suggests that despite her alienation from the
Egyptian Feminist Union, she had achieved a certain social status in society. In
her talk, Doria served notice that she intended to take up the challenge and
continue the struggle. She admonished her listeners:

> Weeping over her loss will not lift the sadness from our hearts. Tears
> will not relieve our great sorrow nor will our pain be great enough to
> console us. This fortieth day of mourning is weighed down by the re-
> membrance of everything that Huda Sha'rawi did on behalf of Egyp-
> tians and all eastern peoples. Remember her, because remembrance is
> useful for believers, and because she fought to create a proud and culti-
> vated society. Remember her until you understand something of what
> you owe her. Because she lived for your sakes and she died for you. And
> I shall see to it that our mourning shall continue what she started. It is
> not sufficient to cry over Huda Sha'rawi because she transcends tears.
> So you must support her fine memory by your struggle. If a woman can
> read or write; or if she goes to the university; or if she stands at the bar;
> or if she goes down to the fields; or if she enters parliament one day—all
> this will serve Huda Sha'rawi's memory much better than our tears or
> our wailing over her death.[30]

8

Carrying the Banner (1948–1950)

Turmoil was raging in my country. Lies had replaced truth. I was revolted. It must change! Before it is too late! But how to attack mountains? Perhaps displace mountains? One had to find the stand from where to begin. It had to begin at the beginning: The Woman! A nation cannot be liberated whether internally or externally while its women are enchained. In the very midst of this earthquake, in this crazy desire for Liberty for a whole nation my feminist movement was born.

When Egyptian troops together with the troops of other Arab states marched into Palestine on May 15, 1948, to forestall the establishment of an Israeli state, a spate of violence erupted throughout Cairo, aiming at nearly everyone—the government, the foreigners, the Jews, and the British. At the outbreak of this, the first of several Arab-Israeli wars, the following editorial appeared in *Bint al-Nil* under the signature of Doria Shafik:

A bloody war instigated by Zionism has shed the blood of the innocent and thus defamed the sanctity of this land. We never heard of a religion becoming a state. While the whole world asserts that religion is for God and the nation is for all, we hear of a religion becoming a state. The most amazing thing about this war inflicted by the Jews on Muslim and Christian Palestinians was that the Jews called for the formation of the Israeli nation forgetting, in their call, that they enjoy their life, not because they are Jews, but because they are citizens of other countries. The screams of American Jews and those of the communist countries overlook the fact that these Jews have other nationalities. What country permits its citizens to create another state? It is no doubt a competition between the Americans and the Soviets. The war in Palestine is neither political nor religious, but a type of Russian and American colonialism to further their own separate aspirations in the Arab world.[1]

This editorial makes no attempt to analyze the roots of Zionism or the persecution of Jews by the Nazis and the outrages of the holocaust that provided Zionists with their moral arguments for a Jewish homeland. Although a ceasefire and a series of armistices were concluded between Israel and various Arab states by March 1949, the masses remained oppressed by feelings of disillusion, humiliation, frustration, and anger. "The Arabs, full of bitterness and rancour, refused to recognize the European *Diktat*, this colonial amputation, which had been imposed on them. Hostilities were only broken off because of their own impotence, which they hoped would be temporary. One way or another the war would go on."[2]

Looking back upon this period, Doria wrote that "the true misfortunes of Egypt began during the Palestinian war, when Egypt was deceived at the highest level by her king in whom the country had such hopes. It was a cruel betrayal at the most sensitive moment of its history, when the country needed a leader worthy of the name. Egypt's fate was decided in the royal gardens of Inchass during one of Faruq's promenades with his private counselor, Karim Thabet, who encouraged the king to enter the war, arguing that once won, Faruq would become the uncontested leader of the Arabs, the new Khalifa."[3] The king, involved in a corrupt arms racket with the chief of staff of the Frontier Corps, authorized the purchase of defective weapons and munitions left behind by the various armies that had fought in the Western Desert and resold them to the Egyptian army at exorbitant prices. Thus equipped and badly officered, the Egyptian army was driven back by the Israelis, until the ceasefire in January 1949: "However, His Majesty, never tiring of devising vainglorious ploys, made our vanquished army march in the streets of Cairo amid cries of victory. Not understanding anything, the people applauded."

Faruq, who had hoped to restore his prestige through a victorious war, was dealt another blow when his wife, the popular Queen Farida, who had progressively withdrawn from public life, sought a divorce: "Faruq seemed to take pleasure in ignoring, ridiculing, humiliating and torturing his wife. At one of the sumptuous receptions of Princess Chevikar, the Queen as usual was not invited. The King's most recent mistress—they were supplanted at a dizzying speed—was seated in the place of honor, between the king and Chevikar. The Prime Minister, Nuqrashi Pasha, was so offended that he considered resigning, but changed his mind, no doubt feeling his patriotic duty was to save what could still be saved."

Farida had given birth to three girls: Ferial, Fawzia (named after the king's favorite sister, who married the shah), and Fadia. Not having produced a male heir undoubtedly contributed to the indignities she suffered during her last years with Faruq. For Doria, the divorce of Queen Farida not only marked the beginning of the end of Faruq's irreparable downfall;[4] it was also a clarion call to the Egyptian woman:

> I speak not of his abdication as King, but of a more serious abdication: that of turning his back on all moral values, even of renouncing his own value as a human being. In exchange for her liberty, Farida gave up a throne, one of the supreme gestures in the history of the Egyptian woman. A Queen descending the stairs of the palace of her own free will, leaving behind the honors, grandeur and even her three daughters, to go and find, under her paternal roof, the most beautiful of all thrones: that of liberty. For the Egyptian woman the hour to leave her prison had struck. The moment had come to break her chains. Awakened from a long sleep, the Egyptian woman was going to rise up in one bound, to rush toward her destiny and be engaged totally in an implacable combat.

The year 1948 not only marked the beginnings of "the true misfortunes of Egypt," but it also witnessed the coming of age of a whole new generation of Egyptians. Extremist political groups became increasingly more visible and more vocal as they organized and prepared their members for the "day of reckoning." The obvious corruption and inadequacy of the monarchical system under Faruq provided the impetus. On the extreme right was the voice of the Muslim Brotherhood, whose rallying cry was that Western imperialism was the source of the country's political, economic, and social problems. The Brothers accused the imperialists of fighting a war against Islam through the Christian missionary schools which concentrated on the education of Muslim children with the aim of implanting doubt, undermining their faith and leaving them neither Christian or Muslim.[5] Their only solution was a return to the Quran, Hadith, and Sunna of the Prophet Muhammad as the primary sources for the reestablishment of an Islamic system of government. The Brotherhood was popular among the masses of the lower-middle classes and by 1948 had established over two thousand branches throughout Egypt. Their anti-British resistance as well as their exemplary battle action in Palestine endowed this group with a certain militancy which found expression in a series of political assassinations on the local Egyptian scene: "Many individual combatants fought bravely, particularly the special commando units of the Muslim Brotherhood who, fighting under the banner of Islam and inspired by the call to jihad, proved to be a more fearsome enemy to the Jewish fighters than the soldiers of some Arab armies. However, two Egyptian officers, Muhammad Naguib (1901–1984) and Gamal Abdul Nasser (1918–1970), acquitted themselves well in the fighting and would soon be heard from again."[6]

On the left were the voices of the ideologically splintered progressive groups, which, although outlawed, were attracting an increasing number of workers as well as young men and women students from the emerging middle class. Preeminent among these groups was the Egyptian National Liberation Movement, a clandestine communist organization founded and led by the charismatic Henri Curiel. National Liberation was an original contribution from Henri Curiel. He had assessed the feeling of national humiliation felt by all Egyptians at the time of the dictate imposed on King Faruq under threat of British guns. He was in Cairo when thousands of demonstrators had chanted Rommel's name in the streets. Although the son of a rich Jewish banker, Curiel understood the Egyptian feeling of betrayal during the 1948 Arab-Israeli war and, unlike so many others, did not sympathize with Zionism nor flee the country. Rather, he was deported by the Egyptian government in the summer of 1950 for his communist activities.[7] For this group, the anti-capitalist struggle in Egypt was not a class struggle but a mobilizing of the radical forces within all classes to join the national struggle against the British.

Although consciously awakened to the broader struggle for national liberation and openly critical of the corruption and social injustice within society, Doria was never sympathetic to the radical ideologies or violent tactics of either the Muslim Brothers or the Communists. Neither were these groups very tolerant of her friendship with Princess Faiza, her fashionable appearance and life-style, her French poetics, or her liberal humanist philosophy. Fundamentalists chastised her for being "too secular and Western" in her interpretation of Islam, while progressives criticized her for being too "bourgeois to be taken seriously." But Doria took herself seriously and began to channel her own deep impulse toward liberation into the fight for women's rights: "For a true liberation of Egypt to occur it would be necessary to begin freeing the Egyptian woman from the tyranny of outmoded traditions and unjust social and economic conditions that were oppressing the majority of women. A country cannot be free if its women are not. The only solution was to build up a feminist movement to demand full political rights for women."

*   *   *

Huda Sha'rawi may have been her inspiration, but it was those "hundreds of letters that I received from my readers, that brought me into direct contact with the unimaginable problems and anguish present within the Egyptian family. Every letter exposed with bitterness the ravages created in their homes by polygamy and unilateral divorce by the husband." She replied to many of these letters in her column, "Let *Bint al-Nil* Solve Your Problems." The more intimate letters she answered personally, and the most tragic cases she invited to her office, which she kept open every Friday especially to receive the women and discuss their problems privately.

Through her employment bureau and network of friends, Doria found work for many, but soon her office was flooded not only "with the destitute seeking financial aid, but also many young men and women students who came to me as an elder sister brandishing their diplomas of higher studies yet unable to find jobs. I made a tremendous effort to provide what they lacked. Some needed money to enroll in school; others a suit of clothes. Each day I emptied out the contents of my purse, including the money set aside for the house, to the despair of my husband." In fact, so liberal was she in spending Nour's money that the subject became a prime source of marital squabbles: "The major arguments my parents used to have seemed to be over all the money Mummy was spending on her *Bint al-Nil* projects. My father kept opening his wallet and handing out money to such an extent, that we jokingly nicknamed him *al-mahfaza* [the wallet]."[8]

Doria soon realized that the problems of these women were too numerous to be resolved on a case-by-case basis. She had neither the time nor the money: "Moreover a solution that stopped at the economic level was not a definitive solution. It left the very essence of the trouble intact: the broken hearts of the women. And even had I been able to find an integral solution to the problems that tortured these several thousand women reading my magazine, what would the million others, about whom I was ignorant, do? I had to find a more permanent solution. Since the equilibrium and well-being of our national life takes its point of departure from family life, a more permanent solution meant establishing new legislation that would guarantee the rights of women."

Doria's growing concern with changing the laws oppressive to women coincided with a great public discussion concerning the acceptance of the New Egyptian Civil Code drafted by the illustrious Egyptian jurist Abd al-Razzaq al-Sanhuri.[9] Nour had been one of his students. Now as a professor of commercial law at the national university, Nour would have been interested in the debate and probably discussed issues with Doria. Given her own interest in reconciling Islam and modernity, it is safe to assume that this public debate supported her contention that Islam in no way opposed the recovery of women's legal and political rights.

In her view the issue of women's rights was not restricted merely to suffrage. She wanted to change the civil laws that prohibited women from running for elected office and serving as parliamentarians, as well as the Islamic personal status laws that allowed the husband unlimited polygamy, the unilateral right to repudiate his wife, and the right of child custody. She wanted to abolish *Bayt al-ta'a*[10] and requested that the measures taken by the police to enact the law also be abolished. She had taken the same liberal stance toward Islam in her doctoral thesis: "The true spirit of the Quran is absolutely against polygamy (except in extreme cases when the woman is unable to bear children or is sick). Islam allows a man to marry up to four wives. But only if he is able to treat them all equally. Since no one will ever be able to treat each with equal fairness or justice, no matter how one tries, this can only be interpreted as an injunction against polygamy."[11]

Her inquiries into how the laws could be changed revealed that two proposals, one limiting polygamy and the other curbing unilateral divorce, had been submitted by Huda Sha'rawi to parliament more than a quarter of a century earlier, "and they still lay dormant in the Egyptian parliament." She attempted to enlist the support of some of the parliamentarians to persuade them to enact laws guaranteeing women greater family security. But her efforts went unheeded. The presence of a woman in the heart of parliament, pleading her own cause, was essential: "What capable hands can rouse them out of their sleep if not those of women? What heart is more susceptible to sympathizing with the sufferings of the woman if it is not the heart of a woman. Women must not only be present when laws concerning them are legislated; they must be involved in writing them. By demanding the totality of her rights, particularly her political rights, which are the very basis of all rights, the woman could bring about fundamental changes in society."

Her desire to resuscitate a moribund movement and her own impatience with the prevailing complacency of the government towards women's rights finally galvanized Doria into action. Barely two months after her eulogy of her esteemed patroness, Doria went on the offensive not with "tears and wailing" but by boldly calling two press conferences (one delivered in French, the other in Arabic) to announce the founding of "a new movement for the complete liberation of the Egyptian woman." It was only natural that Doria would name her movement the Bint al-Nil Union. The symbol of the Nile figured in nearly every facet of her life: her first published poem was an ode to her beloved river, she lived on the Corniche al-Nil, her office was on Kasr al-Nil, and her *Bint al-Nil* magazine was rapidly gaining in reputation and popularity throughout Egypt and the Arab region: "From the beginning I belonged body and soul to Bint al-Nil Union."

Doria believed she was not creating just another women's association but renewing and invigorating the Egyptian feminist movement, which, after the death of Huda Sha'rawi, had become ineffective and inadequate. The two conferences were held at the Semiramis Hotel, prominent remnant of an earlier colonial elegance along the Nile. She opened the French press conference with a bold statement:

DS: The *sine qua non* of Egypt's liberation is women's liberation.

Q: What exactly do you mean by "women's liberation"?

DS: I mean delivering women from servitude to men!

Q: Which form of servitude?

DS: The worst! That which considers women as inferior beings.

Q: What are your means of liberating women?

DS: Primordial means—demanding full political rights for women.

Q: What does primordial mean?

DS: As long as women remain outside parliament, that is, not taking part in the legislation of the laws (men do not care about women's rights)—only women are able to understand the suffering of women.

Q: Tell us, Mme. Shafik, are you happy in your household?

DS: What we are discussing here isn't my personal life. The problem we are dealing with is the problem of all women's inviolable rights!

Q: Don't you think that active feminism will make women less feminine?

DS: Our feminism is completely feminine!

Q: Don't you think Islam is against political rights for women?

DS: Islam is innocent of such allegations. There is not one sentence in the Quran saying this. On the contrary, the true essence of Islam is equality between men and women.

Q: What is "essential equality"?

DS: The essential equality between men and women is the logical consequence of the fact that both of them are human beings, unequivocally "equal" by the very essence of their own nature: human nature.

Q: Are you a barrister?

DS: No. But I am an advocate of women's rights!

If the foreign journalists questioned her about her views on women's political rights, the Egyptian journalists concentrated on her views about polygamy: "The hall was filled with men wearing the familiar turbans of the Azharites, ninety-nine per cent of whom felt personally threatened when I asked for the suppression of polygamy. The conference began with a deafening uproar and ended in a hullabaloo, alternating between the rhythm of the Azharites shouting against my words and their applause in support of the cunning attacks of the journalists. It was literally impossible to be heard. I felt the sting of the dreadful fight that I would face over the next decade. They were terribly powerful."

Doria's press conferences were bombshells, creating a storm of protest from every quarter—criticism she interpreted as centering not so much in the movement as in herself: "People attacked my press conferences because they thought

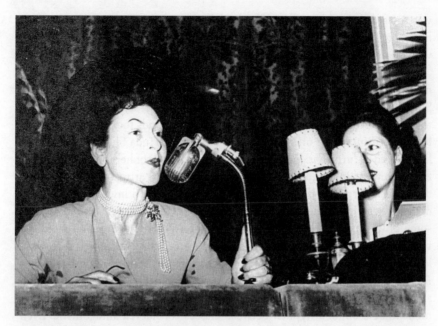

Doria Shafik and Zaynab Labib announcing the founding of the Bint al-Nil Union, at a press conference held at the Semiramis Hotel, January 1948.

I was trying to gain personal publicity. The older feminists bore me a grudge for having seized the banner of women's liberation after Huda Sha'rawi's death: 'How does this nobody, Doria Shafik, who doesn't own a single acre of land, dare pretend to supplant a millionairess?' The Islamic organizations, which persisted in upholding false interpretations of Islam, accused me of going against the teachings of the Quran. Conservatives criticized me for trying to destroy Egyptian traditions; progressives for spoiling Egypt's political life by bringing women into politics."

*   *   *

In the face of this negative reaction, how would she begin and who would respond to her call? There were an increasing number of university women convinced that the tactics of the Egyptian Feminist Union were as outdated as their goals. According to this younger, middle-class generation, the establishment of a health clinic or the distribution of charity was no longer an adequate solution to social problems, nor did equal rights mean only education. In the postwar rhetoric of a younger and more radical generation of Egyptian women, the demand for women's political rights, as well as the need to change the broader socioeconomic system which contributed to the oppression of both men and women, would become the new goals of the women's movement. It was toward this emerging middle class that Doria directed her feminist call, hoping to strike a responsive chord "especially with the youngest among them who offered a certain potential of redressing social justice."

If her movement was to be for all Egyptian women, she needed to attract members from all segments of society and to find a place for them to meet. She persuaded the daughter of Chevikar, who was then serving as president of the Red Crescent Society, to donate the necessary funds to rent the apartment below her *Bint al-Nil* office on Kasr al-Nil Street. Huda Sha'rawi's sister-in-law offered to furnish it. Surplus income from the sale of her *Bint al-Nil* magazine also went into supporting this new venture. To attract members, Doria organized a large reception at her *Bint al-Nil* office and invited several hundred women from different social backgrounds. There were ladies of society, some of whom had strong political connections, others who represented the various benevolent organizations such as La Femme Nouvelle; there were lower-class working women, some of whom Doria had helped through her *Bint al-Nil* employment office; there were the middle-class professional women and young university graduates. From Doria's perspective, "I wanted the movement to be a bond, a hyphen between classes considered antagonistic. Even our meeting was a sort of synthesis, a *sui generis* equality. Women from the lower class were flattered to associate with women of society; highly educated professional women were happy to make friendships with women from powerful families of *la crême de la crême*. In turn society women were pleased to discuss matters of mutual interest with working class women thus discovering an escape from the emptiness of their mundane world. For the first time I did not feel lost in the gaping abyss between our social classes."

To establish a strong organizational structure which could initiate and carry out a program of action, Doria believed it was necessary that she be elected president: "After all, the movement was my baby! I had thought about it, planned it and worked for it. I could best take care of it." However, she needed to convince these women that having a younger, less socially prominent woman as president was not a sign of disrespect. By promising to support their election to the executive council, Doria solicited their votes for the presidency: "It worked. I was elected for life. In turn, the strongest, most interesting women were chosen for the executive council."

Doria was able to recruit an impressive number of powerful personalities into her movement. Listed as members of the executive committee were the wives and daughters of Egypt's most wealthy and prominent men, including the daughter of the assassinated prime minister, Samiha Mahir, and the sister of the head of Egypt's Labor Party, Wasfiyya Shoukri. In addition were the names of distinguished middle-class professional women who had attained public stature through their own achievements. Women like Mufida Abdul

Rahman, the first woman to obtain a law degree. Abdul Rahman had worked with Huda Sha'rawi and later—along with Fatma Nimet Rachad, Zaynab Labib, and Ateyat Shafei—had founded the National Feminist Party. When that organization foundered she joined the Bint al-Nil Union in the late forties.[12] Zaynab Labib, the first woman to be appointed to the Ministry of Foreign Affairs, served as Doria's second-in-command, and Aida Nasrallah, an honors graduate from the Sorbonne, served as editor-in-chief of *La Femme Nouvelle*.

"Doria Shafik awakened those who were asleep," commented Mufida Abdul Rahman; "Not only did socially prominent and professional women respond to her call, but also an increasing number of young middle class university students, including members of the Egyptian Feminist Union, who were attracted by Doria's charismatic charm and energetic personality."[13] Zaynab Fuad, one of the first to join Doria and serve as her personal secretary, wrote a disgruntled letter to the niece of Huda Sha'rawi, complaining that "the [Egyptian Feminist] Union, in my opinion is on its deathbed. Ismaat Hanum [Huda Sha'rawi's daughter and president of the Union] refused to travel to the conference [of the International Alliance of Women] at the last possible moment. The rest of the members are no good at management and the president is busy with her house—I fear that this lofty edifice that your aunt built with her money, health and time until she died, will collapse. The members are useless."[14]

From the moment she announced her decision to go on the offensive in 1948, Doria dedicated herself totally to "pulling the Egyptian woman out of the quandary in which she has suffered for centuries. The attainment of total equality with men was the axis of the Egyptian woman's modern existence and admitted no concession however minimal." The issue of women and politics was always a prominent theme in Doria's writing, but in the early years, Abdu's conservative voice had kept a lid on Doria's volatile ideas. Editorials frequently appeared arguing that the lack of political awareness among the women of her society was explained by the fact that "politics was incompatible with the nature of women":

Women of our generation have as yet not learnt to take control of their lives. They are as yet not ready to enter the arena of politics. What drew my attention to this issue was our society in particular. It is rare to find a woman interested in the goings on of public life, as if Egypt's circumstances and events were issues that didn't affect the household. They are the mothers who are raising a new generation for us and preparing its men for politics or literature. I am referring to our understanding of both domestic and foreign affairs. It is rare to find women who know the names of our politicians. Moreover they don't know the politicians outside Egypt. All of this is information that one can freely obtain from the newspapers that our fathers, brothers and husbands bring home. Most women, however, only read the obituaries and the social news. When asked by their children about a matter that is of public concern they are unable to answer. Instead of making use of social gatherings to participate in serious conversation, they prefer to talk about the latest fashions and gossip. That is what our conversation is wasted on without any women benefiting. I do not ask that women work in politics but I do think that they should be aware of what goes on. We are harming our own children more than anyone if we remain incapable of informing them of the events that take place in public life. In raising our children we should have a comprehensive understanding of political events.[15]

By 1948, the message of *Bint al-Nil* had begun to change in tone and focus, a fact suggesting that Doria was starting to speak out more distinctly in her own voice, uncensored by Abdu and Nour:

Here in Egypt we [women] wage a bitter war not against gambling and alcohol [Shafik is referring to France, where a recently elected female minister of health was campaigning against alcohol consumption in that country] but in defense of the girl who wishes to enter engineering or agricultural school, an educated woman who wishes to participate in public life, one who wishes to apply the constitution and ask for her right to vote for males and one who dares to ask for a share in parliamentary seats or judicial committees. . . . Men in Egypt do not want what is best for their country. They fight us in our efforts to develop our country. At times they do this in the name of religion. We have never heard of a religion that stands between women and their right to life. At other times they say that it is in the name of tradition. What tradition stands between women and their ability to do good? . . . In fact it is the inferiority complex from which some Egyptians suffer which makes them behave in this way. They fear the day when woman holds a position of power which would enable her to ban alcohol and gambling. Gentleman make way for us and let the procession take its natural course.[16]

These two editorials, one written in 1946 and the other in 1948, disclose a definite shift in ideology from "women's nature" to "women's rights." In the latter, Doria's voice is unmistakable, and from this period onward, her editorials are manifestly political in tone and convey a more militant feminist message. She demands that Egyptian men make way for women and permit them to participate in public life, arguing that "Depriving educated women of that which illiterate men enjoy is a sin against Egypt, which will remain an undemocratic society so long as women are deprived of their full political rights.

Men who stand between women and their political rights do not love their country for they insist on depriving Egypt of the services of their women."[17] Continuing in the same vein in August of 1948, she avows: "Since the United Nations has proposed that women all over the world should be given their political rights our demand for political rights has become a non-negotiable issue. His grace, the Shaykh of Islam, was magnificent when he approved the demands of the Social and Economic Council. Islam stands with the cause of women because Islam is the religion of science, understanding, development and freedom. Thank God we have lived to see the day when the Imams of Islam have blessed our cause."[18]

She began to direct her editorials to the men of parliament, "where we had hoped our case would have been brought up, even if it came second to an issue like digging a canal in a village of Qalubiya! Isn't consideration of the destiny of one half of the population as worthy of parliament's time as the appointment of a village shaykh somewhere? Women have reached the highest positions as far as education goes but yet cannot vote like any illiterate shoemaker. What will our men in Paris say when asked about the status of Egyptian women? How would they answer such a question? Do those responsible want us to seek the help of the outside world to obtain our rights for us?"[19] A month later, she asserted: "Parliament opened its new session a few days ago. The speaker ignored the political rights of women assuming that we, the women, are mentally retarded and unfit to take part in public life. This implies that ten million Egyptians (half of the population) do not deserve to participate in civic life. Wretched are the men of Egypt who live in houses that are run by women with no brains and who do not share in public life."[20]

Her editorials continually emphasized the negative consequences to society and the family that arise when women are prevented from participating in legislating for the nation. She argued that Egypt suffered from one of the highest divorce rates in the world: "Out of the homes created at the beginning of the year, one third are destroyed by the end of the year. Accordingly our lives are constantly threatened by a word that could be spoken by an idiot or a drunkard or someone who is ignorant of social and religious manners. For this reason we initiated the Bint al-Nil Union to defend the family. For this reason we asked for the vote, to direct the course of events and of our destinies."[21] She spoke about forming a separate women's party "that can protect and defend our rights and fight for our ideals in life" and called upon the women of Egypt to join her in the struggle:

It is not the goal of women to work in politics in a country that does not have proper direction in social affairs. We need a party that will bring us together to solve the problems that responsible persons were unable to

solve fearing the criticism of reactionary elements who explain everything in terms of religion and tradition. Is it not strange that polygamy
is still a basic principle of marital life? Is it not strange that when a husband quarrels with his wife over a trivial matter, one word from the man
can dissolve any ties between them, even when they have children?
Endless is the list of social wrongs that our party should attempt to set
right. Issues concerning marriage, divorce, inheritance, education, political rights and other things that need to be supported by a party that
has the ability, knowledge and strength to fulfill its mission. Wouldn't it
be an honor if the Bint al-Nil party could do something about these
problems?[22]

We are not demanding, through the Bint al-Nil Union, to work in
politics, as this is defined by politicians and those who join political parties. We are only calling for equality in political rights. Bint al-Nil has no
political aim. But it hopes that when the woman is granted her full political rights she will use them in serving society so that the family would
be guaranteed its rights against the evils of society. There will be no
divorce without the consciousness of its consequences, or marriage for
pleasure alone; no deserted children; no ignorance at home or even at
work that would destroy a woman's health and existence. Women suffer
from these miseries. If we want to cure them we need to choose our
female representatives, or failing that, at least to vote for those males
who sympathize with our cause. We demand these just goals which are
not political.[23]

By disclaiming any pretensions to politics, Doria conveyed a very prudent and
cautious attitude, possibly to avoid any backlash in face of the anarchic political situation in Egypt. For its part, the government had resumed a repressive
campaign against all extremists with numerous arrests of suspected members
of leftist and communist organizations. Martial law was in effect, and the
Muslim Brothers had been formally banned. Although proscribed, they clandestinely agitated against the status quo, using the mosques, al-Azhar, and
the state universities to disseminate their seditious literature. Concentration
camps for the Communists and the Muslim Brothers had opened, and by the
end of 1948, within a few weeks of each other, both the prime minister and
the founder of the Muslim Brothers had been assassinated. Prime Minister
Nuqrashi, who had banned the Brotherhood on December 8, 1948, was himself assassinated three weeks later by a Muslim Brother. Within a few weeks,
Hasan al-Banna, the head of the Muslim Brothers, was himself assassinated.

However, these public disclaimers that Doria's party was not political served
only to nourish the hostile criticism coming from her left-wing opponents.
Inji Efflatoun, an ardent nationalist who was one of those educated elite young

women attracted by communism, belonged to Curiel's clandestine Egyptian National Liberation Movement during the forties and early fifties. Her comments on attempting to work with *Bint al-Nil* emphasize the differences in ideology between Doria's brand of radicalism and her own:

> After the war I tried working with the existing women's organizations except the E.F.U. They had turned into a social organization with no political activism, so I didn't even try. When the founding conference of the Women's International Democratic Federation[24] was held in Paris in 1945, these women's organizations refused to send delegates. That's when we decided to form the Young Women's League of Egyptian Universities and Institutes (Rabitat fatayat al-gami'a wal-ma'ahid al'misriya) and go to Paris. Upon our return we held a press conference at the Lycée Français to publicize the resolutions and information about the Paris Conference. A few months later, after the signing of the Sidki-Bevin agreement in 1946, the government closed down all the progressive and leftist organizations including the *Rabitat*. But they didn't close down the Egyptian Feminist Union or these other organizations. I later tried to join Doria Shafik's *Bint al-Nil* but failed because they claimed to be non-political, which meant they supported the status-quo. They were afraid of any new democratic ideas that might change their goals. It was a right wing group. When Doria Shafik learned that I was a leftist, she immediately dismissed me from the organization. She also published a declaration in *Akher Saa* and *Akhbar al-Yawm* stating that *Bint al-Nil* is fighting these destructive ideologies. So we had to keep re-creating our organization under different names. It was the height of revolutionary fervor in Egypt.[25]

Contradicting this characterization of Doria were the views of Loutfi al-Kholi, who, as a young Marxist lawyer, had worked on the *Bint al-Nil* magazine from the late forties through the early fifties. Al-Kholi recalled how he met Doria Shafik and became involved with her magazine, constructing his own analysis of Doria's evolving yet ambivalent political consciousness:

> In 1946 I joined a secret leftist organization. I was committed to political work that was opposed to the king, opposed to colonialism and my role was to air our Marxist views—to diffuse our ideologies at the university, at conferences, at public gatherings. I went to the journalists. I went to the lawyers. I joined in their discussions to present my point of view. In 1947 Doria Shafik was invited to give the main lecture to the Journalists' Syndicate and I told her that Qasim Amin was not the first man to argue for the liberation of women, but rather Tahtawi and Ali Mubarak. But it was a social point that caught her attention. I argued that there is no

liberation for the Egyptian woman without the political and social liberation of Egyptian society. She asked me to come to see her. For me,
coming from a *petit bourgeois* family, Doria represented the *haute bourgeoisie*, the aristocrat. And I went with a very hostile attitude. But it was
a nice surprise to see that this woman, whom I considered to be high
bourgeoisie, an aristocrat, a "lady of the salon," had a very warm and
deep interest in the people. And it created many contradictions within
me and even with my friends. At that time Egyptian society was very
alive with political and social contradictions, especially within the "leftist world." There were also many political trials at this time, and as a
lawyer I was interested in this, as well as in the syndicalist movement.[26]

During one of those political trials, al-Kholi caught the attention of the well-
known lawyer Maurice Arcache, who admired the young man's defense skills
and invited him to join his law firm. Through this affiliation, al-Kholi met
Arcache's daughter, Germaine, who worked as head of fashions on the *Bint
al-Nil* magazine. She arranged an interview for him with Doria that eventually led to al-Kholi's joining the *Bint al-Nil* staff: "Dr. Ibrahim Abdu was opposed to me. A complete reactionary! But he could not oppose Doria when he
felt that she wanted me to work. Neither could Nour al-Din Ragai. At that
period, Doria was under her husband's ideological influence. He dominated
her thoughts. After a while, not right away, she began to become mentally
independent of those around her. In this early period we entered into many
heated discussions at *Bint al-Nil*, and there were always two sides represented
in our discussions. The conservative or reactionary side, represented by Ibrahim
Abdu, and the progressive side, represented by leftists such as Aida Nasrallah,
Inji and me."[27]

These political currents within the administration of *Bint al-Nil* became a
bone of contention between husband and wife as Doria's ideas shifted back
and forth under the influence of both Abdu and the young al-Kholi. Nour was
caught in the middle, trying to balance his wife's tendency to go to extremes.
Over time, she assumed a more independent perspective as she became more
and more exposed to the social issues of working-class women and factory
workers through her discussions with al-Kholi.

Describing his role in Doria's politicization, al-Kholi commented: "As an
upper-class woman raised to grace the salon, Doria had a very bourgeois understanding of the rights of women. Bourgeois woman wouldn't actually be
equal to bourgeois man, but she would have the right to be educated and to
display this education in the public domain. She wanted to liberate this type
of bourgeois woman (liberate her from being the decorative object). Not all
women, but only this type. But through our discussions and her deep human-

istic feelings, she began to see a different perspective. She took an interest in a class perspective and in time *Bint al-Nil* began to focus more on the linkage between the women's issue and the social issue." [28]

* * *

Doria consciously made every effort to keep the demands for women's political rights in the forefront of people's minds: "Publicity was my primary aim. Even the attacks in the press, however personal, were helping the Bint al-Nil movement to become widely known. The propaganda made against our movement by our enemies surpassed by far what the greatest publicity agencies could do. But it wasn't a question of propaganda strictly speaking. The flagrant injustice from which the women of my country suffered and the necessity for finding a remedy was a profound truth that had to be made known externally as well as internally."

With that object in mind, Doria traveled to Zurich in the summer of 1949, "at my own expense," in order to register the Bint al-Nil Union with "the oldest and perhaps largest feminist organization in the world," referring to the International Council of Women. Founded in 1888 in Washington, D.C., the ICW is represented by an international network of national councils composed of local women's organizations. Its stated aims are "(1) to serve as a medium for consultation among women on those actions necessary to promote the welfare of mankind, the family, children and the individual; (2) to advise women of their rights and their civic, social and political responsibilities; (3) to work for the removal of all that restricts women from full participation in life; and (4) to support international peace and arbitration." But it was not the first time that an Egyptian woman had made such a move. In the early 1920s, under the sponsorship of Carrie Chapman Catt, Huda Sha'rawi traveled to Rome and aligned the Egyptian Feminist Union with the International Women's Suffrage Alliance (later renamed the International Alliance of Women). Founded in Berlin in 1904 under the inspiration of Susan B. Anthony and Carrie Chapman Catt, the AIF has as its stated aims "(1) to promote all reforms as are necessary to establish a real equality of liberties, status, and opportunities between men and women; (2) to urge women to use their rights and influence in public life to ensure the status of every individual shall be based on respect for human personality, without distinction of sex, race or creed, this being the only guarantee for individual freedom; and (3) to take part in constructive work for good understanding between nations."[29]

Doria's decision to affiliate with the ICW would involve her in the broader ideological struggle being waged between the Eastern and Western blocs beyond Egypt's frontiers. And during the late forties, the discourse that unfolded in Egypt around national liberation and women's emancipation, mirrored this cold war ideological struggle. Doria did not consider affiliating with the International Alliance of Women, primarily because the Egyptain Feminist Union was already a member and she categorically dismissed the more progressive International Women for Democratic Freedom as too communist: "These young, radical, Egyptian women were a destructive presence within the heart of my movement. With the Cold War and the infiltration of communist ideas, disorders were born in the world, in my country and in the feminist milieu, leading to total confusion." Doria rationalized her decision to join the ICW in an editorial:

> Our disaster is that the civilized world knows nothing about us and knows nothing about the position and great role of women in creating a new generation and contributing to the foundation of modern Egypt. That is why I decided to register Bint al-Nil Union with the International Council of Women and to announce to the world the relevant history of the Egyptian woman and the significant role that she plays in the life of the Nile Valley during the modern era. I do not intend to introduce a brief summary of the activities of the Egyptian woman but rather, to prove to foreigners that our civilization is a profound one, which our enemies try to deny when they claim, according to the ignorant writings of some of their authors and writers, that the Egyptian woman is still living in the harem. Theirs is an attempt to denigrate our international position by these stories about the "backwardness" of the Egyptian woman these days. It is a pity that our government does not listen to our advice. Egypt is represented at hundreds of conferences and meetings of the United Nations. But all its representatives are males, although many of them do not speak any foreign language. Consequently, many of our intellectual women are forbidden to represent Egypt only because they are females, which is a position similar to the foreigner's image of the harem. This also shows that the Egyptian woman is not up to the standard of any woman in the world and that she is unable to represent her country in any international conference. I was even told that Egypt would be represented by males in any feminist conference held by any government! I advise and keep asking the government to reconsider their position. I recommended that a group of intellectual women should accompany our delegates to participate in international conferences as their appearance in such meetings or conferences will define our country as a member of those nations who respect and know the importance of women's role in the life of nations.[30]

In Zurich, Doria met women from other countries who were also struggling for their rights, "even Swiss women did not have their political rights."

She was particularly impressed by Dr. (Mrs.) Jeanne Eder, the president of ICW, "who was the model *par excellence* of the very highly educated woman in public life, and as I came to know her, was the living example of the very high moral and cultural level that women should aspire to, particularly during moments of international crisis when feminine intuition takes on great importance." Evidently, Eder was equally impressed by Doria, for she recommended that Bint al-Nil Union be invited to form the National Council of Egyptian Women, which meant not only that Bint al-Nil Union would represent Egypt's women's organizations in the ICW organization but also assure Doria Shafik's automatic membership on the Council's executive committee. A rather successful accomplishment from her standpoint, but one that would have later complications.

* * *

From Switzerland, she traveled to Paris to meet her friend, the well-known resistance publisher Pierre Seghers, who had just published her first volume of selected poems, *La Bonne Aventure,* in his highly esteemed series Póesie.[31] Seghers founded his own publishing house during the war to support the writings of such resistance poets as Louis Aragon, Paul Eluard, Pierre Reverdy, and others who were to become among Doria's favorites. Not only did he encourage young foreign poets like Pablo Neruda, Federico García Lorca, and Elsa Triolet, but he also authored several works of his own, including poetry, prose, songs, and films. Following his death on November 4, 1987, Jean Orizet eulogized: "Poetry has lost its most fervent lover, its most active defender. . . . It is still befitting to remember that Seghers was above all the poet of abandon and passion."[32]

Shafik and Seghers had first met in Cairo after the war when Seghers had been sent by the French Ministry of Foreign Affairs to represent the writers of the resistance:

> I was told: "Go and convey to our Egyptian friends the greetings of the French poets, who conducted themselves well against the Germans." Couve de Murville, our ambassador, received me. I lectured both in Alexandria and in Cairo and it was after the occasion of my talk in Cairo, that she came up to me and we talked. She spoke impeccable French. Perfect! And we felt a certain affinity toward each other. We discovered that we had a great deal in common. Following the lecture I remember she invited me to her publishing office, showed me *La Femme Nouvelle,* and read to me some of her poems. We were truly attracted to each other. She told me that she would soon be coming to Paris and indeed, when she came a few months later, I met her and invited her to lunch. Our

friendship began from that first encounter. O Yes! Our friendship was a relationship based on poetry.[33]

If Huda Sha'rawi can be credited for encouraging and supporting Doria's feminist ardor, and Princess Chevikar for offering Doria the opportunity to channel her restless search for a mission into journalism, then Pierre Seghers must be singled out as the one person in her life who recognized, appreciated, and encouraged the soul of the poet smoldering within her. From the moment they first met in 1947, Seghers became her trusted friend, her literary critic, her publisher, but above all, her mentor within the world of modern poetry: "When she came to Paris it was not only to see me. She came for many other reasons. She was busy with her magazines, her publications, her struggle for women's rights. She was extraordinarily active. But I don't think she ever came to Paris without seeing me. And that's another thing. My domain, my sphere of activity, was within the realm of poetry and this is what brought us together, a friendship that became more and more profound."[34]

Through her friendship with Seghers, Doria was encouraged to explore, discover, and give expression to her "inner lyricism," as Seghers once described her special style:

These early poems are a beginning, an annunciation, a preface to her work. They are more radiant, more silky, more smooth than her later ones. They announce; they herald the poet. But you know it is like all the other arts. I think that I cannot say "better" because to say better presupposes that the others are not as good. At the same time I think there is a certain strength, a certain vigor, a certain severity, a certain sobriety and a certain subterranean power in her later work that surpass the first ones. This later poetry goes deeper, much deeper. It is a poetry where thought, reflection and the inner life are, they say, more evident. It is more solemn if you like. The first poetry announces, moreover, a temperament like this. It is still the beginning. But afterwards we feel this gravity, this seriousness which endures until death. From the point of view of Egyptian contemporary poetry in French, Doria Shafik is certainly the first Egyptian woman writer; but as there were not so many, this does mean a great deal. But from the general point of view, men and women together as poets, as poetry, she is a major poet, she is a great poet of Egypt. She is the origin, the profound source of the inner lyricism. She counts among the best. She is not an amateur. You have some who are dilettantes. But she is a serious one.[35]

The publication of her poetry gave her enormous satisfaction in an otherwise hectic and conflict-laden life, and she was thrilled that her work was recognized by one of France's most distinguished publishers: "This need to write poems was as necessary to me as breathing! It is true that I was alive to poetry from my first year of study in Paris—but it is only much later that I was awakened to Poetry—as an expression of the Absolute. The publication of my booklet of poems helped me to give a certain consistency to this Infinity resonating within me, and which I was unable formulate; to this grand flame, whose moving presence I felt but could never reveal."

Over the years, Seghers and Doria exchanged letters and poems—Doria often sending Seghers samples of her work, asking for his criticism, and he, in turn, sending her his published books, often inscribed with warm and affectionate dedications. Doria had begun working on a large opus which she first entitled *Christ Rouge* but later changed to *Rédemption*, metaphors chosen from those childhood memories of the stained-glass windows of the nun's schools. "You are very near to Pablo Neruda as well as to the *Epiphanies* of Henri Pichette," Seghers told her in 1956. "In this union of spontaneity and hard work, they are a lesson to all."[36]

Poetry was not a frivolous diversion for Doria. It was central to her being, and it is through her poetry that we gain an understanding of the woman herself. As Seghers commented, "She was a woman who was a poet. I don't even say that she adored poetry, she was a poet. That's all. With this zeal, passion, ardor. I believe that a man or a woman living passionately is someone who is not calm; there is this demand, this anxiety and this need which are not calm and placid. There is always this ardor, this ardor is like a fire and fire torments itself. She was like that. She was like that because she was an artist; she was a woman of thought."[37] This recognition by one of France's "poètes de l'élan et de la passion" further encouraged Doria to write and she produced a second volume, *L'Amour Perdu* (1954). Many of these poems first appeared on the pages of *La Femme Nouvelle*.[38] As much as *Bint al-Nil* served as the vehicle for her feminist ideas, *La Femme Nouvelle* was the outlet for her aesthetic temperament, as important to her existence as her quest for a political mission.

This tension between the aesthetic and activist within her own persona not only contributed to her enigmatic public image but also reinforced the conservative Muslim belief that Doria Shafik was a tool of Western society trying to undermine the society's Islamic values. Doria's modern ideas about women's role in the life of nations, as well as her own unescorted trip to Europe to affiliate with a Western feminist organization, drew harsh criticism from Islamic fundamentalists, who argued that women's participation in public life was a source of *fitna* (social anarchy).[39] In their view, her affiliation with an international women's organization was just another example of an ongoing conspiracy that combined the motivations and battle plans of colonialism with the goals of international Zionism. The Islamic family structure, the corner-stone of Muslim society, was being attacked by these forces in the guise of the women's movement. Thus any demand for women's right to political power or call for restrictions in divorce procedures and polygamy was perceived as an imperialist plot designed to undermine the Egyptian social structure.

In fact, when Doria returned from her trip to Europe, she experienced the sting of public criticism when one fundamentalist group, the Flame of Muhammad, went so far as to accuse her of being an agent for her country's enemies:

> Colonialism has many games and tricks. The Egyptian Feminist Move-ment, in the shadow of Muslim society, needed a dramatic plot that would give its required thrust and achieve its required goals in the shortest time possible. Therefore it needed a personality that would play the role of opposition in the games of agents in this sphere of women. First there was Huda Sha'rawi, who founded the Egyptian Feminist Union; then there was a second one, who established the national feminist party and renewed the ways of corruption; the third was the Bint al-Nil Party, which seeks to save the woman from the man and recapture the lost rights of women. Who is this personality playing the role of adventurer? None other than Doria Shafik. In 1949 she established the Bint al-Nil Party and within a month she traveled to England, which at the time had 85,000 troops occupying the motherland. There, she was received by heads of state and leaders. The British press received her and shed their light on her and published many talks that depict her as a fighter and the first leader in Egypt for the liberation of women from the shackles of Islam—the restraints of the veil; the scourge of divorce and polygamy. A re-porter from the *Scotsman* iterated the goals of the Bint al-Nil Party as expressed by Doria Shafik: (1) to get the vote and enter parliament; (2) to abolish polygamy; and (3) to introduce European divorce laws into Egypt! The ideas of this "suspected" woman came from colonial instiga-tion and through colonial institutions.[40]

When the Wafd, under Mustapha al-Nahas, returned to power for the third and last time in January 1950, conditions within society appeared ripe for the resurgence of decisive political activity. Martial law was lifted; opposition par-ties, now released from prisons, began to rebuild their forces; nationalist and anti-colonialist movements were reactivated; and university campuses became alive with political activity. Doria Shafik, sensing this more open political at-mosphere, embarked upon a rather ambitious social-reform program, whose prime objective was "to raise the social and cultural level of Egyptian women and prepare them for the worthy use of their rights." Doria hoped "that by rendering a great service to our country perhaps our enemies would no longer be able to level criticisms against us."

Hence, Doria and her comrades began to initiate a number of social and economic activities that were consciously planned and oriented to serve a different class of women, that is, the needy, working-class women of Cairo. Bint al-Nil Union opened a cafeteria and offered subsidized hot meals for working-class women; it established an employment bureau for university students; it established the Bint al-Nil Club, which sponsored concerts and cultural events for the more educated middle-class youth; it promoted theatrical performances for and by university students; and it organized public lectures and seminars "to raise the political awareness of women about their rights and other relevant social issues." Many of these events and activities were "infiltrated by members of the Muslim Brothers who launched carefully orchestrated strategies of disruption and chaos." Jehane talks of being taken to Bint al-Nil as a child to watch some of the plays and witnessing the collapse of the productions due to these outbursts.

However, Doria's most ambitious reform program was her struggle to eliminate illiteracy, so widespread among the adult women of Egypt at that time. Through the initiation of Taha Husayn, who was now Wafdist minister of education, the Egyptian government had enacted laws imposing compulsory education for Egyptian children of both sexes. However, nearly eighty percent of the population, particularly rural and low-income urban women, remained illiterate. Doria argued that since women are destined to become electors and deputies, they must have at least a minimal education: "The first duty of every citizen is to fight illiteracy. Wouldn't enabling our compatriots to read render a great service to Egypt? Wouldn't launching such a campaign raise the general level of the nation, thus confirming to our enemies (or so I thought), the legitimacy of our demands? What use could illiterate women make of their political rights if they were unable to read or write?"

Thus in early February of 1950, an announcement appeared in the *Le Progrés Egyptien* stating that "Doria Shafik and the members of Bint al-Nil Union were going to create the first school to combat illiteracy among the women of Egypt in the popular quarter of Bulaq."[41] Doria appealed to the minister of education for his assistance and blessing. He obligingly authorized the use of Bulaq's government elementary school during the free hours in the afternoon. It was more difficult, however, to convince the adult women of Bulaq to come to this school to learn how to read and write, and "three months elapsed without a single recruit."

To attract the women, Doria resorted to a gambit. One afternoon, after having obtained specific donations from UNICEF, Doria addressed the young girls at the school and exhorted them:

"Tell your mothers and older sisters that each one who presents herself here tomorrow at two o'clock will receive a gift of a scarf, a comb, a piece of soap and a packet of sweets." The next day at the appointed hour, as I entered the street, I saw a crowd at the entrance of the school. Nearly five hundred adult women, with their offspring, waited for their gift. The gate was broken, infants were crying and the directress was scream-ing at the top of her lungs. I climbed on a chair and addressed the veiled and shouting women telling them that each would have her gift as prom-ised but first they had to be calm. Their immediate silence and self-con-trol was the signal of an echo—within their own hearts—of my words. I had the feeling that they trusted me. We divided them into classes ac-cording to age. It was obvious that once they left with their gifts they wouldn't set foot in the place again. So I kept them a moment longer and declared that at the beginning of each session they would receive a dress that they would learn how to make themselves; that during each month, without specifying the date, a new gift would be distributed. We had no problem getting members. I also promised each one a pretty new apron if they dared to circulate without their veils. The initiates of our four classes left without their veils!

Following three months of lessons, public exams were given under the aus-pices of the Ministry of Education, and journalists were invited to participate in the graduation ceremony. According to Doria, eighty percent passed the exam—although one woman's husband divorced her for having dared to par-ticipate in this program "because, also being illiterate, he could not tolerate the idea that his wife would learn a language from which he remained a stranger."[42]

Shortly after this literacy campaign in Bulaq, Doria's photograph appeared on the front page of *Le Journal d'Egypte*, another well-known French news-paper, beneath the banner headline: "According to the terms of a well-pre-pared publicity campaign under the eye of a photographer, Dorreya Chafik has done a Good Deed, where social development is however, nothing but a social uprooting!" This was followed by a scathingly sarcastic article, presum-ably written by Ceza Nabaraoui, impugning Doria's attempts at social reform claiming that she, followed by the camera, "brought a young girl from a poor quarter back to her fashionable apartment in Cairo, had her bathed and dressed in clean clothes, and then gave her some sweets, teaching her modern ways before sending her back home. This only proves that Dorreya Chafik is moti-vated purely by the desire to gain personal publicity rather than to redress any serious social problems."[43]

Representing a different strategy of social reform during this period were the efforts of Ceza Nabaraoui, now president of the Egyptian Feminist Union, and those of Inji Efflatoun, who—along with many other leftist sympathizers—had joined a local organization known as Ansar al-Salaam, or Partisans of Peace. Concerning this latter group, Tareq al-Bishri has written: "Ansar al-Salaam also carefully affirmed that it was not a political party; that it did not adopt any political theory; that it was nothing more than a committee with one objective—to work for world peace, and to unify the struggle of the Egyptian people with the struggle for other peoples in the world to concretize peace. It supported the Communists, Wafdists, nationalists, socialists and Muslim Brothers if their programs included a call for peace, and its politics was the expulsion of colonialism from Egypt and the refusal to accept any military cooperation that would deprive Egypt of its independence or lead her to participate in a war and that its members were a mixture from all political parties."[44]

It was Ceza and Inji who established the *Lagnat al-Shabbat* (Committee of Young Women) within the Egyptian Feminist Union. This young women's auxiliary provided an umbrella for the activities of pro-communist women, who otherwise were not allowed by the government to establish an organization of their own. The incorporation of "young blood" into the EFU was a boost to a sagging organization that was rapidly losing its appeal among the younger generation of women, who were being attracted in increasing numbers to Shafik's Bint al-Nil Union. This committee concentrated its activities in the popular neighborhoods. Their idea was to organize the women in these neighborhoods around specific issues, such as health or education, in a way that would demonstrate to them their political power and raise their consciousness about the responsibilities of the state toward them and about their own rights. The ideology underlying this work was explicitly aimed at politicizing working-class women and providing them with the tools to organize themselves. The link that these progressive women were trying to establish within the popular neighborhoods was an attempt to bring urban working-class women into the changing sphere of politics. This close alliance with the Ansar al-Salaam movement, however, eventually led to Ceza's resignation from the EFU—which continually denied any involvement in politics, claiming it was simply a social organization. Neither Efflatoun nor Nabaraoui were sympathetic to Doria Shafik or the Bint al-Nil Union, and over the next several years they carried on a united and critical attack in opposition to her efforts.

Undaunted by this adverse publicity and certainly aware that literacy was not a matter of distributing scarves, soaps, and sweets among the illiterate poor, Doria and Bint al-Nil Union founded training centers in other districts of Cairo as well as the major provincial capitals "where women were taught the rudiments of reading and writing, some elementary hygiene, and a trade which they could work at in their homes to augment family income. Thirty such centers are now in operation, attended annually by several thousand women. Graduates of the literacy and training programs automatically became members of the movement. The provincial centers were run by local committees affiliated with the Bint al-Nil central committee in Cairo. Each local committee had its own elected officers and submitted an annual report of its activities and budget to Cairo. The goal is to wipe out illiteracy in a few years."[45]

Doria's growing involvement with the Bint al-Nil Union not only fomented criticism of her life-style within society but also drove a wedge between husband and wife. She felt an

> increased sense of estrangement growing between us as I detected a certain unease and a slight wave of sadness entering my home. A sort of emptiness had been dug during my absence. I had left for Europe in spite of Nour's unspoken opposition and Aziza's and Jehane's tears at the airport. They must have felt this departure would be the first of many others; that my new mission would carry me further and further away from our home. The antagonism between my obligation toward this mission and my family, to which, in principle, I had to be everything became more definitive with each passing day. For me it posed a problem not usually faced by men destined to public life: the tug-of-war between my obligations as a mother and wife, which are more uncompromising than those of a father and husband, and the new responsibilities of this mission, no less intransigent and already profoundly woven into my destiny.

This tug-of-war between her love of family and her own sense of personal mission seemed to mirror the larger political turmoil raging around her. Despite this dissonance, Doria would not abandon her feminist struggle. "Those who demand much must give much" was her personal motto.

By the end of 1950, the name of Doria Shafik began to spread throughout Egypt and the Middle East, due mostly to the growing success of her two prestigious magazines. *Bint al-Nil* was becoming more widely known, not only among women from the educated middle- and upper-classes of Cairo and the provincial towns but also among the poorer women from the popular urban quarters. Among the many millions of poor and destitute peasantry, however, the name of Doria Shafik, as well as the names of other activist women, remained virtually unknown.

That Doria personally enjoyed a national reputation at this time is beyond dispute. And it was as much her fame as her militant tone that led some of her critics to renew their accusations that she was "a foreign agent" supported by Western imperialist forces trying to undermine the values of Islam.[46] She was not only beautiful and magnetically charming, but had developed influential social and cultural contacts across both Egyptian and foreign milieux. She moved in society with unusual freedom and did not fear being photographed, for example, in the company of the great actors of the time: a photograph showing her surrounded by an all-male ensemble of Egyptian actors—Youssef Wahby, Mukhtar Othman, and Husayn Riad—at the old Cairo Opera House is now displayed in the historical museum of the new Opera House. News about her, whether critical or favorable, continuously appeared on the front pages of the major newspapers and journals and led to the construction of a controversial public image.

To her friends, who worked closely with her in the Bint al-Nil Union, "She was a famous personality, the glorious lady in Egypt. She was in all the newspapers, always looking beautiful and always invited by Princess Faiza, by the great people, by the personalities; all the embassies were very proud to receive her. She was well known among the social elite. They looked up to her as though she was Indira Gandhi. Some from the lower class knew her through the literacy schools and the middle class knew her through the magazines. She was not with any political party. She said all the rulers and all the people must work for the welfare of Egypt no matter what their party, like Bint al-Nil Union. She was Bint al-Nil!"[47]

To the majority of others, who knew her only by what they read in the newspapers, Doria was a paradox, difficult to categorize or understand. At the same time that she cultivated close ties of friendship with Princess Faiza, she was the liberal spirit, fighting openly against social injustice inflicted by the very palace regime she befriended. Her poetry was published along with those who belonged to Cairo's postwar literati,[48] yet among some intellectuals of the period, she was considered a lightweight: "Her impetuosity conveyed an impression of superficiality. She followed a lot of paths. She was like a kaleidoscope, never staying with one idea or following one direction in depth. The way she dressed was very avant-garde. Doria was too different, too elegant, too beautiful to be regarded as other than a 'lady of the salon.'"[49] This was an image that was hard to shake, and it remains to this day in the minds of many Egyptians as an accurate depiction of the "real" Doria Shafik. Her political efforts over the next seven years, however, offer contrary evidence!

9

Storming the Parliament (1951)

The freedom granted so far remained on the surface of our social structure, leaving intact the manacles which bound the hands of the Egyptian woman. No one will deliver freedom to the woman, except the woman herself. To seize this freedom by force since our polemic over the past three years has led to zero. To use violence towards those who understand only the language of violence. I decided to fight to the last drop of blood to break the chains shackling the women of my country in the invisible prison in which they continued to live; a prison, which being invisible, was all the more oppressive.

By the early fifties, political unrest in the country took a more violent turn. In addition to the protests instigated by both the left and the Muslim Brothers, there was a growing conflict between the forces of nationalism on the one hand and the British and the Egyptian crowns on the other. In fact, the two developments were connected in the sense that the radical groups rejected any compromising solution to the British occupation. Nahas reiterated his assertion that the 1936 Anglo-Egyptian Treaty had lost its validity and that the total evacuation of the British was essential to Egyptian independence. The British, on the other hand, with three times the number of troops stipulated in the treaty, intensified attacks against the various Egyptian resistance groups.

It was during this period that a more radicalized Doria Shafik emerged, voicing a more militant feminist protest than had yet been heard within the Egyptian women's movement. According to al-Kholi, "By the beginning of the early fifties she began to use a political and social language which, in my estimation, flabbergasted Nour al-Din. She began to enter the political fight. She transformed Bint al-Nil from being a movement whose only aim was to liberate bourgeois women, into a movement that related the liberation of women to the larger political struggle. From here emerged the linkage of democracy to social justice, to social development. Doria began to have a more political agenda. By degrees she became convinced, for the first time, of the idea of protesting in the streets."[1]

Three years had elapsed since the founding of her movement, and Doria was fed up and impatient with al-Nahas's inability or lack of will to fulfill the Wafd's campaign pledge. In an editorial titled "A Free Man Fulfills His Promises," Doria ironically asked her readers: "Why are we doubting the prime minister's words? Didn't His Excellency, Mustapha al-Nahas, announce last summer that the Wafd's primary goal was to grant the Egyptian woman the right to vote? Who can deny that His Excellency is a man of principles? His Excellency was one of the leaders of the national movement and he saw for himself the Egyptian woman's share in the national struggle, whether political, social or economic. Our case is in the hands of somebody who knows how to fulfill his promises." She decided that the time had come to change tactics, "to assail the men; surprise them right in the middle of injustice, that is to say, under the very cupola of parliament."[2]

*   *   *

Nothing that Doria had yet attempted would take her society by surprise, catch the imagination of both the national and international press, and intensify the hostility of her enemies as greatly as the carefully constructed and successfully executed plan to storm the Egyptian parliament on the afternoon of February 19, 1951. With nearly fifteen hundred women at her side, Doria left Ewart Memorial Hall of the American University in Cairo, marched the few blocks south along the main street of Kasr al-Aini, forced her way through the gates of parliament, and orchestrated four hours of boisterous demonstrations before finally being received in the office of the vice president of the chamber of deputies and extracting from the president of the senate a verbal promise that parliament would immediately take up the women's demands.

That such a daring act of public defiance against the bastion of male authority could actually be organized and executed was a tribute to the strategy of secrecy and surprise followed by Doria and her small circle of coconspirators, who had sworn a solemn oath on the Quran not to divulge their plans to anyone, not even to their husbands. It was "an affair that concerns us only. Why mix the men up in it?" A month before the demonstration, during the course of a meeting with the executive council of Bint al-Nil, Doria remarked to the great surprise of those assembled, "We are only playing." Then she got up, banged her fist on the table and exclaimed, "We must go out into the streets!" She sat down and, in a low voice, added, "Why don't we organize a demonstration?" A profound silence fell over the room. One woman asked, "And if we fail?" "Then we will be the only ones responsible for our failure. But you must guard this secret!"[3]

And effectively the secret was kept for a month as preparations were made for what was ostensibly to be a large feminist congress. The element of surprise was maintained until the moment Doria stood on the podium in Ewart Hall and announced:

> Our meeting today is not a congress, but a parliament. A true one! That of women! We are half the nation! We represent here the hope and despair of this most important half of our nation. Luckily we are meeting at the same hour and in the same part of town as the parliament of the other half of the nation. They are assembled a few steps away from us. I propose we go there, strong in the knowledge of our rights, and tell the deputies and senators that their assemblies are illegal so long as our representatives are excluded, that the Egyptian parliament cannot be a true reflection of the entire nation until women are admitted. Let's go and give it to them straight. Let's go and demand our rights. Forward to the parliament!

This was indeed an historic moment not only for Doria but also for the women's movement. The Egyptian press, who followed the events surrounding Doria's audacious manifestation closely, remarked: "This was the first public meeting organized conjointly by two groups who have identical aims yet a different history. The first is the Egyptian Feminist Union founded by Huda Sha'rawi, who joined the battle thirty years ago when the spirit of national revolution animated the land. The second is the Bint al-Nil Movement which marches under the banner of youth. But the two organizations are resolved to collaborate. They have declared themselves in favor of unified action."[4]

It is testimony to her seriousness that Doria Shafik would invite Ceza Nabaraoui—"with whom I had believed I had definitely made peace"—to join her in the demonstration in order "to unite the largest number of women regardless of their ideological and temperamental differences, to prove to society the solidarity of all women in their demand for political and civil rights and to demonstrate through this solidarity women's ability to have a major impact on society."[5] Ahmad al-Sawi, Doria's calamitous former 'aris (legal fiancé) and outspoken critic, was fully aware of the antipathy between the two women, and commented in al-Ahram newspaper: "It is inconceivable that there would come a day when we would see Ceza Nabaraoui and Doria Shafik exchanging kisses in the street, but that is exactly what happened yesterday."[6]

Doria's rebellious march resulted in a feminist delegation's being able to proclaim within the hallowed halls of parliament for the first time its specific demands: first, permission to participate in the national struggle and in poli-

Doria Shafik with members of the executive council of the Bint al-Nil Union during a planning session for the march on parliament, February 1951.

tics; second, reform of the personal status law by setting limitations on polygamy and divorce; and third, equal pay for equal work. When a group of women, headed by Doria, finally forced their way into the chamber of deputies, they were met by the vice president, Gamal Serag al-Din,[7] who remonstrated with them as to the legality of their actions.

To which Mme. Shafik answered: "We are here by the force of our right."

"Tell your girls to hold their tongues," countered the vice president.

"For over two years we tried to make ourselves heard in a correct manner. It is time that you listen to us. They will not keep quiet before I have a promise on your part," threatened Mme. Shafik. Seeing that the president of the chamber refused to meet the delegation himself, she decided to meet the president of the senate, His Excellency, Zaki al-Urabi Pasha, and present her grievances. Unfortunately he was ill that day and had not come to the session. Mme. Shafik entered the Senate and did not hesitate to telephone him: "Excellency, we have forced open the door of parliament. I am calling you from your own office. Over a thousand women are outside demanding their political rights, based on your own interpretation of Article 3 of the Constitution, which states that all Egyptians have equal civil and political rights. You yourself have declared that 'Egyptian' designates women as well as men. Nothing in the constitution stands in the way. Only the electoral law discriminates against women. We are convinced you will not go against your own words."

In the face of such a barrage the president of the senate, in an effort to appease Mme. Shafik, replied that he would take this question personally in hand.[8]

Doria was placated by the pasha's assurance and repeated his words to the throng outside: "'Our negotiations have won a solemn promise that the Egyptian woman will have her political rights!' From the crowd a voice shouted, 'We'll see that he keeps his word!' We left the parliament feeling victorious."

The following morning, Doria found a letter from the wife of the Indian ambassador, apologizing for not having attended the congress of the day before and explaining that she was ill. She ended her note with: "Bravo! Allah helps those who help themselves."[9] Later that day, Doria and Ceza headed another delegation to Abdin Palace, where they deposited copies of their demands—then to the office of the prime minister, where a meeting was arranged for the following week. One week after the assault on parliament, a draft bill, amending the electoral law granting women the right to vote as well as run for parliament, was formally submitted to the president of the chamber of deputies, by a Wafdist representative, Ahmad al-Hadri.[10]

All seemed to be going well until the prime minister reneged on his promised appointment with the feminist delegation. The initial feelings of euphoria were tempered by the realization that once again, oral promises were being broken. Having felt cheated by the prime minister, the members of the delegation demanded that the *chef de cabinet* remind his excellency that (1) his August 1949 election pledge had posited the realization of feminist demands would figure as a top priority in the Wafd program when they returned to power, and (2) Egypt was one of the signatories of the UN Charter, in which the first article accorded equality to all human beings without distinction of sex. They left the office refusing the traditional cup of coffee.[11] The London *Times* described this incident as "Nahas Pasha's Snub to Suffragettes."[12] By now, the foreign as well as the Egyptian press had taken up Doria's "storming of parliament" as a major media event. The *New York Times* ran a five column feature on the event including two photographs of Doria, one looking through a book with Jehane and Aziza, and the other, leading the march on parliament. The headline read: "Rising Feminism Bewilders Egypt: Muslim Conservatives Shocked by Suffragettes' Behavior in Invading Parliament."[13]

Doria was summoned to appear in court on March 6 to hear the public prosecutor's formal accusations: "I assume full responsibility for everything that has happened and I am even ready to go to jail!" she declared. Because of the extraordinary nature of the case, a number of lawyers, particularly women, volunteered to defend her. At this time, women lawyers in Egypt were fighting male opposition that still placed barriers before their admission to the Tribunals. Appointments to judgeships were absolutely denied to them. Although there were a few hundred women lawyers in Egypt during this period, these obstacles functioned to discourage women from entering the profession, and their numbers were not increasing. Those who did come were from as far away as Samalout and Alexandria as well as from Cairo. But it was the eminent Mufida Abdul Rahman, a successful career-woman and mother of nine children, whom Doria selected to defend her case. Under the banner headline "*Bint-al-Nil* in Court: The Case of Mme. Doria Shafik Will Be the Defense of the Egyptian Feminist Movement," *La Bourse Egyptienne* declared on its front page that the case had "stirred the enthusiasm of Egyptian feminists and roused their energies. The true object of the flimsy accusation against the founder of Bint al-Nil is the entire feminist movement. The case to be pleaded on April 10, 1951 is not just a matter of conscience but a political affair that is destined to have repercussions nationally and internationally. The dynamic Egyptian feminists are certainly not going to waste the opportunity of using this unexpected tribunal to plead their cause with the government."[14]

In response to questions about how she was going to conduct her defense of Doria's case, Mufida Abdul Rahman commented:

It appears to me that there is no crime in going to lodge the petition in parliament. As regards having forced the gates: We know that the public is not banned from parliament. Sessions may be observed by people who have invitations. But is there a law that says one must have an invitation? Such a law does not exist. The women went to parliament to demand their property, to demand the right which is denied them and which they cannot obtain by other means. The door of parliament ought to be open like other doors—those of factories, of the professions and of higher education. All women, literate or not, have the same right as men to participate in the social and political life of the nation.[15]

As a symbolic gesture of solidarity, four female Egyptian university students submitted a petition written in their own blood to King Faruq, demanding equal rights for women.[16] Two days later, the council of administration of the Association of Sunnites submitted an anti-feminist petition signed by the chairman, Muhammad Hamid al-Fiki, to the palace, requesting the king to "Keep the Women Within Bounds!"

The feminist movement is a plot organized by the enemies of Islam and the bolshevik-atheists, with the object of abolishing the remaining Muslim traditions in the country. They have used women, Muslim women, as a means to achieving their goal. They made the woman leave her

realm which is the home, conjugal life, maternity. They have followed
these hypocrites in participating with them in acts of charity which are
nothing other than evil and corrupt. Not content with their exhibitions,
hospitals and dispensaries, now they have created associations and parties that strive to demand equality with men, the limitation of divorce,
the abolition of polygamy and entry into parliament. Your majesty, protect the orient and Islam.[17]

The king, who was not at all amused by all this feminist fuss in the wake of
Doria's assault on parliament, told her husband, whom he frequently met at
the Automobile Club, "Let your wife know that as long as I am king, women
will not have political rights!"

The trial was set for April 10. In anticipation, feminists and anti-feminists
were carrying on a war of petitions. Doria meanwhile went to Athens on March
26 with Zaynab Labib to represent Egypt at the congress of the International
Council of Women. She had been invited to present a talk on the results of
Bint al-Nil Union's literacy project among the urban poor. As a consequence
of the dramatic situation awaiting her back in Egypt, she remarked ironically
to the assembled delegates, "I noticed that the day after we stormed parliament in Egypt, the Greek government granted the women of Greece the right
to vote. Others profit from our work!" She ended her speech by presenting a
motion "requesting UNESCO to help all those countries who fight for the
education of illiterate women."[18]

Following her return from Athens and on the eve of her trial, Doria faced
renewed public criticism from Ceza Nabaraoui and Inji Efflatoun, her erst-
while allies during the march on parliament. They published two articles in
the Egyptian press (one in French, the other in Arabic) accusing Doria "of
sharing a point of view contrary to the policy of the country and its national
interests because Doria Shafik voted for an ICW resolution approving the occupation and supporting the argument of Great Britain concerning the maintenance of her troops on the Suez Canal under the pretext of defense."[19] Doria's
answer was swift and direct: "I did not participate in any resolution about
armaments, which would have been contrary to the principles of the peace
charter, but simply to a motion supporting the right of every country to have
its own system of defense."[20] This debate reveals how feminist issues became
embroiled with cold war ideological struggles.

Finally the day which many Egyptian feminists were impatiently awaiting
arrived, and Doria appeared before the tribunal, "dressed in a somber gray
flannel suit, totally feminine, poised and charming. How delicate the president of Bint al-Nil appeared, surrounded, almost to the point of being carried
off her feet, by lawyers enveloped in their austere black robes. Far from let-

ting herself be intimidated by this solemn entourage, she personally defended the cause so dear to her heart and for which she struggles with so much energy. Because of the justice of the cause and its strong defense by these lawyers, who have honored the Egyptian Bar, the case was postponed *sine die.*"[21]

In addition to Mufida Abdul Rahman, there were other lawyers "honoring the Egyptian Bar." They included Abdul Fatah Ragai, Doria's father-in-law, who had helped her with the al-Sawi saga; Maurice Arcache, a prominent political lawyer from an upper-class Syrian-Lebanese background; and al-Kholi, the young Marxist, who commented that "Doria's storming parliament surprised Nour al-Din and it came as a shock to him when she was arrested. In my opinion her storming of the parliament was a landmark."[22] Doria Shafik was acclaimed a national celebrity by the press, but for her, the battle had just begun as she, along with other Egyptians, were swept up by the events surrounding the national struggle, events that would shape the course of her fight for women's rights in the years to come.

* * *

After months of negotiations with the British government, the Wafd unilaterally abrogated the treaty on October 8, 1951. This was followed by the outbreak of a full-fledged guerrilla war against the British which intensified over the next three months, particularly in the Suez Canal cities of Port Said and Isma'iliyah, and unleashed a moment of tragic violence in Egypt's modern history. By autumn 1951, as the armed clashes between Egyptian guerrilla squads and British army units intensified, Doria called for women's participation in the national liberation struggle against the British:

> Egypt, country of our birth, who has taught us the meaning of freedom, is calling her sons to fight for her dignity. This is a call from our Great Mother, that should move the whole nation to sacrifice for her. I am calling upon the women of Egypt to fall into the line of battle and to carry guns in order to save their nation from its enemies; so that she can occupy an honorable place under the sun. Come on, turn the wheel of history, and take your place at the head of the troops doing your utmost for the sake of Egypt. You have no choice but to answer the call of the present hour, which states that women have a responsibility towards their nation—their own blood should be shed for their nation, not only the blood of their husbands, sons, and brothers. This blood will nourish the tree of honor, which will reach to heaven itself.[23]

Bint al-Nil Union organized "the first female military unit in the country to prepare young women to fight alongside men; to train field nurses and provide first aid training to over two thousand young women. It opened a subscription campaign to give financial aid to workers who lost their jobs in the Canal Zone."[24] Through these actions, Doria intended to demonstrate that by sharing equal responsibilities with men in armed struggle, the Egyptian woman would show herself worthy of her right to occupy her proper place in the political and parliamentary life of the nation.

On November 13, 1951, the anniversary of the 1919 revolt, a large demonstration against the continued occupation of Egypt by the British was organized. Along with hundreds of thousands of other Egyptians, Doria Shafik and the members of Bint al-Nil Union marched alongside Inji Efflatoun, Ceza Nabaraoui, and the members of the Women's Committee of Popular Resistance. When the guerrilla war broke out in the summer, Inji Efflatoun along with other leftist women like Aida Nasrallah, Latifa Zayyat, and Ceza Nabaraoui established an ad-hoc Women's Committee for Popular Resistance (al-Lagna an-nissa'iyah lil-muqawama al-sha'abiyah), with Nabaraoui as president. This committee sought to support popular resistance in the Canal region by providing medical care and military assistance for the guerrillas; to mobilize women, and the general public, in backing the struggle against the British; and to establish branches all over Cairo, and even set up a secret branch in Isma'iliyah.[25] This was the last time that all the women's organizations transcended their differing ideologies to unite together toward a common goal.

Doria described that November 13 as a day in which "the world witnessed the gathering of millions of people silently marching in the streets of Cairo, proving that Egyptians, though deeply frustrated by the occupation, could succeed in controlling their anger. A people who experience the tyranny of the English and can still control their feelings, are truly great."[26] Ten years later, while writing her memoirs, she remembered this autumn of 1951, when "I, like several of my companions from Bint al-Nil, was in the grip of this fever. Like tens of thousands of others we were carried along by the spontaneity of our nationalist zeal."

In the midst of the excitement and turbulence of this historic autumn of 1951, Doria was in the process of completing her one published novel, L'Esclave Sultane (1952). One is tempted to speculate how far she might have identified with its heroine, that extraordinary thirteenth-century Mameluke slave Shagarat al-Durr, who through sheer determination, willpower, courage, and naked ambition imposed herself as the first woman sultan of Egypt, when the Ayubid dynasty was succumbing to the Mamelukes. Their names are linked by the same Arabic root durr, meaning "pearls." Shagarat al-Durr literally means "tree of pearls," and durriya (from which the name Doria derives) means "sparkling," "brilliant." Doria introduces her novel with the admonition that "this history of Shagarat al-Durr is not fictional. I have adhered to reported facts. And if the astonishing destiny of Shagarat al-Durr, so closely linked to that of Egypt, has inspired some writings already, never, I believe, until this present work, has anyone based their research on anything except the most anecdotal of incidents. I have produced this work with the intention of restoring the personality of an enigmatic woman, which events, most certainly of an exceptional nature, have rendered spellbinding."[27] These words as well as the novel itself are touchingly prescient in terms of Doria's own life. Like her heroine, Doria lived through a moment when Egypt had arrived at one of its turning points: "when two dynasties, one dying the other dawning, meet each other and collide head on."[28] Only for Doria, it wasn't the magnificent Ayubids succumbing to the powerful Mamelukes, but rather an enfeebled *ancien régime* crumbling in the face of the rising tide of nationalism.

Personifying this nationalism that was sweeping through the Middle East was the Iranian hero Muhammad Musaddegh, popularly known at the time as the liberator of Iran. Musaddegh became the prime minister of Iran following the assassination of General Ramzar in March 1951. Soon afterwards, he nationalized Iran's oil, an action he justified under a parliamentary law he himself had promoted prior to assuming power. Thus to many Egyptians, including Doria at that moment, Musaddegh symbolized the very spirit of nationalism. Musaddegh was also to be the victim of the Cold War struggle. In 1953, the CIA and other Western powers successfully fomented a right wing take over, and Musaddegh's freely elected government was overthrown and he himself put under house arrest. The shah, Muhammad Reza Pahlevi, heading a regime more friendly to Western political interests, was returned to power.

In the fall of 1951, Musaddegh was on his way home from New York, where the Security Council of the United Nations was debating the issue of nationalization, and he stopped off in Cairo. Doria, who caught him for an interview, was "mesmerized by his unbelievable way of reasoning, his great faith in duty and deep confidence in his nation, which he has raised above all nations. He is someone who is a true man of revolt. He is a symbol of his country's struggle against foreign exploitation and an example that should be followed all over the world."[29] Little did she realize that in a few months, her own country would embark on a similar path.

10

A False Dream (1952–1954)

More than one idea of emancipation was germinating in Egypt. All the aspirations of the Egyptian people whatever their background, cause or motive—spontaneous or planned—converged around the hard core of nationalism. But this concept was veiled by the most diverse interpretations: from the pure flame mounting in our hearts to foreign intrigues diffusing directives of destruction in the heart of our nation under the camouflage of a false nationalism.

By early January of 1952, demonstrations and student strikes spread throughout the country, expressing increased popular opposition to both government and king. Furthermore, several of the demonstrating students publicly displayed arms and used them against the police. The government realized that subversive and seditious elements had by now decided to use the Anglo-Egyptian crisis for their own political ends. British troops in the Canal Zone, in an impossible situation, responded to the guerrilla attacks and on January 25, 1952, surrounded the auxiliary police headquarters in Isma'iliyah and gave the occupants one hour to surrender. On orders from Minister of the Interior Fuad Serag al-Din, the police commander rejected the ultimatum, and the Egyptians resisted bravely until over fifty policemen and gendarmes had been killed; many more were wounded. The next day—Black Saturday—a large part of central Cairo was burned and looted by the enraged populace; at least thirty lives were lost and several hundred people were injured.

In looking back upon this period, Doria reflected, "I was verging toward violence, toward a military spirit of which my inner nature had a fundamental horror. Illogical! It is only in looking back, now as I am writing, that one realizes how inconsistent one can be." But did Doria feel she was "being illogical" or "inconsistent" when on January 23, 1952, she led twenty young, uniformed girls from the Bint al-Nil military unit across the street from her office to "surround Barclays Bank and stop all its activity for twenty-four hours"? Given that armed struggle was raging in the Canal Zone and that in her editorials she was calling on women to "shed their own blood for their nation," it should have come as no surprise that some of the young girls of the Bint al-Nil militia would want to fight alongside the men. But feeling "responsible for the safety of these young women who were still unprepared for armed confrontation," Doria decided on a "new genre of battle . . . a peaceful protest against a dominant symbol of English colonialism, which would provide an outlet for their nationalist ardor, yet minimize the physical danger."

In point of fact, her peaceful demonstration attracted a large and unruly crowd, including a group of organized agitators shouting slogans and inciting people to violence: "The excitable crowds were getting out of control and I thought they would attack the bank. One girl placed a chair in front of the door of the bank from which to harangue the crowd. Before she could move, I climbed on to the chair and shouted to my girls: 'Close ranks and let no one break the cordon. Our manifestation is peaceful!'" Finally the security police arrived, dispersed the crowds. and carted the "agitators," as well as Doria and her "militia," off to the police station. Doria was then driven to the office of the minister of the interior, where she found Nour, "who was furious with me for having concealed my plans from him." Most probably out of consideration for Nour, a highly respected university professor and lawyer as well as a Wafdist sympathizer, and perhaps bemused by what he felt was Doria's well-intentioned naiveté, the minister released her from custody and freed her young companions.

Three days later, around eleven o'clock in the morning on Black Saturday, while looking from her office window, Doria "saw thick, black smoke coming from nearby Opera Square. One of the staff came rushing in and announced, 'the foreign establishments are burning, mostly English!' Nour telephoned: 'Cairo is burning! Come home immediately! I'll pick up the children.' I was frantic. Had these rampaging mobs attacked the school where my two daughters were? I ordered the staff to go home, locked up the office, rushed to pick up Aziza and Jehane only to discover they had already been sent home by the headmistress. Nour and the girls were at home when I arrived."

*   *   *

Aftershocks reverberated throughout Egypt in the months to come. The country was put under martial law. The king dismissed Nahas and recalled Ali Mahir, but Mahir only lasted five weeks. After that episode, Egypt had four different governments in as many months; it was becoming difficult to find anyone capable of forming a government. The corruption and extravagance of Faruq and his entourage were a source of scandalous amusement to the world and of shame to most Egyptians. The chaos—the breakdown of order—was complete, and the conditions for a coup d'état were ripe.

These events also had their repercussions on a personal level. Realizing that her daughters were suffering from the hostile taunts of British children at school and wishing to protect them in case of further anti-British demonstrations, Doria withdrew them from the Gezira Preparatory School and enrolled them instead in the small private school Cours Morin, which attracted many from the more "Westernized" elite Egyptian families. Owned and run by a French Jewish couple, the school was selective in its enrollment and liberal in its philosophy of education and its discipline.

Doria perceived a certain tragic irony in the juxtaposition of the burning of Cairo following so soon after her symbolic protest at Barclays Bank, and in her memoirs she reflected on the question of responsibility or what she called "a case of conscience": "Could I have imagined that disaster would follow three days after my protest? Is it possible to foresee that a spontaneous gesture could provoke acts of violence, indeed, even criminal ones? How much are we responsible for the acts of others when these latter have been subjected, either from near or far, to our influence? I saw how easy it was to slip imperceptibly, without being aware, into demagoguery and violence. I made a vow: always to act 'sincerely,' never 'blindly.' I recalled Gandhi and his example and philosophy would exert a strong influence on my future line of conduct."

*   *   *

This did not mean that Doria retired from her struggle; on the contrary, it was only a few weeks after the events of Black Saturday that Doria dreamed up yet another tactic of confrontation with the government. Only this time, it concerned the issue of women's right to participate in elections rather than the British occupation, and it was planned and staged from her hospital bed (where she was recovering from an emergency appendectomy), rather than in the streets.

As part of the preparation for general elections to be held later in October, toward the end of March the new government announced that there would be revisions to the election laws. Doria was encouraged by reports suggesting that in revising the electoral lists, the government might modify voting qualifications to exclude illiterates and include literates, both men and women. People close to the government had mentioned feminist demands as one reason for scrapping the old electoral lists and starting anew. Never one to let an opportunity pass her by, Doria went into action, convinced that her demands contradicted neither Islam nor the constitution—"we had proved that on more than one occasion." However, she was aware that this new prime minister had the reputation of being "excessively anti-feminist," so Doria decided "that there was absolutely no way of restoring our rights through good manners. A *fait accompli* was the only recourse."

She convened a meeting of the executive council in her hospital room and proposed that the members act as if they had rights of suffrage: "Each of us will choose a district and present our candidacy as a future member of parliament, deposit the one hundred and fifty pound campaign fee and, in effect, put the government in front of a *fait accompli*." On March 30, 1952, still confined to her bed, Doria submitted her registration papers and money to run for election as the candidate for the popular district of Abdin, where her office was located. She accompanied her papers with a letter stating that "I take this right myself since I refute the article in the electoral law which is against the constitution that declares that all Egyptians are equal in their political rights, without the mention of sex."[1] The head of the district sent her papers on to the minister of the interior, who kept them beyond the date for registration and then returned them to her, stating that she could not be a candidate because only men were eligible to run for office and women did not have the right to vote. Doria replied by filing a suit before the state council to amend the electoral law. Meanwhile, "hundreds of women from the poorer classes of Abdin came to the clinic with long lists of names (or thumb prints) to give me their votes for the coming election! I was deeply moved. It was another proof that women, even illiterate women, value the importance of political rights."

Not only the government but the religious authorities were becoming more openly vocal in their opposition to Doria's demands. Within a few weeks, the *ulimas* (authorities in Islamic law) of Damietta, a town at the mouth of the eastern branch of the Nile, issued a *fatwa* (an argued opinion on any issue related to an interpretation of Islamic law) under the leadership of Shaykh Kamal al-Hudra, dean of the Azharite Institute, which categorically stated: "Votes are degrading to women and against their nature."[2] Riled by these Islamic scholars, Doria went to the minister of education, Taha Husayn, to demand that he formally protest this ruling to the prime minister. She channeled into the Egyptian press the text of a dissenting *fatwa* sent to her by Abdul Hamid Badaiuni, chairman of the Association of Ulimas of Pakistan, regarded as a much greater authority on Islamic law than the shaykh from Damietta. The Pakistani scholar declared: "History reveals the diversity of roles which women undertook in times of war and peace and Islam acknowledges their role and accords to women all rights accorded to men. At the present time Egypt seems to be passing through a confusing stage where much of the debate centers around the right to vote, unlike Pakistan where the right is both secured and practiced."[3]

Doria wrote an editorial arguing that "The excuse of the conservatives has been proven false since women in Syria, Turkey and Pakistan—all Islamic countries—have won their political rights. Islam does not require that women be deprived of their rights. So what is the excuse of the conservatives now?"[4] Concerned about her appeal to religious liberalism, the grand mufti of Egypt,[5] the conservative Shaykh Hassanayn Muhammad Makhluf, issued another *fatwa*, condemning feminist agitation in Egypt and rebuking Doria personally.

The mufti was a graduate of al-Azhar University, the thousand-year-old intellectual center of Islam, and an authority on Islamic jurisprudence; his opinion carried considerable weight among Muslims throughout the world:

> The bearded and turbaned patriarch, with great traditional prestige, expressed himself in terms of pained reproach rather than anger. "The wives of the Prophet Muhammad," the aged Grand Mufti stated, "were veiled. The Prophet did not touch the hands of those women who came to acknowledge him as the Prophet of God. Islam had built barriers to protect women from being abused. Thus it forbade a woman to be alone with strangers (men) and it prohibited her from showing her beauty. Women, the Grand Mufti admonished, were not permitted by the early Caliphs to call to prayer from the minarets. Islam did not make it compulsory for women to pray publicly in mosques." He then asked: "Does woman now want to cross the barrier and join men in the chambers of parliament, in elections, in propaganda, in committee meetings, in calling on ministers and traveling to conferences and other matters more serious than being a judge between two opponents, which was however denied them in early Islam?" Answering his own question, the Grand Mufti stated categorically: "No one can accept this nor can Islam approve this. No one would take a decision contrary to his conscience and religion."[6]

Such views from the grand mufti dealt a serious blow to Doria's feminist struggle, and she was not about to let them go unchallenged. Yet to contradict his religious opinion on women's rights publicly was very daring on her part, as it meant contradicting the highest religious authority on matters related to the interpretation of the Quran itself. But so convinced was she that Islam was not against the political rights of women that she felt bound to answer the mufti's arguments.

Displaying her characteristic defiance and courage and basing her rebuttal on evidence from the Quran as well as the views of other religious scholars, Doria entered squarely into the polemical debate that raged around Islam and women's constitutional rights:

> Professor Hassanayn Muhammad Makhluf's article published last Friday has stirred many readers. The article clearly lacked sound quotations in support of his views which were both important and essential by

virtue of his position in the religious world. Readers had hoped that his views would be more relevant to their daily concerns particularly because many of the daily issues have been the source of long debates among religious scholars. On the other hand, a group of religious scholars maintains a different opinion and claim an opposing view. The Mufti's article has moved some of them to write back voluntarily supporting their position with religious sources.[7]

Over the next months, as Egypt was heading into revolution, Doria kept the women's rights issue at the center of public discourse, making herself the target of an ever-moving crescendo of anti-feminist pronouncements from the conservative religious establishment. Voices of support for her liberal interpretation of Islam came from both within Egypt and beyond. An eminent Egyptian religious figure, Dr. Ahmad Zaki Bey, wrote several articles outlining point by point how the mufti "has not only taken literal meanings of verses but has added his own prejudices. Islam has not placed a class of selected individuals to act as mediators between man and his Creator. Every individual has a mind that can understand and grasp the Quran and as a *hadith* expresses it, can read, understand and evaluate with his God-given faculties. . . . Mind and Reason."[8] The Indian minister of education, Mawlana Abul Kalam Azad, translator of the Quran from Arabic to Urdu and champion of women's rights, also sent articles—which Doria was later to publish in her *al-Kitab al-Abiyad* (1953)—that flatly declared: "Islam is not against women's political rights."[9] A committee of the mufti's *ulimas*, echoing the sentiments of the grand shaykh, issued yet another *fatwa* on June 11, 1952, repudiating feminist claims on the ground that "Women are by instinct made to follow a particular path dictated by nature. A woman's role as mother has a particular effect on her. It affects a woman emotionally in the sense that it weakens her moral spirit, her determination, her capacity to fight for her ideas, her capacity to defend her ideas; all this no woman can deny."[10]

Several religious associations convened an Islamic conference to endorse the position taken by the mufti's committee of *ulimas*. Printed invitations specified that women attending the meeting "must wear long sleeves and the veil that God gave them to honor them."[11] A ten-point manifesto opposing women's rights was published in the papers. Among other statements, the manifesto declared: "Women's claim to political rights is an outrageous breach of religion. The government regards *this movement as a serious threat to society's stability and solidarity* and is insistent on the maintenance of Islamic rule."[12]

Prime Minister Ahmad Naguib al-Hilali Pasha and his cabinet, apparently under pressure from this strong religious opposition, withdrew from their earlier position and took a firm stand against the introduction of political rights for women as part of the government's electoral reform. The then-independent newspaper *al-Ahram* reported that the cabinet's decision to reject women's suffrage had been based on an article in the Egyptian constitution making Islam the "religion of the state." Consequently, the ministers were obliged to heed the opinion of the highest Muslim authorities in this matter.[13]

* * *

The government's action was a great disappointment to Doria, and she strongly objected to the unfavorable Quranic interpretations handed down by the *ulimas* demanding "that the government, instead of taking cover behind religion, should state its real reasons for denying women's rights" and announced that "Bint al-Nil Union will contest the constitutionality of women's exclusion from political life before the Council of State as soon as a new electoral law is promulgated."[14] However, these debates as well as the forthcoming election were soon totally eclipsed by the unfolding of the broader political events which culminated in the military coup d'état on July 23.

The straw that finally broke the camel's back and led the army to revolt was a struggle of authority between the king and his own army. The king wanted to dismiss the duly elected General Muhammad Naguib as president of the Officers Club in Cairo and nominate one of his own entourage. The army refused, thus for the first time directly challenging the authority of the king. He responded by ordering the club closed and, against all advice to seek a compromise with the army, attempted to impose General Sirry Amer—the Free Officers' chief enemy, detested for his part in the Palestine arms scandal—as minister of war, rather than General Naguib. On the night of July 22, the army moved from its barracks in Heliopolis and occupied army headquarters in Cairo. Only two private soldiers were killed in the entire operation. By July 23, the capital had fallen like a ripe mango, and General Muhammad Naguib was made president of the Revolutionary Council.[15] Having been asked to form a new government, Ali Mahir, the same man who had helped Faruq to mount the throne, was sent to Alexandria to demand his abdication: "On July 26 the king sailed for Italy on his royal yacht, accompanied by Queen Narriman, their infant son, Ahmad Fuad and Farida's three daughters, who were unable to say good-bye to their mother, plus two hundred and four pieces of luggage."

During this "bloodless revolution," Doria and Nour were in Cairo. Normally they would have been in Alexandria, where Doria sent Aziza and Jehane every summer, accompanied by Mme. Marie, to stay at her sister Soraya's villa. The evening following the coup, Doria and Nour dined with Ahmad Abul Fath, editor-in-chief of *al-Masri*, the newspaper which had supported her debates with the mufti. Abul Fath was also closely linked, through kinship, to one of the Free Officers, and he assured Nour and Doria that the Free Officers wanted nothing more than to change the cabinet and make Naguib commander-in-chief. Like the majority of the Egyptian people in the aftermath of the military coup, Doria "enthusiastically supported 'the liberators of the people,' as they were called, believing that Egypt was entering a new era of love and liberty, a period of true Liberation, of true Equality, of true Peace."

And so, it seems, did all the old party leaders. As the historian P. J. Vatikiotis has explained: "In traditional political style, all hastened to congratulate the army for ridding the country of the tyrant Faruq and to swear undying loyalty to the revolution. Nahas, 'the beloved and sole leader of the nation,' raced back from his European holiday to do the same. What they did not understand was that the Free Officers were not their clients. They had come to power by force in order to purify the country of all the elements that had contributed to its plight since the Second World War."[16]

Doria too wasted no time in presenting her views. Within two weeks of the military takeover, the outspoken feminist leader was in Naguib's office, not only offering her congratulations to the Free Officers but also reminding Naguib that he had accomplished only half of the revolution; the liberation of the woman remained:

> Naguib was most cordial but advised that I risked setting loose the conservative elements against the regime if I called too quickly for women's political rights. He argued that hastiness could cause harm to the beginnings of the new era, which ought to begin calmly. I agreed and promised to keep quiet for some time. However, I cautioned him not to make me wait too long. Anwar al-Sadat was present at this meeting. I remember the scene—Naguib's eyes, full of confidence in the future of the revolution and in his companions, contrasted with the closed face of Sadat, who had complete control over Naguib's conversation. At one look from Sadat, Naguib held his tongue or changed the subject.

Agreeing that the "champions of liberation" needed time to get rid of the corrupt vestiges of the former regime in order to build a more egalitarian base for Egypt's renaissance, Doria placed a moratorium on her confrontational tactics to force women's rights.

However, this did not mean that she abandoned her struggle, and in early October—a few weeks after the new "law of political parties" appeared on September 10, 1952, decreeing that every party must declare publicly their political programs, internal organization, and party funds to the Interior Ministry—she declared to the Ministry of the Interior (headed now by Gamal Abdul Nasser) that Bint al-Nil Union was reorganizing as a political party and listed herself as president of the party. Her request was accepted, and the first meeting of the Bint al-Nil political party was convened on December 11, 1952:

"For the first time in the history of the women's struggle, the government officially recognized the practice of party activities for women as on a par with men." Doria affirmed her faith in the revolution in a speech delivered before five hundred girls and women at the first general assembly of the Bint al-Nil political party:

> Today is truly a happy one, because the general assembly for the Bint al-Nil political party has joined the dawn of our blessed national movement that liberated the country from an age of darkness and will liberate woman from past slavery. The Ministry of the Interior has accepted the notification of the Bint al-Nil political party, and has not differentiated between our party and men's parties. . . . It is a decisive step in the history of the Egyptian woman, after which she will achieve a lot. The only thing following this step is her political right permitting her to share in the legislation of laws and in steering the course of government in parliament.[17]

With the recognition of Bint al-Nil Union as an official political party, Doria founded another monthly supplement, called *Bint al-Nil al-Siyassa*, through which she intended to awaken the Egyptian's woman's consciousness to the broader events unfolding in the world. Doria believed that the women's rights issue had finally attained legitimate status under the military government and that it would only be a matter of time before the new regime would formalize these rights. She thus turned her energies toward supporting the revolution, through the pages of her several magazines. For example, she took a rather defensive line "against our enemies who started publishing nonsense concerning our revolution, which regained our dignity in front of the whole world. It is our obligation, therefore, to explain our revolution by good deeds at home and publishing news about it through publicity channels abroad."[18]

The following message appeared in a special issue of *La Femme-Nouvelle* which Doria published under the title "Egypt's Renaissance," and in it, her enthusiastic acclaim for Naguib and the revolution could not have been more wholehearted:

> The *coup d'état* of Muhammad Naguib is much more than a simple revolution. Not only did he put an end to a régime, not only did he rid Egypt of the most revolting of dictators, but he set the foundations of a new edifice on the principles of liberty and equality. Only a few months have elapsed and social reforms of the highest importance are beginning to emerge and take shape. The first was agrarian reform—to bring rapport between the social classes by limiting property; then there was the abolition of titles which, from a moral point of view, produced an effect as important as social reform from an economic point of view. The govern-

ment proceeded to lower prices to the great relief of the people. Now it will be the turn of a new Constitution on the basis of new ideas: liberty and equality. Thus Egypt has turned one of the most beautiful pages of its history, where the people, guided by their liberator, Muhammad Naguib, have learned to break with the past, work with unfettered hands for the Egypt of tomorrow.[19]

Backing up her rhetoric with action—"to explain our revolution by good deeds at home" and "to work for the Egypt of tomorrow"—Doria presented a project to General Muhammad Naguib outlining a plan to "combat illiteracy among men and women in Egypt, and eradicate this disease of ignorance among our citizens within the next three years."[20] Ragia Raghab, a member of Bint al-Nil's executive committee and responsible for one of these schools, estimated that "during this period Bint al-Nil Union had nearly eighty centers spread throughout the four corners of Egypt, attended by several thousand women."[21]

But for Doria, "they were only a beginning. In a country of 23,000,000 where the majority are illiterate, to teach a few thousand was but a drop in the bucket. It was necessary to find a method that would cover the entire country, and include both men and women." Her scheme would utilize the broad readership of *Bint al-Nil* magazine and also involve the cooperation of the government and popular organizations. She was not complacent about this project.

Doria Shafik describing her literacy project to Nehru's sister at the Bint al-Nil Union office, December 1953. Mustapha Amin, Egyptian journalist, is at right.

Well aware that it had been successful in other countries such as Mexico and Turkey, she was tempted to try it out:

I made it clear to the officials that the government, along with the various voluntary, popular organizations, must have a large share in directing and guiding the project because it should be the duty of every person who can read and write, to teach a certain number of illiterate people. A law should be passed to punish those who are able to teach people but have not offered their services, because teaching people of the nation is a duty on every good citizen. What I'm making today through our magazine, *Bint al-Nil*, and with the cooperation of "Fax" schools, is only an experiment to demonstrate that the eradication of illiteracy in Egypt is something within our grasp and which will not require a lot of money. This experiment will prove that anyone who can read and write is able to be a teacher if he follows the guidelines that we publish in a number of issues of our magazine in the three months starting from today. With this, we guard against exorbitant financial requirements for the appointment of technical teachers in a period in which we're seeking austerity and economy. The formation of a class for male and female students will not cost anything above the ability of those participating in the coming three months. This is an experiment that I present to the nation, and I believe that its success will confirm the correctness of our programs and the ability of the Egyptian population to get rid of illiteracy within three years, and let God be the guardian of success.[22]

While Doria was exhorting her readers to assume their duties as good citizens, the Free Officers were preoccupied with solidifying their own authority. They annulled the 1923 constitution, nationalized the press, abolished political parties, and confiscated the parties' funds. Naguib appointed a fifty-*man* commission, headed by Ali Mahir, to draft Egypt's new constitution. Later, a smaller founding committee of five would be appointed from this larger commission to decide on the form of government that would rule Egypt. Doria was still hopeful that "The Egyptian woman will obtain her complete political rights in the near future. I have faith that the officials have come to realize fully that allowing complete rights to Egyptian women is a correction to the situation, as there won't be any progress for a population half of which is paralyzed and inactive. The champions of the liberation movement will not be reluctant to restore rights to people who deserve them as this is a part of their mission."[23]

In the spring of 1953, she traveled to England to attend the meeting of the executive council of the International Council of Women in Reading, where she faced a hostile British delegation who automatically assumed she was one

Doria Shafik with Gisela Shaw of Argentina at Reading University, England, during the opening session of the meetings of the executive and standing committees of the International Council of Women, September 1952.

of the instigators of Black Saturday. It took Doria's charm and the persuasive skills of Jeanne Eder, the president of ICW, to allay their hostility. The *Daily Express* attacked Doria, accusing her of "being in the front row when the Wafdist government was inducing and stimulating people to murder a number of British people in Cairo. Doria Shafik (fanatically anti-British at that time) announced and confessed to one of our colleagues that she really loved the English and said: 'We cannot but depend on the English.'"[24]

Of course, this article aroused negative reaction in Egypt: "This is a lie as Doria Shafik has spent her life serving her country and her principles would not allow her to say what the colonial newspaper claims. No colonial newspaper should dare to distort our patriotism and unity by utilizing falsehood in propaganda against us."[25] At the same moment and on the other side of the Atlantic, Doria was being hailed as the model suffragette:

Last week, as every week, Doria Shafik was sallying forth to fight twelve hours a day every day for equal political rights for Egyptian women. Last week she came closer to victory when a special group of the Constitutional Committee recommended an end to political discrimination against women. Tall, slim and ultra fashionable in appearance with arched eyebrows and bangs, Doria Shafik looks more like a Parisian model than a suffragette. But her beauty conceals an Arab warrior's spirit, undaunted by the enmity of the Muslim leaders who cite the Quran to place a curse on female participation in public life. The elders of Islam have proclaimed her an "infidel" and her life has been threatened by young Muslim zealots.[26]

But opposition to Doria was not limited to conservative Islamic scholars or a hostile English press. Egyptian women criticized her for wanting to appear on the pages of the local and international press. They portrayed her as being oriented more toward European society than toward her own Egyptian community. Although extremely sensitive to these allegations, she firmly believed that cross-cultural understanding was not only possible but necessary if Egypt was to take its place as a modern nation. Because of her familiarity with the liberal humanist tradition underlying both cultures, she was more perceptive of Egypt and the West and consequently sought to accentuate the values connecting them. It is true that whenever she traveled to Europe, as she often did to attend meetings of international women's organizations, she was lionized by the press. But it is equally true that, given the emergent political significance of Egypt in the Cold War politics of the postwar era, to the Western world she was the most public symbol of the "new" Arab woman. A letter from Lady Margery Corbett Ashby, honorary president of the International Alliance of Women reveals just how significant:

Dear Madam and President:

I have read with a lively satisfaction the stories that were carried in the Swiss press of your energetic action towards your authorities regarding the new constitution. The situation between our countries makes any action here dangerous for your cause, but I can assure you that we would very much like to declare ourselves your enthusiastic colleagues in your fight for the dignity of the Egyptian woman.

That the woman of Egypt with its secular civilization is refused the right to vote whereas so many other countries have accorded her this minimal right is truly regrettable. Unfortunately reactionaries always use the pretext of religion to cling to rights that no longer correspond to the exigencies of the time.

If Bint al-Nil Union would like to become a society within the Alliance maybe we could make a campaign for you, if this would be of use to you. Do you have an article to send me? I would be happy to make the voice of the Egyptian woman heard in our journal which is widely distributed throughout the world.

You know that Mme. Ceza Nabaraoui is no longer a member of our Executive Committee. She has chosen the Communists as colleagues and although we acknowledge the great service that she formerly rendered our feminist cause, her activities in the Democratic Federation make her impossible as a member of our Committee.[27]

Give me your news, dear Madam, take care of your health as you are very precious to us. I would have written sooner but both my husband and I have been a little unwell.

I send you, dear Madam, my very sincere friendship and my wishes that your great General has the courage to stand up to the forces of reaction and that he will allow the Egyptian woman and especially you, to take the place in society that the needs of the country itself cry out for.[28]

Later that year, Doria was elected to the Executive Council of the Alliance at its meeting in Naples. This was against all precedent because, by statutory regulation, Bint al-Nil Union was already a member of the ICW and therefore not allowed to join this organization. Upon returning to Cairo from this meeting, Doria discovered that an Egyptian magazine had published two photographs showing her face-to-face with an Israeli delegate, with Hebrew scrawled across the photographs. Still technically at war with Israel, Egypt had adopted an official policy neither to recognize the state of Israel nor to have any direct formal contact with its citizens (a situation that persisted until Sadat's historic visit to Jerusalem in November of 1977). To depict her as having subverted her government's boycott at an international meeting was to publicly undermine Doria's credibility as an Arab nationalist. Knowing that Naguib understood Hebrew and wanting to correct this negative image, Doria asked Nour to send President Naguib copies of the photos through one of her husband's contacts with a military officer. The latter reported back that the president was amused since the text referred to her storming the parliament in 1951, "revealing that the photos had been doctored and reproduced in order to slander me." Doria was convinced that Ceza Nabaraoui ("who took every opportunity to call me pro-colonialist, then pro-Zionist; to tell stories right and left that I was a mannequin, more interested in my make-up than my nationalist spirit") was behind this episode.

Al-Kholi commented that he had tried to reconcile Ceza and Doria: "I couldn't bring them together. And in my estimation, despite Ceza Nabaraoui's reputation as a socialist/leftist, I believe, in fact, that Doria Shafik was on her way to becoming the much more politically active person. She studied, she read, and she analyzed to strengthen and to educate herself socially and politically."[29]

By the end of 1953, social and political events began unfolding at such a dizzying pace that the country's attention would be focused elsewhere than on women's rights. Egypt had been declared a republic and General Naguib appointed as its first president. Supreme authority in Egypt was now vested in the Revolutionary Command Council and the newly formed National Liberation Rally, which would serve as Egypt's sole political organization over the next three-year "transitional period," to end on January 16, 1956. The *ancien régime* and its former political leaders were either neutralized or destroyed.

Doria still held out hope that the new regime was being persuaded to her cause and firmly believed that the battle for women's political rights had entered its final stages when a decision was made to allow women to join the militia of the National Guard: "We are overjoyed that the leaders of this nation have begun to agree with us. This is evident in the statements they have been making since the revolution and most recently in their latest statement about the right of women to join the militias of the National Guard. The immediate implementation of this decision means they have recognized women's right to equality with men. Everything points to the nearing of the time when our pleas and calls will be answered. We deserve these rights and they in turn deserve us."[30]

Over the next three years, however, Doria's optimism turned sour in face of her growing reservations: "In place of a renaissance movement leading to women's rights, there was a flagrant transgression of the liberty of other people, heading in the fundamental direction of a progressive negation of human freedom on the individual, national and international levels. Toward what abyss is my country heading?"

11

Divergent Paths (1954)

I have taken my decision to begin at noon today, March 12, 1954 in the Press Syndicate, a hunger strike until death, in protest against the coming formation of a founding committee to create the new constitution in which no woman has been included. I refuse to be governed according to a constitution in whose drafting I have not participated. I make my strike at the Press Syndicate because the latter, by its very essence, is intimately connected with every movement of liberation. Signed Doria Shafik.[1]

Doria began the new year convening the first general assembly of the Bint al-Nil Union, which she unabashedly described as "our first parliament." Representatives of the Union's branches in all cities, provinces, and governorates of Egypt participated:

How sorry I am that those who oppose women's rights could not have witnessed how these representatives, displaying independence of will and political awareness, ran the session in a true democratic spirit. Intense and heated discussions voicing their various points of view were held in an organized, precise and comprehensive manner. To the extent that I have witnessed this attainment of awareness, strength of character and ability to shoulder responsibilities in this, our first parliament, I am more determined than ever to continue the struggle to obtain the rights of the Egyptian woman for the sake of Egypt and the sake of participating in the movement to rebuild Egypt. A liberated Egypt is only as productive as her liberated daughters.[2]

Doria's editorials discuss the common cause shared between women's liberation and national liberation. In the piece published in February, she asserts:

In the national struggle that is gathering momentum day by day in Morocco and Tunis against colonialism, in the growing national awareness in the Sudan, East Jordan, Libya and Iraq against colonial conspiracies, and in the revolution that Egypt declared against the forces of both colonialism and reaction, what is the role of the Arab woman? The immediate answer can be found in the images of the national resistance in Morocco and Tunis in which the woman participates for the sake of her country's freedom. It shows in the militant resurgence in Sudan, Jordan and Iraq. It shows in the examples of progress and civilization of women in Lebanon and Syria. The Arab woman today has to understand fully that there is no road to her liberation without her participation in the liberation of her country. Because there are no enslaved women in a free country.[3]

About this time, Doria received a letter from Lady Corbett Ashby, the president of the International Alliance of Women, who, despite her influential position, reveals a considerable lack of understanding of existing political realities. Such views add credibility to those critics who challenged Doria's affiliation with this sort of international women's organization. The letter contains an indirect attempt to co-opt Doria and the Bint al-Nil Union to recruit for the Alliance, which itself appears insensitive toward the nationalist sentiments of Arab women:

We are enchanted to have Bint al-Nil Union among our associations. Have you done a little propaganda for the Alliance on your tours? You have the political sense and I know that I can write you in total confidence. Our associations in the Near East do not give any sign of life and yet there are women in Syria and Iraq who need our friendship and help. They can't think about anything except the poor Palestinian refugees at present and are offended by our lack of support. But you are in politics, you can understand that after having tried many times to attract the attention of our governments to the fate of these wretched souls, the Alliance does not have the resources to come to their aid. I am sure that you have the confidence of these women and that little by little you could attract them to us. But if you can give us your advice on this subject we would be very grateful.[4]

One does not know what Doria answered to such a letter, if indeed she answered it. But her March editorial continues her plea for the formation of a league of Arab peoples: "I discussed with the brotherly people of Beirut, Amman, Jerusalem and Ramallah, the importance of uniting the feminist struggle with the national struggle in order to win the Arab case. Thus I had

Doria Shafik with Camille Chamaoun, president of the Lebanese Republic, during her visit to Beirut, where she gave a lecture titled "Women and the Arab Cause," February 6, 1954.

the idea of creating a league for Arab peoples. The mission of this league is to express the will of the Arab peoples and to link the Arab struggle among all our striving people for the sake of their freedom. The league will be the arena that unites the men and women of the Arab world in carrying the banner of the sacred battle."[5]

While Doria was arguing, through her editorials, that women's liberation was a logical extension of the authorities' call for national liberation, the regime was facing its own problems trying to contend with the most powerful movement in the country at this time—the Muslim Brothers. The latter had infiltrated deep into all sectors and strata of Egyptian society, particularly the student population, the poorer urban masses generally, and even the army. Despite their survival as a political-religious organization, they were no nearer to direct participation in the military-controlled government. Thus in mid-January 1954, the Muslim Brothers made their move to take over. Using the occasion of a memorial meeting to honor the dead in the Canal disturbances of 1951–1952, they incited their student followers to demonstrate: "Clashes followed between these and pro-junta student members of Liberation Rally. Within forty-eight hours the government arrested the leaders and several members of the Brethren, dissolved its organization and proscribed all its activities. The Brethren went underground and soon came to control a secret apparatus in the army, which constituted an even more serious threat to the regime."[6]

The challenge to the new regime did not come only from the outside. The junta also suffered from splits within the Revolutionary Command Council, particularly from differences between Colonel Nasser and General Naguib, who was by temperament more inclined to favor a return to a constitutional government. He resented the RCC's dictation of policy and criticized the summary sentences passed by the revolutionary tribunal on political leaders of the *ancien régime*. On February 24, 1954, Naguib was said to have resigned as president, prime minister, and chairman of the RCC, while Nasser proclaimed himself chairman and prime minister. "Led by Khaled Muhieddin, an original member of the Free Officers Executive and of the RCC, the cavalry officers proceeded to challange the Nasser faction in favor of Naguib's return to office. . . . Within twenty-four hours Naguib was reinstated as president but Nasser retained the premiership. The universities were closed down and on March 1 some one hundred and twenty arrests were made including several Muslim Brethren, Socialist Party (the old Young Egypt) extremists, as well as some Wafdists and communists."[7]

These divisive political pressures, both internal and external, forced the military junta to make certain concessions toward parliamentary democracy by announcing the formation of a constituent assembly to be elected the coming July. Although martial law was to remain in force until one month before elections, there was an immediate lift on censorship. Naguib was reinstated as prime minister and chairman of the RCC, with Nasser serving as his deputy prime minister.

It was precisely during these politically volatile moments that Doria decided to go into action. As events unfolded, her patience was stretched to the limit, and she became increasingly skeptical about the prospects of women's political rights under the new military junta, although only a year earlier, she had enthusiastically hailed it "as the beginning of a renaissance for women." Like many others of liberal persuasion, she believed in the effective return of parliamentary and constitutional life. Thus when the newspapers announced the approaching formation of a constitutional committee on which no woman was given a place, she revolted immediately in exasperation. She claims to have been "inspired by Gandhi, whose philosophy of non-violence always comforted me in dark moments. I remembered one of his sayings in which he stressed, 'if non-violence is the law of our being, the future is with women. Who can make a more effective appeal to the heart than women?' And it was Gandhi who showed me the way, which I followed that very day after reading the newspapers."

It was March 12, on a Friday, the Muslim Sabbath. After Nour had left the

apartment to join friends at his favorite coffeehouse and the two girls had
gone to swim at the nearby sporting club, Doria packed her small valise and
rushed to the elevator. Mme. Marie, startled by this sudden departure, asked
Doria where she was going. "On a trip to Alexandria for a few days," she
answered. But instead, she drove to her Bint al-Nil office and dictated a dramatic telegram to an astonished private secretary, with explicit instructions
that it be dispatched immediately to all members of the constituent assembly,
the responsible persons in the military government, the rector of al-Azhar,
the president of the Council of State, the members of the Press Syndicate, as
well as to all local offices of the Egyptian and foreign press in Egypt.

She then told her driver to head for the Press Syndicate, where she feigned
an appointment with the chairman. "But he is not here, Madame Shafik."
"Then I will wait for him in his office." She took her overnight case from the
driver, then handed him a letter to be delivered to Nour informing him of her
decision. Once again she would confront her husband with a fait accompli,
which she knew would "cause him pain as I always did with every one of my
manifestations. But I could not do otherwise to obtain the rights of women.
And what about my children, now ten and twelve years old, the age where one
is so sensitive, the age at which I lost my own mother? What if something
should happen to me, leaving them orphans, exposing them to a life of torment
such as mine? Did I have the right to infringe on the happiness of others?"

Within a matter of hours, her worried and distraught husband arrived on
the scene in the company of Naim Abu al-Fath, the secretary-general of the
Press Syndicate, who was concerned for his position in case of trouble. This
was the brother of the owner of *al-Misri* newspaper with whom Nour and
Doria spent the evening of the coup in July 23, 1952. Nour tried to convince
Doria to come home and reproached her for making this hunger strike alone.
At that very moment, the door opened and in walked Ragia Raghab, her friend
and comrade from the Bint al-Nil Union, who had learned of the strike in the
afternoon papers, "and my husband has no objection to my joining you."
Shortly thereafter, Doria's journalist friend Fathiya Falaki arrived (her two
young daughters, about the same age as Aziza and Jehane, were to join the
Ragai household for the duration of the strike). By evening, eight women had
come to the Syndicate to demonstrate their solidarity with Doria.[8] They sent
another telegram pledging "to hunger unto death unless our demand for the
representation of women on the Founding Committee and all other legislative
committees are met."[9] A telephone call from the Bint al-Nil Union in Alexandria announced that five women wanted to come to Cairo and join the protesters. Doria advised them to go to the Press Syndicate there and carry out
their strike. Many telegrams of support began arriving—including one from
Samiha Ahmad Mahir, daughter of the assassinated prime minister, and an-

other from Amina Shoukri, a well-known personality in the field of voluntary welfare and former associate of Huda Sha'rawi, who joined the protesters
in Alexandria.

What began as the dramatic protest of one woman soon became a major
media event that continued for the next ten days. Barely liberated from two
years of censorship, the local press had a field day. The sensation of seeing
prominent Egyptian women appearing in front of the nation bundled in their
bathrobes and adorned with hair rollers was too rich an opportunity for the
critics and skeptics to let pass unnoticed, and several mocked and ridiculed
Doria and her compatriots in scathing caricature:

> Being surrounded by male journalists, cameramen, TV people, we pre-
> sented a spectacle never before seen in the Orient. It started rumors about
> our conduct: that we were undressed before men—even foreign men—
> and had no morals. Even Taha Husayn put his pen to paper and wrote an
> article about *al-abathat* [the irresponsible women]. The rumors surround-
> ing this point were the most dangerous attack. Nour received telegrams
> from religious bodies ridiculing him for not being strong enough to "beat
> his wife and take her home." On the basis of these rumors, others ac-
> cused us of not being sincere in our strike, for staging it for publicity
> only. One newspaper even said we were not only eating surreptitiously,
> but eating "candied chestnuts." Another accused us of spending the night
> with the male journalists! These rumors were designed to ruin our repu-
> tations, those who concocted them knowing that in Muslim countries
> this is the most dangerous ground.

However, there were other newspapers and journalists who paid serious attention to the hunger strike. The prestigious newspaper *al-Ahram* published
daily accounts of the "battle of wills" and the "war of nerves" being waged
between the women strikers and the steady stream of Naguib's unofficial representatives, who argued, implored, cajoled, and finally, to avoid serious deterioration of their health, ordered the women transferred from the Press Syndicate to a government hospital.

The public discourse surrounding this hunger strike clearly reveals that
Doria Shafik and the women protesters had not only maneuvered the women's
rights issue into the forefront of public consciousness but also challenged
Naguib and the military rulers with an embarrassing and confounding situation. This was the moment of deep schism between those who favored a return to civil rule and the reestablishment of parliament and those who, fearing that the old power groups would return, favored surrendering all power to
the military junta. With the political situation in society at large so volatile,
they were concerned that any major public demonstration would ignite more

general unrest. On the other hand, they didn't want to appear unsympathetic to the issue of women's rights and immediately dispatched Ali Mahir to the Press Syndicate to meet personally with the women and try to convince them to abandon their strike. In Doria's view, "Our hunger strike offered a perfect cover up for the convulsions that were taking place within the junta. By focusing on us, attention was distracted from what was taking place in the shadows."

The argument between Doria Shafik and Ali Mahir revolved around the issue of representation on the founding committee mandated to construct the new constitution. Doria demanded that women be represented "because women cannot accept the rule of a constitution in which they have had no say." Mahir replied in equally categorical terms that "women cannot be appointed on the founding committee since this nomination can only be decided by the duly elected constituent assembly. The new constitution's project has tentatively approved giving political rights to women. It is up to the founding committee to put forward its proposals concerning the matter. Wait and see and do not take such rash actions."

Shafik reiterated her argument: "Women are more than one-half the population. The constitution equates men and women. It is the law of elections that is the source of differentiation." To which Mahir countered: "This situation has existed for thirty years and now there is hope for change and therefore no reason to protest."

But Shafik was not mollified: "The women of Pakistan were members on the founding committee and the women of Egypt want a legal solution to the issue and that is the reason for our hunger strike." In exasperation Mahir pointed out that "The strike is in no way helping the country and my committee can only defend the rights of women and the protesters in front of the elected constitutional assembly. The woman has won the first round and should relax and wait for the second round." Shafik persisted: "We have waited long enough. We want our constitutional rights immediately, and I think it is in keeping with the logic of our revolution."[10]

Ali Mahir ended the conversation by admitting to the press that "there was no immediate solution." However, within twenty-four hours he returned to the Syndicate, armed with a formal statement about the political rights of women. Choosing to remain in his car, he designated an aide to deliver the following text to the protesters:

The Egyptian woman joined the country's men in the 1919 revolution and showed her patriotism thinking that in its aftermath she would gain her full cultural, social and economic rights. Now she is working side by side with men in government offices, businesses and even in academic posts in universities. She lacks only her political rights. The committee convened for the preparation of our constitution has specified that women must ask for their right to vote. Many see this as a way of pushing women into public life before they are fully prepared to face it. That is why voting has been made obligatory for men but not for women.

The general policy of this nation, which is in keeping with documents issued by the U.N. concerning human rights, "is to offer and gladly accord political rights to the Egyptian woman." It is therefore only fitting that the elected body should place the right to vote for women in our new constitution. We are proud of India's victory in the U.N. which was achieved with the appointment of Mrs. Pandit Nehru. I am sure that with our new policy the Egyptian woman will achieve victory.[11]

Doria's response was uncompromising: "Tell His Excellency that we refuse! We have a faith that we shall never abandon and we shall not budge from the syndicate until we get a written guarantee of our constitutional rights." That night, hundreds of women supporters organized a demonstration surrounding the building of the council of ministers demanding to see Naguib and shouting: "Give the strikers their demands!" The syndicate "was like a marketplace. The boardroom where we were staying was a replica of a studio set with the huge lamps of cameramen and TV people and walls littered with press cuttings and photographs from newspapers all over the world."

Strong reactions both for and against the striking protesters began to polarize. A group of religious agitators demonstrated around the building shouting: "Let the whores get in there with them! Let their husbands beat them. The Quran authorizes it!" Some stormed the building but were arrested before they could attack the women. Yet the brother of Shaykh Hasan al-Banna, founder of the Muslim Brothers, wrote a letter of support that included a few lines from his own poetry. Delegates from women's organizations criticized the hunger strike as futile and useless "because it is not fitting for today's Egyptian women to enter an election campaign." A few like Samia Tewfik, vice president of the League of Arab and Eastern Women, and Fatma Nimet Rachad, president of the National Feminist Union, attacked Doria personally, arguing "that at such an unsettled time in Egypt, demanding women's rights was against the interests of the country": "I was shocked to hear women accusing me of working against the country, that it was not the time! I told them there is never a special time for demanding women's freedom. Our freedom goes hand and hand with the freedom of the country. There can be no free Egypt with enslaved women."

However, on the whole public reaction, was supportive. The Egyptian Red Crescent Society sent the protesters four beds. A delegation representing ten different women's organizations waited "from seven in the evening until one in the morning to meet with President Naguib to convey his opinion to the protesting women in order to reach some sort of compromise." The president refused to see them. Telegrams of support from home and abroad began arriving. Among those individuals and organizations represented were the Association of Liberation for Social Services, the National Women's Union, the La Femme Nouvelle Association, the Committee of the Rights of Lebanese Women, the Omdurman Women's Union, the Nubians of Egypt, the Union of Female Graduates of Alexandria University, Edith Sumerskill, one of the first women ministers in the British government, and Lady Corbett Ashby, president of the International Alliance of Women. Even some American television stations sent their representatives. One hundred and twenty students from the American University in Cairo signed a petition to President Naguib calling for an "end to reaction and the granting of full political rights to women. Fifty-six countries have given women the right to vote and it is now an impossibility for any country to claim that it is a modern state without having first given full political rights to over half of its citizens. It is therefore the responsibility of the revolution and its council to give women their rights."[12]

Muhammad Husayn Haykal, the highly respected Egyptian man of letters, entered the debate, commenting that "It is obvious that the days when women sought the help from men to improve their lot are gone; yet I am still surprised at the persistence of the protesters, especially after the promising statement made by Ali Mahir." Rendering his opinion on the distinction between the power of the founding committee and that of the constitutional assembly. he pointed out:

> The constitutional assembly has decided by a near consensus that women should have their full political rights. Yet these women want to participate in the founding committee as candidates and electors. The mission of the constitutional assembly is only to make suggestions. The law for the founding committee and for its elections is not a constitutional matter but one which is decided by the present government. Should the government support women's rights, so will the founding committee and vice versa. Even so I do not think that women believe that, if they are nominated, they will win a majority of seats. Women in England, France and the U.S.A. have the right of nomination and have not yet won many seats. Do our women protesters think that however many seats they win, this will be a show of their strength and capacity to defend women's rights? That may be so. But we must also see that by joining the founding committee they may be able to win men over to support their cause rather than maintaining a position of blind prejudice

against then. The president of the constitutional assembly has fulfilled his duties. It is now up to the government and the protesters to find a solution to this complicated problem.[13]

But neither the protesters nor the regime seemed willing to compromise. Then the unexpected appearance of Charlotte Weller—an American journalist who learned of the strike while traveling through Egypt with her husband George, himself a veteran foreign correspondent for the *Chicago Daily News*—"added an international tinge to our manifestation. I was delighted when the American asked to join us. This gesture of solidarity demonstrated that political rights were not just a question for Egyptian women but for women in general." Under the headline "Newsman's Wife Getting in the Act as Ladies of the Nile Starve to Win Vote," George Weller wrote:

For five days these women—five brunettes and two blondes, all but one married and one wearing her husband's pink pajamas—have been uncomfortably sharing four mattresses crowded together on the floor of Cairo's Journalists' Union. Two of the original nine have toppled over due to weakness, but none have yielded. The military junta ruling Egypt has tried to snub the strike hoping that it will collapse quietly. But Doria Shafik, who after having two children still preserves a Marilyn Monroe figure, told me: "I'm sticking it out till they give us a written guarantee." Unofficially Naguib has sent a series of fatherly men to wheedle the women into giving up. I watched the Daughters of the Nile rout both Naguib's legal advisor, Soliman Hafiz, a small dark attorney, and the suave governor of Cairo, Mahmud Nour. Arabic phrases flew, broken by French and British terms such as "unilateral rights" and "taxation without representation." Naguib's spokesmen pleaded: "You have aroused sympathizers all over the world and warned us of your feelings but it is time to end your fast. Otherwise your strike will be considered crude pressure on the government." Mme. Shafik replied hoarsely: "This government when overthrowing Faruq made plenty of laws in 48 hours. What makes it so sensitive about passing another to give rights to half the Egyptian population?" Naguib's fixers retreated after declining Mme. Shafik's *demand that promises be put in writing.*[14]

Two days later, Charlotte Weller filed her own story:

An Egyptian army colonel and the vice-governor of Cairo solemnly entered the hunger strike headquarters of the "Daughters of the Nile" Thursday morning and ordered the suffragettes to hospital. The ulimas of al-Azhar said the strike was tantamount to an attempt at suicide, which is condemned by the Muslim religion. They asked the government to take a firm hand against what they called the "frivolity of certain women." While the ladies argued, one of them, the poetess Amani Farid, fainted and had to be carried out to the waiting ambulance on a stretcher. As they left for the hospital, Doria announced that the suffragettes would stay together.[15] She led those remaining to the ambulance. Doria walked out with the dignity of a queen, modestly clutching her bathrobe as she withstood the stares of Egyptian males on the sidewalk. Not being an Egyptian citizen I cannot occupy a bed in the government hospital with the suffragettes. But from her hospital bed, Doria kissed me good-bye and whispered, "I will continue to fast until the government gives us a written guarantee that women can participate in Egypt's new constitution."[16]

Much to the consternation of the government, the women continued to fast: "After six days, the health of the women protesters has undergone serious deterioration, to the point that some women have had to be force-fed with tubes and given glucose shots. But they swear they will go on fasting in hospital."[17]

The headmistress of Aziza's and Jehane's school conveyed to Doria that "the school was in a turmoil as the children were repeating what their parents were saying: 'Doria Shafik was going to die.' Jehane and Aziza were in tears and their mother shouldn't let them suffer so."[18] And indeed, for the two young sisters, although accustomed to Doria's periodic absences from the house, the sensationalism surrounding their mother's hunger strike provoked very deep feelings of pride, bewilderment, ambivalence, and anxiety:

> I remember she had a friend, whose two daughters came to stay with us during the strike . . . so in a way there was not so much anguish as we were with other children who were sharing the same plight. Papy would take us to visit her at the Press Syndicate, but not every day. It was full of lots of people, newspaper men and journalists, and all the time people taking photographs. We were always being photographed. I remember the mattresses everywhere on the floor, the women were all dressed in bathrobes and Mummy would stay and talk with us a bit. I kept asking her, "When are you coming home, Mummy? When will all this end?" There was so much going on that we would stay for a short while and then leave. It was not like going somewhere where I felt a lot of anxiety at least at the beginning. Yet I was taken by surprise. All of a sudden all this was happening. And there was such a sensation around town. Everywhere we'd go, there would be Reuters. She was front page. At school the teachers would ask us questions and always refer to us as the "daughters of Doria Shafik." We were proud. Yet it was worrying, because at

school we would hear that she had died. There was an aspect of sensationalism but at the same time one of anxiety. Not total anxiety. It was only toward the end when they were taken to hospital and on the brink of death . . . at that moment there was plenty of anxiety.[19]

In utter dismay, Nour implored Doria to call off the strike, arguing that she was not strong enough to continue: "'Have you thought how much our children are suffering?' At any other time it would have been difficult to hold back the tears. But now I had passed beyond emotion. I was living with my soul, forgetting my existence as a human being with feelings and weaknesses. This region of the Absolute which I had reached did not leave a place for anything else . . . not even that which made me love my children more than myself. Nothing counted except my freedom!"

Mahmud Nour, the governor of Cairo, arrived at the hospital and informed Doria that he carried an oral message on behalf of President Naguib: "'I am charged to inform you that the new constitution will guarantee women's full political rights.' My answer was swift: 'I want this statement written on paper.' Beside himself, the governor pleaded, 'But I am the official representative of the government. I have been sent to tell you this. It is impossible to demand such a paper from the government, Madame Shafik.' I hesitated a moment then said, 'But we can do something. Give me in writing that you come to speak as a delegate from the president of the republic.' He acquiesced."

When the newspapers announced the breaking of the hunger strike, "hundreds of well wishers crowded the hospital ward to offer congratulations to the strikers, who were ordered to remain in hospital for three more days until they recovered sufficient strength to return home."[20] Doria herself had shed twenty-five pounds, "but in this ecstasy where I made a fast for eight days I felt in my heart I had equated the freedom of women with the freedom of humanity. When my husband and daughters came to visit me I took them in my arms feeling that I had returned from a long, long voyage. I was happy. I had my girls and my husband near me . . . I had a written promise for women's political rights . . . I had gone through the greatest experience of my life and it had brought me in touch with the Absolute."

Despite these expressions of bliss at having touched the Absolute, her impromptu and theatrical political actions, of which the hunger strike was the most flamboyant, placed a great deal of stress on Nour and Doria's marriage, which was already showing signs of strain. As her husband, friend, and financial advisor, Nour was a continuous and dependable source of support to Doria, offering his material and legal help whenever she turned to him for advice in the management of her magazines. However, as she became more politicized and committed to her "mission," Doria often made decisions without consultation and with which Nour totally disagreed.

Such was particularly the case over the financial management and editorial policy within *Bint al-Nil* magazine. Al-Kholi recalls:

Around 1954, a serious fight erupted. At that time I was very active politically and both Abdu and Nour al-Din warned Doria that I could endanger the image of *Bint al-Nil*. The government might close down the magazine because I was a known Marxist rebel who had been arrested several times. I remember Nour pulled me aside one day and warned me: "You are a political man and we cannot be responsible for you. You are a political liability and pose a threat and I want you to leave this magazine." But Doria told me No! She was a great lady. Really, she was open. She could have been one of the greatest women leaders. In any case I left; yet I kept on working for her. Sometimes I would write some of her speeches. I wrote without signature. They used to pay me fifteen pounds a month, but after I left she paid me twenty! Symbolically I was not on *Bint al-Nil* but in fact I was in very close contact with Doria. But it was not known, not publicly. I used to go to *Bint al-Nil* or to the office of *La Femme Nouvelle* late in the evening when no one was there and write the articles. This arrangement went on for a few years, until I was arrested and put in prison for a long period.[21]

Never inclined to argue in public, Nour and Doria's disputes were reserved for the privacy of their home, creating a rather turbulent domestic scene, punctuated by fierce arguments and strained marital relations. As Aziza recalls:

Ever since I can remember, from the very beginning, my parents would argue a lot. Their clashes were not over the fact that our mother was spending a good deal of her time out of the house being a public figure. No; the clashes were more around the many aspects of their everyday lives. I mean for instance my father was the financial advisor of the magazines and there were many things that they didn't agree upon. He was very involved in the business without really being in charge. She was in charge of running the whole thing but relied very much on his financial support, and at the same time she did not accept many of his views. So there were clashes on that level. And then there was another side to it. He was a very gregarious person. He enjoyed other people. She was probably more of a private person and so there were arguments. It was not a happy household. You see, there was always this contradiction, this wonderful outside picture that was very glamorous—both bright, very much admired etc. . . . and the reality at home which was something else.[22]

As only their closest friends knew, "nineteen fifty-four would mark the beginning of the end of Nour and Doria's marital relationship."[23]

In front of the press, both Doria and Nour kept up appearances. Whenever she was asked whether her husband approved and supported what she was doing, she maintained: "My husband and I have a mutual understanding and respect for each other's opinions and I am confident of his support." And indeed, despite his profound disagreement with some of her decisions, especially those threatening to bring her into direct conflict with the ruling authorities, Nour never publicly criticized or undermined his wife's actions. "In fact," commented Aziza, "he was very supportive of my mother. He accepted the fact that he had a wife who was a public figure. He was very sure of himself. I mean she was no threat to him. He never, never suggested that she stay at home. He knew that was out of the question."[24]

There is no doubt that Doria enjoyed basking in the glamour of the publicity that followed her hunger strike, and in fact, the media attention given to it would catapult her into the ranks of international celebrity, particularly in the United States. In a letter to Doria, Charlotte Weller comments:

Two American television stations gave nationwide pictorial coverage of the hunger strike on their evening news television programs. The story of the strike seems to have made just about every U.S. paper. Your friends in Beirut and Damascus think your strike most effective, but I am wondering where you stand now that the government has withdrawn the proposal for early elections including "full rights for all citizens." I shall not forget the privilege of participating, if only for 48 hours, in Egypt's political development. Please let me know when you are planning on coming through Rome. I should like so much to have you stay with me and let me introduce you to the Romans who are eager to meet you, including our ambassador, Clare Boothe Luce. Please give my warmest regards to Ragia, Amani, Bahija, Fathia and both Muniras. I should like to thank you again for allowing me to share your experience with you.[25]

Her Egyptian critics challenged the attention given to this alleged victory for the women of Egypt, claiming that the whole escapade was nothing but a publicity stunt that had ended in failure: "The position of the women protesters was a hard lesson for Egyptian women. Their failure was a result of their obvious haste. Is it possible that after all the efforts made and the propaganda given to them by the world media, they will be satisfied with having their problems merely 'looked into'? This is the failure we regret and which the protesters and the press wish to project as a victory. Where is the victory?"[26]

Doria was not long in responding to her critics:

My hunger strike was not a feminist demonstration pertaining to women's rights only, and if some illiterates and weak-minded people tried to defame it by making fun of us, at least the whole international press received it with all of its larger and deeper connotations including women's rights. The international press found in it a historical event that forecasts the strength of the democratic current and the firm roots of a new popular consciousness in Egypt. . . . this consciousness that cannot tolerate government without a parliament, without a constitution and without liberty. The whole world already knows the truth that nobody here dares to discuss: It is that democracy is a whole that cannot be divided and that incomplete democracy is a futile distortion and a travesty. Free peoples do not accept such a state of affairs and it will not satisfy them. I said from the very first moment that we do not acknowledge a foundation assembly in which women are denied the right of participation and we still stick to our opinion. . . . And we, the Egyptian women, will not permit being ostracized and enslaved anymore in this era of knowledge, enlightenment and freedom. . . . We will find a way to win our rights. The hunger strike is only a warning. It is the first step and will be followed by other steps![27]

For a brief moment following the hunger strike, it appeared that Naguib and his supporters had gained the upper hand in the internal power struggle. Resolutions were decreed, announcing the restoration of political parties, and Naguib promised to dissolve the Revolutionary Command Council after the forthcoming election of the constituent assembly. However, within seventy-two hours, barely a week after the hunger strike ended, these and all other previous resolutions were formally rejected—an action which meant not only the renewal of martial law, the return of censorship, and the dissolution of all political parties, but also the postponement of elections until the end of the "transitional period" (that is, until January 1956).

By mid-April, the Nasser-led faction had emerged victorious in the junta struggle. Surviving an assassination attempt on his life by the Muslim Brothers in late October, Nasser consolidated his position as the unrivaled leader of the country. On November 1, 1954, a new revolutionary tribunal was appointed to try those accused of treason, and many "leftist" officers were either purged or put in prison, along with suspected Communists and the previously arrested Muslim Brothers. On November 14, Naguib was placed under house arrest, thus eliminating any further challenge to Nasser's claim to leadership within the military junta.

By the end of 1954, Nasser had tightened his control and consolidated his power over the country, and for the next two decades, the future of the Arab region would be shaped by this powerful and charismatic leader. For the citizens of Egypt, however, this date marked the beginning of the collapse of democratic institutions, as measures were taken to centralize and industrialize the economy in pursuit of the "socialist experiment." Wealth was sequestrated, land redistributed, and industries nationalized. Nasser also clamped down on freedom of expression by abolishing political parties and placing the once open and free press under state control. For Doria Shafik's independent and assertive temperament, this was a path she could not follow, and in less than three years, she entered into direct confrontation with Nasser and his regime.

Pursuing the Absolute (1954–1957)

Resolved to go to the end of the road . . . without hesitation . . . without turning back. But what would this road be like? With all my love of truth and freedom (two concepts that were but one for me), I would discover the way. The way could not be imagined beforehand, once and for all. The way is made of sweat and blood, of battles and tears. A way of thorns and love. In the pursuit of the Absolute, one may finally find it.

— *Shafik, "Memoirs" (1960), 358*

Flight around the World (1954–1955)

Conquète de mon âme	Conquest of my soul
course affolée	frenzied flight
vers le ciel	toward heaven
pour y voler	to steal
un peu	a little
de feu	fire
de quoi me ranimer	with which to revive myself
et notre terre qui se meurt	and our land that is dying
comme toi, ô Prométhée	as you, o Prometheus
au Vautour	exposed
exposée[1]	to the vulture

I welcome this trip so that I may explain the important role played by the Egyptian woman in building the glory of modern Egypt and ridding the civilized world of the nonsense that still clings in its mind from the dead weight of the past.[2]

The enormous national and international publicity in the wake of her celebrated hunger strike opened a new chapter in Doria Shafik's life, forcing her to redefine her fight for women's rights in the context of the broader struggle for democracy in Egypt. The circumstances that brought about this redefinition proceeded from the events leading up to and following her voyage around the world at the end of 1954 and beginning of 1955. From this point onward, she irrevocably followed a course of action that would result in a defiant confrontation with Gamal Abdul Nasser and his policies.

Intending to participate in the important June meeting of the International Council of Women in Helsinki, Doria planned a stopover in Rome to visit Charlotte Weller. However, later in May, she received another letter that sparked her smoldering desire "to leave the country for a time, to make a long voyage, *not* with the intention of running away, as in my youth; *not* in quest of diplomas with which I had armed myself to the teeth. But to travel around the globe! To fly through the very high spaces in order to contemplate the world without perceiving its pettiness. Perhaps then, I could catch a glimpse of the Absolute."

The letter which offered her the chance to fulfill her ardent dream came from Garland Evans Hopkins, vice president of the board of directors of the American Friends of the Middle East, an organization that emerged shortly after the Second World War and was spearheaded by such luminaries as Dorothy Thompson, Dorothy Kenyon, Philip Hitti, and Lowell Thomas—all of whom had strong values and ideas about the prospects of Arab-American relations. It was officially established in 1951 as a nonprofit, private organization whose basic philosophy and objective was to open up the American public consciousness to a special awareness and understanding of the Arab world. Supported by voluntary contributions from individuals as well as generous donations from American oil companies, the AFME tried to accomplish its goal not only by conducting a program of guest lectureships in the United States but also by establishing ways to bring Arab students to the United States for study and training. However, "beginning in the late 1950's, the CIA began to infiltrate this organization by supplying monies and using 'agents' to exploit the 'good offices' of the AFME. As this became public knowledge among Middle Eastern governments, they became suspicious of the organization and particularly in the 1960's, refused to use it as a means for sending students to the United States for education and training. Other organizations had sprung up as the AFME fell into disrepute. Garland Evans Hopkins was never part of this and certainly not Doria Shafik."[3]

In his letter, Hopkins proposed that Doria come to the United States on a six-week tour from the Atlantic to the Pacific to lecture on issues and problems facing the contemporary Arab woman. She was delighted at the opportunity but wondered how she could arrange to continue her journey around the globe. Relying on her own ingenuity and Nour's seemingly endless generosity, Doria devised a scheme by which she could return to Cairo over the Pacific rather than back through Europe. First she needed several hundred pounds, "an amount which was not unbearable for my husband's purse," to add to the round-trip ticket from Cairo to San Francisco already offered by the American Friends of the Middle East. What remained were her living expenses while on tour. To minimize those in the Far East, she immediately wrote back and accepted invitations from Japan, India, Pakistan, and other countries of the region, which had poured in after her hunger strike. As for the expenses required for passage through the European capitals, "Nour, who never refused me anything that was within his means, would provide them." Conferences or formal speaking engagements were arranged for Doria in Rome, Paris, and London on the way to America and Tokyo, Calcutta, New Delhi, Colombo, Karachi, and Beirut on her return journey to Cairo. By June, plans were well underway for the American stage of the trip in the early fall.

Charlotte Weller, the American journalist who had joined in the hunger strike, was most anxious to see Doria and wrote: "I am delighted that you are going to the US and when you pass through Rome in September I hope you will be able to stay with me more than just a few days. If I can be of help introducing you to editors just let me know. Don't worry about writing to me in French, I can read it perfectly but have trouble speaking it without a horrible American accent. I cannot spell it at all!"[4]

Everything seemed to be moving along smoothly when Doria received a telegram, a month before her intended departure, inquiring whether she knew English sufficiently to deliver lectures. "And in what language did you think you would speak to the Americans?" teased Nour gleefully. Doria was in a quandary as she knew only a few words of English, and those certainly not at a level that would allow her to express herself freely. She cabled back the executive secretary of the American Friends postponing her arrival and immediately embarked on an intensive English-language course on gramophone records. With the help of her daughters and Mathilda Greiss, a friend who had learned English at the American Girls College, she set to work and prepared herself "by learning one lesson each day."

In preparation for her speaking engagement in London, Doria wrote to Lady Margery Corbett Ashby asking her advice about possible topics for her presentation. In her response, Lady Margery reveals an interesting perception of what the English would be most likely to want to hear from Doria:

> Since you so kindly asked me my advice I believe that a lecture on "Women and Islam" would attract the most attention, or even "The Woman in the New Regime of Egypt." The lecture you have prepared on "The Mission of the Woman in the Spiritual Life of the World," would attract more attention in the United States than with us. Our experience after 1918 with the participation of women in politics shows us the progress realized in the social sphere a little more than the progress in the spiritual sphere. Also the English, although very sentimental, prefer political and practical lectures.[5]

A second letter arrived shortly thereafter in which Lady Margery wrote that she had

> secured a hall for your lecture on October 28 at six in the afternoon. Everyone is thrilled at the idea of listening to you. Could you make your

lecture on the "Status of the Woman Under the New Regime," because now that relations between our two countries are so friendly one wants to hear more about the subject? I thought of offering you a tea with some personalities before the lecture and arranging a dinner with some of the women parliamentarians at the House of Commons after the meeting because the session will be at Church House, Westminster which has a beautiful restaurant near the House.[6]

Finally the day of Doria's departure arrived, and at the airport she held back her own tears as she tried to comfort her teary-eyed daughters, who were just emerging from their trauma over her recent hunger strike. "Don't worry, three months will fly by quickly," she assured them. Although he supported her decision to travel, Nour was none too happy at the prospect of this, their longest separation. With a wave to her family and her comrades from Bint al-Nil Union, who had come to see her off, Doria boarded a BOAC plane on October 19, the very day that Nasser signed the Evacuation Treaty with England, stipulating the withdrawal of all British troops from the Canal Zone within twenty months.

To the readers of *Bint al-Nil*, Doria explained the reasons for her world tour. Her language discloses how clearly she perceived herself as an ambassador of the Egyptian woman throughout the world, with a mission

to make propaganda for our nation and to raise its reputation everywhere. During this month, I will begin a trip around the civilized world. This trip is not a promenade or a pleasure trip and is not geared towards private gain. The trip is part of the mission that I took upon myself for the sake of the Egyptian woman's case and for the sake of making it known everywhere. It is now clear to everyone who possesses two eyes and insight that no society whose women are chained can prosper, and no nation will remain chained when its women are free. We have been affirming this fact to our people during six years of stiff struggle.[7]

She held an impromptu press conference at the Rome airport, where journalists bombarded her with questions: "How many Communists are there in Egypt? How far does Islam oppose women's rights? What do you think of women's entry into the public sphere?" The Egyptian embassy representative, worried that she was not prepared for these questions, suggested postponing her answers until the formal press conference later that evening. But Doria refused: "I preferred not to delay, afraid to give the impression of being unable to answer, which might affect my future conferences. So I answered their questions by posing other questions. How do you count Communists? They are invisible! As for women's entry into the public sphere I think it is

Doria Shafik with Lady Margery Corbett Ashby at the London meeting of the International Federation of Women, October 29, 1954.

the most powerful event of the twentieth century after the invention of the atomic bomb."[8]

It was in Paris that she felt her journey around the world would begin: "Perhaps because Paris was closer to the heart of Europe or maybe because I had lived and been educated there, that I felt my success in the other countries of the world would depend on my success in Paris." To this end she mobilized the Egyptian community in Paris to distribute a thousand invitations, "in the hopes that half would turn up." She persuaded the Egyptian embassy to help defray the costs of sponsoring a large public conference at the elegant Hotel Plaza, where she was staying. Among the many personalities who attended that evening's lecture was her friend Pierre Seghers, who had just published her second volume of poetry, *L'Amour Perdu*. "It was a long time ago," he avers, "but I remember Doria gave a conference on the first floor stage of the Hotel Plaza. It was a lecture on 'Woman and Egyptian Poetry.' She gave this lecture in French and it was indeed a great success. She was a very representative person: she was really the best Egyptian ambassador, if one can say so. First she was a very beautiful woman, she had glamour and she was very active. She was truly in fine form . . . a vigorous woman!"[9]

In the discussion that followed her lecture, Doria was bitterly attacked by one of the French journalists for her excessive nationalism: "I criticized France's continued occupation of Morocco, which was struggling towards national sovereignty under King Muhammad V. The journalist made me understand that I was an undesirable visitor, because I expressed what I believed to be true and just, despite the fact that I had been educated in France and had many friends there. I answered that she must not forget that I was an Arab."[10]

On the eve of her departure for London on October 26, the Muslim Brothers made their unsuccessful attempt to assassinate Gamal Abdul Nasser in Alexandria, an act which evoked a great deal of speculation in the foreign press about Nasser's political control. The regime's response left little doubt that democracy in Egypt was on the wane; hundreds of citizens were arbitrarily arrested and accused of treason, several Muslim Brothers were executed, and within the next months, nearly three thousand political prisoners had filled the Egyptian jails.

Egyptian political events would follow Doria throughout her trip, as the media, the Western press in particular, hounded her for commentary on the social and political conditions unfolding in her country, often forcing her into the uncomfortable role of having to defend a regime of which she now disapproved. She was placed in the paradoxical and ambivalent situation of wanting simultaneously to be ambassador-at-large for the Egyptian-qua-Arab woman, at the very moment when her own country seemed to be moving in a direction antithetical to her own deep commitment to "truth and freedom." She studiously tried to avoid any mention of her government, "something for which the Egyptian authorities would never forgive me." As the London newspapers were speculating about the arrests in Cairo, Doria was being interviewed on BBC: "Noting my anxiety when the conversation touched upon the troubles in my country, the journalist asked, 'Isn't it terrible to live in such a tense atmosphere?' What could I answer?"

But Doria's greatest anxiety came when her ability to communicate in a newly acquired language was put to the first test. She stood on the podium at Westminster to deliver "my first public lecture in an unfamiliar language in front of several members of parliament, many celebrated feminists (some of whom had been comrades of Emily Pankhurst) and a crowd of journalists, always on the watch, ready to criticize." Although she had a prepared text, "I decided not to read it; a read lecture is a dead lecture." She put away her papers and, in her usual flamboyant style, launched into an extemporaneous talk "using the few English words I knew, substituting French ones when I was stuck, and if they didn't understand me, I gestured with my eyes, hands and body until my audience, discovering the word, would shout it to me. Communication was established. We created the conference together because it was the same feminist experience which we shared whether narrated by an Egyptian or an Englishwoman. I met with the same experience in America."[11]

Doria commented later in her memoirs: "If Paris is the heart of Europe and London the fountainhead of feminism, then New York was like a poem. I fell into America as if out of the blue and remained open-mouthed. A mad frenzy surrounded me. Where am I? People walked too fast for my oriental step. People spoke too fast for my limited English. Do these Americans speak through their noses?"

Her first encounter with America was at a press conference where she was questioned about censorship in Egypt:

> The journalist seemed to know we had censorship and posed the question to bait me. "I speak. Moreover, I am here to speak." In this way I defended my government (although I totally disapproved). But I was not about to criticize my country in front of strangers. It was not from fear, but from a reluctance to wash our dirty linen in public. If your family deceives you, it is still your family. Everything that touches it, touches you. "My country is obliged to censor for a short while—a matter of security." My interlocutor answered: "If we had censorship, for even 24 hours, the government would fall." Fortunate country. I shut up!

But she didn't shut up when it came to letting the American public know about the struggle and achievements of the Egyptian woman in the modern world. During her first thirty days in America and with her customary gusto and limitless energy, Doria traveled back and forth between New York and Washington and other major towns in between, giving over forty public speeches, holding press conferences, being interviewed on New York television, taping radio interviews, and conferring with different women activists and groups.

She was convinced that through these efforts, "The world has started to see in the modern Egyptian woman the old strong Egypt, and it has realized that times have come full circle, when our women exhibit accomplished minds, strong hearts and deep awareness. The world now believes that the 'daughters of the Pharaohs' have emerged from the dark ages and they will not return to them again. No power on earth can stand in the way of their progress."[12]

Nevertheless, Doria was impressed by what she perceived as the American woman's enjoyment of complete freedom and equality with men. To her readers back in Egypt, Doria portrayed the American woman as "Commander of the Situation," in rather utopian and idealistic language:

> Whenever I ask about the American woman, I find her everywhere: in the fields and factories, in the courts and the legislature, in the lowliest

and in the highest jobs. She is the spirit and beauty of American society. She is a kind mother and a good wife. Her work does not hinder her from struggling for the sake of her people, nation and children. I now know the reason for the glory that the United States is enjoying. . . . It is the woman who contributes in this active nation, the woman, for whom the man pleasantly makes room, without being fidgety or resentful. I came to the United States after the elections. Everybody is happy because all the women nominated won without exception. This society can announce to the whole world that it repeatedly gives preference and full rights to the woman, and generously gives her a seat in the congress. . . . I came here to speak to the people about the emancipation of women in Egypt, in particular, and in the Arab world in general. I was a bit shy, because there is a wide gap between us and the Americans. When a comparison is made, it is very painful. Yet, they have passed through the stage that we are now experiencing. They have simply moved faster and taken the lead in acknowledging the service of their women. They were not miserly in encouraging and inspiring them. They saw in the liberty and independence of their women the liberty and independence of their nation. We should not be depressed, for the day will come when the Egyptian woman will march with the American woman shoulder to shoulder and this day is near, as long as the Egyptian woman knows her right and exerts herself for the sake of this right.[13]

Doria had come to the United States right after the 1954 by-elections for seats in the Senate and House of Representatives, and Eisenhower was still in office during this period. She was taken on a visit to Congress, where she attended one of the sessions of the McCarthy hearings—"a stain on the face of this country of freedom and democracy," she remarked in her memoirs. Although Doria was surprised "by McCarthy's ability to speak in such an artful manner, he did not make the best use of this skill for the public good. He was an example to the whole world that there is no real success without principle and faith!"

In marked contrast, Mrs. Edith Sampson was "the one American woman who left a deep and lasting impression on me." Sampson was a prominent black lawyer, chairwoman of the Committee on International Relations of the National Council of Black Women and a member of the executive committee of the United States commission to UNESCO. In 1952, she was appointed by Eisenhower to serve as an alternate of the United States to the seventh session of the United Nations General Assembly. In April of 1955, two months after Doria's return from her world trip, Sampson arrived in Cairo on the first leg of a two-month AFME sponsored lecture tour throughout the Middle East: "She was a personality who truly honors and raises the status of women. I couldn't have guessed that she would be so elegant and good looking. What made her very special in my eyes is that she was the first to attack Senator Joseph McCarthy and confront him without giving any importance to the 'terror campaign' he led against her on the pretext of protecting the country against communism. Her example made me aware of women's bravery in the face of tyrants. And I felt it would be great to be like this woman and have her courage."[14] How prophetic these words would be.

Interestingly, however, many Americans saw in the figure of Doria those very same qualities she so admired in Sampson. John Gunther described her as "one remarkable personality. She is a poetess of distinction, a journalist and publisher—one of her magazines has a position comparable to that of the *Ladies Home Journal*—the leader of the Egyptian feminist movement, a signal political force, and, together with all this, one of the most exotically beautiful women in the Middle East."[15] *Holiday* magazine portrayed her as "A Tempest in the East": "Mundane and chic, Doria Shafik is a startling and attractive contrast to the traditionally veiled figures of most of her countrywomen. Explosive and courageous, a single-minded lady in a hurry, the elegant Dr. Doria Shafik fights implacably for women's freedom in her fast-changing and newly-aroused country. Here is a very modern story of an exciting personal battle against tradition, ignorance and the awful weight of the past."[16]

Harper and Brothers, a publishing house, wrote to her immediately following the appearance of this article, commenting that she "must have a fascinating personal story to tell if she could be persuaded to tell it."[17] And for the next two years, Doria unsuccessfully tried to write her life story in a manner that the publishers thought would "appeal to Americans." Writing her chapters in French with someone else translating them into English produced stilted narration. She sought help from Charlotte Weller and sent drafts to Garland Evans Hopkins for his counsel. But whatever she produced just did not click with Harper and Brothers, and the whole project was dropped by the summer of 1956, when the chairman of the editorial board wrote: "I am afraid that the editor's letter to you of May 24 will come as a disappointment. There does seem to be a big difference in the reaction of American readers compared to Egyptian readers. In the event that you would like to send us more material, we'd be glad to read it. However my frank advice would be for you to approach a new publisher who would come fresh to your manuscript."[18]

It was Doria's living persona, more than her autobiographical jottings, that would leave a lasting imprint on the memory of those Americans she met during her six-week sojourn. For some, it was almost infatuation: "Just a short note to accompany the enclosed *Holiday* article. Would still enjoy receiving an autographed picture from you. Thank you for the copy of *Poésie*. I also saw your picture in the *Nippon Times*. Am much more relaxed now *grace à vous*."[19] For others, she was an inspiration: "We have enjoyed reading about you as you have progressed along your trip. Recently at the United Nations on December 15 I was delighted to hear the wife of the Egyptian Ambassador, Mme. Aziza Husayn, giving practically your same talk about the status of women in Egypt and Islam."[20]

* * *

But Doria's visit to America would come to signify more than the froth of publicity surrounding her beauty, or a fascination with the woman question in the Arab East, or a curiosity about her own life, which was still very much in the making. Given the critical juncture of Arab-American relations during this particular historical moment, Doria's success with the Americans would become a liability back in Egypt. During her visit to America, Naguib had been placed under house arrest: "The newspapers made no comment. However it was easy to surmise what had happened. In the heart of the military junta, power had followed its course. My country was advancing toward the abyss." Cold War politics entered a new stage where the growing influence of Nasser's pan-Arabism appeared on a collision course with Dulles's policy of Russian containment, directly affecting Egyptian-American relations in the months and years to come.

As Doria was preparing to leave the United States in late December 1954, the executive secretary of AFME was writing a letter to the regional representative in Cairo suggesting that he watch out for Doria's return and perhaps make an opportunity to talk with her: "As you undoubtedly know, Doria Shafik is now concluding her tour as AFME's guest lecturer in the United States. She has been well-received and her visit here has, in general, been most successful, bordering at some points on the spectacular, as you may well imagine, if you know Doria. She has picked up while here some interesting ideas that she hopes to develop on her return concerning the use of radio and television, particularly in regard to the possible use of television in a literacy campaign. It would be well worth her while to talk with you when she returns."[21] During her stopover from New York to Seattle, Doria spent a few hours in Washington, where "I met Henry Byroade, Under Secretary of State for Foreign Affairs and the next US ambassador to Cairo, and suggested to him the possibility of using TV in my campaign against illiteracy in Egypt. The idea first came to me during one of the many sessions on TV that populated my days in the USA and I thought: TV must not only reach people, it must teach them.

Doria Shafik delivering a lecture titled "Modern Women of Egypt" at Somerset House, Pakistan Karachi, January 9, 1955.

This seemed to interest the Secretary and for my part I was enthusiastic for a meeting likely to aid in the establishment of TV in Egypt, which we still did not have."

As she headed westward, she felt the pangs of homesickness: "I long for a quick return to my beloved country as my tongue keeps repeating the immortal words of Shawki: 'If my body has been deflected from my country, then my soul will bring it back.'"[22]

Her journey through Asia was as educational as it was exhausting: "In Japan I had the feeling of landing on a see-saw. A land exposed to earthquakes and tidal waves, I was dazzled by its beauty. I was thrilled to meet women parliamentarians, but perplexed by their fatalistic acceptance of the geisha system. In Hong Kong I was astonished to learn that women were taken by men at will and kept as possessions as long as they pleased them. I concluded that polygamy is not a specialty of Muslims! What a consolation!"

Over the course of the next four weeks, Doria admonished the Japanese parliamentarians to work toward legislation to put an end to the geisha system, harangued the women of Hong Kong to start demanding their rights, and, in Pakistan, openly rebuked Prime Minister Chaudry Muhammad Ali for taking a second wife. In response to the specific requests of the women's associations of India, Ceylon, and Pakistan, she focused all her public lectures

Doria Shafik meeting with Fatima Ali Jinnah, sister of the founder of Pakistan, January 10, 1955. Egyptian newspapers described the encounter: "Two Leaders: One from India, One from Pakistan. Doria Shafik in the Salon of Fatima Jinnah, First Lady of Pakistan."

on the injustices of polygamy: "My conferences took a tragic turn in Pakistan, provoking even worse disorders and tumults than those occasioned in my country by the Muslim Brothers." She met Fatima Ali Jinnah, the sister of Muhammad Ali Jinnah, the founder of the modern state of Pakistan:[23] "A certain asceticism surrounded her with an aura of moral grandeur that I could not but admire, yet so much religious fanaticism. I left her feeling very uncomfortable about the future of Pakistan."

But the country to which she was spiritually drawn was India, "the land of Gandhi! My Master! *Satyagraha*, power of truth, non-violence! I approached this land with the respect one feels only toward sacred places. Mystery of a country that Gandhi forever vitalized by his absolute gift of self. I met with Jawaharlal Nehru, and through his conversation, felt the ineluctable presence of Gandhi. I lived in a dream world, a dream of truths." When Doria heard, by chance, that Prime Minister Nehru was passing through Calcutta on his way to New Delhi at the same time as her visit, she requested, through the good offices of the Egyptian consul-general in Calcutta, that a meeting be arranged.

Mukhtar Zaki recalled his first encounter with Doria Shafik in 1950, when he returned to Cairo from the Egyptian Embassy in London to assume the post of deputy director of the press of the Ministry of Foreign Affairs:

> Doria came to see me with a request for the ministry to purchase 1,000 copies of *La Femme Nouvelle* to be sent to all Egyptian embassies around the world. Because Doria was always in debt producing this magazine I convinced the ministry to purchase 500 copies. I was able through the secretary of the Bengal government to get her an appointment with Nehru, who was aware of Doria Shafik and her efforts for women's rights and of the fact that India had expressed great interest in the revolution that was taking place in Egypt. The meeting was held at ten o'clock in the evening and Nehru stayed with her for over two hours. When she returned to the consulate after the meeting she took care not to discuss any details so that it would not be reported back to Cairo.[24]

Doria Shafik with Prime Minister Nehru of India, following an hour-long interview in Calcutta, December 25, 1954.

Before her meeting with Nehru, Doria played with the idea of visiting Communist China:

I regretted not having visited any communist country on my voyage. Until then I had always condemned communism, only knowing it through the destructive elements within my country. But can one judge things from such a distance? Before condemning something isn't it necessary to try to have an idea by approaching the truth as closely as possible? No problem can be solved if one knows only one side of the conflict. I needed to know both sides before making judgments. I conferred with the consul-general about my plan and he was absolutely against it, arguing that aside from my being taken for a "communist," such a visit would greatly displease our government. I decided to open the question with Nehru but a sort of timidity restrained me. I felt it would not be elegant to ask a favor from someone I had just met for the first time. My project collapsed.

Little did she realize what significance this encounter with Nehru would have on her own destiny when she returned to Egypt. On the eve of her departure from India, she was "trembling with fear of returning to my country empty-handed . . . without having anything to report of my flight toward the Absolute." From her hotel room in New Delhi, she looked out upon the gardens beneath and experienced a kind of mystical union with life itself: "I felt the leaves trembling, as I was trembling, realizing the communion of all beings, on every scale of life. I felt profound sympathy for the least vibration of all these beings, evoking Gandhi's hymn: 'That one, whom the arrows of love bewitch, knows the power of that love.' The spirit of truth, in its immanent universality, the principle of love, of goodwill, non-violence. The way is there. I had found my way: Truth. It is not just a word. It lives. It is to become. The fire-builder, taking me by the hand leading me toward the ultimate hope, the ultimate goal: Freedom."

She stepped off the plane in February into the loving embraces of her husband and children and the proud congratulations of her Bint al-Nil Union comrades. Brimming with excitement, presents, and stories, she was too happy at being reunited with her family to realize how profoundly the Egypt she had left just three months ago was moving in a direction that she could not or would not follow.

13

The Beginning of the End (1955–1957)

O, Liberté	O, Freedom
Je te fais don	I make you the gift
de mon coeur	of my heart
sans toi	without thee
pour moi	life is
nulle	worthless
vie!	for me!

From the moment of my return I entered into a new struggle, one that had taken on fresh meaning since my voyage around the world. A meaning infinitely more far-reaching with regard to the question of freedom. Renunciation of self, the fundamental building block of the very concept of freedom. Without this total fusion with the world, without this absolute abnegation for the common good, do not speak of freedom. A regime in which the fundamental importance of the human being does not constitute the beginning and the end, cannot speak of freedom.

Throughout her voyage around the world, Doria was careful to maintain a determined silence about Nasser and the new regime—a silence which was interpreted by the authorities in Egypt as an implicit form of challenge. The generous media coverage surrounding her public appearances in the various capitals of Europe, America, and Asia reinforced the growing feeling in certain quarters back in Egypt that Doria was "in league with the centers of reaction who were against the revolution." And upon her return, she became a target for the press, reinforcing her feelings of estrangement from a society that was growing more and more populist in the wake of the broader political struggles of the Cold War. In Mustapha Amin's view:

Doria began to journey to all parts of the world publicizing the case of the Egyptian woman. She traveled East and West and met with leaders and rulers. Prime Minister Nehru invited her to be his guest during her visit to India. In 1954 news agencies said that Dr. Doria Shafik was one of the most important women in the world and *The Daily Mirror* described her "as wanting to be a twentieth century Cleopatra." The authorities in Egypt were not too thrilled by her activities which went beyond certain limits, and newspapers and magazines began to attack her, calling her the "perfumed leader."[1]

Nasser had ascended onto the world stage at the very moment when the Western powers, led by America and Great Britain, were becoming deeply concerned about communist penetration into the vital regions of the Middle East, particularly the coveted oil reserves of Iran, Turkey, and Iraq. To impede that spread, U.S. Secretary of State John Foster Dulles and British Foreign Secretary Anthony Eden initiated a strategy of Russian containment, known as the Baghdad Pact, hoping for Egypt's participation. Nasser, smarting from the humiliation of an Israeli raid on the Gaza strip and its subsequent occupation, refused to join, not only because he was offended by the neocolonialist tinge of this obviously anti-Soviet pact, but also because he felt it would compromise his pan-Arab nationalist aspirations.

In April 1955, Nasser left Egypt for the first time in his life to attend the founding meeting in Indonesia of the non-aligned countries, known as the Bandung Conference. There he met Tito, Pandit Nehru, and Chou En-lai, who introduced him to a Soviet connection for the purchase of arms. Dulles, alarmed that Nasser was flirting with the Communists (and furious at the arms deal) decided to give him the lesson that non-alignment was counterproductive. He reneged on his previous promise to aid Egypt in its plans to build the High Dam at Aswan. The World Bank and International Monetary Fund shortly followed suit by withdrawing their financial support.

In an impassioned speech on July 26, 1956, that aroused the fervor of the Arab world, Nasser announced the nationalization of the Suez Canal Company. On the following day, an enraged Eden described Nasser as "another Adolf Hitler who has his hand on our jugular"[2] and secretly joined France and Israel in preparations that ultimately led to the outbreak of the first Suez War on October 29, 1956, otherwise known as the Tripartite Aggression. President Eisenhower refused to support such naked aggression and used his influence to negotiate a cease-fire and withdrawal of foreign troops. Israel continued to maintain troops in the Sinai. Nasser emerged from this crisis as a nationalist and populist hero for the Egyptian masses and for the several anti-colonialist people's movements taking place throughout the Arab world during this historic moment. However, for Doria these years "began to mark my country and my heart with a profound wound, a single and incurable wound, shared with a world racing headlong toward nothingness—an Egypt wedged between a Russia, already infiltrating into the depths of our social structure and an America, wanting to replace England and play a major role in the Middle East, arriving among us with its fluctuating policies or rather, its absence of policy. More than one signal announced the tearing in two of a haggard world. In one bloc as in the other, along with those who believed they could stay in the middle, there was this horrible sensation of falling into the abyss."

As Nasser rose to the peak of his personal power, hoping to make Arab nationalism a political force not only in the Arab region but throughout Africa and the Islamic world as well,[3] the democratic institutions in which Doria fervently believed and ardently struggled to extend to women began to collapse. From the perspective of her own Bint al-Nil Union, Doria was aware that the future of civil society was at great risk under Nasser's centralist bureaucratic philosophy and socialist experiment: "From the point of view of the political rights of women it was the beginning of the end, we had returned to our point of departure." The state co-opted the Bint al-Nil movement by taking over all the various women's organizations and centralizing their activities through the Ministry of Social Affairs. Hoping to win over the support of women from all classes and to take the wind out of the movement's call for equal political rights, Nasser gave women the right to vote. Shortly thereafter, all efforts to organize around feminist or class issues, whether liberal or progressive, came to an end, and the dynamism and self-confidence that the women's movement had contributed to civil society from the era of Huda Sha'rawi to that of Doria Shafik would soon disappear.

It is within this context that Doria, in her quixotic pursuit of the Absolute, would wage her final, solitary battle against this process of disempowerment by an emergent authoritarian regime within Egypt: "Almost from the moment of my return, I felt I knew not what indefinable malaise in the atmosphere around me: within my magazines, within the executive board of Bint al-Nil Union, even within the bosom of my family." By the time she got back, Ibrahim Abdu—dismissed from his teaching post at Cairo University for being a reactionary Wafdist—had left the country to work for an Arab publishing house in Kuwait. To finance her projects as well as the expenses of her public life and maintain the household with two teen-aged daughters, Nour had to devote more time to his private law practice. His increasingly frequent travel outside Egypt removed him from any further involvement in the management of the magazines, but it also fueled local gossip "that he had taken a mistress and was spending less and less time at home, because his home life was so intolerable, always discussions about Doria's political involvement and the large financial expenditures on her feminist movement; all she wanted was publicity and to be glorified."[4]

Disturbing changes were taking place within her Bint al-Nil Union as key posts were taken over by pro-regime elements. As Zaynab Labib, vice president of Bint al-Nil Union, recalled:

> At the beginning we had many members, but after the revolution, several grew afraid, because the regime was against Doria; that is, they didn't approve of her activities or her tactics. And in time things began to disintegrate. Economic pressures threatened her magazines. Since all publicity was controlled by the state, she could not get advertising and thus was in constant need of money. All her projects: the Bint al-Nil clubs, the literacy schools, the cafeteria for working women, the employment office, all were on the verge of collapse from lack of funds and the bureaucratic red tape.[5]

This disintegration of Doria's projects was reflected in the local media, which never tired of making her the center of attention, however they chose to portray her. After all, she was glamorous, elegant, a dramatic newsmaker and the first Egyptian woman to have undertaken such a world tour.

Nevertheless, all this did not generate much enthusiasm among those sympathetic to the new regime, who tended to look upon Doria as merely a vestige of the "old feudal society," "a lady of the salon" who did not really have much contact with, or empathy for, the masses. And following her world tour, the local press took on a more sarcastic and at times openly hostile tone towards her. At a reception held at the Press Syndicate, organized by some of the major personalities of Egyptian art, theater, and dance, she was presented with a statuette portraying her standing astride a replica of the globe, "presumably glorifying my trip around the world." "But," she mused, "why was this being given to me by artists and belly dancers rather than women journalists, writers or educators?" Within days, her photograph appeared in one of the largest weekly magazines, doctored in such a way that "my head had been superimposed on the top of the body of a belly dancer in a very obscene pose. It had the taint of blackmail. The worst propaganda for a Muslim feminist leader!"

This was the first time that the press had been so openly crude in their ridicule and derision of her and she was provoked into writing a defensive rebuttal:

> There is a big difference between criticizing me and insulting me. Criticism is an important national act that comes out of every honest observer. However insults are a matter that I personally don't like to describe, especially when they are published in a newspaper or magazine. Newspapers and magazines are enlightening to those who know the value

of journalism and are able to understand the greatness of their message. For ten years *Bint al-Nil* journal has been every home's magazine, informing every woman about her duties toward her husband and her son and it has never gone one foot beyond its message. I remember the calumny that Huda Sha'rawi endured when she inaugurated the first salon to which men and women were invited. Those who had engaged in attacking her were the worst of scoundrels who had been paid to sell lies in the place of truth. I never realized in all I have read about women's movements, that the leaders of such movements are supposed to be pale-faced, messy-haired and shabbily dressed. That is why I am surprised that the defect of the women's awakening in Egypt, to some of its opponents, is concentrated around the fact that those who are carrying on the renaissance are women who know their duties toward their country and their home and don't neglect their elegance as women.[6]

But Doria regretted having spoken out and vowed "never again to allow myself to sink to the level of my adversaries." For reasons that are linked as much to the changing political climate as to her own enigmatic persona, particularly her many connections with the West, the Egyptian press, now under government control, increased their critical attacks, some dismissive of her literacy program, others derisive about her political naiveté, and all skeptical about her true Arab nationalist intentions.

When she attempted to introduce the use of radios in her project to combat illiteracy, the Egyptian press mocked her: "It seems that Dr. Doria Shafik is tired of striving for women's political rights and has now decided to do something else: to trade in radios. The Bint al-Nil Union has become like a commercial shop in which appliances are sold in gross and in retail."[7]

When she received official permission from the government publishing house on July 2, 1955, to publish yet another journal, which she chose to call *Doria Shafik*, the reaction from the press was both sarcastic and scornful. To a regime on the road to a statist socialist structure, Doria's pamphlet seemed a throwback to an outmoded bourgeois liberalism: "Doria Shafik claims that her reason for founding this new journal was that she looked around for a magazine that expressed her opinions, and agreed with her orientations, but she couldn't find one. Thus she decided 'to publish a magazine that would carry my name meaning that I would be responsible for everything that was published.' Then, we ask ourselves, does this mean that *Bint al-Nil* magazine doesn't express her opinions despite the fact that she owns it?"[8]

The semi-official newspaper *al-Gomhouria* published a very critical article and a copy was sent to her, with a caustic note typed in French on the top saying: "This article is offered to Mme. Doria Shafik and for the best comprehension let someone translate it for her. With our compliments." The sarcasm implied in sending the Arabic article with a French note, as well as the content of the article itself, is obviously a thinly veiled criticism not only of Doria and her French education but also of what is perceived as her intellectual superficiality:

> Did you see it? It's a new magazine and its name is *Doria Shafik*. And I have one in front of me and it is the third that I know that bears the first name of a lady after Rose al-Yusuf, and Marilyn Monroe. Doria Shafik is an original lady `and the magazine that bears her name is her latest creation. No matter what the new magazine deals with, this magazine is a specimen of her writing and we have seen an example of her critical approach from her own social and political life. It is enough to describe it with the words: "Collective Poisoning: The Solution to the Problem of Mothers-in-Law." We refer to the perils of *subiya* [a cheap drink of slightly fermented rice, sugar, and water, occasionally tainted, that used to be sold in very poor districts]. Now did I succeed in presenting this new magazine? I hope you agree.[9]

While some Egyptians were mocking Doria Shafik for her shallow political analysis, others, francophones for the most part, were bestowing accolades on the success of the special summer issue of *La Femme Nouvelle*. She titled this issue *Mon Pays* (My country); it was a beautiful representation of Egyptian culture and heritage, complete with colored photographs, art works, prose, and poetry. The sale price of this issue was ten Egyptian pounds, so the segment of society having access to it was primarily the upper-class French-speaking elite. However, the Cairo office of the general secretariat of the Islamic Congress requested ten copies of this issue. Egyptians as well as foreigners were of one mind in describing the issue as an "aesthetic and artistic triumph." Some comments bordered on the euphoric:

> Thank you for your thoughtfulness in sending me the latest issue of *La Femme Nouvelle*. Thank you for the dedication, so warm, so friendly and above all thank you for the extraordinary effort you have made to put together such a beautiful work. It is not only that you plunge your readers with both feet into Egypt; you are also the first to put our nostrils there as well, if I may so express myself. The aromas, all the sweetness of our marvelous country is released from your poems. They are all so beautiful, but there is one that is so delicate, so subtle, so fine, so poetic that one cannot stop reading it. It is the *Poupée de Sucre* [The sugar doll]. What a dream, what an escape and how one feels your soul and all your grace. Thank you for having felt it; for having dreamed it and for having written it.[10]

Among a certain group of francophone poets in Egypt, Doria was regarded as "a woman of remarkable activity. A prolific bilingual writer who has written poems of an engaging simplicity, where interior landscapes and Egyptian impressions are stated in a few touches, rapid but sure."[11] She was invited to contribute several of her poems to an anthology, which also included the work of such Arab literary luminaries as Andrée Chedid, Georges Henein, and Albert Cossairy.

The Egyptian press, on the other hand, enjoyed depicting Doria in metaphors that stressed her enigmatic public persona. Qualities that had attracted a following several years earlier were now seen as superficial and out of step with the changing political agenda of the new regime. An article titled "The Leader of Candied Chestnuts Discusses Love, Dancing and the Ph.D." appeared in the prestigious *Rose al-Yusuf* magazine toward the end of 1955. In a rather lengthy interview, the reporter portrays Doria in less-than-flattering terms:

> There is no doubt that those who will write the history of the Egyptian woman will remain puzzled a long while by Doria Shafik as I remained perplexed by her for a full two hours. Is she a person who is as simple as she seems? Is she as cultured as she cares to be? I do not know. But what I do know is that she is, on the whole, a person whose elegance, conversation and perfume are beguiling. Doria Shafik is an excellent "lady of the salon." She knows how to choose her words, whether in Arabic or in French; she knows how to choose her topics of conversation, whether about herself or her Bint al-Nil Union. She always likes to be the center of attention, to be the most important person wherever she goes. She is known more for her hairstyle than for her women's association. She expressed an air of "aristocracy" in the way she moved and the way she sat. Was she affirming this aristocracy when she offered candied chestnuts to the board members of Bint al-Nil during their long meetings?[12]

For Nasser and his regime, Doria was less an enigma than a vexation. Her class affiliation and her many connections with the West, particularly America—at the moment when Nasser was trying to steer a course of anti-imperialism and non-alignment—irritated him. Given Doria's position and visibility as the recognized leader of one of the more active women's movements in the Arab region, she had captured the attention of many different groups and public figures during her voyage.

Throughout the following two years, Doria received innumerable letters either announcing the visit of some dignitary, or requesting her assistance in setting up meetings with other personalities in the region, or scheduling a private interview with a major foreign newspaper or journal, or asking her to lend her name to some particular political cause. Daniel Baroukh, the director of one such organization, the International Council on Arab Refugees, tried to persuade her to "accept the honor of inclusion on its committee of patronage." The main goal espoused by this organization—championing the pro-Zionist position of "trying to find a permanent and satisfactory solution to the 300,000 Arab refugees in the Gaza Strip, who represent a continual danger and drain on UN funds. ICAR is devoted to the goal of repatriation of some to Israel and the absorption of others into Arab countries"[13]—was diametrically opposed to the general Arab position calling for the establishment of a Palestinian state to which refugees would return.

There is no evidence suggesting that Doria ever responded to or accepted Baroukh's offer, but it is clear from her correspondence that many foreign organizations wished to honor her "efforts to obtain for the Egyptian woman and perhaps for all Arab women equal rights with men."[14] Prime Minister Nehru sent Doria a personal message through his ambassador in Cairo, "asking me to convey his deep thanks for your congratulations on the steps India is taking to enhance the status of women in India. He also wants me to tell you that he read your telegram with pleasure."[15] In August of 1955, Doria was in correspondence with Ambassador Ali Yavar Yung planning a return trip to India: "Your idea to speak on polygamy is an excellent one and I think you should visit Bombay and Hyderabad for this purpose. My boat arrives in Bombay on the fourteenth and I shall be in Hyderabad on the fifteenth and will sound the people out and let you know."[16] This trip never materialized.

She continued to receive enthusiastic fan mail, particularly from readers of the American press admiring her cause: "I have just read Anne Sharpley's story about you and the women of Egypt in today's Cincinnati Post. How can I be of help? Who knows but that the salvation of the whole world may hinge on the outcome of your extremely important endeavors."[17] However, it was mainly through the "good offices" of the American Friends of the Middle East and the newly established Arab World Information Center, who were seeking ways to foster friendship and understanding between the peoples of Egypt and America, that Doria was drawn into a network of prominent women leaders and personalities from America.

To a regime moving rapidly in the direction of pan-Arabism and non-alignment, this link to the West and America in particular seemed to add support to one popular view that "The ideas of Doria Shafik came from colonial instigation and through colonial institutions."[18] Doria, on the other hand, firmly believed that these connections were furthering the cause of Egypt: "Our country is passing through the most critical epoch in its life, thus it needs all the publicity and propaganda it can get. The Egyptian woman is half the nation and her role in this new era is to appear to the world to be standing in the

front row. That is why I traveled, and I think that my lectures about my beloved nation, along with all my private and general connections with the authorities in these different countries have realized the aims and objectives of
my journey."[19]

Within weeks after her return, these "authorities" began arriving in Cairo.
Eva Deane Kemp, then the liaison officer of the Arab World Information Center in New York, wrote: "Through the recommendation of Dr. John Badeau,[20]
the wife of a general of the U.S. Marine Corps is bringing a group of prominent American women to the Middle East and will be in Cairo March 6–22,
1955. They are particularly interested in meeting outstanding women in the
Middle East who are leaders in civic and cultural affairs. Naturally I thought
of you and believe this group would profit greatly from a visit to your editorial offices and literacy schools."[21]

Others who would follow in rapid succession and call upon the good services of Doria Shafik to set up meetings and make connections with prominent Egyptian women included Edith Sampson; Mrs. Theodore Waller, director of the *Herald Tribune*'s International Forum;[22] and most notably, the
outstanding American journalist, Dorothy Thompson, co-founder and first
president of the American Friends of the Middle East from 1951–1958.[23] Although totally committed to Zionism in the thirties, Thompson was appalled
at the injustices perpetrated upon the Palestinians with the creation of the
State of Israel and wanted the American public to be more informed about
Arab point of view.

The American Friends of the Middle East was set up to fulfill this purpose.
Aziza distinctly remembers Dorothy Thompson's visit at home, "where a
large number of women, mostly Bint al-Nil members, were present." Doria
and Nour often invited guests to their home. In fact, lunches at the Ragai
household were like mini-seminars on the current events of the day: "Every
afternoon around two or three, we would have lunch with our parents and
there was always some invited guest, either a famous journalist like Dorothy
Thompson, or some visiting dignitary like John Gunther, whom my mother
or father knew. We were never asked our opinion nor did we articulate our
feelings, but we listened to the discussions which were always centered around
politics, what was going on in the country and the world. It was very stimulating."[24]

It was during one such lunch that Doria and Dorothy Thompson came to
know each other on a more personal level. Although from different cultures
and backgrounds, these two women shared certain things in common. They
held similar convictions about the "truth" of liberal democracy, and they both
possessed a single-mindedness, an indomitable will and the courage to do battle

for the causes in which they each believed.[25] And the cause in which Doria believed, and for which she would soon pay a heavy price, was that of individual freedom.

On January 16, 1956, a new constitution was promulgated. It consisted of 196 articles and replaced a parliamentary form of government by a presidential republican system in which the president could appoint and dismiss ministers, a power that the deposed King Faruq exercised with great abandon. The constitution envisioned a new unicameral National Assembly, but it wasn't until July that a law was decreed which provided for election of 350 members from 350 districts and an organization called the National Union, which was to screen and select nominees for election to the National Assembly. There were to be no political parties, perceived by the leadership of the country as divisive. The new constitution was vague in its specifics toward universal suffrage, saying that "women shall have their rights," a statement which was understood to mean that women had won the right to vote and to stand for political office. But voting was not made obligatory for women as it was for men—an issue which Doria would focus on as discriminatory against women. By having to apply in order to vote or to run for office, women would have to demonstrate their literacy (a condition not required of men). Even some political analysts of this era seem to have interpreted the constitution as equivocating on women's suffrage: "The electoral law of 3 March 1956 had provided for universal *male* suffrage at eighteen years of age and gave franchise to military personnel on active duty."[26]

When that long anticipated moment for the announcement of the new constitution finally arrived, Doria sat by her radio at home rather than attend the mass rally in Liberation Square, where hundreds of thousand had gathered to listen to Nasser make his speech: "I was not pleased with what I heard and turned off the radio with such anger that it flew on the floor. I felt my hands chained even more than ever. Not only as a woman but as an Egyptian and above all as a human being. More than ever I felt betrayed over that which I held most dear: freedom." When she was asked about her reaction to the new constitution by the press, she responded categorically: "'A catastrophe!' 'Can we quote you?' 'What I say to the press is not a secret.' But our press did not make any allusions to this conversation. Moreover an absolute silence in the local press shrouded my name." However, the foreign press picked up on her remarks almost immediately:

Feminist leader Doria Shafik pressing her relentless one-woman campaign against Nasser's constitution declared: "I would fail in my mission if I were to approve this constitution without reserve." She said: "The constitution doesn't clearly define complete rights of women. The promise of women's political rights doesn't even exist in the text of the constitution." She added: "My primary duty is to take an uncompromising stand concerning the totality of women's political rights." She objected to the fact that Nasser promised women the right to elect but not the right to be elected. She said she would continue to oppose the constitution in spite of "a campaign of defamation" against her in the "government controlled press." She concluded: "I had hoped things would be different in Egypt, now that we have people of the constitution!"[27]

Doria immediately convened a meeting of the executive council of Bint al-Nil Union, and "against the advice of a vocal minority including my best friend," she inserted a resolution into the *procès-verbal* expressing Bint al-Nil Union's disapproval of "the confused and uncertain way that this new constitution treats the political rights of women, and demands that these rights be the object of an explicit declaration that does not leave any doubts about the true intentions of the government on this subject." She threw down the gauntlet and publicly challenged Nasser and his government, which the American press was quick to report:

Mme. Doria Shafik, a fighter for women's rights, has refused to rejoice over the government's pledge that Egypt's "female citizens" may be allowed to vote for the first time. Nasser's declaration of January 16, 1956, says that "women will have their rights." Later official statements that women will have the right to vote but not to hold public office satisfied her even less. These proclamations arose out of a vaguely defined article in the constitution pledging "to secure for the female citizens means for reconciling their family duties with their public responsibilities." What kind of rights are these, asked Mme. Shafik. They cannot force Mme. Doria Shafik to accept such half-way measures. Doria Shafik will continue to fight until she dies for the full emancipation of Egyptian women, for their rights to hold office, to make laws and to share the responsibility of running the nation equally with men. Mme. Shafik rarely uses the first person singular when referring to her feelings on such matters. She has used her self-assurance, her husband's money and tremendous energy to promote her position as a feminist leader. Her enemies say it is for self glorification. A tall attractive woman whose well plucked eyebrows are severely arched and give her a look of perpetual astonishment, she does not shrink from describing herself as extremely popular, dynamic and indomitable of will and one whose personality is a conflict of romantic sensitivity and volcanic emotions. A hint at the government's concern over Mme. Shafik's influence can be seen, however, in the press attacks that have appeared since she refused to take the lead in expressing gratitude to Premier Nasser for having "liberated Egyptian women." For example the semi-official newspaper *al-Gomhouria* called her the "perfumed leader" who has no interest in the common women of Egypt. None of her criticisms of the provision in the new constitution regarding women has been published in the censored local press.[28]

Her reasoning was simple. If women had to register on electoral lists and men did not, this was unjust and illegal. Therefore, as a way of protesting, Bint al-Nil Union members would not submit to the requirement and refused to register.

The government in retaliation made an announcement: "Members of Bint al-Nil were prevented from presenting their names for candidacy for election to parliament because they did not appear on the electoral lists. I told them: 'Is it for a parliament like this that we have fought so much? To acquiesce would be like breaking our fast with an onion.'" One member from Alexandria, Amina Shoukri, decided otherwise, broke rank and registered. Although stricken from the membership of Bint al-Nil Union, she became one of two women to be popularly elected to the first Egyptian parliament in July 1957.[29]

To defy Nasser publicly in such confrontational language only isolated Doria more from mainstream political sentiments and led many of her former comrades to conclude she had gone too far. To her colleagues within the Bint al-Nil Union, Doria's persistence in demanding full political rights under a regime that continued to curtail everyone's democratic freedoms seemed not only pointless but also very dangerous. Those who had not already left Bint al-Nil Union when the movement began slowing down after the revolution were certainly quick to desert her and her cause after this latest move. In effect, she lost the support of even those she had energized into action over the past eight years. To the older generation, Doria represented a risk under a regime that had concentrated power in the hands of one man. To the younger generation of middle-class youth, mesmerized by Nasser's charisma, Doria seemed somewhat irrelevant to the growing populist sentiments in Egypt. To the regime, which felt it had pandered enough to the cause of women, Doria's continued criticism and public demands appeared downright irksome and unsympathetic in the face of the growing external threat of Western, particularly American, neocolonialism.

But to Doria Shafik, seeker of the Absolute, who "loved freedom more than life itself," the concentration of power in the hands of one man, the lack of a free press, "where vitality can't reside except in free expression," the fear of the growing influence of communism, the political arrests and detentions, the destruction of her projects, the disappearance of everything she had committed her adult life to defend, "for a constitution that was not worthy of the name," all were clear signs of the "slow death of democracy, of Liberation." Yet her categorical rejection of the constitution's granting women the right to vote turned out to be a tactical error in that she lost whatever remaining credibility she might have retained among her dwindling supporters. Politically, it was a disastrous move. She signed her own death warrant by flouting Nasser.

However, convinced of the infallibility of her own position and imbued with a mystical sense of "the fusion of my destiny with that of the world," Doria— unable or unwilling to compromise—decided on a course of action that she hoped would awaken the Egyptians to what she perceived as the clear and present danger facing her country: the destruction of human freedom.

L'Absolu est là	The Absolute is there
au bord	At the edge
de ma conscience	of my conscience
n'y touchez pas	Do not touch it
vous détruirez l'HUMAIN	You will destroy HUMANITY
l'Infini	The Infinite
sur terre	on earth

14

A Woman Alone (1957)

Could an individual alone lead the flustered crowd and thwart the intrigue of universal destruction? Could an individual alone, say to the masses: Stop! This is not the path. It is not the truth! Could an individual alone move mountains? Could a woman alone stand against the human tide? A woman alone who had never taken up arms but who had, however, the most powerful weapon, her heart?

The Egyptian authorities were astonished by the news in the early afternoon of Wednesday, February 6, 1957, that Doria Shafik had entered the Indian embassy, several blocks from her apartment building in Zamalek, "to hunger unto death as a protest against the two enemies of my human freedom." She had written a declaration and addressed one in Arabic to Gamal Abdul Nasser, and the second, in French, to the secretary-general of the United Nations, announcing that

> Given the hard times that Egypt is now enduring I have decided, with determination, to hunger unto death in order to gain my external and internal freedom. As an Egyptian and as an Arab, I demand that the international authorities compel the Israeli forces to withdraw immediately from Egyptian lands and reach a just and final solution to the problem of the Arab refugees. Second I demand that the Egyptian authorities give back total freedom to Egyptians, whether male or female, and put an end to the dictatorial rule that is driving our country towards bankruptcy and chaos. And if I sacrifice my life for the liberation of my country, I alone take responsibility for this action. And I leave my husband, Dr. Nour al-Din Ragai, and my two daughters. If anything should happen to them I surrender to world public opinion and to Egyptian public opinion the responsibility for what would ensue. Doria Shafik.[1]

Doria Shafik's decision to embark upon what would ultimately be her last act of public defiance was not reached after long weeks of introspection and indecision. In fact: "The idea of a hunger strike was imposed upon me as a necessity," she was later to record in her memoirs, "on a day when my heart boiled over, as a river leaps its banks. I had to renounce everything to maintain the flame of my mission. I don't remember the exact circumstances that pushed me to it on that particular day, except this absolute necessity of my freedom, a contact with infinity, a veil torn away—to liberate myself or die." To grasp Doria's quixotic pursuit of the "Absolute" in the face of an emergent authoritarian regime after her return from her voyage around the world more fully, one needs to keep in mind that the verb "to renounce" connotes the double meaning of "to abjure, deny, repudiate" as well as "to sacrifice, surrender, give up."

The day began like any other, except that Aziza woke up with a fever of nearly 103 degrees. Doria hesitated momentarily, questioning whether she should delay her strike or stay at home with her daughter: "Then I would have to change the dates, retype the telegrams, put them in new envelopes—another day would go by with the risk of letting the whole plan collapse. It can't be helped. I'll make the strike, leaving my sick child, demonstrating to the world, that the absolute of freedom was dearer to me than my life, dearer than my children, dearer than everything."

Doria always waited until Nour left home before embarking on her dramatic gestures, preferring to confront him with a fait accompli rather than risk his preventing her from carrying out her plan. So, as usual, she left him a brief note informing him of her intentions. However, she felt it necessary to inform her daughters of what she was going to do: "'You are old enough to understand. Be equal to the sacrifices that I am obliged to impose on you.' As I was leaving, Jehane came running to give me a biscuit. 'Eat, Mummy,' she said, 'before you go out.' I felt the tears coming and shut the elevator door quickly so as not to weaken."

Both daughters were perplexed and anxious after this unexpected decision on their mother's part:

I remember I had a fever. She was getting ready to go to the Indian embassy and had told nobody. She just packed her bag and told Hasan, the servant, to call a cab. And she came into my room. I think she couldn't leave without explaining herself to me because she felt that I was ill and she was going out and I could tell that she was tortured. She told me: "You are too young to understand what I am going to do now, but one of these days you'll understand the sacrifice that I am making." Then she told me what she was going to do. I pleaded with her and I felt panicky.

Then she left. I said to myself: "Here we go again!" and at that point enough was enough. The next day I opened the newspapers and there was no mention of it. I did not expect the reaction would be total silence. I was surprised and at the same time relieved.[2]

I remember it was the day after my father's birthday. She was wearing her mink coat and carrying her overnight bag. She said she was going out and I asked her: "Where are you going, Mummy?" She answered: "I am doing something for Egypt" and then she left. I remember I was eating some biscuits and I rushed to the door and gave them to her: "Here, Mummy, take these biscuits." The next day everybody was asking: "Where is Doria Shafik?" Tante Soraya came from Alexandria and seemed very worried. Everybody was worried. I went to school and my French teacher asked, "Où est votre maman?" There was an uneasy, anxious atmosphere, unlike the first hunger strike when everything was open. Now there was nothing about it in the newspapers. My father was very worried. There seemed to be this feeling of catastrophe.[3]

The authorities were extremely irate—first, because the Egyptian police could not enter the embassy and arrest Doria; second, because the international press was giving Doria's strike and her demands for the end of dictatorship in Egypt high visibility. The London *Times* filed a report on February 9, 1957, under the headline "Egyptian Feminist's Hunger Strike: 36 Hours at the Indian Embassy," and the German newspaper *Die Welt* carried a full-page story titled "A Woman of the Nile Has Raised the Banner of Resistance against Abdul Nasser." Finally, what really annoyed Nasser was that Doria's dramatic act took place within the Indian embassy during a moment when he was engaged in rather delicate negotiations with the Indian government. Prime Minister Nehru intervened and sent a request to President Gamal Abdul Nasser to allow Doria to leave the Indian Embassy—free—and return to her house without arresting her. And Abdul Nasser agreed to detain her under house arrest in her apartment in Zamalek.

Doria's hunger strike, although admittedly a spontaneous act, was not a haphazard undertaking. It reflected her perception of the historical moment and, given her penchant for the dramatic, seemed totally in character. She realized she had to do it alone: "No one will follow me this time, that is certain. But it doesn't matter. I have this powerful inner voice within me." And anticipating that "my strike might be stifled by censorship, I decided to inform the foreign news agencies."

She chose the Indian embassy because "India was a neutral country and thus, I could not be accused of favoring one camp or the other." A few Egyptians have voiced the opinion that she sought political asylum in the Indian embassy because it was handling the affairs of the British following the outbreak of the Suez War when diplomatic ties between London and Cairo were severed: "India was the country of passive resistance, the homeland of Ghandi, my master." And Doria had met Nehru in Calcutta in 1954, and entertained his daughter, Indira, when she came to Cairo in 1955 to lecture on the emancipation of Indian women; Doria also considered the Indian ambassador, Ali Yavar Yung, and his wife her personal friends. When packing her valise for her vigil, Doria selected three books from her private library to accompany her on this solitary journey: the Quran, a biography of Gandhi, and a collection of poems by Pierre Reverdy.

Each reveals an aspect of Doria Shafik's sense of self and mission and offers some insight as to what she might have been thinking as she prepared "to go all the way" in her demand for her two freedoms. She was a believer who felt deeply about her religion, and during moments of crisis or stress, the Quran was always her source of comfort and sustenance: "Whenever I read verses from the Quran or listened to the call to prayer from the minaret, my anxiety was soothed and my heart was lightened." We know Ghandi's life and philosophy inspired her. But it was Pierre Reverdy—the French poet, essayist, critic, novelist, and short-story writer—with whom Doria felt an affinity of the heart. He too was on a quest in pursuit of the Absolute. Seghers described him as "a volcano of the profound life and of refusal, of restrained violence, rages and the blood of a bullfighter. Snarling but warm, friendly but reserved, alone. One of the greatest, most ardent poets of our time."[4]

On that fateful day, Hasan, the servant, left Doria at the Indian embassy door with the parting words, "May God give you health and safety." The ambassador's daughter welcomed her and immediately escorted her to her father's office. Hearing of Doria's intentions, Ambassador Ali Yavar Yung tried, unsuccessfully, to dissuade her. The situation was very critical for him; indeed, he had an appointment with Nasser for the next day. To Amina al-Sa'id, the ambassador—"who was a close friend of Abdul Nasser and many thoughtful Egyptians, including me and my husband"—revealed the details of Doria's request for political asylum in the Indian embassy:

> The ambassador said, "Doria Shafik suddenly entered the embassy without previous notice and announced her determination to undertake a hunger strike unto death if the President would not abandon his rule. At the moment of her arrival the halls of the embassy were packed with foreign reporters with whom she had already got in touch. As I was a personal friend of Abdul Nasser's and my country had good relations

with his, I found I couldn't do anything else but get in touch with Nasser and be advised as to what I was supposed to do. But he answered very placidly and pleasantly: 'Why do you mix me up in this affair? It is more appropriate to ask her husband's advice for he has more right than myself.' It was very late. It was difficult to find her husband and I postponed the whole affair to the next day. My wife and I accompanied the guest to her bedroom and left her to settle in. She had a large Quran in her hand, its cover was embossed with a golden design. And we returned to sit with her. It was time for supper and she refused to go to the dining room to eat. So we ordered her dinner as well as our own to be served in the bedroom. We tried to convince her to have her dinner but she refused. After that we left her to sleep and we got in touch with her husband and informed him of Nasser's opinion. He came immediately and convinced her to return with him and he took her to the hospital, where she spent some days allegedly suffering from nervous exhaustion."[5]

Doria's memoirs affirm that there were several calls back and forth to Nehru, "who told the ambassador that Doria Shafik was to be considered a guest of the embassy and could stay as long as she wished." The ambassador's wife brought her fresh bedding, made her comfortable, and called Aziza and Jehane to calm them about their mother. She invited her to dine with them that evening, but Doria politely declined and remained in the room prepared for her. The following day, while Ambassador Ali Yavar Yung was at his meeting with Nasser, Doria received a call from the council of the president, ordering her immediate departure: "I learned much later that the government's intention was to take me, as soon as I crossed the threshold of the embassy, to an asylum in order to declare to the press that my strike was the result of a mental breakdown. Nour, who was with me at that moment, turned pale at the idea of my being hunted down like this. 'Do you see what a situation you have placed us in?' I told the caller that I would not quit the embassy. Nour turned to me and said in a quiet tone, 'I am going to look for a solution, a place where you can continue your strike. Don't move until I get back.'"

By the third day, despite the blackout in the local press, Cairo was buzzing with the news of Doria's latest action. Radio Monte Carlo had broadcast the news of her protest strike and referred to Doria as "the only man in Egypt." The foreign press agencies in Cairo, having received copies of her telegram, filed reports back to their respective papers: "The exact whereabouts of Dr. Doria Shafik, wife of a prominent lawyer and mother of two young girls was not immediately known. Her husband, Nour Al-Din Ragai, said he wanted his wife 'to stop her hunger strike for health reasons, but I cannot say where she is.'"[6]

Actually, Nour had negotiated with Dr. Abdul Wahab Mooro, a famous Egyptian surgeon, to have Doria transferred from the embassy to his clinic, where she continued her fast for eleven more days under the supervision of the family physician. But it was Nehru who gave the order that Doria not leave the embassy except in an embassy car and under the ambassador's diplomatic protection until she reached the clinic. On February 9, the London *Times* reported : "Public criticism of the regime, in terms such as those chosen by Mrs. Shafik, can hardly fall sweetly on the ears of the authorities, but it is understood that they are not disposed to invest the incident with much importance. Mrs. Shafik according to her husband has not yet fully recovered from the hunger strike she staged three years ago in support of political rights for women." Several other foreign papers also filed reports on this event.[7] By February 10, according to the *New York Times,* "signs of weakness appeared today as Doria Shafik entered the fourth day of her hunger strike against the dictatorial regime in Egypt, for a withdrawal of Israeli forces from Sinai and the settlement of the Palestinian problem."[8]

On the sixth day of her hunger strike, an article appeared in the French newspaper *Le Figaro*: "After her reproach to Nasser, will Mme. Doria Shafik join the opponents who overflow the jails of her country? Will the 'bikbachi' treat her with a gallantry, which is not his usual manner, or will he deduce that he can no longer allow her to starve? Even if no sanction menaces her, the Egyptian feminist gives an example of courage. As she wants to obtain the end of a disastrous dictator, she risks at least that the stubborn colonel will decide to wait, taking her threat seriously, except that she will be in no state to savor her victory."[9] On February 17, the *New York Times* reported, "Mme. Doria Shafik left the hospital for home on a stretcher today—the eleventh day of her hunger strike in protest against Egypt's 'dictatorial regime.' She was told by her attending physician that "if she remains another twenty-four hours on this fast she will surely die." Her husband said he was taking his wife home in the hope that "the moral pressure of her daughters will convince her to stop the strike."[10] And the next day, the *Times* reported that Doria had ended her fast.[11]

While in the hospital, Doria was closely guarded by the police and was allowed no visitors except her attending physician, her husband, and one friend, her comrade from the Bint al-Nil Union, Ragia Raghab. Ragia was the only person, out of all those with whom Doria had worked over the years, who had the courage to come to the clinic:

> I had no idea what Doria was going to do because this time she hadn't telephoned any of us. My husband, who was always on the side of the underdog, told me that Doria was in the Indian embassy on a hunger

strike against Nasser. And he said "Ragia you must go to her. She is your friend and she is in a very bad situation. We don't know what they will want to do with her but you must go and see her." When I went to the Mooro clinic she was still on her hunger strike and her first words to me were, "You have nothing to do with this affair." But I said, "I only want to help you. Why have you done this? I don't understand. Why did you do this when sentiment in Egypt now is all with Nasser and we know that the war of 1956 was not a failure for Egypt." She answered: "I do this from faith. We must stand against the Communists. I am not with the Americans. I am not with anyone, but as an Egyptian it is my duty to protest and to ask the ruler of Egypt where he is leading us. It is the moment. If we don't do something now, we will never escape from under Nasser." She was against Nasser because she was afraid of communism coming into Egypt, especially when Nasser made the arms treaty with the Russians. When I went to the hospital she was reading the Quran and she was happy that I had come. I was the only one. She said to me: "Please, if any of the women of Bint al-Nil want to visit me, tell them I don't want to involve them in this affair." She knew that she was in a very bad situation.[12]

Ragia was also in trouble, for as soon as she left the clinic, she was visited at home by the *mukhabbarat*, a special internal intelligence agency that Nasser had set up to gather information on enemies of the revolution.

Day after day, for several weeks, Ragia was harassed by these intelligence men, who were convinced that the American embassy was behind Doria's hunger strike:

They threatened me through my family saying, "Your husband has no work, your son is in the military and you make trouble for your brother, Hasan Raghab." My brother was then secretary of war. They asked me "What did Doria Shafik tell you?" I said, "Nothing! She was reading the Quran." They kept asking again and again: "Who is the force behind Doria Shafik?" I answered: "God. She has faith. She is afraid her country will turn communist. She is motivated by her love of Egypt. Don't you understand what love of country is? We send our children to war to die for the land of Egypt. Nasser is the ruler and someone must tell him. Why can't you understand that a woman could do that to herself? She has done this alone, not with the women of Bint al-Nil. I had nothing to do with this affair."[13]

Finally, Ragia was on the verge of a nervous breakdown, and her husband spoke to the *mukhabbarat*: "I am the husband of the woman but please, we are Muslims. You can't hurt a lady, you mustn't. She's just a housewife. She joined Bint al-Nil and the Red Crescent only to help Egypt. Why do you persecute her? If you want anything from my wife, if she has done something wrong, then take me, I am responsible and I will talk to you."[14]

There were some Egyptian intellectuals who, when they became aware of what Doria had done, secretly applauded her courage. Galal al-Hamamsy—former deputy director of the government newspaper *al-Gomhouria* during the early years of the revolution and one of Egypt's most highly respected journalists—was an open critic of Doria's activities during her struggle for women's rights. But as early as 1957, he became alarmed at the direction in which the country was heading as Nasser rode the wave of popular support following the Suez war of 1956:

> Doria Shafik was an enigmatic figure. Was she really serious? It was when she faced Nasser that I changed my mind and truly felt she was a courageous woman. Her courage in publicly defying Nasser made me realize that she was able to see more clearly what was happening. By that defiance, she acted out what many felt in their hearts but did not dare do. Her defiance forced Nasser to give up the idea of putting her in jail and that made him think and reflect upon what his response to her defiance should be. The fact that he did not put her in jail, means that he feared a broader public reaction. In my view to have accomplished this or to have forced Nasser to examine the consequences of his own action was a positive achievement.[15]

Following a visit to Yugoslavia with Nasser, Galal admitted privately to his wife that "We are headed toward chaos and I am dismayed with this man, Nasser. He is a liar and leading Egypt to destruction."[16]

However, not all Egyptians shared this point of view. Ironically and tragically as it actually turned out, Doria's solitary stance, which she believed to be an act of self-sacrifice for the sake of her country, was in turn repudiated by several of her own countrywomen as an act of treason. There were women like Inji Efflatoun, who felt that Doria's action was self-serving and very poorly timed in the face of Egypt's military situation at that point:

> In front of the world she made it appear as if all Egyptian women were against Nasser. I heard many from the foreign embassies saying that the Egyptian woman is fantastic; that Egyptian women are against Nasser. Well, since all the Europeans, the French, the English and Americans were against him, it wasn't the time to open another front against Nasser when we were still occupied by Israel. So we responded immediately and drafted a petition showing that not all Egyptian women supported Doria

Shafik. We sent it to all the outside news agencies but it was never published in Egypt. Maybe Nasser was afraid to publish it and draw more attention to the issue. And you know, Nasser didn't put her in jail; he just put her under house arrest. Normally anyone who had done what she had done would have been put in prison. Nasser was very clever, for once, because Doria Shafik wanted to be a martyr. I believed and still believe that she did this because she was expecting there would be a *coup d'état* (there were a lot of plots against Nasser at this time), and she would come out a heroine.[17]

This petition, "Egyptian Women Renounce the Position of Doria Shafik"—bearing the names, but not the personal signatures, of twenty-seven women representing more than a dozen different women's groups, professions, and syndicates—was circulated by Ceza Nabaraoui and Inji Efflatoun. The names appearing on the list read like a "Who's Who" of women's groups in Egypt at the time. There were some women, perhaps more sympathetic to Doria, who were under the impression "that the government ordered all the women's organizations that were under its control to sign a declaration opposing the position of Doria Shafik against Nasser."[18]

The substance and objective of this petition was to publicly discredit Doria's political act against Nasser and his regime and to offer a critical assessment of her role in the feminist movement during this stage of Egypt's military struggle against Israel and the West. Pointedly addressing her as "Mrs. Shafik," the petition declared:

On February 7, Mrs. Doria Shafik announced a hunger strike until death stating that, "in the face of the severe circumstances of Egypt" she implores the international authorities to intervene in order to: (1) ensure Israeli withdrawal from all Arab lands; and (2) reach a just and final solution for the problem of the Palestinian refugees. And in addition to that Mrs. Doria Shafik has implored the internal authorities to (3) regain freedom for all Egyptians—men and women alike—and end the dictatorial rule that can only lead our country to a state of bankruptcy and corruption. She finally asserts that such an act (her hunger strike) is her own initiative and that she is willing to sacrifice her life for the freedom of her country. "I am sacrificing my life in order to free my country and I alone bear the responsibility."

We women of Egypt were amazed by Mrs. Doria Shafik's announcement and we strongly condemn such an act which injures our feminist movement's reputation abroad. We hasten to state that our feminist movement has entered a new phase since our national revolution of 1952 and since the Egyptian woman has fully gained her political rights under the new constitution. Our feminist movement is a people's movement, far removed from the individualistic trends which characterized prerevolutionary feminist movements based on personal publicity.

There is much evidence to suggest that Mrs. Doria Shafik has isolated herself from the modern feminist movement and from the female population of Egypt and that one way of confessing her isolation was through her statement: "I alone bear the responsibility of this work. I alone am responsible for this deed."

We wish to ask Mrs. Doria Shafik her reasons for making such an announcement at this particular time, in which Egypt and many Arab countries are facing the dangers of disintegration caused by foreign powers; a time in which Egypt and the Arab countries face the conspiracies of the occupation that undermine the solidarity of the Egyptian people and the Arab peoples in order to make it easy for the occupiers to enslave and deceive us.

We wish to ask Mrs. Doria Shafik, what she means when referring to "international authorities" when stating her conditions for the immediate withdrawal of the Israeli forces from the Egyptian lands. Is she addressing the United Nations? In this case, is she not aware that the UN unanimously, except for Israel and France, condemned the Israeli aggression and asked Israel to withdraw? Does Mrs. Doria Shafik really believe that her hunger strike will be more effective in forcing Israel to withdraw and take action than the UN? We wish to ask Mrs. Doria Shafik, on what grounds has she the right to seek a "final and fair solution to the Arab refugee problem"? Have not the Arabs and the refugees themselves refused to reduce the Palestinian problem to a refugee problem?

In whose interests is Mrs. Doria Shafik doing all this? In whose interests does Mrs. Doria Shafik, who doesn't represent anyone but herself, describe Egypt's present rule as a dictatorship that would eventually lead the country to "corruption and bankruptcy"? Does Mrs. Doria Shafik consider the policy of an independent government, the policy of a government that has liberated its economy from foreign domination to be heading towards "bankruptcy and corruption"? Is Mrs. Doria Shafik aware that foreign broadcasting stations in Israel and the colonial powers have used the very same phrases in provoking the anger of the Egyptian nation—men and women alike—strengthening their solidarity with Gamal Abdul Nasser's independent government? Would it not have been better if Mrs. Doria Shafik had expressed her concern over "her country's freedom" by joining feminist committees resisting the foreign invasion of Port Said? Instead, she preferred to be isolated.

And what has Mrs. Doria Shafik done, in practical terms, in order to "sacrifice her entire life for her country's freedom"? Where was her real sacrifice? Her concern over the "lost democracy" which she claims is not present—is it not the same tune which Israel and other powers are singing? This is only a game pursued by colonial powers to distract the nation from its real struggle. Have the colonial powers given us a chance to look to our internal affairs? Mrs. Doria Shafik should feel quite comfortable concerning the fate of democracy in Egypt. We assure her that the Egyptian nation will be keen to secure its democratic rights under the new constitution. A differentiation is sensed between the "democracy" which foreign broadcasting stations are claiming and between the democracy backed by a united independent nation and government.

Finally, Mrs. Doria Shafik has shown the world her hunger strike, which she claimed would last "until death," ended in just 48 hours after which she was sent to Mooro Hospital for glucose treatment. She has returned home a free citizen despite the fact that her act has harmed the interests of the country and the Egyptian woman—So what sort of freedom is she seeking?[19]

Amina al-Sa'id, who represented the new voice of feminist journalism under Nasser's revolutionary regime and whose magazine, *Hawa*, was overshadowing *Bint al-Nil* by this time, appeared on the list of signatures to this petition. She later disclaimed any support of this crusade against Doria. In a strongly worded article written many years later, al-Sa'id explains:

I was contacted by Ceza Nabaraoui, who was one of Nasser's enthusiastic supporters and had angrily turned on Doria Shafik for her stand against him. She wrote a memorandum and distributed it to all women in Cairo in order to gain their support against Doria by signing this petition. When it came my turn and Ceza asked for my signature, I refused completely and I said to her: "Maybe I'm on bad terms with Doria but I am NOT somebody who will 'bring out the knife when the cow is down' [meaning that she would not do a person further injury when he or she was already suffering]. Besides I respect her intellectual courage and freedom of thought although a lot of people think that what she has done is not right. But I have my opinion and I won't change it." And Ceza challenged me and we plunged into a heated discussion, but I refused to

concede and stuck to my point of view. Ceza reported my position regarding Doria to the responsible authorities and when they came to in-
terrogate me I repeated everything I had said to Ceza.[20]

Ironically, Doria's political stance of isolating herself—"I am sacrificing my
life in order to free my country and I alone bear the responsibility"—ultimately led to her final exclusion from Egyptian social and political life. Gamal
Abdul Nasser immediately ordered her to be placed under house arrest. On
February 28, her Bint al-Nil comrades expelled her from the Bint al-Nil Union,
an organization that was "my baby and for which I had sacrificed blood, sweat
and tears, in the struggle for the political rights of the Egyptian woman." The
government appointed a committee of five women to replace her, issued a decree closing down her publishing house, and saw to it that her magazines were
destroyed or gradually discontinued.

This totally unsympathetic public response to Doria underscores the deep-
seated opposition to her not only among those women who represented the
progressive left but also among those sympathetic to the Nasserist regime.
From their point of view, Doria appeared too committed to the liberal-human-
ist values of the imperialist West, with its emphasis on legal reform and social
transformation based on a democratic system of parliamentary government—
a system that in Egypt had allowed absolute power to fall into the hands of the
few. During the struggle against the tripartite aggression, which had culminated in the Israeli occupation of Arab land, progressive forces were organizing resistance groups among the lower classes within the orbit of the general
struggle against imperialist domination, class hierarchy, and economic inequality. Meanwhile, Doria, increasingly alarmed at the erosion of democracy in
Egypt, was on her own tack. Through the pages of her *Bint al-Nil* editorials,
she showed open hostility to both communism and the rise of dictatorship
which she considered anathema to her fundamental value of individual freedom. She had consciously avoided joining any political party except her own
Bint al-Nil Union and Women's Party, a gesture which many considered inef-
fectual and futile in the face of the national anti-imperialist struggle. Her open
challenge to Nasser when Egypt was under direct aggression by France, Great
Britain, and Israel was interpreted by her opponents as sufficient evidence
that she was "playing into the hands of the enemy."

Despite being under house arrest, she appealed the decree banning her magazines on the grounds that, as the owner of *Bint al-Nil* and *Katkout*, she had an
authorized license from the organization of publications. She argued that the
government had based its decision on a decree of martial law issued by the
Ministry of the Interior at the beginning of the year, and hence was constitu-

tionally illegal. The government claimed that Doria's editorials were not in the best interest of the country as she warned of a communist invasion of Egypt and the Middle East and implored people for the sake of religion to consolidate efforts to prevent this danger. The last three editorials that appeared in *Bint al-Nil* bore the titles "The East and Communism" (April 1957), "Colonial Communism" (May 1957), and "International Communism and Freedom" (June 1957).

"The court rejected her appeal on the grounds that her editorials would deter cordial relations between Egypt and her communist allies during this very critical period. And in July 1957 the police entered her *Bint al-Nil* office, seized all the issues ready for distribution and destroyed her private papers."[21] Her publications confiscated by the state and her name officially banned from the Egyptian press, Doria withdrew into the shadows.

Solitude (1957–1975)

Poetry!
In this desert
where I am drowning,
you open more than one way.
In this silence,
the horrible silence
that encircles me,
in the torment of my becoming
you permit me
to act!

—*Shafik (from "Hors-Temps")*

15

The Interior Life

These poems are entitled "Hors-Temps" because they were conceived and written in an atmosphere escaping our perceived time, that external, narrowly measured time. The setting of these poems is timeless. It is an immediate apperception of our interior life whose essence belongs to infinity, to the unlimited. The profound meaning of these poems is in the expression of interior music that emerges from the depths of our own hearts, when our heart is pure, transmitting the echoes of our soul which, when it is elevated to the lofty heights of purity, becomes capable of capturing the Absolute.[1]

Doria's house arrest abruptly ended a public career which had spanned nearly thirty years, beginning in 1928 when she first stood beside Huda Sha'rawi on the platform at the theater of Ezbakiya Gardens and delivered her impassioned, and in some ways prophetic, eulogy of Qasim Amin: "Do men believe that traditions that are useful for a certain time can be adapted to the current of modern life? Or is it that they do not understand the absolute value of liberty?"

Ironically, her final defiant act in defense of that single principle resulted in her entering an eighteen-year period of near total seclusion, in many ways more painful and tortured than life in the harems she witnessed as a child growing up in Mansura and Tanta: "What miseries the depths of the harems have hidden and for how long! What experience can one acquire if one has only crept from one part of the house to the other? And in her torpor, the woman was not aware of her captivity, having always led the same life, she did not think she could liberate herself."[2] Doria believed that the woman could indeed achieve that liberty, and the result of her ensuing struggle ended with her remaining until the end of her life secluded in an apartment on the sixth floor of the Wadie Saad building in Zamalek. Her voice effectively silenced,

Doria eventually disappeared from public consciousness until her tragic death on September 20, 1975, brought her name back onto the front pages of the Egyptian press.

Withdrawn from public view, abandoned by her former comrades, and denounced by her society as a "traitor to the revolution," Doria Shafik was only forty-eight years old when she embarked upon her final and most difficult battle: the struggle against the isolation and solitude that this banishment to the world of internal exile imposed. How did she live out these eighteen years of near total withdrawal and seclusion? What impact did these years have on her family, and what meaning did they have for her life? Understandably, the French memoirs are silent about the details of her long internal exile; in fact, she ceased writing them in 1960. But we do have the narrative accounts of her daughters, who lived through this ordeal with their mother, as well as the recollections of those few contemporaries who were in touch with her. However, it is essentially through her poetry, "that voice of interior music," that we can catch a glimpse of what Seghers often referred to as "her most authentic truth." In this brief homage to her favorite poet, we can feel her mood:

O, Reverdy	O, Reverdy
quelle résonnance!	what resonance!
Le coeur en silence	the heart in silence
se tait	holds its tongue
et laisse parler	and lets others
les autres . . .	speak . . .
Il n'a plus rien à dire	There's nothing more to say
Il a tout dit	It has all been said
(ce qu'il fallait dire)	(that which one must say)
Et son Silence	And its Silence
à travers l'absence	through the absence
de veritable vie	of a genuine life
erre	wanders
dans le désert	in the desert
de la melancholie.	of melancholia.
Mais le poids de	But the burden of anguish
l'angoisse tasse	boxed in
en barricade	against a wall
se découvre	discovers itself
soudain	suddenly
et se révolte	and revolts
sans bruit sans vaine parade	without noise or vain display
levier inexorable	unyielding lever
des HEURES *de matin.*	of the HOURS of morning.

And in this silent lament is her message to the world outside her prison:

> Don't be surprised
> That I write you in verse
> When the customary prose is there
> It is, you see,
> That I have suffered some setbacks
> Hemmed in by walls
> Not of stones, it is true
> But worse—I hope you understand
> And only poetry
> Friend of passionate souls
> Should explain to you
> My name begins with D
> and I am a woman . . .
> Daughter of the Nile
> I have demanded women's rights
> My fight was enlarged
> To human freedom
> In a world of oppression
> I have dared to demand
> This freedom
> And what was the result?
> I have no more friends
> So what?
> Until the end of the road
> I will proceed alone
> Without hesitation, without turning back
> What does loneliness matter?
> Nausea—disheartening torture
> I feel my heart is big
> So big that it overflows
> The barriers of treason
> And rejoins, in the four corners of the world,
> All Souls of Good Will. [3]

"Three years have passed since my strike—years of isolation or encircle-ment. Forever distanced from the milieu for which I struggled so much, that I have loved so much that I have accepted its hate in exchange for my love. Betrayed, wounded by this same milieu for which I have given everything, except my inner freedom. Sooner or later they will understand." Even when the ban on her house arrest was finally lifted, Doria chose to remain secluded from the society she felt had betrayed her. Mustapha Amin, who lived in the flat facing hers, related how "Doria Shafik remained half imprisoned in her sixth-floor apartment without anyone visiting her and without her visiting anyone. Her former supporters had forsaken her for fear of their own positions; her friends had deserted her for fear of her arrest or because they themselves were put under surveillance. The newspapers were forbidden to mention her name—even when they were reporting the decision to give the Egyptian woman the right to vote and the entrance of women into the parliament and the appointment of the first woman to the Ministry of Foreign Affairs."[4]

During those first three years, a guard was posted at the front door and Doria was literally prohibited from leaving the confines of her apartment, although Nour and the daughters could come and go as they pleased. The fact that there was a policeman at the door whenever the daughters came or went seemed not to have bothered them particularly. "I, personally, did not feel stigmatized because of that," says Aziza; "I remember I was just happy with my friends. All the group or class of people whom we were with sort of regarded what my mother did in a very positive way, even though some of them did not acknowledge it. I did not feel that I was paying for what my mother did or something of that sort. Never. Never."[5]

However, Nour suffered from the retaliation of the regime in response to Doria's challenge to Nasser. The police immediately surrounded his law office and arrested any clients coming to seek his counsel as well as anybody who wanted to employ him for a case. According to Nour's friend Mustapha Amin,

> the government declared war on the husband of the leader, following him, tapping his telephone, opening his letters and harassing him with bureaucratic delays when he needed to travel to defend a client in an Arab country. And if he got into his car, he found another car following him; and if he sat in a public place he found an informer sitting in a seat behind him. Nour Eddin Ragai did not object to the bold steps that his wife had taken. She felt that it was her right to publicize her political decisions without consulting her husband. She refused to ask her husband's permission before dropping her bombs. Despite the fact that some of the shrapnel from these bombs would hit her innocent husband.[6]

The tensions that had developed between Nour and Doria over her "bombshells" in public life became even more intensified under the stressful conditions of her house arrest and the government's harassment of his professional career. The pressure kept building and, at the height of one particularly heated argument in September 1959, they decided to divorce.

Jehane remembers this moment quite vividly because it coincided with her trip to Lebanon. She was an honorary guest of the Gezira Club's swim team, which was participating in the Mediterranean Games in preparation for the Olympiad in Rome, where Jehane was expected to enter the breaststroke competition. In 1960 when she was to travel to Rome with the Olympic swim team, the military regime refused her permission to travel despite the fact that she had set a new Egyptian record for this event for women. The minister of Social Affairs at that time was Husayn Shafei, a distant relative through marriage to Doria Shafik, and a former member of the Muslim Brothers, who defended his decision prohibiting Jehane's departure on the argument that Egyptian Muslim women should not be allowed to display their bodies publicly in such events. Most probably, it was another way for the regime to punish those close to Doria for her challenge to Nasser. Jehane recalls:

> My father liked to go out a lot, but because of her house arrest Mummy couldn't go out at all for two or three years and then afterward she decided that she wouldn't go out anymore. Whether it was her own will or she was afraid to go out or because she had lost the habit, I don't know. So he had his own life and gradually they drifted apart, as in Victor Hugo's poem "Le vase est brisé." Once the relationship is broken it is difficult to repair. There was some anxiety at home resulting from the financial strife and the quarrels between my mother and father. In spite of this, there was still a lot of affection between the two and a lot of respect. This divorce was something done on the spur of the moment lasting less than a month because when I returned from Beirut, they were both at the airport and it was all patched up.[7]

Virtually prevented from practicing his legal profession in Egypt, Nour began looking for clients from the surrounding Arab states, which meant that beginning in the nineteen sixties, he was traveling a great deal outside Egypt. Doria, of course, remained at home:

> Every voyage outside Egypt was naturally excluded for me. For these past three years, I have been prevented from leaving my country to attend the annual meetings of the International Council of Women. I remember flying into a rage when I was prevented from participating at the special meeting of the executive council to be held in Vienna in 1959. By what right? I still had the illusion of speaking about rights in my country. My anger pushed me to send a message to the Secretary General of the United Nations, spelling out for him, through A+B, the ineffectiveness of this great international organization as it remained impotent to safeguard individual liberty, foundation of all liberties, around the four corners of the world. I knew very well the uselessness of my act, not even being sure that my message would reach Mr. Dag Hammar-

skjöld. My gesture was nothing more than that of a drowning woman clinging to the slightest hope.[8]

Doria closes her 1960 memoirs by expressing her deepening concern about the peril that human freedom faces at all levels of existence, and in a melancholy mood she writes:

From this isolated ambiance, where my enemies believe that they have driven me back to a slow death, I nevertheless have discovered the most beautiful windfall: my own existence as a free being. At what door can I knock in order to leap over these invisible bars of my prison? Invisible even for those, who up until this point, were near to me, and had the habit of seeing clearly. Here I am hunted down on the moving sand, encircled by wolves and vipers. In this indescribable desert where my optimism at every trial still pushes me to hope, I advance in the void, echoing my own call. I speak to the deaf. Where are the people? I belong to them! I am made of the same stuff! Human! One can be made to do anything but no one can oblige me to go against my conscience. There I affirm myself as Absolute. There I exist in the most elevated sense: I am free. At the end of three years of seclusion, at the end also of my years of struggle, I have discovered you, Liberty, essence of my being, by the sole victory over myself, and by that victory over everything that can aspire to your negation. Liberty! You give the unique meaning to this work. I have dedicated this work to you and to all those who, like me, have suffered from privation.

On the final page she sculpts these lines of verse in homage to another of her beloved poets, Paul Eluard, from whose immortal poem she borrowed her title and to whom she dedicated her work:[9]

O LIBERTÉ
Je te fais don
de mon coeur
Sans toi
pour moi
nulle
vie.

Despite the removal of the soldier from her door in late 1959, the apartment continued to define the boundaries of her physical and social world, and it was largely the warmth and affection of her daughters and, later, her first-born granddaughter, Nazli, that enabled Doria to cope with her self-imposed seclusion and to maintain a tenuous connection to the human world beyond those "invisible bars." Jehane and Aziza, vibrantly attractive and popular teenagers, were always surrounded by friends; hence the apartment was continuously filled with the chatter and laughter of young people.

Jehane recalls that when she was training for the Rome Olympiad with the swim team,

> there were all these boys swimming with me, and Mummy would be very open-minded. We'd swim, train all day and we'd come home in the afternoon and she'd welcome us all, prepare us tea and things. Television had just come to Egypt around this time and I'd have all these swimmers home watching TV. She never said no to anything that pleased us. For instance we had a Malaysian friend, who was a student with us at university and couldn't find a place to stay. We invited her home thinking it would be for a week or two, but she ended by staying with us for four months and Mummy never said a word. She was always very open and receptive to our friends. And in that sense it created a balance with all the other things.[10]

This dramatic shift from Doria's being away from home all the time to her being at home all the time also created a new situation for both mother and daughters—one in which for the first time the daughters began to feel their mother's presence and the significance of her influence on their lives: "Whenever I or Aziza was sick, she was there for us. I remember in 1958 when I had malaria and they didn't know whether I had typhoid or not, she was in tears. But she never allowed herself to cry in front of me. She would go out of the room and then come back; she didn't leave me one minute. Once Aziza had a terrible boil on her back and it was quite serious, Mummy was with her all the time. Aziza couldn't walk and Mummy used to half drag, half carry her. She was there. We felt her love very much!"[11] Aziza has other memories to share:

> When I was very young I tended to look upon her with a lot of veneration. I mean she was more like a movie star and I was very proud of her. But later on I became aware of her vulnerability. She was an extremely sensitive person. She was the one major influence in my life—much more so than my father or anybody else. Her value system was something unattainable in the real world. She always believed that the goal in life was to strive to attain the ultimate good in things and instilled in us the importance of being truthful, honest and compassionate. And she was not the least bit materialistic and always warned us not to be seduced by such things. To those who equate being beautiful, having lovely clothes and taking care of her looks with her being materialistic I'd answer that it was her sense of beauty that motivated her, not the accumulation of things. And toward the end of her life she either threw away or gave away everything she possessed.[12]

By any standard, Jehane and Aziza were brought up in a very liberal house-hold, where both parents emphasized the importance of obtaining a college education and having a career:

> Compared to the rest of our family, whether on my mother's or my father's side, we were brought up very differently. My mother was much more liberal in our upbringing than my father, who started off being very conservative. But she changed that completely, which shows you the influence she had on him. Because they were taken up with their own careers, they did not direct our lives. We grew up early on in a way, free from them and their own mold. Even when she ended up staying at home all the time she gave us free rein. I mean the trust she put in us made us very responsible early on.[13]

The decade of the sixties brought major changes in the domestic life of the Ragai family. By 1966, Aziza had spent a year in America following her gradu-ation from the American University in Cairo, where her outstanding scholas-tic achievement earned her a fellowship to pursue further studies in material science at Carnegie-Mellon Institute in Pittsburgh. Nour was traveling more frequently to Kuwait on business, and Doria tried to keep her mind active and busy. As Jehane recalls, "she continued to receive dozens of different newspa-pers in Arabic, French and English, but now she had more time to study them and she would read them all every day. Later she started to learn Italian so she could read Dante in the original, then she added Spanish and German. She even took up bridge." The learning of languages was basically her own idea, but it was Jehane who went to the major cultural centers to make the neces-sary arrangements for registration: "I remember Mummy telling me how happy she was to be learning. You know, she used to work very intensively on her languages all the time. She had to attend courses and to take exams. It kept her busy for a good while."[14]

And when Aziza and Jehane graduated from the American University in Cairo, Doria returned to Ewart Hall, where fifteen years earlier she had elec-trified her society by leading the audacious march on parliament. Now she sat anonymously, forgotten and unrecognized, among the audience, but smiling with pride, as her daughters were accorded the highest scholastic honors the university could bestow. But the years of isolation had begun to leave their mark. Muhammad Zaki Abd al-Qadir, the eminent Egyptian journalist, whose own daughter was also graduating from AUC, described his encounter with Doria: "The last time I saw Doria Shafik was in June of 1966 at the com-mencement ceremonies at AUC, where her daughter, Jehane, was among the graduates. She, if I remember well, was chosen as the ideal student at the uni-versity. I saw Doria and I didn't recognize her because of what the days had done. But she recognized me and greeted me in the gentle and kind manner for which she was famous throughout her life."[15]

Soon thereafter, Doria began to lose interest in the company of others. It came quite gradually. One day Mme. Morin—the owner of the French school which Aziza and Jehane had attended until the Suez War of 1956, when the Morins were forced to leave—returned to Cairo for a visit and asked to meet Doria. After she left, Doria confided to Jehane, "Do you know what Mme. Morin said? *Vous semblez mener une vie trés austère.* It was a lonely life for Mummy but there were our friends." However, whenever Jehane and Aziza did bring their friends home, "she would interact very little and then go back to her room. She had no real friends, except Ketty Efthyvoulidis, a Greek-Egyptian who was Mummy's bridge teacher and used to visit from time to time. But Mummy had cut herself off completely. She was not seeing anybody." She even stopped communicating with her old friend Pierre Seghers:

> I didn't meet Doria Shafik often but when I did, we talked of poetry and poets. I corresponded with her but I never went back to Cairo. She sent me her poems and I sent her my books as a friend and because she was a poet. The later years of her life were horrible. She was unable to leave her apartment. She was unable to publish, or do anything. It was a great scandal, you know. She had her own ideas, beyond the struggle for women, ideas which were not those of Nasser. Thus she was unwanted there within her society and she had an aura surrounding her, yes, it was a sentence of death.[16]

Shortly after the news of her house arrest reached Seghers, he sent her this personal note: "For you, Doria, who will always remain the very image of beauty, the flame and the passion. Living poetry! For you, who are your country and to whom I remain so near. With the most faithful friendship, Seghers."

For ten years after her house arrest, Seghers faithfully continued writing to his friend and sending her copies of his latest books of poetry, in which she would find an affectionate inscription, such as "To Doria, The art of always being able to keep oneself company," "For Doria Shafik, these stones from the same temple, With my loyal memory," "For Madame Shafik, this architecture that time has never reached, With my faithful remembrance," "For you, Doria, whosoever sings his trouble, enchants it!" But Doria never responded, and Seghers eventually stopped writing. Doria possessed a profound sense of moral propriety and according to the daughters "was always very strict with herself. She was a very attractive woman and certainly must have had men running after her. But she never encouraged anyone. She had a lot of intrinsic honesty."[17]

The year 1967 was a catastrophic one, both for Nour and Doria and for the

Egyptian people. The circumstances leading up to this *nakba*, as the Egyptians refer to the Six-Day War, began somewhat earlier when, in 1965, Nasser made sweeping changes in his policy and embarked upon a radical reappraisal of his relations with the West. Signaling this change on the internal level were a series of punitive actions against all those, even his personal associates, who were thought to hold pro-Western sympathies. In general his attitude towards his associates had come to show an ever-increasing arrogance and disregard, especially of those who deeply, and rightly, believed that what he was doing was wrong and foolish.

Mustapha Amin, who was Nasser's personally selected liaison with the CIA, was arrested in 1965 for allegedly having abused his position as Nasser's close friend to pass on to the Americans sensitive information that he had no authority to divulge. According to Anthony Nutting:

> However ill-advised Amin may have been in some of the things he discussed with Bruce Odel, his CIA contact, Nasser should have known he was no traitor and that at any moment, before or after the trial, a word from the presidency could have spared his former friend further mental and physical suffering. Consequently this cruel farce was played out to the end and Mustapha Amin was sentenced to life imprisonment, and for Nasser, it was the start of a sorry progression of errors and miscalculations which was to leave him to face disaster in the course of the next two years with hardly a single friend in the Western world.[18]

Furthermore, a considerable rightist reaction was developing within the dispossessed bourgeoisie, and when the old Wafdist leader, Mustapha al-Nahas, died in September 1965, "the enormous crowds which followed his funeral cortège served notice on the regime that the Egyptian populace had remained predominantly conservative in outlook, despite every effort to change them. Then, when the residue of the old reactionary Muslim Brotherhood chose this moment to erupt in violent demonstrations against the police in one of Cairo's suburbs, the authorities promptly proclaimed martial law."[19] A vigorous campaign of internal suppression of dissent through imprisonment and death penalties ensued.

On the external front, Nasser's new shift in foreign policy had proven less than successful, and conditions did not bode well for the future. The Arabs were in a state of total disarray, brought about by squabbles among the states surrounding Israel as to the best strategy towards the war in Yemen and the continual struggle for the restoration of Palestinian lands. By February 1967, according to his biographer, Nasser had brought upon himself a series of circumstances which were to make him an easy target for his Israeli enemies in a few months' time. The most imperiling event for Nasser was Egypt's signing of a mutual defense agreement with Syria, in which an attack on one state would mean an attack on both. Israel could not have been more pleased, and events unfolded with such rapidity that on June 5, 1967, Egypt suffered one of its worst political and military disasters of modern history. By contrast with the disarray which prevailed in the Arab camp, the Israelis presented the very embodiment of military preparedness. Unlike their fragmented neighbors, the Israelis had used the years since the Suez War not to squabble among themselves but to work out and perfect plans to recover all and more than they had been obliged to abandon after their victory in 1956. In other words, more than ten years of planning had preceded the assault which Israel launched against Egypt and her allies in 1967.[20]

These broader political conditions would also have their repercussions on the personal lives of Nour and Doria, when in the early weeks of February 1967, the *mukhabbarat* arrived in the middle of the night to arrest Nour on the charge that he was involved in some subversive plot against Nasser and the regime. Aziza explains that "it all boiled down to this oppressive system where they were trying to shut everybody up. In this particular instance there was some lawyer, either a Kuwaiti or a Saudi, who was criticizing the regime. Either as a result of torture or blackmail he just blabbered out the names of some Egyptian lawyers, who were also criticizing the regime. So they were all rounded up and put in prison."[21] Jehane adds: "My father was among a group of nine that were thrown into prison and we didn't hear from anyone or know where and how they were for nearly four months. Everything had been sequestrated and nationalized a few years earlier so we didn't have a penny in the bank. Of course my father's legal firm suffered because he was away for nine months. Thank God we had some money at home and were able to keep going."[22]

These months were very stressful on the rest of the family, and it was only in May that Doria learned her husband was in Tura prison, south of Cairo, where the regime confined most political prisoners, except the Communists and Muslim Brothers who were isolated at another prison in the desert near Kharga Oasis.[23] Although no visitors were allowed, Nour was able to get messages to his family until his release. "The only reason my father came out of prison," says Aziza, "was because of the Six-Day War, after which the internal secret police came under severe attack. The people criticized the regime for spending all its time locking up Egyptians when it ought to have been investigating what was going on in Israel. It was only after the defeat that they started looking into the case of these political prisoners and freeing some of the people who were imprisoned. My father could have been lost and been in prison for many years. Later the government published a formal apology to these lawyers in the press."[24]

Although he never openly complained, it was clear to his daughters that Nour was depressed after his release. His law practice had been destroyed a second time, he had very little money, and his country had just suffered its worst military defeat in modern history. If he were to start again, it would have to be outside Egypt. Thus began a period of prolonged absences in Kuwait, absences which placed further stress on an already fragile relationship that over the years was characterized more by tension than by companionship. Doria had almost totally withdrawn from social life and, realizing that there was very little left to sustain their marriage, finally asked Nour for a divorce.

On October 21, 1968, barely a year after Nour's release from prison, the couple entered the divorce court at Abdin, where Doria was asked by the shaykh whether she agreed to this second divorce. She assented, the formal papers were signed, and their marriage of thirty-one years ended. Although there was a three-month period during which they could be legally reunited, there was no doubt in either of their minds that this separation was final. "My mother was very much in love with my father," Jehane explains, "and this divorce evoked disturbing memories of her childhood. My father told me that during the divorce, my mother kept remembering the death of her own mother and she broke down and wept during the proceedings. Whenever Mummy talked of her mother, she always spoke about her as a queen." Although Nour remarried soon after his divorce from Doria, "my mother and father were always very civilized to each other and I never heard either one of them speak against the other."[25]

Friends also observed that "neither of them opened their mouths to give a word that would hurt their old lover."[26] One of the last times the two were to meet publicly was at Aziza's wedding in February 1969, and Jehane, who had married the previous February and was at that moment pregnant with the first grandchild, has related that "it was a small wedding held in our Wadie Saad apartment and both our parents were there and it was as if there hadn't been any divorce or anything." However, to some members of the wedding party, Doria seemed remote and distant, avoiding meeting or conversing with Nour. Perhaps because of her own hurt pride (it was just a few months after the divorce, and Nour had recently remarried), she did not go out of her way to mix freely.

Nour's imprisonment followed by the divorce placed Doria in a critical financial situation. Nour continued to provide her with as much money as he could afford, but at the beginning, it was minimal, due to his own personal circumstances. Doria's pride would not allow her to accept anything directly from Nour after the divorce. So he used to give money to Jehane, who would see that her mother did not lack for anything. Jehane once had the idea of asking her father to place the apartment in her mother's name, as a kind of financial security, for Doria was now living alone in a flat that was not hers: "There was no point, now that my father had remarried, in the flat remaining in Papy's name. He was very gallant and totally agreed. But she was very proud and said, 'No, I don't want you to do that. You are just presupposing that something may happen to your father and I just don't want to think about it and whatever comes, comes. But I don't want any of these considerations.' And that was that. When she reacted like this, I didn't pursue it any further. For me it was just giving her a kind of security. But for her, it was a matter of pride."[27]

Both daughters experienced the pain that comes with the divorce of one's parents. They adored their father and realized that his remarriage was making him happy and content. Yet, at the same time, they were keenly aware of their mother's vulnerability and her perceived sense of abandonment. However, according to Jehane and Aziza, their mother never made them feel they had to choose sides. As Aziza avers, "Of all the people in the world [the ones] that she would never in any way turn against or feel betrayed by [were] me and Jehane. The whole world could go to blazes, everyone could betray her but not us, whatever we did, she never felt that way. When she talks about the absolute of love as being the love that one carries for one's children, she really means it." Jehane remarks concerning her mother at the time: "I could feel her sensitivity. I was very close to her then and I don't think she was easily hurt because there was no one around to hurt her. She would never ask indiscreet questions. For instance, my father was remarried and we would visit him often. Mummy would never embarrass us by asking questions. She never said a word. Never asked us anything. A lot of discretion on her part."

There's no doubt that 1969 marked a critical turning point in Doria's struggle against her solitude and loneliness. Divorced, both daughters married and starting families of their own, she was now living totally alone. And later that summer, Aziza and her husband Hamed al-Lozy, like many other educated young Egyptians of their social backgrounds during the sixties, decided to immigrate to the United States to continue their doctoral studies and begin a new life. Jehane distinctly remembers the date of their departure:

It was the 24th of August, because Nazli was 20 days old. When Aziza left, Mummy was forbidden to travel because it was during the time of Abdul Nasser and it was very difficult. I was the closest person to her those last years, no doubt. I mean she would open up to me and I felt that she would trust me more than anybody else. And at the same time I knew how sensitive she was. I was always careful, you know, not to say anything that could hurt her feelings. She was not at all the complaining

type. She lived on almost nothing, you know. It's not that she had nothing. I mean the apartment was very nice, she always had a servant. But
the expenses were minimal and she managed. I used to make some of
her clothes. And at the same time she was an extremely generous person
and liked to spend money. Her philosophy was *isrif ma fil geb ya'ti ma
fil ghaib* [spend what's in your pocket and what's unknown will come].
She was not at all the kind that cared about or wanted money. It was just
a means to an end for her, that's all.[28]

Doria never wanted to feel dependent on anybody, and if she needed money,
then she would look for work. When her situation demanded, she managed to
find different translation projects through the help of Jehane's contacts with
the various cultural and archaeological research centers in Cairo: "They would
send her the texts at home and Mummy would translate them. And she was
happy for a while because this work brought her in a small income, but at the
same time it was taking too much of her time and she saw that it was stifling
her own creative writing."[29]

She eventually stopped seeking work, completely minimized her physical
needs, and entered into a phase of her life that could only be described as as-
cetic. She led a very simple life— according to Aziza, "perhaps carrying it to
extremes. First of all she became a vegetarian. She didn't like meat anyway
but at the end she gave it up completely. She limited herself to the very few
things that she owned. She wore simple clothes and refused to wear jewelry,
most of which she had either thrown or given away." Jehane remembers that
"Mummy was always reading from the Quran, especially from the Surah
Yassin, which she knew by heart. She used to tell me, 'If you need anything or
are facing any crisis, read it forty times and your problem will be solved.'
When I had difficulty during Nazli's birth, Mummy sat by my bed and read
the Quran. She always fasted at Ramadan. She used to say 'It keeps me company.' She never asked for anything. She never complained about anything.
She was very strict with herself."

Despite her obviously lonely and austere way of life, Doria conveyed the
feeling to those around her that she was at complete peace with herself and,
according to her daughters, "during those last few years, she seemed to have
reached a certain inner tranquillity and equilibrium." Even to those less close,
Doria imparted "a very strong mystical quality. She was so near to reaching
communion with the divine. If she had met a guru, he may have helped, but
she was so near. How could one so close to spiritual grace convey such a different personality to the outside world?"[30]

*   *   *

Primarily what helped Doria maintain this semblance of serenity in the face of total solitude was her writing, which throughout her life had always been her faithful companion, "as necessary to me as breathing." During the course of her many years of seclusion, she produced over sixteen books, including many volumes of poetry, several philosophical essays, two versions of her memoirs, and a novel. She spent a good deal of her time translating the Quran from Arabic into French and English. As Mustapha Amin remembers, "She wrote poetry in French about Qays and Layla and about the love of Isis for Osiris. She wrote a book in French, *Avec Dante aux Enfers*, and she compared the hell that Dante lived with the hell of her life. And when she wrote about Layla and Isis, she wrote about her love."[31]

Doria had her writing, her long walks beside her beloved Nile River, and her regular Sunday lunches with Jehane. But it was the arrival of her first-born granddaughter, Nazli, in 1969 that provided a new and different fulcrum to Doria's daily life. As a young child, Nazli looked like a small replica of her grandmother, and the two were to develop a very special relationship: "I suppose all grandmothers find granddaughters very remarkable, but Mummy adored Nazli. Every year, in spite of her limited financial situation, she always bought Nazli an elegant birthday cake from Simonds. It was all white, with birds, like a wedding cake, but smaller." When Nazli was about three years old, she began her schooling at a French kindergarten, the Franciscaines. Since Jehane was working as a laboratory instructor in the chemistry department at the American University in Cairo, Doria would go every day at noon to pick Nazli up from school:

> Mummy's big outing for the day was to get Nazli from the school and take her to Simonds to choose her favorite cake. And Nazli always looked forward to this daily outing with her Nona Doria. They would return to Wadie Saad, where Nazli would cuddle up on the couch, suck her thumb and listen to Mummy tell her stories until I arrived in the afternoon. Sometimes they'd play cards together but mostly Mummy told her stories in French. Once Mummy told me that Nazli cried after hearing one of her stories. It was about this fish and how it was caught. "And what did they do with the fish?" Nazli asked. Mummy replied, "They cut it up in small pieces, put them in boxes and made tuna." "Goodness," she said, "Nazli burst into tears and I didn't know what to do to console her." I told her to forget it and I would make another ending to the story.[32]

Nasser died of a heart attack in September 1970, and Anwar al-Sadat became the third president of Egypt. Soon after Sadat came to power, foreign travel restrictions on Egyptians were lifted, and Doria immediately made plans to visit Aziza and Hamed in the United States. Thanks to the generosity of her daughters, who provided her with the tickets, she traveled to North Carolina in June of 1971 in order to be present during the birth of her first grandson, Sharif. She made a second trip in the summer of 1973, after Aziza and Hamed had both obtained their doctorates in material science and had moved to New York, where Hamed had accepted a position with IBM. During both these trips, Doria did not remain more than a month or six weeks at the most.

As the Sadat open-door policies began to crystallize after the October War of 1973, there were those who suggested that Doria Shafik come out of her self-imposed retirement and resume her previous work. Aziza's father-in-law, who was one of Doria's great admirers, told her that things were different now and that she should become involved once again and pick up where she left off. She categorically refused. She argued that the very raison d'être of the Bint al-Nil Union was the struggle for women's political rights. Now that women had the right to vote and to be elected to parliament, what was the point? Furthermore, she maintained, the same military regime was still in power; despite the shift in leadership, the principle was the same. As Jehane recalls, "She used to say, 'Now it's finished. I'm not going to start again. This is my way, to be alone to show passive resistance. Just staying out of politics is a negation.' That was her way of resisting, of reacting to the revolution as a whole. So she refused to be part of it. Although for me, I used to say, My God, being years and years on your own like this, it's no life."[33]

A few years later, a small column in *Akhbar al-Yawm* contained the following query from a reader in Qalubiya province to the editor: "Dear *Akhbar al-Yawm*, Where did Doria Shafik go and why has she completely disappeared?" The paper carried a brief answer that outlined her past activities and ended by saying, "A decision was taken to close her journals and feminist union under the pretext that she was a danger to public security! And she has been secluded in her apartment for eighteen years. And she believes that silence is more effective then speaking."[34]

Amina al-Sa'id claims that after Sadat came to power, Doria called to congratulate her for refusing to accept a post in the new government:

One day as a consequence of changes in the government, Doria Shafik got in touch with me in my office by telephone and I was surprised to find her congratulating me on refusing to accept a ministerial post, although no post was offered to me. And I never had refused any position at all. And when I tried to explain this truth to Doria she didn't believe me no matter how much I tried to convince her. Doria accused me of denying being offered a ministerial post because of fear of the authorities. I swore that I was telling her the truth. It was impossible to convince her and she insisted that I was a heroine for refusing the position.[35]

In the spring of 1973, Jehane decided to pursue her Ph.D. and formally registered to study with the distinguished professor of physical chemistry, Dr. K. S. W. Sing, of Brunel University in London. Later that June, after her mother had safely departed for New York to visit Aziza, Jehane, five months pregnant with her second daughter, Hedy, left for England to begin a month's research work under the guidance of her major professor. When Sing and his family visited Cairo the following year, he specifically asked to meet Doria Shafik. When Jehane conveyed this request to her mother, she agreed to arrange a tea in his honor. He was deeply impressed by his encounter with the former feminist and wrote Jehane to that effect. Aside from this rare moment of sociability, Doria continued to shun people. Of course, there were the times when she took bridge lessons and all those language lessons, and she took up golf briefly.

But near the end of her life, her only outings were to pick up Nazli or take her usual two-hour walks along the Nile. Jehane commented that "toward the end she seemed less sure of herself, maybe shy. For instance when Aziza would come in the summer to visit and we would all go to the airport. There would be me, my father, the in-laws and friends waiting. I felt she was a bit lost. But she never complained." Even Jehane's short trips to England during the summers seemed to intensify Doria's sense of loneliness: "Mummy used to be very sad every time I left, but she put up a brave front for my sake. She never made me feel guilty about anything." To the contrary, Doria conveyed the impression that, despite her altered situation following the divorce, she had come to some sort of reconciliation within herself those last few years. However, it was becoming increasingly more obvious to those who were close to her that she was sliding into a deep depression. The many years of seclusion and withdrawal from social life eventually began to take their toll, even though, as Aziza commented, "the last three or four years of her life seemed to have leveled off. She seemed at peace with herself, although I sensed she was depressed, I mean she was going through a depression. She was a very sad person. The sense of tragedy had begun to set in during those last six months. I couldn't bear it. I really couldn't. It was very painful. It was almost like seeing someone drowning without being able to do anything about it."[36]

As Doria withdrew further into herself, she struggled harder against the encroachment of her loneliness through the only means left open to her. More than ever she relied upon that voice of interior music, her trusted muse, who became both her mistress and companion and through whom she could express the anguish of her loneliness—as her poem "Rythme de Vie" makes clear:

Comment vivre sans
Poésie?!
Comment
sans ce rythme de vie
supporter
l'écoulement des jours
vides de contenu,
et ces départs sans retour
départs
de tous nos espoirs?
Comment vivre sans
cette musique intérieure
qui seule nous permet
de porter le poids lourd
d'indicibles douleurs?
Comment vivre sans
cette respiration profonde
qu'est la Poésie
amie
de ceux qui souffrent
de ceux
au coeur grand trop sensible,
de ceux qui veulent
et insistent à vouloir
faire de leur vie
une Oeuvre d'Art?

How to live without
Poetry?!
How
without this rhythm of life
to endure
the passing of the days
empty of content and
these departures without
return
departures
of all our hopes?
How to live without
this interior music
which alone permits us
to bear the heavy burden
of inexpressible sorrow?
How to live without
this profound breathing
that is Poetry
friend
of those who suffer
of those
with too sensitive a heart,
of those who want
and insist on wanting
to make of their life
a Work of Art?

Unyielding, she continued through her poetry to denounce oppression, hatred, and violence. Under these conditions of separation and loneliness that
became more and more difficult for her to endure, she proclaimed her attachment to freedom, to good, and to love. She filled thousands of blank pages
with words that now gushed forth in a stream of consciousness, revealing the
slow process of a self disconnecting from the world of social and family ties,
drifting slowly toward the ultimate fusion with the Absolute.

After her divorce from Nour and Aziza's departure to America, Jehane and
young Nazli became the central source of warmth and affection that still connected Doria to the human world. But it was especially Jehane, who lived near
her, who worried about her and preserved her, and to whom Doria was able to
open up, as much as she could open up to anybody, and share her innermost
thoughts during those last anguishing months:

Every Sunday was so sacred that I'd never give it up for anything. It was her day, you see. On Tuesday, for instance, the children and I would have lunch with Papy. Normally she'd get Nazli from school but there was this one day when someone else picked her up. I'd love going to her because I would stay with her before lunch and we would sit and chat. Sometimes she would recite to me some of her poems, like *La Poupée de Sucre* and *Action de Grâce*. When she recited *Heures du Caire*, especially the last cantos, she had tears in her eyes. And there was also *Le Nil*. She adored the river. Whenever we went walking together along its banks, she would always say, "Sometimes when I feel anxious or upset, I look at the Nile and I forget my misery." And there were moments when we would laugh together. By the way, she used to have a good sense of humor. It was only towards the end that I read any of her poems. I mean that she would invite me to read her poems, like *Larmes d'Isis*. It was just once, before she died. We were sitting together on the sofa and she said: "Voilà! I have finished writing this. If you wish to read it you may." It was the only work I read, except the few things she would recite to me. And she would very often refer to this other poem, *Rédemption*, and to her memoirs that she was writing. But she would never invite me to read anything that she was working on at the moment.[37]

Doria spent a very lonely summer in 1975, when Jehane left for England, taking Nazli with her: "Nazli had grown to be very shy and I was afraid that my leaving her every summer would affect her, so I took her with me." Before they left, Doria confided to her daughter how terribly depressed she was feeling. Jehane's departures had always provoked a certain sadness within Doria, but for the first time, Jehane noticed that her reaction seemed intensified:

Every time I'd see her, she was almost in tears. I tried to assure her by her telling her it was only forty-five days, that they would pass quickly, that I would write and so on. Even though Ali, my husband, and Hedy went to her for lunch every Sunday I was away, when I returned she said, "I've never felt so lonely; I cried almost every night. And now that you are back, I feel that everything is going to be all right." Then two weeks later, she felt very low, very depressed, and she said, "I don't understand, I mean for these past few years, I've felt at peace." And its true, she seemed, in spite of her loneliness, to have reached a kind of tranquillity and equilibrium. She had a lot of inner strength because nobody could have coped with all this.

Aziza analyzed the situation: "My mother may have looked within herself and felt that everything had crumbled and all her sacrifices may have been for nothing but she would never admit it openly to anyone. During her moments of depression, she would never agree to seek help, that would have been admitting weakness, that was out of the question."[38]

However, those last few weeks of the summer, Doria finally confided in Jehane and admitted that she was feeling very low and that perhaps she should see a doctor. Jehane could not possibly realize the import of what her mother was saying:

> She seemed relatively healthy. She was writing a lot. I never, never remember her not writing, except when I came back from the States around the middle or end of August. When I returned she said "I felt so depressed two days ago." "How?" I asked. "Well I just have these black ideas [ces idées noires]." "Quelles idées?" "I don't know, there are moments when I don't feel like living any more." I didn't know whether she meant, j'ai envie de mourir [I long to die]. You know sometimes you have uncontrollable moments like this when you feel down and you make a comment like this and it is not meant seriously.

On the advice of a friend who was also suffering from bouts of depression, Doria contacted Dr. Ahmad Okasha, a well-known Egyptian psychiatrist, with whom she had two or three meetings. He prescribed some pills, which were supposed to calm her down a bit but actually seem to have produced another kind of reaction. One day she acknowledged to her daughter that "Something strange is happening to me. I got down from the taxi and I found myself in front of the house and I didn't know where I was. For a long while I didn't know where I was. It worried me." Obviously she was having a much more serious nervous breakdown than Jehane, or anyone else, ever imagined or could understand during that last month. Sania Sha'rawi, the granddaughter of Huda Sha'rawi, related how she often encountered Doria Shafik returning from one of her long solitary walks along the Nile: "She seemed so very alone but I felt her presence. She had this psychic quality, this child-like quality, shy, gentle. One day when I saw her, I approached her and asked if I might come to see her soon to talk with her about my grandmother. She most graciously agreed. 'But of course, anytime.' I felt she was genuinely pleased to be asked, yet there was this sense of her terrible aloneness. I regret I never fulfilled my promise as she died a few weeks later."[39]

Her neighbor, Mustapha Amin, who used to see her from time to time in the elevator of the building, commented, "She was without any makeup, without any paint, in a plain dress. And before she had been a beauty, the queen of elegance. Her face was pale; her eyes were crying without tears; her lips were quivering without uttering a word; her heart was bleeding without blood; her soul was shouting without a voice. This woman was closer to being a ghost; a dead woman that walks; mute despite her song. And I used to see her dilemma in her sad eyes."[40]

Jehane relives their final moments together—moments which she had no way of knowing would be the last time she would ever see her mother alive:

> I remember very vividly it was a Friday. I stopped by to see Mummy on my way to have lunch with Granny that day, as Friday was always Granny's day.[41] I sat on Mummy's bed and she whispered, "Yesterday I felt very low and I packed away all my writings in my suitcases and I want to entrust these to you." "Why?" I asked. "Maybe you will take out your books again and you will start writing again." I then prepared lunch for her. She wasn't sick or anything but she felt, you know, just tired. When I brought in the lunch tray, I told her she must eat. We sat together for awhile and then she said, "You know I'm feeling better now. Maybe I'll take out a book or two and start working again." Then she turned to me and queried, "You know, I'm wondering if all this, my struggle, my writing, my whole life has been for nothing. Throughout it all, I wanted my life to be a work of art." Then as an afterthought she pondered, "I don't know what is going to happen to me." And I said, "Nothing will happen to you. I am here and you know I'll take care that nothing happens to you." And I remember I was wearing a big turquoise ring, which I took off and I told her, "Take this and it will bring you good luck," because she would always keep my things saying that I always brought her good luck. She put it on saying, "Now I am already feeling much better. *Tu sais tu es mon âme*, Jehane."[42]

The next day, Saturday September 20, 1975, Jehane called her mother very early in the morning, "and her voice was very low, almost inaudible. And I asked, 'Mummy, what's wrong?' And she kept repeating, 'I have a headache, I have a very bad headache.' And then I spoke to her again from the university. 'Do you still have your headache? *Toujours mal à la tête?*' And her voice was very low and she said, '*Oui, téléphones moi avant de venir.*' And that was it. That was maybe around one o'clock in the afternoon. And then, it's very strange, as I went out from university around half past one I said something has happened to Mummy. It's funny because it was a feeling, just a feeling."

At approximately the same moment that Jehane was having this uncanny feeling of tragedy surrounding her mother, one of her close friends and colleagues at the university, who lived in the Wadie Saad Building, was returning home for lunch and was the first to learn the sad news:

On that Saturday I arrived home from university around one o'clock and I noticed the doorkeeper at the left of the entrance of the apartment building opposite to my own. Knowing that I was a very good friend of the Ragai sisters, he came running toward me screaming, "Come quick! The lady has just jumped!" He covered the body with newspaper but he didn't know what to do next. I rushed immediately to Jehane's husband, who was working just a few blocks away. Ali then called Nour al-Din at his office and told him there had been an accident. When we returned to Wadie Saad a crowd had begun to gather.[43]

Mustapha Amin recalled that same afternoon in these words:

I returned to my house after lunching at one of the hotels. In the entrance way in front of our building, I saw a crowd of people surrounding a white sheet. I asked what happened. They said, "The lady has thrown herself from the balcony of the sixth floor." I looked under the white sheet and I found the body of my neighbor, Doria Shafik, this woman, who filled the world with noise and declarations, this woman, upon whom the world's lights were directed wherever she went, this woman, who was the star of Egyptian, Arab, European and American society. People forgot her charge into parliament, demanding the right to vote; they forgot her hunger strike in 1954 for the rights of women and they forgot that she lost her freedom and her magazines, her money and her husband because she demanded human rights for the Egyptian people. She paid a horrible price for her resistance when other people gave up. She paid a horrible price for her boldness when all those around her quivered in fear from the sword and the whip.[44]

16

Life as a Work of Art

This song possessing me since my earliest childhood had finally to be sung. Not only throughout my life, which I tried as much as possible to make a work of art, but also through a rhythm, for which I searched a long time in vain. First, as a child, the song of my soul escaped between my fingers at the keys of the piano at Mansura and Tanta; then in Paris during my years of study when I wanted to take lessons on the cello or indeed painting. I was searching for something without being able to define it. Art, yes! But a little more than art. An art that at the same time would be a philosophy; that is to say, essentially an attitude, a route, a way opening to the future.

As the news of Doria's tragic death, her falling from her sixth-floor apartment in Zamalek, appeared under banner headlines on the front pages of all the major Egyptian newspapers, the name and deeds of Doria Shafik once again burst upon the local scene and then spread like wildfire across the national and international media. Journalists, Egyptian and foreign, male and female, wrote touching tributes to this woman who had so vexed her society during a turbulent moment in Egyptian history. "There was a day when Doria Shafik was the only man in Egypt," wrote Fatma Abd al-Khalak. "We were then all silent out of fear, our mouths were gagged and our tongues cut. We were 'struck dumb.' Suddenly Doria Shafik emerged in 1957 to tell us that we were on our way to dictatorship, that our liberties had to be restored, that we had to rid ourselves of this dictatorship. That day Egypt's women and its feminist organizations came out to protest and attack her. She was labeled a traitor because she had asked for an end to this dictatorship. She paid the price, but Doria Shafik did not bend her head. Now that our press is liberated, that our tongues are back in our mouths and our lips are unsealed, we owe this woman the credit she deserves!"[1]

Al-Ahram's front-page coverage of the death of Doria Shafik, September 21, 1975.

Muhammad Zaki Abd al-Qadir made this declaration:

Fate willed that her exit would be so tragic in order to deepen our feeling of loss for her. For Doria Shafik, with her life and her struggle, was not an ordinary event on the Egyptian scene. Rather, she was the breaking of stagnation in a time when it was nearer stagnation than movement. She led a serious campaign to awaken Egyptian women to assert their rights to freedom, emancipation and equality. And her movement was not the only one at the time. For there were many scattered efforts, but hers was the most effective and the strongest and the one attracting the most attention by virtue of her dedicated distinction and assertiveness and by virtue of her wide culture and excellent academic background. Then Doria Shafik disappeared and she resorted to imposed silence or the silence to which there was no alternative and which was not suitable to the movement and the call and the struggle. Dr. Doria Shafik will never be forgotten whenever the rights of women are mentioned or even whenever the freedom and struggle for these rights are mentioned. I hope that those who attacked her when she was still young and struggling—I hope these people know how unfair they were.[2]

But as during her life, so in her death, Doria Shafik's final dramatic act was shrouded in ambiguity and contradiction. Several articles from the Egyptian press expressed the public perplexity about the circumstances surrounding her fall from the balcony of her sixth-floor apartment. The last person to see Doria alive was her servant, Ahmad Muhammad Taha, who very simply and clearly stated, "I used to arrive every day around nine in the morning and leave by two thirty in the afternoon. On the day of the incident, I asked if I should make her breakfast, she refused. I asked if I could get her some tea, as it was her habit to have tea a half hour after her breakfast. She refused the tea also. She asked for a glass of water which I brought to her. She went out into the kitchen seemingly busy with something and then sent me out on an errand to buy something for her lunch. When I returned I found the crowds surrounding this white sheet."[3]

Amina al-Said, who was never in total sympathy with Doria, wrote nearly fifteen years later: "I learned from a few friends, who had been in close touch with Doria, that she was suffering from depression and that her health had deteriorated. It was a deep depression that led to her suicide. This friend, who lived in the building facing Doria's balcony, told me that on that horrible day, she saw Doria standing on her balcony immersed in thought. She stood immobile for a while and then went into her room and brought out a chair. Instead of sitting on it, she did the opposite. She stood on the chair and she jumped to the ground below. Thus the tragedy occurred. Had it not been for the eye-witness accounts, there would have been rumors and different stories about the cause of her death."[4]

The most bizarre rumor that circulated around Doria's death suggested it was neither a suicide nor an accident, but the willful act of some Nasserist or fundamentalist who wanted her out of the way. Most journalists, however—perhaps out of sensitivity to her memory or in deference to the fact that suicide is not condoned in Islam—chose to focus their obituaries on her life's accomplishments. In his book on outstanding Egyptian women, Abd al-Halim described Doria Shafik's life as "consisting of a series of explosions, which continued until the last explosion when she fell from the sixth floor ending her life on September 20, 1975. Did Dr. Doria Shafik commit suicide after having lived more than eighteen years in the shadows, or was she the victim of an attack of low blood pressure causing her to lose her balance while standing on the balcony and fatally fall to her death at the age of 65? Whether we take the first or the second possibility, the truth is that in both cases, on that fateful day the last explosion occurred in the life of Dr. Doria Shafik, the head of the Bint al-Nil Union."[5]

From the pen of one of her journalist friends, who was not in total sympathy with Doria's earlier political struggle, came these lines:

I invite you to cry with me, Doria Shafik. A simple note in the press, accident or suicide? I refuse to know. I refuse even to know the true causes and circumstances of this brutal death that put an end to a destiny, nourished by intelligence, by refinement and by the most absolute dignity. Where had you disappeared then, Doria Shafik? A huge human misunderstanding seems to have decided to isolate her from society. There are beings who refuse to come to terms with life. Intuitive, cultivated and intransigent, I suppose that Doria Shafik could not bear for long a world that had no more to offer except choice and battles. Had she suddenly wanted in her "dizziness," to follow that old dream which had escaped her or, rather, had she lost herself in that total annihilation, which for certain elite beings, assumes the form of a new wager with destiny?[6]

Four years later, in an editorial discussing the attitude with which the Sadat government handled its opponents, this same writer circulated a critical tract to Arab and foreign embassies violently opposing the ratification of the proposed peace treaty between Egypt and Israel and conjured up the memory of Doria Shafik: "And I suddenly measured the change that has occurred in our society since the epoch of my friend, the great militant, Doria Shafik, editor-in-chief of La Femme Nouvelle, who having deposited an anti-Nasserist tract in the letter boxes of the foreign press agencies, had to seek refuge in the Indian embassy in order not to endure the worst brutality on the part of the 'centers of power' and information services of the period. If she had lived until our day, she surely would have been heartened by all our reconquered liberties!"[7]

The young journalist Madiha, who had interviewed Doria Shafik nearly twenty years earlier, describing her as "The Leader of Candied Chestnuts," wrote an eloquent obituary in *Rose al-Yusuf* under the title "The Leader Outside Her Time":

> Although I once called her "Leader of Candied Chestnuts," due to her elegance and aristocracy, I cannot forget that Doria Shafik was one of the pioneers of the Egyptian women's movement and one of the first who demanded women's political rights; and those who came after her asking for the rights of the Egyptian women in the field of politics were either her comrades or her students. It should also be noted that *Bint al-Nil* magazine, which she originally founded and edited, was very popular in all centers. I remembered all these efforts of Doria Shafik when I read the news of her death. Here ends the life of one of the pioneers of feminist work in Egypt and a leader who chose the wrong time but not the way, because she prepared the way for those who followed her and carried the same torch. Doria Shafik, one of Egypt's working women in the field of service and of knowledge has departed for good. She gave a great deal of her money and her effort, even though her work was not completed. But she paved the way for the progress of Egyptian women. Yet she died with no word of remorse from those who shared in the effort with her, neither from a comrade nor a student. No word of "Goodbye," without friendship or comradeship. May God bless her.[8]

There were a few among her old comrades and students who remembered Doria Shafik and shared their sentiments in private letters to her daughters. One of them wrote:

> Useless to tell you how much the death of your mother has touched me . . . but you cannot know what she represented for me. I have always considered her my ideal and I have lived in her wake, following her as closely as my absence from Cairo and Alexandria would permit me. She was an extraordinary woman who could combine courage and audacity in order to fulfill the dream that Huda Sha'rawi and Egyptian women wanted to realize for a long time. It is through her and her alone that we have achieved the right to vote. It was with Bint al-Nil that the fight against illiteracy began. And if today the Egyptian woman can be a minister or member of parliament or head of a section at the university, it is in large part due to Doria Shafik. In a word, she was a great lady and a fervent Egyptian, hence her disappearance is an enormous loss. What consoles us is that she accomplished her mission toward Egypt and the world.[9]

Ragia Raghab, Doria's most loyal comrade and friend in the Bint al-Nil Union, categorically denied that Doria Shafik could have ever taken her own life and argued that "she had an illness that resulted in vertigo. She was going out to her balcony to see if her cook was returning and she fell. I was the victim of this illness once and I felt that I was falling. I tried to get away from the window. It stayed with me for a year." When it came to assessing Doria's life and the impact she had upon her society, Ragia was steadfast in her belief:

> Doria Shafik had faith, principles and courage. She was ready to do any-thing for her country. Eccentric, yes. But a woman like her had to be. She was not common. She was on another plane, not like me who had family name, financial security, money. Doria was middle class, no family name behind her, no inherited wealth. She was an upstart, an outsider to those women who clustered around Huda Sha'rawi and they were jealous. She was an idealist, clean and courageous. Even her enemies never accused her of anything immoral or corrupt. She was truly a messenger. She represented the Egyptian woman to the west in such a way that one could be proud of being an Egyptian. She was a pioneer in the sense that she did new things that nobody thought of before. But she chose the wrong moment! She had bad timing. An individual must fight within his own possibilities; he must know his own limits and not go beyond them. And she went beyond her own limitations and the result was that she failed. Her life was broken and she spent her latter years in seclu-sion, all alone. [10]

While the public pondered her death and hence the meaning of her life within the context of her political struggle in recent Egyptian history, Doria Shafik's inner personal project, her yearning to make life a work of art, went unexamined. If we are to understand Doria's life, then it must be in the sense in which she consciously intended to live it. It was Oscar Wilde who once said that a life, in order to be beautiful, must end in disaster; that tragic beauty is enhanced when there is a sad ending to the life. But it was Pierre Seghers whose choice of metaphor to describe Doria Shafik seems more germane to her own quest: "She was a woman smitten with the Absolute; a woman who had her own convictions, her own beliefs and who always defended them. Her spirit never broke, she never left the battle. Perhaps she had the demon of the Absolute in her heart."

In the midst of our interview, he got up from his desk and pulled out a copy of Louis Aragon's *Aurélien*: "Never has anyone written a text on the Absolute so powerful, so lofty. You know, this text on the Absolute will remain at all times the most beautiful text that one could write. This is why I cite it. It is a text which can be very well applied to Doria Shafik at the end. This quest for the Absolute. That's it. She was one of the noble hearts. It was exactly her. It was something I had given her during our correspondence."[11] Then he read this passage to me:

> There is a passion so devouring that it cannot be described. It consumes whoever contemplates it. All those who take from it are taken by it. No one can sample it and then recover. One trembles to name it: it is the taste for the Absolute. We can say it is a rare passion, unhappily for those enthusiastic amateurs of human greatness. One must not be deceived. It is more widespread than the common cold, and if one recognizes it better when it affects noble hearts—it has sordid forms that show its ravages with ordinary people, with dry hearts and impoverished temperaments. Open the door, it enters and installs itself. Logic matters little to its simplicity. It is the absence of resignation. If one wishes, one can appreciate what it has enabled men to do; the reaching for the sublime that such dissatisfaction has engendered. But it is only to see the exception, the monstrous flower and even then look into the heart of those that it transports to the borders of genius, you will find this internal shriveling, these stigmata of devastation, which are the only signs of its passage on individuals less privileged then the angels. By the same token, he who has the taste for the Absolute renounces all happiness. What happiness could mean anything at these dizzying heights? On this never ending quest?[12]

"You know," Seghers went on, "I have met many poets, but I had a great regard for Doria. I held her in the highest esteem because she was a very brave woman. Besides her poetry, she was a woman of great valor, who was struggling politically; she was a fighter and I appreciate this attitude very much. I knew that she would have many, many difficulties because she absolutely rejected the idea of compromise. Truly a woman who gave wholeheartedly and then, I don't know, relations with her husband had been difficult. At a certain moment he gambled a great deal with Faruq. I know this because she confided in me and trusted me. It was very, very difficult."[13]

Looking at her life, as well as her uncommon death, through this prism, we can better understand the basis for the complex and turbulent relationship she had with society. It is not so much that she was a "leader in an inopportune time" as a woman who lived out her life passionately. She was very demanding, exacting, wanting to go beyond her limits, to surpass her own strengths. To some, she was an eccentric interested only in being in the limelight. To others, she was an ideal of what an Egyptian Muslim woman could become. To those who knew only her public persona, she was perceived as *dûre* (hard, harsh, difficult, tough), *froide* (cold, chilly, cool), *enfermée* (shut in, locked up, enclosed within herself), *majestueuse* (majestic, stately), *hautaine* (proud, haughty). To those who knew her poetic self, she was, in Seghers's words, "like a fire and a fire torments itself. She was like that because she was an artist and she was a woman of thought."[14]

There was this aura of contradiction surrounding Doria Shafik. Here was an ardent Egyptian but with a French education, thinking and writing in French, a woman of acknowledged femininity and beauty, struggling to liberate her compatriots who could neither understand her modernity nor fully accept her political struggle. Doria experienced that inevitable chasm that often arises between those who want passionately to bring innovative ideas to their society and those to whom these ideas are addressed. They are not necessarily understood or followed. Those who upset the established order or who speak of a new order embarrass others. Such people are disturbing. Such has been the case not only with Doria Shafik, as Emma Goldman reminds us: "the iconoclast in whatever line—is fated to be misunderstood, not only by her own kind but often by her own comrades. This is the doom of all great spirits; they are detached from their environment. Theirs is the lonely life—the life of the transition stage, the hardest and most difficult for the individual as well as for a people."[15] All those who are innovators must go through a period of struggle which one cannot say hardens the individual, but it does seem to debilitate one and to set one's nerves on edge. As Seghers said with regard to Doria, "To pass one's life defending poetry is not easy. She was a woman who was a poet. I don't even say she adored poetry. She was a poet with zeal, ardor and passion. That's all."

And herein lies the tragic beauty of her life. First, she had the temperament of the poet. This implies an ardor and an inner fire within a conscience. Secondly, being a woman, she saw major injustices around her in Egypt—it was the female condition. Because of her social background and early experiences, she could not remain an indifferent witness. Being a poet, she proclaimed this injustice. There was a correlation between her origins as a poet, the voice of the poet, and the flagrant injustice which she saw around her and wrote about. And then poetry enabled her to reach her inner self, the interiority of the person, in a sort of reflection, a sort of expression that others around her did not generally possess. Being a poet, she was able to speak, to express herself. For Doria Shafik, it was always a question of conscience. Wrote Seghers: "She had become a conscience, an unrelenting gaze, an unbearable presence, a voice who spoke for all. The temporal powers were no longer able to tolerate her. You have silent consciences because they do not have the means or are not able to express themselves. But she, as a poet, had a conscience. Her ability to write could have become for her a kind of exorcism and could have spared her the kind of death that she eventually had; but the outer political conditions were such, for her, that she could not withstand them. These [political conditions] killed her. In the words of Pierre Reverdy 'There is no suicide, there are only assassins,' would be worth contemplating here."[16]

Through her writings, we discover that her struggle was as much a reflection of her own deep commitment to individual freedom as it was an expression of Egypt's longing for national liberation. Her feminist consciousness was shaped as much by her commitment to the moral values of a liberally interpreted Islam as it was to secular Egyptian politics. Her vision of the "just" society reflected as much the ideas of Egyptian liberal thinkers like Qasim Amin, Taha Husayn, and Lutfy al-Sayyid as it did the signers of the Magna Carta, the philosophy of Rousseau, and the poetry of the French surrealists.

Her aesthetic voice was French, yet her metaphors were profoundly Egyptian and Islamic. Her activist voice was Arabic, yet her metaphors were deeply feminist and modernist. Her public persona was daring, proud, self-centered, and strong-willed; her private self was shy, sad, over-sensitive, and vulnerable. Her passionate attitude to life, accompanied by an unwavering pursuit of the Absolute, took her to the brink of disaster in 1957. Misunderstood and repudiated by her compatriots but unable to compromise on her fundamental convictions, she remained estranged and alone.

Doria Shafik epitomizes the dilemma of the double bind of the feminist cultural critic. In Doria's case, the more she refuted the stereotypes created by European ignorance and romantic images of the East by expressing herself as "the new woman," the more she was criticized by her own society as not being oriental enough. The more she attempted to be a "bridge," a "messenger," between two cultures, not as an imitator but as a mediator, the more she was distanced from her own society. Her predecessors, like Huda Sha'rawi, stayed within the cultural boundaries of expected oriental custom. But Doria Shafik—with her modern dress code, her public protests to gain access to the restricted domain of male power, her fluency in French and her feminine beauty—was "too western, too modern."

At the same time that she was trying to render to the West the nationalist/feminist message about Egyptian civilizational greatness (with the expressed purpose of altering the negative image of the Egyptian woman), she was engaged in challenging those patriarchal barriers that curtailed the human freedom of the Egyptian woman in her own society. In other words, she was simultaneously engaged in a cultural defense and a social criticism. She wanted to change the Western image of the Eastern woman and at the same time create a new ("modern") image for the Eastern woman. The more she persisted, the more she was impugned for being an agent of Western colonialism and imperialism. These strands of nationalism, modernism, and feminism within her endeavors placed her in opposition to the rising tide of religious conservatism as well as the new revolutionary ethos that after 1952 dominated the politics of the country. Caught between the images of her own creation ("the new woman" and "the daughter of the Nile"), Doria Shafik struggled for her own sense of self until the state finally brought an end to the general movement for the emancipation of women and Nasser permanently silenced her voice of protest. As Irene Fenoglio Abd al-Aal observed, "After the agitation surrounding Doria Shafik, there was in effect no more general movement having a definite project of freedom of the Egyptian woman and her desire for institutional equality with men. The state had co-opted the movement and hence had muted feminist expression."[17]

Having finally exhausted her strength, she arranged her papers and unpublished books, packed them neatly into several old suitcases, and entrusted them to her younger daughter. She had not yet reached her sixty-seventh birthday when she walked out onto her balcony and stepped off into the void. Yet, as Seghers has averred, "In the heart of the typhoon, the eye of destiny lay in wait for her, but was not able to deny her the final victory, that of the written word." Indeed, there are thousands of pages of Doria's unpublished manuscripts—works ranging from prose poems in English to a novel in French, from philosophical essays to a historical piece on Egyptian women, from French and English translations of the Quran to more than a dozen volumes of French poetry. From this enormous output, only a few poems have been published posthumously. "One must take the poems of Doria Shafik as they are," Seghers maintains, "notations, scribbles on the pages of a desk diary, dashed off, directly in French, without corrections. They comprise the journal of interior exile of a poet-prisoner, surrounded by high invisible walls. They are questions and answers seized in flight within the confusions of an epoch."[18]

As the biographer Phyllis Rose reminds us, "life is as much a work of fiction as a novel or a poem and the task of the biographer is to explore that fiction. The metaphors may vary, but the need to shape expectations about experience does not: past, present and future would be inassimilable, perhaps an unlivable blur, unless we projected upon it a structure of meaning to sift certain moments as significant, some experiences as crucial. Each of us, influenced perhaps by one ideology or another, generates her own symbolic landscape."[19]

This biography does not presume to be a truer story than Doria Shafik herself tried to convey through her various writings; rather, it is an attempt to demonstrate that one age, through the art of biography, can understand another, can touch and be understood and hence persist. It does not presume to explain Doria Shafik but to try to grasp the meaning of her life, and perhaps, only fleetingly, to disclose a possible way of being.

Notes

Preface

1. Eliot, "Little Gidding," *Four Quartets*, 58.

2. See Shafik, *La Femme Nouvelle en Egypte* (The new woman in Egypt); *Tatawwur al-Nahda al-Nisa'iyah fi Misr* (The development of the renaissance of women in Egypt); *al-Kitab al-Abiyad li huquq al-mar'ah al-siyasiyah* (The white book on the political rights of women); *al-Mar'ah al-Misriyah min al-Fara'niah ila al-Yawm* (The Egyptian woman from the pharaohs until today); *Rihlati Hawla al-'Alam* (My trip around the world).

3. Shafik, *Larmes d'Isis* (Tears of Isis) and *Avec Dante aux Enfers* (With Dante in Hell).

4. Shafik, "Poésie," *Avec Dante aux Enfers*, 4.127. This and all subsequent material from Shafik's work is translated by the author.

5. Mills, *Sociological Imagination*, 3. Mills argued that the major challenge facing the social scientist was the cultivation of the turn of mind he described as the sociological imagination, which "enables its possessor to understand the larger historical scene in terms of the inner life and external career of a variety of individuals. It enables us to grasp history and biography and the relation between the two" (1961: 34).

6. Sujut K. Das, "In Defense of Taslima Nasreen," *Economic Political Weekly* (Jan. 29, 1994): 235.

7. Rose, *A Woman of Letters*, ix.

8. Elizabeth Lawrence to Shafik, Dec. 16, 1954.

9. Lawrence to Shafik, May 24, 1956.

Chapter 1

1. The *katb-il-kitab* is a stage in Muslim religious marriages when the marriage contract between two families is negotiated and signed in front of the shaykh by male representatives of the two families. The groom's family provides the *mahr* (dowry), while the bride's family is charged with furnishing the trousseau. The actual consummation of the marriage, called the *dukhla*, can take place at a later date. In front of society, however, the contract signifies a legal marriage and cannot be rescinded except by divorce.

2. The institution of slavery legally ceased in Egypt in the latter part of the nineteenth century. Many notable families, including Khadiga's, established a *waqf* (endowment), the revenues of which were given to slaves at the moment of their libera-

tion to enable them to live independently. However, some slaves, women mostly, preferred to stay on with their owner.

3. The religious *imam* sings the call to prayer from the minaret of the mosque five times a day, according to Muslim religious practice. Doria wrote several poems using the minaret as an image.

4. Heyworth-Dunne, *History of Education,* 374–75.

5. After the Muslim conquest of Egypt, Tanta reached its zenith as a commercial center in the heart of the Delta. It played a heroic role when its citizens, led by Muslim shaykhs, defeated Napoleon Bonaparte's invasion forces in October 1798, forcing them to withdraw from Gharbiya. Today it is a strategic industrial and commercial center of Egypt, boasting the greatest railway network in Egypt. From Tanta, one can travel by train anywhere in Egypt—from Alexandria in the north to Aswan in the south. The people of Tanta celebrate October 7 not only to mark the humiliating defeat they inflicted on the French but also to commemorate the Egyptians' crossing the canal to destroy the Bar Lev line of the Israeli army in 1973.

6. Muhammed Khalil Subhi, *Tarikh al-Hayat al-Niyabiya fi Misr,* 226–27.

7. In ancient Pharaonic times, the arrival of spring was celebrated by throwing a young virgin into the Nile as a sacrificial gift to Osiris, the river god. In modern times, it is an occasion for families to gather together in the countryside and feast on *fasikh* (a salted fish that has been aged) and *basal akhdar* (fresh green onions).

8. According to Islam, a Muslim who worships in a church is considered an apostate. Given the government's sensitivities over the possible proselytizing intentions of some of these Christian missions in Egypt, Muslim students attending foreign mission schools were not allowed to participate in any form of Christian religious education.

9. The passage to which Doria refers is from Sura XIX Mary.

10. There are two feasts which follow *Ramadan: Little Bairam* and *Grand Bairam.* The former follows right after the month of fasting and is celebrated by family gatherings and festive foods. The latter comes some forty days later and is associated with the period when Muslims make the Hajj to Mecca.

11. The sacrifice of a sheep by the Muslims during the feast reflects the ancient tradition associated with Abraham (related in the Quran), who sacrificed a sheep in place of his own son. Another belief, associated with the magical traditions of rural Egypt, holds that the blood flowing from the sheep—immediately after the reciting of the Quran—not only redeems the soul of the dead but protects against the evil eye and thwarts misfortune.

12. Layla Ahmad Chafik, personal communication, June 19, 1986.

13. In 331 B.C., having conquered Syria and Egypt, Alexander ordered the construction of a city in the only place in Egypt by nature well-situated to commerce, with access to the sea and to the river. Alexandria was the New York of the ancient world, the first world-city, enormously rich—"the greatest emporium in the inhabited world," Strabo claimed. Like Manhattan, it was bordered by water, and its streets were laid out in unvarying straight lines intersected by stately avenues. It, too, was the meeting and melting point of diverse races, languages, cultures, and religions, and was the city with the largest Jewish population in the world. For more than three centuries, Alexandria

was the most learned place on earth. Here, man first surmised that the earth was round and that it revolved around the sun. The great library is reported to have contained four hundred thousand scrolls. Yet that city—which was once described as having four thousand palaces, four thousand public baths, and four hundred theaters—no longer existed in 641 when the Arab conqueror Amr Ibn al-'As ("a sensitive and generous soul," according to Forster) took Alexandria, which yielded almost without a struggle. Under the Arabs, the grandeur of the city disappeared, and by the time of Napoleon, it was but a simple fishing village. The modern city was built in the nineteenth century by European entrepreneurs, who controlled most of Egypt's industry and commerce. They were exempt from taxation and from what under Egyptian law was known as the capitulations, which gave them economic advantages in trading and special legal protection. They were subject not to the laws of Egypt but to those of their own country of origin. With its face turned northward toward Greece, Italy, and France, and away from the southern hinterland of Africa, Alexandria continued to be a more Mediterranean, cosmopolitan, politically radical city than Cairo. It was the city of Cavafy, Forster, and Durrell, where East and West met, mingled and mutually inspired. As Jane Pinchin has asserted, "Alexandria, her landscape, her peoples and the spirit of place had, perhaps more than any other city of this century, the power to excite mythic visions" (*Alexandria Still*, 7). E. M. Forster spent three years in Egypt as a medical orderly during the First World War and in 1961 published a minor classic on the city, *Alexandria: A History and a Guide*—a work in which the heroic Macedonian conqueror, the strange dynasties of the Ptolemies, the librarians of Alexandria, the poets, the astronomers and mathematicians, the church fathers, Amr ibn al-As, and Napoleon wander across the pages like the characters of a forgotten ghost city. Forster struck up a friendship with Constantine Cavafy, "the great Greek poet who so poignantly conveys the civilization of his chosen city." For Cavafy, Alexandria was a city of antiheroes—ambiguous, indolent, decadent, forever fin-de-siècle—the same themes which Lawrence Durrell developed in his *Alexandria Quartet* (1959).

14. In the French system of education, the Brevet élémentaire follows upon the completion of the Certificat d'étude, which is awarded upon the successful completion of an exam after six years of primary education. The Brevet usually takes three years of study. Following the successful completion of an exam, the student is allowed to continue on for the *bachot* (baccalaureate), which is in two parts: the *deuxième* (one year) and *première* I and II (two years).

15. In a newspaper interview given after Doria's death, her elder sister, Soraya, mentioned Doria's silver medal "in recognition of her achieving second place and being the youngest ever to complete the bachot."

16. For further details about Huda Sha'rawi's own formation as a feminist, see Badran's translation of Sha'rawi's *Harem Years* (1986). On the history of the women's movement in Egypt, see Khater and Nelson, "al-Harakah al-Nissa'iyah: The Women's Movement and Political Participation in Modern Egypt."

17. See Ahmed, *Women and Gender in Islam*; Baron, *Women's Awakening in Egypt*; and Badran and Cooke, eds., *Opening the Gates*.

18. Sha'rawi, "Eulogy to Qasim Amin," *L'Egyptienne*, 8.

19. Shafik, "Un Petit Mot," *L'Egyptienne*, 13.

20. The Druze are an offshoot of Shi'ism found in southern Iraq and Lebanon. In Sunni Egypt, the term means "the stranger."

Chapter 2

1. Shafik, "L'Enfant du Nil," *L'Egyptienne*, 26.

2. Among those traveling with Doria were Naglaa Khalil, Bahia Othman, Nazira Nakoula, Helen Sidarus, Kawkab Hifni Nassif, and Karima al-Sa'id. Helen became the first woman gynecologist in Egypt, and Kawkab became the first female head of Kitchener Hospital. Kawkab's letters to her friend Mai Ziadeh were collected and published by her sister (the well-known writer/feminist of the early 1900s, Malak Hifni Nassif). Kawkab's brother, Magdy Hifni Nassif, served as Huda Sha'rawi's secretary. Karima Said, who pursued a diploma in history from Westfield College, returned to take up a post in the Ministry of Education and became the first woman deputy-minister of the Ministry of Education in the 1960s. Her sister, Amina al-Sa'id, was one of Huda Sha'rawi's disciples and one of the first women to enter Cairo University in the late 1920s.

3. Shafik to Huda Sha'rawi, Aug. 17, 1928. I am indebted to Sania Sha'rawi Lanfranchi, Huda's granddaughter, for sharing these letters with me. All the translations from the original French are by the author.

4. Taha Husayn's most articulate argument for a Europeanized Egypt, *The Future of Culture in Egypt*, was published in 1938. He devoted his life to scholarship and educational reform and was primarily interested in the application of modern research techniques to the study of Arabic language. As minister of Education before the revolution and minister of culture during the early years of the Nasser regime, he had a major impact on the extension and reform of education in Egypt. His autobiography has been translated into English in two volumes, *An Egyptian Childhood* (1990) and *A Stream of Days: A Student at al-Azhar* (1948).

5. Although silent about her inner emotions in her memoirs, Doria would later write an essay entitled "Rêverie d'une femme d'aujourd'hui" [Dream of a young woman of today], in which she explores the dilemma facing the young woman who wishes to reconcile love with personal ambition.

6. Shafik, "L'Enfant du Nil," *L'Egyptienne*, 26.

7. Shafik, "Une Femme a-t-elle le droit de philosopher?" *L'Egyptienne*, 25.

8. The *Agrégation* is a state competitive examination used for the recruitment of secondary school teachers. In publishing this letter, Nabaraoui states, "We are proud and happy to reproduce this letter that has been addressed to us and is done so without any comment."

9. Shafik to Huda Sha'rawi, Oct. 1, 1930.

10. She is referring here to Muhammad Shamseddin Hafez, a fourteenth-century mystic poet whose ostensibly literal style is the vehicle for a heavy philosophical message. The interpretation of Hafez's poetry encouraged poets to invest deep spiritual meaning in poems that appear quite straightforward and mundane on the surface. In some ways, the reading of Hafez is similar to that given the *I Ching* of ancient Chinese philosophy.

11. *Moulid al-Nabi* is a Muslim feast celebrating the birthday of the Prophet Muhammad.

12. Shafik to Huda Sha'rawi, July 16, 1932.

Chapter 3

1. Shafik, "Rêverie d'une femme d'aujourd'hui," *L'Egyptienne*, 15.

2. Quoted in Mitchell, *The Society of the Muslim Brothers*, 30.

3. In 1932, a conversion to Protestantism of a student at the American University in Cairo, allegedly the work of a clergyman on the faculty there, unleashed indignant emotions. The Egyptian government (under Sidki) cut off subsidies to the university. See Vatikiotis, *Modern History of Egypt*, 327–29.

4. Ceza Nabaraoui to Huda Sha'rawi, Aug. 29, 1932; in the Hawa Idris Papers, Rare Books and Special Collections Library, The American University in Cairo, Cairo, Egypt.

5. Note the similarity between Shafik's title and Jean-Jacques Rousseau's *Les Rêveries d'un Promeneur Solitaire* (1782).

6. Shafik, "Rêverie d'une femme d'aujourd'hui," *L'Egyptienne*, 19.

7. Nabaraoui, "Réponse aux Réactionnaires," *L'Egyptienne*, 5.

8. Ibid., 8.

9. Shafik to Huda Sha'rawi, Oct. 15, 1932.

10. Shafik to Huda Sha'rawi, July 9, 1934.

11. Reprinted in special number of *La Réforme Illustrée* published in 1950, on the occasion of the twenty-fifth anniversary of the magazine.

12. "Glissez mortels" is a French expression whose meaning—literally, "slippery mortals"—leaves us wondering what Doria had in mind.

13. Mustapha Amin, personal interview, 1986. Amin is one of Egypt's leading journalists and the co-founder, with his twin brother Ali, of the major Egyptian newspaper *al-Ahkbar*.

14. *Piaster* is the term for the Egyptian penny. The Quran stipulates that the *mahr*, sometimes referred to as *sadaq*, is a basic constituent of the marriage contract. According to the teachings of Islam, twenty-five piasters is the absolute minimum a groom must offer his bride. It is viewed as a gift symbolizing the husband's role to provide financial security to his wife. Also written into the marriage contract is the *muta'akhkhir*, a substantial amount of money the husband agrees to pay his wife if he should divorce her. Marriage in Islam passes through several steps, each qualified by certain rights and duties and specified by a particular Arabic term. The term *khatib/khatibah* refers to the status of the couple signing the contract; *'aris/'arusah*, literally meaning legal fiancé/fiancée, refers to the period of the relationship prior to actual consummation. After that the term *zawj/zawjah* is used to refer to husband/wife.

15. Mustapha Amin, "The Beautiful Leader," 59.

16. In Egypt, to describe someone as a *sai'idi* is to imply that the individual is not only very conservative and traditional but also blockheaded and stubborn about his or her beliefs.

17. Mustapha Amin, "The Beautiful Leader," 61.

18. As one scholar has cogently observed, "The decade of the 1930's was a crucial period in the political evolution of Egypt for its effects were permanently damaging to

the hoped for development in parliamentary government. More important, this period laid the foundations of more violent politics in the country; alienated political leaders from the monarchy; and the public from all normal orderly government. It made it easier for extremist, fanatic political groups to emerge and be organized as well as to attract new elements of the population to their ranks. It permitted the Muslim Brethren, for instance, to strengthen their organization and experience a period of great development" (see Vatikiotis, *The Modern History,* 282).

19. Said, *The Question of Palestine,* 17–18.

Chapter 4

1. It is not entirely clear when Doria actually wrote this poem, but I believe it belongs to a series of poems she wrote during her years of "internal exile" and gathered together under the title "Hors-Temps."

2. See Rose, *Jazz Cleopatra: Josephine Baker and Her Time.*

3. See Stuhlman, ed., *The Diaries of Anais Nin: 1931–1934.*

4. See Lewis, *Dada Turns Red.*

5. Isabel Naginsky, personal communication, 1987.

6. I am indebted to Jane Bond-Howard and Armand Hoog for their personal insights into the backgrounds of these professors.

7. The Magna Carta is a document signed by King John of England in 1215 to secure the nation's liberties. John had overridden, or sought to override, all law, and in January 1215 the barons demanded the confirmation of the old charter issued by Henry I, promising to observe "the good laws of Edward the Confessor." The barons were largely guided by the archbishop of Canterbury, Stephen Langton, and the king was compelled to set his seal to the Great Charter on June 15, 1215, at Runnymede.

8. Traditionally, the woman had no right to get a divorce without her husband's consent unless, at the time of the marriage contract, she had asked "to have the *'isma* in her hand." This phrase refers to the introduction into the marriage contract of the right of the woman to divorce her husband if certain circumstances should arise that make life between them impossible. If the woman does not have the *'isma* and can prove that her husband is either mad, impotent, unable to support her, or extremely cruel, she has the right to go to a judge and seek a divorce. The man can divorce his wife with no justification of his action simply by pronouncing the *talaq* ("I divorce thee") three times in front of witnesses, and the divorce is legal.

9. See chapter 3, note 14.

10. Nour al-Din Ragai, *De la condition légale des sociétés anonymes étrangères en Egypte* (On the legal condition of anonymous foreign companies in Egypt), a thesis pertaining to commercial law.

11. Raymond Weill, cited through the courtesy of the Archives Nationales, Académie de Paris documents library, Sorbonne University, Paris, France. Special acknowledgement to M. Laurent Morelle and Dr. Gina Gourdin-Serveniere.

12. Capart, "Revue," *Chronique d'Egypte: Bulletin Périodique de la Fondation Egyptologique Reine Elisabeth,* 96. I am indebted to the late Bernard Bothmer for bringing this article to my attention.

13. Maurice Halbwachs, cited through the courtesy of the Archives Nationales, Académie de Paris documents library, Sorbonne University.

14. Ceza Nabaraoui, "La Jeunesse egyptienne et ses tendances," *L'Egyptienne*, no. 157 (July–Aug. 1939): 22.

Chapter 5

1. Ahmad Bahaa al-Din, personal interview, 1987. Bahaa al-Din is a Nasserite journalist with *al-Ahram*.

2. Helys, "Commentary," *L'Egyptienne*, 7.

3. Abdul Monein Tanamly, personal communication, Jan. 29, 1987.

4. Cited through the courtesy of the Archives Nationales, Académie de Paris documents library, Sorbonne University.

5. *L'Egyptienne*, no. 163 (March 1940): 34.

6. Soheir el-Qalamawy, personal communication, Jan. 1988.

7. Ahmad Amin was one of a handful of liberal intellectuals whose writings and ideas were to have a significant impact on the generation that witnessed the 1952 revolution. Leaving al-Azhar, Amin reconciled himself to the life of teacher and worked in both Tanta and Alexandria. He joined the national university in 1926, where he lectured in Arabic literature and conducted historical and philosophical research on Islamic civilization. He married at the age of thirty and saw his wife for the first time after the wedding ceremony; he later stated in his autobiography, "the marriage was a lottery." His prolific intellectual writings focused on the social and cultural implications of modernization (East-West relations, problems of education, decline of parental authority) and on great historical personalities.

8. *Egypt: Imperialism*, 462.

9. Abd al-Halim, "Dr. Doria Shafik," *Nis'a fawq al-Qima*, 58.

10. Amin did actually resign from his post in 1941 when the minister of education transferred some professors from Fuad I University in Cairo to Farouk University (now called the University of Alexandria) without consulting him.

11. Mme. Munira Qassim, personal communication, 1987.

12. Mustapha Amin, personal communication, 1986.

13. Layla Takla, personal communication, June 1988.

14. Shafik, "Ma Grandmère et Moi," *La Femme Nouvelle*, (Dec. 1947): 56–57.

Chapter 6

1. Naguib, *Egypt's Destiny*, 78.

2. Vatikiotis, *The Modern History*, 348

3. Naguib, *Egypt's Destiny*, 77–78.

4. Shafik, *La Femme Nouvelle en Egypte*, 8. All citations from this work are translated from the French by the author.

5. Ibid., 10–12.

6. Ibid., 75.

7. Princess Chevikar (1873–1947) married Fuad in the mid-1890s, long before he had any pretensions to the throne. Spoiled and capricious, Chevikar was as well-born

as her husband and considerably richer. Their marriage nearly cost Fuad his life. As a young man, Fuad was an impoverished playboy who owed money everywhere. His Italian upbringing had given him a taste for gambling and mistresses, but he had very old-fashioned ideas about the seclusion of Muslim women, and Chevikar deeply resented being kept in the harem from morning until night. In 1896, Chevikar gave birth to their only son, who died in infancy. After the birth of her second child, Princess Fawkieh, she decided she could no longer bear her husband's violent temper and finicky habits, and returned to her family in Constantinople. Her husband got her back, as he was entitled to do under Muslim law. But Chevikar had an elder brother, Prince Sayf al-Din, who swore to deliver her from this tyrant. On May 7, 1898, Sayf al-Din rushed up the stairs of the Khedival Club, found Fuad in the Silence Room, and shot him several times before anyone could stop him. Fuad was so badly wounded that his doctors decided to operate there on the floor. They took a bullet from his ribs and another from his thigh, but one lodged in his throat too near an artery to be removed. From that day until his death, the future sultan/king of Egypt was left with a permanent disability in his speech that has been described as a high spasmodic bark. Fuad divorced Chevikar, and the criminal court committed her brother to a mental asylum in Ticehurst, Sussex, near Tunbridge Wells, where he stayed for nearly twenty years. Many years and several husbands later, Chevikar, having inherited an enormous fortune, returned to Egypt.

8. Shafik, *La Femme Nouvelle en Egypte,* 80.

9. It was only in 1944 that La Femme Nouvelle Society came under the patronage and presidency of Princess Ayn al-Hayat's infamous niece, Princess Chevikar.

10. Shafik, *La Femme Nouvelle en Egypte,* 84.

11. Inji Efflatoun (1924–1989) became a well-known painter and was imprisoned by Nasser in 1959 for her communist activities. She died of cancer in 1989. Latifa Zayyat (1923–) is presently a professor of comparative literature and chair of the National Committee for the Protection of Egypt's Cultural Heritage; she published her first feminist novel, *Bab al-Muftuah* (The open door), in 1960. See Botman, "The Experience of Women in the Egyptian Communist Movement, 1939–1954," and Khater and Nelson, "al-Harakah al-Nissa'iyah," for a more detailed analysis of these different feminist projects. See also *al-Ahram Weekly,* July 18, 1991, for a commentary on Latifa Zayyat.

Chapter 7

1. It was Winston Churchill who sounded the alarm of the Cold War in 1945, when he first named the split in central Europe as "the iron curtain." As the United States was emerging as a major post-World War II power in the West, the USSR was becoming the leader of the Eastern bloc. As the United States developed its policy of "containment," the USSR pursued its policy of support to the "wars of liberation" (or nationalist struggles) erupting throughout the third world.

2. Anwar al-Sadat, *In Search of Identity,* 242.

3. Amina al-Sa'id, "Experiences." Al-Sa'id (1914-1995) was a well-known Egyptian editor, journalist, and feminist writer. She contributed to the highly respected publishing house Dar al-Hilal, founded by Zeidan. She wrote a special column, "Isa'luni" (Ask

me), for the prestigious *al-Mussawar*, in which Egyptian women wrote in their problems and al-Sa'id offered advice. (See Nelson, "Changing Roles in a Changing Society," for a content analysis of these letters.) Al-Sa'id served as editor-in-chief for two women's magazines, *Hawa* and *Elle*, throughout the Nasser era and beyond. She was considered one of Egypt's leading journalists and TV personalities from the early 1950s until her death.

4. Inji Efflatoun, personal communication, Feb. 1987.

5. See Fenoglio-Abd al-Aal, *Defense et Illustration*; Badran and Cooke, eds., *Opening the Gates*; and Baron, *Women's Awakening in Egypt*.

6. *Tatawwur al-Nahda al-Nisa'iyah fi Misr* (The development of the renaissance of women in Egypt), Cairo: Maktabat al-Tawakul, 1945, and *al-Mar'ah al-Misriyah min al-Fara'niyah ila al-Yawm* (The Egyptian woman from the pharaohs until today), Cairo: Maktabat Misr, 1955.

7. Ibrahim Abdu, personal communication, March 31, 1985.

8. Amina al-Sa'id, "Experiences."

9. Khalil Sabat, personal communication, Nov. 14, 1985.

10. Ibrahim Abdu, personal communication, March 31, 1985. Also see Khalifa, *al-Haraka*, 173–76.

11. Lacouture, *Egypt in Transition*, 156.

12. "We Want Rights Not Equality," *Bint al-Nil*, Jan. 1946.

13. "An Orphan Nation," *Bint al-Nil*, March 1946.

14. "The Great People," *Bint al-Nil*, April 1946.

15. "Evacuation—without Bloodshed," *Bint al-Nil*, July 1946.

16. Dar al-Hilal was founded by the Lebanese Christian George Zaidan in 1892. As Muhammad Salmawy explained in *al-Ahram Weekly* in 1992: "Dar al-Hilal is more than just a publishing house. It is an Egyptian institution. Imagine a combination of Penguin publishing, *Encounter* magazine and a half dozen other publications, then we would have a picture of what Dar al-Hilal is."

17. Foreword, *La Femme Nouvelle*, Dec. 1947.

18. "The New Woman," *La Femme Nouvelle*, Dec. 1947.

19. "Message to the Reader," *La Femme Nouvelle*, June 1946.

20. "The New Woman as Message," *La Femme Nouvelle*, Oct. 1948.

21. "A Bond between Civilizations," *La Femme Nouvelle*, Dec. 1949.

22. "Always the Beginning," *La Femme Nouvelle*, May 1948.

23. "Crises of the Self," *Bint al-Nil*, June 1946.

24. Jehane Ragai, personal communication, Oct. 28, 1986.

25. Aziza Ragai, personal communication, Sept. 5, 1986.

26. Gallagher, *Egypt's Other Wars*, 116–79.

27. Groppi's is a very famous tearoom and pâtisserie owned and operated by a Swiss family. During the 1930s and 1940s, it was a favorite spot of the British and Egyptian elite, and to this day continues to be a popular meeting place for foreign residents as well as Egyptian students, poets, and intellectuals.

28. Sania Sha'rawi, personal communication, March 1986.

29. Shafik, "A Short Speech of Doctor Doria Hanum Shafik," in *Memory of the Lost One of the Arab Cause, Thou Bearer of Power: To the Most Honourable Huda*

Hanum Sha'rawi: A Collection of Speeches and Poems (Cairo: Shirkit fann al-Tiba'a, 1948). This volume also includes many articles that were written about Huda Sha'rawi in the local and foreign press. I am indebted to Sania Sha'rawi Lanfranchi, her granddaughter, for bringing this reference to my attention and for providing the translation.

30. "A Short Speech," 107–8.

Chapter 8

1. "In the Lands of Religion," *Bint el-Nil*, June 1948.

2. Rodinson, *Israel and the Arabs*, 40.

3. The term *Khalifa* means "successor to the Prophet." The caliph had absolute power (religious and temporal) over all the Muslims.

4. Faruq later married Narriman Sadek, an Egyptian commoner, who bore him a son, Ahmad Fuad, the impatiently awaited male heir to the throne. According to Doria, Narriman's irresponsibility greatly aided Faruq's ultimate collapse.

5. Stowasser, "Liberated Equal or Protected Dependent?" *Arab Studies Quarterly*, 276.

6. Mansfield, *Nasser's Egypt*, 31.

7. Perrault, *A Man Apart*, 88.

8. Jehane Ragai, personal communication, June 18, 1988.

9. For a more in-depth discussion of the debate surrounding the New Egyptian Civil Code constructed by al-Sanhuri, see Hill, *al-Sanhuri and Islamic Law*.

10. *Bayt al-ta'a* (literally, "house of obedience") refers to the right of the husband to force his wife to return to his house through the use of the police if necessary.

11. In her dissertation, *La Femme et le droit* (67), Shafik refers to Quran Surah 4 ("Women"), verse 3: "And if ye fear that ye will not deal fairly by the orphans, marry of the women, who seem good to you, two, three or four; and if ye fear that ye cannot do justice to so many then marry one only."

12. See Khater and Nelson, "al-Harakah al Nissa'iyah."

13. Mufida Abdul Rahman, personal communication, Nov. 1988.

14. Zaynab Fuad to Hawa Idris, May 11, 1948; in the Hawa Idris Papers, Rare Books and Special Collections Library, The American University in Cairo.

15. "Ourselves and Politics," *Bint al-Nil*, Nov. 1946.

16. "Make Way," *Bint al-Nil*, Jan. 1948.

17. "The Time Has Come," *Bint al-Nil*, May 1948.

18. "Our Obligation toward You," *Bint al-Nil*, Aug. 1948.

19. "Is It a Mirage?" *Bint al-Nil*, Nov. 1948.

20. "Our Rights Are Not a Mirage," *Bint al-Nil*, Dec. 1948.

21. "Let Our Enemies Listen," *Bint al-Nil*, June 1949.

22. "The Party of Bint al-Nil," *Bint al-Nil*, Feb. 1949.

23. "Non-Political Aims," *Bint al-Nil*, May 1949.

24. The Women's International Democratic Federation was founded Dec. 1, 1945, in Paris. Its aims are "(1) to unite women regardless of race, nationality, religion and political opinion, so that they may work together to win, implement and defend their rights as mothers, workers and citizens; (2) to defend the rights of children to life, well-being and education; (3) to win and defend national independence and democratic free-

doms, eliminate apartheid, racial discrimination and fascism; and (4) to work for peace and universal disarmament." (*Encyclopedia of Associations*, 29th ed., 1995, 1338.)

25. Inji Efflatoun, personal interview, Nov. 21, 1986.

26. Loutfi al-Kholi, personal interview, July 17, 1987. Formerly a member of the communist party, al-Kholi is one of Egypt's more prominent and outspoken intellectuals and political analysts. He writes regularly for both the opposition newspaper *al-Ahli* as well as for the moderate government-controlled *al-Ahram* newspaper. He represented Egypt at the Arab-Israeli peace dialogues in Madrid and is a staunch advocate of Palestinian rights. He is married to Liliane Arcache, the daughter of Maurice Arcache, an eminent lawyer of the forties and fifties.

27. Ibid.

28. Ibid. His comments appear to contradict Doria's own views as discussed in chapter 6.

29. *Encyclopedia of Associations: International Organizations*, 29th ed., Washington, DC: Gale Research, 1995, 1316–17.

30. "Some of Our Obligations," *Bint al-Nil*, July 1949.

31. The Poésie series also included the volumes of the poetry of the French surrealists Paul Eluard, Tristan Tzara, and Louis Aragon, as well as the short books of verse by Lewis Carroll and Henry Miller.

32. Jean Orizet, "Adieu a Pierre Seghers," *Le Monde*, Nov. 7, 1987; translated by the author.

33. Pierre Seghers, personal interview, Sept. 10, 1986.

34. Ibid.

35. Ibid. The "later poetry" to which he refers is that contained in Shafik's volumes *Larmes d'Isis* and *Avec Dante Aux Enfers*, both of which he helped her daughters publish in 1979 after her death.

36. Seghers to Shafik, Oct. 1956.

37. Seghers, personal interview, Sept. 10, 1986.

38. "Le Caire," "La Nuit," "Nil," "Automne," "Couples et Minarets," "Retour des Champs," "Le Joueur de Flute," and "La Sakkieh" were later published in *La Bonne Aventure* (Paris: Pierre Seghers, 1949). "Crepuscule" and "Grâce à Dieu" appeared in 1949, as well as a short tale on Shagarat al-Durr called "Le Destin," which Doria would later develop into her first novel, *L'Esclave Sultane* (1952). "Le Maktoub" and "Le Zikr" appeared in 1950; "Le Fou de Laila" and "Les Larmes d'Isis" in Dec. 1951; "Le Sacrifice" and "Hymne au Nil" in 1952.

39. See Fatma Mernissi, *Behind the Veil: Male-Female Relations in Morocco*, for a more detailed discussion of women as a source of *fitna* in Muslim society.

40. Abd al-Wahab cited in Muhammad Mahmoud al-Gohari's *Al-Ikhwat al-Muslimat* (1980), 259–64. I am indebted to Akram Khater for his help in this translation. In a scathing attack against al-Gohari, Amina al-Sa'id asserted: "The author not only attempts to destroy seventy years of the contemporary Egyptian woman's struggle but also attacks the symbol of the Egyptian woman's movement and a prominent nationalist, who is Doria Shafik" (see "Amina al-Sa'id Requests the Detainment of Author in Mental Institution" [in Arabic], *Hawa*, Oct. 1993, 16–25). An interesting reversal of opinion for someone who had severely criticized Doria Shafik earlier on.

41. *Le Progrés Egyptien,* Feb. 6, 1950; this publication was one of the popular French dailies in Egypt. Suzanne Mubarak initiated a project on the upgrading of primary education in this same school during the early 1980s.

42. "One Drop May Form a Heavy Rain," *Bint al-Nil,* April 1950.

43. "Actualité, July 22," *Le Journal d'Egypte,* July 25, 1950. Although this article was not signed, it was probably written by Ceza Nabaraoui, who made vague reference to it while severely criticizing Doria in a letter to Hawa Idris, the niece of Huda Sha'rawi.

44. al-Bishri, *al-Harakah,* 440.

45. Shafik, "Egyptian Feminism," *Middle East Affairs,* 236.

46. See al-Gohari, *al-Ikhwat al-Muslimat.*

47. Ragia Raghab, personal interview, June 1986.

48. See Moscatelli, *Poètes en Egypte.*

49. Chafik Chammas, personal interview, Feb. 1991. Chammas is founder and editor of the contemporary and prestigious cultural magazine *Aujourd'hui l'Egypte.* He knew Doria during the late forties and early fifties, when he was a member of the Jean Moscatelli group of Egyptian writers and poets.

Chapter 9

1. Loutfi al-Kholi, personal interview, Sept. 1987.

2. "A Free Man Fulfills His Promises," *Bint al-Nil,* Feb. 1950.

3. Cited in "How the Suffragettes Were Able to Assault the Parliament: Details of the Plans of the 'Crocodiles of the Nile,'" *Akhir Saa,* March 2, 1951.

4. "How the Suffragettes Were Able to Assault the Parliament," *Akhir Saa,* March 2, 1951.

5. Shafik, *Rihlati,* 201–8.

6. Ahmad al-Sawi, cited in *al-Ahram,* Feb. 20, 1951. This is the same al-Sawi whom Doria divorced some fifteen years earlier.

7. Gamal Serag al-Din was the cousin of Fuad Serag al-Din, at that time the secretary of the Wafd and the minister of the interior.

8. "Feminists Storm Parliament," *La Bourse Egyptienne,* Feb. 20, 1951.

9. Mme. Ali Yavar, cited in "Women Disrupt Parliament," *Akhir Saa,* Feb. 27, 1951.

10. Reported by UPI in the *New York Times,* Feb. 28, 1951.

11. "Feminists Snubbed by Prime Minister," *La Bourse Egyptienne,* Feb. 28, 1951. In Egypt, the refusal of a cup of coffee, the traditional symbol of hospitality, is considered a serious cultural and social affront. The women, signaling their hurt and disillusionment, were returning the prime minister's snub.

12. "Nahas Pasha's Snub to Suffragettes," *London Times,* March 5, 1951.

13. "Rising Feminism Bewilders Egypt," *New York Times,* March 5, 1951.

14. "*Bint al-Nil* in Court," *La Bourse Egyptienne,* March 13, 1951.

15. Mufida Abdul Rahman, cited in *La Bourse Egyptienne,* March 13, 1951.

16. *La Bourse Egyptienne,* March 14, 1951.

17. Muhammad Hamid al-Fiki, cited in "Keep the Women in Check," *La Bourse Egyptienne,* March 16, 1951.

18. Shafik, cited in "Bint al-Nil Addresses International Women's Congress," *La Bourse Egyptienne,* March 30, 1951.

19. "Doria Shafik Against National Interest," *al-Masri*, April 10, 1951; "Doria Shafik Accused of Pro-Zionist Sympathy," *La Bourse Egyptienne*, April 10, 1951.

20. Shafik, cited in "Une Mise au Point de Mme. Doria Chafik," *La Bourse Egyptienne*, April 12, 1951.

21. "This Morning Mme. Doria Shafik in Court: The Public Prosecutor Presents His Accusations," *La Bourse Egyptienne*, April 10, 1951.

22. Loutfi al-Kholi, personal interview, Sept. 1987.

23. "The Egyptian Woman in the National Struggle," *Bint al-Nil*, Nov. 1951.

24. "Bint al-Nil Organizes Female Military Unit," *New York Times*, Oct. 30, 1951.

25. Inji Efflatoun, personal interview, Nov. 12, 1986.

26. "The Mastering Month," *Bint al-Nil*, Dec. 1951.

27. Shafik, *L'Esclave Sultane*, 7.

28. Ibid., 7.

29. "The Mastering Month," *Bint al-Nil*, Dec. 1951.

Chapter 10

1. Shafik, cited in "Egyptian Woman to Run," *New York Times*, March 31, 1952.

2. Cited in "Islamic Scholars Rile Suffragette," *New York Times*, April 20, 1952.

3. Abdul Hamid Badaiuni, cited in *al-Masri*, April 19, 1952 (as cited in Shafik, *al-Kitab al-abiyad*, 36).

4. "Complete Representation of the People," *Bint al-Nil*, April 1952.

5. The mufti is a salaried appointee of the state who gives legal opinions, *fatwas*, in answer to questions pertaining to Shari'a, or the sacred law, submitted to him by judges or private individuals. It is an independent office constituting part of the judicial system. Under Egyptian criminal law the mufti reviews judgments before a sentence is passed, to ensure that Islamic principles are not violated.

6. "Grand Mufti Admonishes Egyptian Feminist," *New York Times*, May 3, 1952.

7. Shafik, cited in *Akhir Lahza*, May 5, 1952 (as cited in Shafik, *al-Kitab al-abiyad*, 39).

8. Ahmad Zaki Bey, "Mufti of Islam Stumbles," *Akhbar*, May 10, 1952.

9. Mawlana Abul Kalam Azad, cited in Shafik, *al-Kitab al-abiyad*, 20.

10. "Ulimas Repudiate Feminists' Claims," cited in *Akhbar*, June 12, 1952.

11. "Egyptian Mufti Issues Fatwa against Feminists," *New York Times*, June 14, 1952.

12. Cited in Shafik, *al-Kitab al-abiyad*, 53 [italics mine].

13. Shafik, *al-Kitab al-abiyad*, 55.

14. Ibid., 58.

15. Mansfield, *Nasser's Egypt*, 43–45.

16. Vatikiotis, *Modern History of Egypt*, 379.

17. Shafik, "The General Assembly," *Bint al-Nil al-Siyassa*, Jan. 1953.

18. "Publicity by All Means," *Bint al-Nil*, Dec. 1952.

19. Shafik, "Egypt's Renaissance," *La Femme Nouvelle*, 27–28.

20. Shafik, "This Contest," *Bint al-Nil al-Siyassa*, Feb. 1953.

21. Ragia Raghab, personal interview, June 4, 1986. Mme. Raghab, born in 1917, is a member of a wealthy Muslim family from Alexandria. Her brother is a former min-

ister of defense and now heads the Hassan Raghab Papyrus Institute, which he founded in his name; her sister, Zohra, was one of the first women to enter parliament after 1956. Ragia married into a politically prominent Cairo family; her husband, Muhammad, was the son of Abd al-Qadir Hamza, founder and editor of the pro-Wafdist newspaper *al-Balagh,* and was imprisoned along with several other journalists for his opposition to King Faruq.

22. Shafik, "Only a Beginning," *Bint al-Nil al-Siyassa,* Feb. 1953. With the help of Ecole Fax (a Swiss language institute that had outlets all over Egypt), twelve lessons were divided over a three-month period and appeared in the March, April, and May 1953 issues of *Bint al-Nil.*

23. Shafik, "I Have Faith," *Bint al-Nil al-Siyassa,* Jan. 1953.

24. "Doria Shafik States: We Cannot But Depend on the English," *Daily Express,* May 22, 1953.

25. Rauf Salama, "English Spread Lies about Doria Shafik," *Rose al-Yussuf,* June 1, 1953.

26. "A Model Suffragette," *Newsweek,* June 22, 1953, 22.

27. Ceza Nabaraoui's name still appeared on the stationery as being a vice president of this organization. During this same period, Ceza also revolted against the Huda Sha'rawi group and was forced to resign.

28. Margery Corbett Ashby to Shafik, Nov. 24, 1953; written in French, translated by the author. Ashby was also the president of the AIF's Commission on Peace and Human Relations as well as the editor of the journal *International Women's News.*

29. Loutfi al-Kholi, personal interview, July 17, 1987.

30. "Last Hope," *Bint al-Nil,* Dec. 1953.

Chapter 11

1. Verbatim text of a telegram.

2. "Our First Parliament!" *Bint al-Nil,* Jan. 1954.

3. "The Role of the Woman in Arab Revival," *Bint al-Nil,* Feb. 1954.

4. Margery Corbett Ashby to Shafik, Feb. 20, 1954; written in French, translated by the author.

5. "Towards the League of Arab Peoples," *Bint al-Nil,* March 1954.

6. Vatikiotis, *Modern History of Egypt,* 383.

7. Ibid., 384.

8. In addition to Ragia and Fathiya, there were representatives from three different women's organizations: Bahiga al-Bakri, of the Association for Women's Liberation; Soad Fahmy, of the Philanthropic Organization for Liberation; and Munira Hosni, of the National Association of Women. Also participating were Amani Farid, a poetess; Hayam Abdul Aziz, an artist; and Munira Thabet, the prominent publisher and owner of *al-Amal* magazine ("Nine Women Undertake Hunger Strike at Press Syndicate," *al-Ahram,* March 13, 1954).

9. Cited in "Nine Women Undertake Hunger Strike," *al-Ahram,* March 13, 1954.

10. Ali Mahir, cited in "Prime Minister Meets with Shafik," *al-Ahram,* March 14, 1954.

11. Mahir, cited in "Prime Minister Delivers Ultimatum," *al-Ahram*, March 15, 1954.

12. Cited in "Students Issue Protest," *al-Ahram*, March 16, 1954.

13. Muhammad Husayn Haykal, cited in "Do the Strikes Serve Their Cause?" *al-Ahram*, March 16, 1954. Haykal is credited with having written the first truly Egyptian novel, *Zaynab*, in 1914. He was editor of the liberal party's *al-Siyasa* and a leading constitutionalist in the country during the twenties. By the thirties, he was retreating from his earlier position of secular liberalism and the adoption of European culture. Effectively abandoning the liberal values of Western civilization as an ideological foundation for a modern Egypt, Haykal published a series of books on the life of the Prophet and the first orthodox caliphs (see Vatikiotis, *Modern History of Egypt*, 303, 323).

14. George Weller, "Newsman's Wife Getting in the Act as Ladies of the Nile Starve to Win Vote," *Chicago Daily News*, March 16, 1954.

15. Doria had heard that they were going to be sent to three different hospitals—"a deliberate plan to split us up. I told the governor of Cairo that we would not accept being separated." They were then taken to Kasr al-Aini hospital, where they were isolated from the press and allowed visitors only with special permission.

16. Charlotte Ebener Weller, "Feminists Keep Up Fast—in Hospital," *Chicago Daily News*, March 18, 1954. Charlotte Weller served as a news correspondent in China and Southeast Asia after World War II, where she met and married George Weller. She is the author of a book entitled *No Facilities for Women*, based on her experiences as a reporter. Her brief encounter with Doria led to an interesting correspondence between the two women over the next few years.

17. Similar commentaries were carried in both the Egyptian press, "Shafik Vows to Continue Fast," *al-Ahram*, March 18, 1954, and the English press, "Feminists Continue Fast," London *Times*, March 19, 1954.

18. Mme. Marin as cited in Memoirs, 1960.

19. Jehane Ragai, personal interview, Oct. 26, 1986.

20. "Feminists End Hunger Strike," *al-Ahram*, March 20, 1954.

21. Loutfi al-Kholi, personal communication, July 1987.

22. Aziza Ragai, personal communication, Sept. 1986.

23. Mustapha Amin, personal communication, 1986. Amin lived next door to the couple and was in a position to know them more intimately than most of their other friends. He published a short biographical essay on Doria Shafik called "The Beautiful Leader" in a book entitled *Masa'il Shakhsiyya* (Personal matters) (1984).

24. Aziza Ragai, personal communication, Sept. 1986.

25. Charlotte Weller to Shafik, April 5, 1954; written on stationery from the Rome bureau of the *Chicago Daily News*.

26. Fatma Nimat Rashid, president of the National Association for Women, cited in "Where Is the Victory?" *al-Ahram*, March 23, 1954.

27. "Our Strike, the First Step," *Bint al-Nil*, April 1954.

Chapter 12

1. Written in Shafik's 1960 memoirs.

2. "Trip for the Sake of the Nation," *Bint al-Nil*, Oct. 1954.

3. Herman Eilts, former ambassador to Egypt and Saudi Arabia, personal communication, June 27, 1988. In 1977, the AFME (American Friends of the Middle East) was superseded by the AMIDEAST (American Middle East), whose aims were "to further human resource development in the Middle East and North Africa and to promote understanding between the peoples of the region and the United States" (Entry 15572, *Encyclopedia of Associations*, 26th ed., 1992).

4. Charlotte Weller to Shafik, June 5, 1945.

5. Margery Corbett Ashby to Shafik, no date—but presumably in late August or early September 1954.

6. Ashby to Shafik, Oct. 9, 1954.

7. "Trip for the Sake of the Nation," *Bint al-Nil*, Oct. 1954.

8. Shafik, *Rihlati Hawla al-'Alam*, 11.

9. Pierre Seghers, personal communication, Sept. 10, 1986.

10. Shafik, *Rihlati Hawla al-'Alam*, 33.

11. Ibid., 59.

12. "From Overseas," *Bint al-Nil*, Nov. 1954.

13. "The American Woman: Commander of the Situation," *Bint al-Nil*, Dec. 1954; written in and sent from New York on Nov. 24, 1954.

14. Shafik, *Rihlati Hawla al-'Alam*, 63–64.

15. Gunther, *Inside Africa*, 185.

16. *Holiday* 17:52, Jan. 1955, 53–55. Shafik's name, photograph, and biographical data were published for the first time in *Current Biography* (H. W. Wilson Co., 1955).

17. Elizabeth Lawrence, chief editor at Harper, to Shafik, Dec. 16, 1954.

18. Cass Canfield to Shafik, May 28, 1956.

19. David Collier to Shafik, Jan. 21, 1955. Dr. Collier was director of the AFME's regional office in Chicago.

20. Eva Deane Kemp to Shafik, Jan. 14, 1955.

21. William Archer Wright, Jr., to Barry Mahool, Dec. 13, 1954.

22. "A Short Letter," *Bint al-Nil*, Jan. 1954; written Dec. 22, 1955, in Tokyo.

23. Muhammad Ali Jinnah (1876–1948), an Indian nationalist Muslim leader, founded the modern state of Pakistan after the partition of India and Pakistan in 1947–1948.

24. Mukhtar Zaki, former consul-general in Calcutta (1952–1956), and his wife, Eva Zaki, personal interview, Nov. 7, 1985.

Chapter 13

1. Mustapha Amin, "The Beautiful Leader," *Masa'il Shakhsiyya*, 63.

2. The quote is taken from a lecture delivered by Keith Kiley at AUC, April 1992, and sounds ominously similar to the rhetoric of George Bush regarding Saddam Hussein and the Gulf War of 1991. The major difference is that the Suez Canal belonged to Egypt and it was the foreign-controlled Suez Canal Company—which was under a ninety-nine-year lease (1869–1968) and run mostly by the French—that Nasser nationalized.

3. See Nasser, *The Philosophy of the Revolution*.

4. Isis Fahmy, personal communication, Sept. 1986. Fahmy, an Egyptian, was a journalist at the time.

5. Zaynab Labib, personal communication, Feb. 1987.

6. "Settling My Accounts," *Bint al-Nil*, March 1955.

7. "Doria Shafik Now Trades in Radios," *Rose al-Yusuf*, Aug. 1955.

8. "News of Personalities," *Rose al-Yusuf*, Oct. 17, 1955.

9. "A New Magazine from Doria Shafik," *al-Gomhouria*, Oct. 27, 1955; translated by Hasna Makdashi and the author. At this time, Anwar al-Sadat was the general director and Galal al-Din al-Hamamsy the vice director.

10. Beppo al-Hakim, an Egyptian friend, to Shafik, April 11, 1955; translated from the French by the author.

11. Moscatelli, *Poètes en Egypte*, 204.

12. Interview with Shafik by a "Madiha," "The Leader of Candied Chestnuts Discusses Love, Dancing and the Ph.D.," in *Rose al-Yusuf*, Aug. 1, 1955. Twenty years later (Oct. 12, 1975), this same "Madiha" would write an obituary for Doria Shafik in *Rose al-Yusuf*, which she entitled "The Leader outside Her Time."

13. Daniel Baroukh to Shafik, April 16, 1955.

14. Letter from the Stockholm-based "Letter Writers' Round Table," to Shafik, April 22, 1956.

15. Ali Yavar Yung to Shafik, June 4, 1955.

16. Yung to Shafik, Aug. 7, 1955.

17. Elbert Greenberg to Shafik, Sept. 11, 1956.

18. Muhammad Fahmi Abd al-Wahab, 53.

19. "Interview with Doria Shafik," *Rose al-Yusuf*, Jan. 24, 1955.

20. John Badeau was an American missionary whose long years of service in the Middle East began in Iraq in 1928. He came to Egypt in 1936, where he taught at the American University in Cairo, serving as its president from 1945 until 1953 when he left to become president of the Near East Foundation. He was appointed ambassador to Egypt in 1961. Because of the trust his lengthy years in Egypt had inspired, the basis of a genuine rapprochement in American-Egyptian relations was created during the Kennedy administration.

21. Eva Deane Kemp to Shafik, Feb. 1955.

22. Under the patronage of Helen Rogers Reid, owner and editor-in-chief of the *New York Herald Tribune*, the International Forum organized meetings of youth in different countries of the world on themes of peace and disarmament as a way of lessening the tensions of the Cold War and fostering friendship and understanding among young people from both East and West. Mrs. Waller called upon Doria for her help and participation during the April 1955 meeting of the Forum held in Cairo.

23. As a journalist expelled from Germany in 1934, Dorothy Thompson spent the next six years warning the American public about what was going to happen to the Jews under Hitler. She later became an opponent of the State of Israel, which she predicted would bring about "perpetual war" in the Middle East. She believed that the extermination of the Jews could not be laid at the door of the Arabs. Herman Eilts commented that "Thompson became a close confidant of Gamal Abdel Nasser and most

probably helped him write *Philosophy of the Revolution*" (personal communication). It was Helen Rogers Reid who in 1936 urged the *New York Herald Tribune* to offer Thompson a column, "On the Record," to run alongside that of Walter Lippmann. Her column was intended to present important issues from and for women's points of view. Its combination of solid reporting, sharp opinion, and naked emotion caught on. Thompson would write "On the Record" three times a week for twenty-two years. She wrote regularly for the *Ladies Home Journal* until her death in 1961. See "Wonder Woman," *New York Review of Books*, Aug. 16, 1990, 37–40; and "The Woman Who Interviewed Hitler," *New York Times Book Review*, July 29, 1990, 12.

24. Aziza Ragai, personal communication, 1986.

25. See Furth, *American Cassandra*.

26. Vatikiotis, *Modern History of Egypt*, 387. The constitution was approved and the president elected on June 23, 1956. The Suez crisis and related events delayed the actual implementation of the election of the National Assembly until July 1957.

27. Text of a UPI cable to London, Jan. 19, 1955.

28. "Cairo Feminist Minimizes Gains," *New York Times*, Feb. 17, 1956. Next to the story on Doria was a short article describing how the Egyptian government of Premier Gamal Abdul Nasser "has long held that the flowing dress of Egyptian men and women, its pattern almost unchanged through centuries, is impractical and unsanitary. Wing Commander Abdul Latif al-Boghdadi has ordered the formation of a joint committee to investigate the abolition of the colorful costume of the Egyptian people in favor of a uniform national dress."

29. Sullivan, *Women in Egyptian Public Life*, 39–45.

Chapter 14

1. Copies of this declaration were sent to all the foreign press and news agencies in Cairo.

2. Aziza Ragai, personal communication, Sept. 1986.

3. Jehane Ragai, personal communication, Oct. 1986.

4. Seghers, *La Résistance*, 263–64. Son of a highly literate wine merchant, Pierre Reverdy (1889–1960) was educated in Narbonne. In 1910 he arrived in Paris, where he met Guillaume Apollinaire, Max Jacob, Pablo Picasso, and Georges Braque. He became editor of the journal *Nord-Sud* in 1919. From 1926 until his death, he lived in seclusion near the Benedictine monastery of Solesmes near Le Mans. R. R. Hubert has written that "Reverdy introduced into poetry the splintered persona, the multiple perspective, and other forms of discontinuity that have become central to postmodernist poetics. Poetry has led him on an arduous and obscure path, bereft of that inexpressible reward so devoutly sought by the mystics" ("Reverdy," *Encyclopedia of World Literature*, 26–27).

5. Amina al-Sa'id, "Experiences."

6. "Hunger Strike Begun by Egyptian Feminist" *New York Times*, Feb. 8, 1957.

7. In *Le Monde*, Feb. 9, 1957, the story was headlined "Un leader féministe égyptien entreprende la grève de la faim pour mettre fin á la dictature de Nasser." In *France-Soir*, Feb. 9, 1957, there appeared "La Fondatrice des 'Filles du Nil' fait la grève de la faim."

8. "Egyptian Feminist Continues Her Hunger Strike," *New York Times*, Feb. 11, 1957.

9. Raymond Millet, "La Grève de la faim de la suffragette egyptienne: Mauvais présage pour Nasser" (The hunger strike of the Egyptian feminist: a bad omen for Nasser), *Le Figaro*, Feb. 12, 1957.

10. "Hunger Striker Goes Home," *New York Times*, Feb. 17, 1957.

11. "Cairo Feminist Ends Fast," *New York Times*, Feb. 18, 1957.

12. Ragia Raghab, personal interview, May 31, 1986. Raghab's husband, Muhammad Abdul Qader Hamza, was the son of the famous pasha who founded the newspaper *Balagh*, the favorite newspaper of Saad Zaghlul. He was the vice president of the Press Syndicate before the 1952 revolution.

13. Ibid.

14. Ibid.

15. Galal al-Hamamsy, personal interview, Feb. 9, 1986.

16. Chafika al-Hamamsy, personal communication, Nov. 14, 1988.

17. Inji Efflatoun, personal interview, Nov. 21, 1986.

18. Munira Qassem, personal communication, Dec. 10, 1986.

19. Undated document, but more than likely it was circulated within days of Doria's dramatic act of protest.

20. Amina al-Sa'id, "Experiences."

21. Samir Subhi, "Doria Shafik."

Chapter 15

1. Preface, "Hors-Temps."

2. Shafik, "Un Petit Mot," *L'Egyptienne*, 13.

3. The preceding poems are part of "Hors-Temps," an unpublished collection of poems that Shafik wrote and translated during her eighteen years of semi-seclusion.

4. Mustapha Amin, "The Beautiful Leader," 59.

5. Aziza Ragai, personal communication, Sept. 1986.

6. Amin, "The Beautiful Leader," 61.

7. Jehane Ragai, personal communication, Oct. 1986. Under Muslim divorce law, a husband may divorce his wife and then under certain conditions take her back without any ceremony, providing that he does so before the end of the *idda*, the period of waiting required by law prior to the woman's possible marriage to another man (Quran Surah 2, verses 228, 232).

8. Shafik refers to her letter of July 7, 1959, to Dag Hammersjköld, secretary-general of the United Nations, which contained her manifesto on human liberty.

9. According to Seghers, "the theme of Eluard's poem and his own life can be recaptured in these two lines that define better than all that one could say: 'Pour la recherche la plus haute / Un cri dont le mien soit l'echo. For the sake of the highest pursuit / A cry in which the echo is my own.' In his most famous war poem, *Liberté* (1942), he wrote about the prevailing frenzy for freedom, searching for it in school notebooks, in jungles and deserts, in his daily bread, writing the word 'liberty' in the rising sun and in the sea and mountaintops" (*La Résistance* 2:150–52). Paul Eluard (1895–1952) joined Breton and Aragon in the 1920s in launching the surrealist movement in France:

He provokes the power of extended vision through verbal imagery demonstrating the theory that in Surrealism the objective is not so much the creation of unusual images as the cultivation of the power to provoke sight, of making the invisible visible. Above all he writes about love, the cult of woman, and the engulfing power of the eternal feminine. He also wrote prose poems, coupling the abstract with the concrete, in the manner of symbolists. If he is a comrade of Breton he is also a descendant of Baudelaire and Paul Verlaine in the translucence he can achieve and in the richness of meaning he obtains through lexical simplicity. Eluard shared the Surrealist's belief in the need for revolution, and identified with their struggle for political, social and sexual liberation." (*Columbia Dictionary,* 229.)

At some time during her "internal exile," Doria wrote a long prose poem, which she varyingly called "Liberté," "Redemption," "Le Christ Rouge," in homage to Eluard.

10. Jehane Ragai, personal communication, Oct. 1986.

11. Ibid.

12. Aziza Ragai, personal communication, Sept. 1986.

13. Ibid.

14. Jehane Ragai, personal communication, Oct. 1986.

15. Muhammad Zaki Abd al-Qadir, "Remembrance," *al-Ahram,* Sept. 22, 1975.

16. Pierre Seghers, personal communication, Sept. 1986.

17. Ibid.

18. Nutting, *Nasser,* 378.

19. Ibid., 379.

20. Ibid., 392–93.

21. Aziza Ragai, personal communication, Sept. 1986.

22. Jehane Ragai, personal communication, Oct. 1986.

23. For an account of what political imprisonment was like under the Nasser regime, see Hetata, *The Iron Eyelid.*

24. Aziza Ragai, personal communication, Sept. 1986.

25. Jehane Ragai, personal communication, Oct. 1986.

26. Mustapha Amin, "The Beautiful Leader," 68.

27. Jehane Ragai, personal communication, Oct. 1986.

28. Ibid.

29. Ibid.

30. Personal communication from an Egyptian acquaintance of Doria's, who was herself a member of a Hindu Ashram in India and a disciple of Krishna Murtti.

31. Amin, "The Beautiful Leader," 66.

32. Jehane Ragai, personal communication, Oct. 1986.

33. Ibid.

34. Nany Mubarak, "Letters to Editor," *Akhbar al-Yawm,* June 14, 1975, 21.

35. Amina al-Sa'id, "Experiences."

36. Aziza Ragai, personal communication, Sept. 1986.

37. Jehane Ragai, personal communication, Oct. 1986.

38. Jehane Ragai, personal communication, Oct. 1986; Aziza Ragai, personal communication, Sept. 1986.

39. Sania Sha'rawi, personal communication, Jan. 23, 1986.

40. Amin, "The Beautiful Leader," 66.

41. "Granny" was Jehane's mother-in-law. As Sunday was Doria's day and Tuesday Nour's day, Friday was Granny's day to have lunch with Jehane, Ali, and the children.

42. Jehane Ragai, personal communication, Oct. 1986.

43. Fadel Qassabgui, personal communication, Nov. 1992.

44. Amin, "The Beautiful Leader," 68.

Chapter 16

1. Fatma Abd al-Khalak, "Doria Shafik, the Only Man in Egypt," *al-Ahram*, Sept. 21, 1975.

2. Muhammad Zaki Abd al-Qadir, cited in *al-Ahram*, Sept. 23, 1975.

3. Ahmad Muhammad Taha, cited in Sohayr Abd al-Sitar, "Doria Shafik Requests the Publication of Her Works," *al-Ithnayn*, Sept. 23, 1975.

4. Amina al-Sa'id, "Experiences."

5. Abdul Abd al-Halim, "Dr. Doria Shafik," 58.

6. Lita Gallad, "Je Vous Invite," *Le Journal d'Egypte*, Sept. 22, 1975.

7. Gallad, "Temps nouveaux, temps democratiques: C'est Sadat lui-même qui assurait la plus large publicité aux tracts qui circulaient sous le manteau" (New time, democratic time: It is Sadat himself who assured the greatest publicity to the tracts circulated under cover), *Le Journal d'Egypte*, Oct. 6, 1979.

8. Madiha, "Leader Outside Her Time," *Rose al-Yusuf*, Oct. 12, 1975. See chap. 13, above.

9. Letter from Mme. Labib Habashi to Jehane Ragai, Sept. 22, 1975. Mme. Habashi served as the Egyptian director of the American Research Center in Egypt, during this period when diplomatic relations were severed between Egypt and America. Her husband, Labib Habashi, was one of his country's foremost Egyptologists.

10. Ragia Raghab, personal interview, June 14, 1986.

11. Pierre Seghers, personal interview, Sept. 13, 1986.

12. Louis Aragon, *Aurélien*, chap. 37. I find it somewhat ironic that Seghers selected Aragon (1897–1982) as the poet most closely epitomizing the interior life of Doria Shafik. Politically, Aragon and Shafik were poles apart. Aragon—one of the founding members of the surrealist movement in France in the 1920s—joined the Communist Party in 1927. Under the influence of his future wife, the Russian-born writer Elsa Triolet (1896–1970), Aragon finally abandoned surrealism to fight for the Russian Revolution under the banner of socialist realism. He wrote a poem, *Front Rouge*, that caused the French police to indict him on charges of incitement to murder and provoking insubordination in the army (see Lewis, *Dada Turns Red*, 97–118).

13. Seghers, personal interview, Sept. 13, 1986.

14. Ibid.

15. Emma Goldman, cited in Falk, *Love, Anarchy and Emma Goldman*, frontispiece.

16. Seghers, preface to Shafik's *Avec Dante aux Enfers*.

17. Fenoglio Abd al-Aal, *Défense et Illustration*, 37.

18. Preface to *Avec Dante aux Enfers*.

19. Phyllis Rose, *A Woman of Letters*, viii.

SELECTED BIBLIOGRAPHY

Abd al-Halim, Abdul Z. "Dr. Doria Shafik: The Piece of Candied Chestnut and Eighteen Years of Oblivion" (in Arabic). In *Nis'a fawq al-Qima* (Women above the pinnacle), 57–64. Cairo: Dar al-Faisal, 1987.

Abd al-Wahab, Muhammad F. *Al-Harakat al-Nissa'iyya fil-Sharq wa silatuha bi-isti'mar wa-sahyuniyya al-alimiyya* (The woman's movement in the East and its connection to colonialism and world Zionism). Cairo: Dar al-'itsam, 1979.

Ahmed, Leila. *Women and Gender in Islam: Historical Roots of a Modern Debate.* New Haven: Yale University Press, 1992.

Alloula, Malak. *The Colonial Harem.* Translated by M. and W. Godzich. Minneapolis: University of Minnesota Press, 1986.

Amin, Mustapha. "The Beautiful Leader" (in Arabic). In *Masa'il Shakhsiyya* (Personal matters), 59–68. Cairo: Tihama Publications, 1984.

Amin, Qasim. *Al-mar'ah al-jadidah* (The new woman). Cairo: n.p., 1901.

———. *Tahrir al-mar'ah* (The emancipation of women). Cairo: Dar al-Ma'arif, 1899.

Antonius, George. *The Arab Awakening.* Beirut: Khayats, 1938.

Badran, Margot, and Marilyn Cooke, eds. *Opening the Gates: A Century of Arab Feminist Writing.* London: Virago Press, 1990.

Badran, Margot. "Dual Liberation: Feminism and Nationalism in Egypt, 1870–1925." *Feminist Issues* 8 (1988): 15–34.

———. "The Feminist Vision in the Writings of Three Turn-of-the-Century Egyptian Women." *British Journal for Middle Eastern Studies Bulletin* 15, nos. 1–2 (1988): 11–20.

Baker, Raymond. *Egypt's Uncertain Revolution under Nasser and Sadat.* Cambridge, Mass.: Harvard University Press, 1978.

Baron, Beth. *Women's Awakening in Egypt: Culture, Society and the Press.* New Haven: Yale University Press, 1994.

Beck, Lois, and Nikki Keddie, eds. *Women in the Middle Eastern World.* Cambridge, Mass.: Harvard University Press, 1978.

Berque, Jacques. *Egypt: Imperialism and Revolution.* Translated by J. Stewart. London: Faber, 1972.

al-Bishri, Tareq. *Al-Harakah al-siyassiyyah fi Misr, 1945–1952* (The political movement in Egypt, 1945–1952). Cairo: al-Hayah al-Misriyyah al-'Ammah lil Kitab, 1972.

Botman, Selma. "The Experience of Women in the Egyptian Communist Movement, 1939–1954." *Women's Studies International Forum* 11, no. 2 (1988): 117–26.

Capart, Jean. "Revue." *Chronique d'Egypte: Bulletin Périodique de la Fondation Egyptologique Reine Elisabeth*, no. 31 (January 1941): 96.

Dekmejian, R. Hrair. *Egypt under Nasir: A Study in Political Dynamics.* Albany: State University of New York Press, 1971.

Durrell, Lawrence. *The Alexandria Quartet.* London: Faber and Faber, 1959.

Eliot, T. S. *Four Quartets.* New York: Harcourt, Brace, 1943.

"Eluard, Paul." In *Columbia Dictionary of Modern European Literature*, 229. New York: Columbia University Press, 1981.

Falk, Candace. *Love, Anarchy and Emma Goldman.* New York: Holt, Rinehart and Winston, 1984.

Fenoglio Abd al-Aal, Irene. *Défense et Illustration de L'Egyptienne: Aux Débuts d'une Expression Féminine.* Cairo: Cedej Publications, 1988.

Flaubert, Gustave. *Flaubert in Egypt: A Sensibility on Tour.* Translated and edited by Francis Steegmuller. Boston: Little, Brown, 1972.

Forster, E. M. *Alexandria: A History and a Guide.* New York: Doubleday, 1961.

Furth, P. *American Cassandra: The Biography of Dorothy Thompson.* Boston: Little, Brown, 1990.

Gallagher, Nancy. *Egypt's Other Wars.* Syracuse: Syracuse University Press, 1990.

al-Gohari, Muhammad M. *Al-Ikhwat al-Muslimat wa bina al-Usrah al-Quranyah* (The Muslim sisters and the foundation of the Quranic family). Cairo: Dar al-Dawah, 1980.

Gunther, John. *Inside Africa.* London: Hamish Hamilton, 1955.

Hatem, Mervat. "The Enduring Alliance of Nationalism and Patriarchy in the Personal Status Laws." *Feminist Issues* 6, no. 1 (1986): 19–43.

———. "Through Each Other's Eyes: Egyptian, Levantine-Egyptian and European Women's Images of Themselves and of Each Other (1862–1920)." *Women's Studies International Forum* 12, no. 2 (1989): 183–98.

Helys, Marc. "Commentary." *L'Egyptienne*, no. 111 (March 1935): 7.

Hetata, Sherif. *The Iron Eyelid.* London: Zed Books, 1989.

Heyworth-Dunne, James. *Introduction to the History of Education in Modern Egypt.* London: Frank Cass, 1968.

Hill, Enid. *Al-Sanhuri and Islamic Law.* Cairo Papers in Social Science 10, no. 1 (1987).

Hourani, Albert. *Arabic Thought in the Liberal Age.* London: Oxford University Press, 1967.

Hubert, R. R. "Reverdy." In *Encyclopedia of World Literature in the Twentieth Century.* New York: Continuum, 1989: 26–27.

Husayn, Taha. *An Egyptian Childhood.* Cairo: American University in Cairo Press, 1990.

———. *The Future of Culture in Egypt.* Translated by Sydney Glazer. Washington, D.C.: American Council of Learned Societies, 1954.

———. *A Stream of Days: A Student at al-Azhar.* Translated by E. H. Paxton. London: Longmans, Green, 1948.

Khalifa, I. *Al-Harakah al-Nissa'iyah al-haditha fi-Misr* (The modern woman's movement in Egypt). Cairo: Dar al-Kuttub, 1973.

Khater, Akram, and Cynthia Nelson. "al-Harakah al-Nissa'iyah: The Women's Movement and Political Participation in Modern Egypt." *Women's Studies International Forum* 11, no. 5 (1988): 465–93.

Lacouture, Jean, and Simone Lacouture. *Egypt in Transition*. London: Methuen, 1958.

Lane, Edward. *An Account of the Manners and Customs of the Modern Egyptians*. London: East-West Publications, 1978.

Lane-Poole, Stanley. *Social Life in Egypt: A Description of the Culture and Its People*. New York: Collier, 1894.

Lewis, Helen. *Dada Turns Red: The Politics of Surrealism*. Edinburgh: Edinburgh University Press, 1990.

Mansfield, Peter. *Nasser's Egypt*. London: Penguin Classics, 1965.

Mernissi, Fatma. *Behind the Veil: Male-Female Relations in Morocco*. Cambridge: Schenckman, 1975.

Mill, J. S. *The Subjection of Women*. London: Oxford University Press, 1969.

Mills, C. W. *The Sociological Imagination*. New York: Grove Press, 1961.

Mitchell, Richard P. *The Society of the Muslim Brothers*. London: Oxford University Press, 1969.

Moscatelli, Jean. *Poètes en Egypte* (Poets in Egypt). Cairo: Les Editions de l'Atelier, 1955.

Nabaraoui, Ceza. "Réponse aux Réactionnaires." *L'Egyptienne*, no. 83 (1932): 2–8.

———. "Echos d'Orient" (Echoes from the Orient). *L'Egyptienne*, no. 163 (March 1940): 34.

Naguib, Muhammed. *Egypt's Destiny*. New York: Doubleday, 1955.

Nasser, Gamal Abdel. *The Philosophy of the Revolution*. Introduction by Dorothy Thompson. Cairo: National Publication House, n.d.

Nelson, Cynthia. "Changing Roles in a Changing Society," *Anthropological Quarterly* 41, no. 2 (1968): 57–77.

———. "Islamic Tradition and Women's Education: The Egyptian Experience." In *World Yearbook of Education: Women and Education*, edited by Sandra Hacker et al., 211–26. New York: Nicholar Publishing, 1984.

———. "The Voices of Doria Shafik: Feminist Consciousness in Egypt, 1940–1960." *Feminist Issues* 6, no. 2 (1986): 15–31.

Nerval, Gérard de. *Journey to the Orient*. Translated by N. Glass. New York: New York University Press, 1972.

Nowaihi, Mohammed. "Changing the Law on Personal Status in Egypt within a Liberal Interpretation of the Shari'a." *Middle East Review* 11, no. 4 (Summer 1979): 40–49.

Nutting, Anthony. *Nasser*. London: Constable, 1972.

Perrault, Gilles. *A Man Apart: The Life of Henri Curiel*. London: Zed Books, 1987.

Pinchin, Jane L. *Alexandria Still*. Cairo: American University in Cairo Press, 1977.

Ragai, Nour al-Din. *De la condition légale des sociétés anonymes étrangères en Egypte* (On the legal condition of anonymous foreign companies in Egypt). Paris: Les Presses Modernes, 1939.

Reverdy, Pierre. *Grande Nature*. Paris: Editions Seghers, 1925.

Rodinson, Maxime. *Israel and the Arabs*. Baltimore: Pelican Books, 1968.

Rose, Phyllis. *Jazz Cleopatra: Josephine Baker and Her Time.* New York: Doubleday, 1989.

———. *A Woman of Letters: A Life of Virginia Woolf.* New York: Harcourt, Brace, 1978.

al-Sadat, M. Anwar. *In Search of Identity.* New York: Harper and Row, 1978.

Said, Edward. *Orientalism.* New York: Pantheon Books, 1978.

———. *The Question of Palestine.* New York: Pantheon Books, 1979.

al-Sa'id, Amina. "Experiences from the Tape of Memories" (in Arabic). *Akhbar al-Yawm,* Nov. 4, 1989, 3.

al-Sayyid-Marsot, Afaf Lutfi. *Egypt and Cromer: A Study of Anglo-Egyptian Relations.* London: John Murray, 1968.

———. *Egypt's Liberal Experiment: 1922–1936.* Berkeley: University of California Press, 1977.

———. "The Revolutionary Gentlewoman in Egypt." In *Women in the Muslim World,* edited by Lois Beck and Nikki Keddie, 261–76. Cambridge, Mass.: Harvard University Press, 1978.

Seghers, Pierre. *Chanson et Complaintes.* Paris: Editions Seghers, 1958.

———. *Les Pierres.* Paris: Editions Seghers, 1958.

———. *Piranese: Poems de Pierre Seghers.* Paris: Editions Seghers, 1960.

———. *La Résistance et ses poètes.* Vol. 1, *France 1940–1945;* vol. 2, *Choix des poèmes.* Paris: Marabout Editions, 1978.

Shafik, Doria. *L'Amour perdu* (The lost love). Paris: Pierre Seghers, 1954.

———. *L'Art pour l'art dans l'Egypte antique* (Art for art's sake in ancient Egypt). Paris: Paul Geuthner Press, 1940.

———. *Avec Dante aux Enfers* (With Dante in Hell). Paris: Pierre Fanlac, 1979.

———. *La Bonne Aventure* (The pleasant adventure). Paris: Pierre Seghers, 1949.

———. "Egyptian Feminism." *Middle East Affairs* 1 (Aug.–Sept. 1952): 233–38.

———. "L'Enfant du Nil" (Child of the Nile). *L'Egyptienne,* no. 53 (December 1929): 25–27.

———. *L'Esclave Sultane* (The slave Sultana). Paris: Editions Latines, 1952.

———. *La Femme et le droit religieux de l'Egypte contemporaine* (Women and religious law in contemporary Egypt). Paris: Paul Geuthner Press, 1940.

———. *La Femme nouvelle en Egypte* (The new woman in Egypt). Cairo: Schindler Press, 1944.

———. "Une Femme a-t-elle le droit de philosopher?" (Does a woman have the right to philosophize?). *L'Egyptienne,* no. 64 (December 1930): 18–28.

———. *Al-Kitab al-abiyad li huquq al-mar'ah al-siyasiyah* (The white book on the political rights of women). Cairo: Maktabat al-Sharqiyya, 1953.

———. "Hors-Temps." Unpublished collection of poems, n.d. Private collection of Jehane Ragai and Aziza Ellozy.

———. *Larmes d'Isis* (Tears of Isis). Paris: Pierre Fanlac, 1979.

———. "Ma Grandmère et moi" (My grandmother and me). *La Femme Nouvelle* (December 1947): 56–57.

———. "Memoirs." Unpublished manuscripts. 1956 (in English); 1960 (in French); 1975 (in English). Private collection of Jehane Ragai and Aziza Ellozy.

————. "Un Petit Mot" (A small word). *L'Egyptienne*, no. 35 (June 1928): 12–14.

————. "Rêverie d'une femme d'aujourd'hui" (Dream of a young woman of today). *L'Egyptienne*, no. 82 (1932): 15–19.

————. *Rihlati Hawla al-'Alam* (My trip around the world). Cairo: Maktabat al-Sharqiyya, 1955.

Shafik, Doria, and Ibrahim Abdu. *Al-Mar'ah al-Misriyah min al-Fara'niah ila al-Yawm* (The Egyptian woman from the pharoahs until today). Cairo: Maktabat al-Misr, 1955.

————. *Tatawwur al-Nahda al-Nisa'iyah fi Misr* (The development of the renaissance of women in Egypt). Cairo: Maktabat al-Tawakul, 1945.

Sha'rawi, Huda. "Eulogy to Qasim Amin." *L'Egyptienne*, no. 35 (June 1928): 8–12.

————. *Harem Years: The Memoirs of an Egyptian Feminist*. Translated by Margot Badran. London: Virago Press, 1986.

Stowasser, Barbara. "Liberated Equal or Protected Dependent? Contemporary Religious Paradigms on Women's Status in Islam." *Arab Studies Quarterly* 9, no. 3 (Summer 1987): 260–83.

Stuhlman, Gunther, ed. *The Diaries of Anais Nin: 1931–1934*. New York: Swallow Press, 1966.

————, ed. *The Diaries of Anais Nin: 1934–1939*. New York: Swallow Press, 1967.

Subhi, Muhammed Khalil. *Tarikh al-Hayat al-Niyabiya fi Misr*. 6 vols. Cairo: Matbaat Dar al-Kutub al-Misriyya, 1939.

Subhi, Samir. "Doria Shafik: Her Dissertation *Women and Islam*" (in Arabic). *Nifs al-Dunya*, no. 2 (December 1994): 2.

Sullivan, Earl L. *Women in Egyptian Public Life*. Syracuse: Syracuse University Press, 1986.

Vatikiotis, P. J. *The Modern History of Egypt*. London: Weidenfeld and Nicolson, 1969.

White, Hayden. "The Burden of History." In *Tropics of Discourse*, edited by Hayden White, 27–50. Baltimore, Md.: Johns Hopkins University Press, 1960.

INDEX